ADDITIONAL PRAISE FOR

THE
ROAD
TO
CAMELOT

"The most compelling book on JFK in the year of his centennial."
—*The Daily Beast*

"Thomas Oliphant and Curtis Wilkie, both veteran political journalists, re-
tell the story of this momentous campaign, reminding us of now forgotten
details of Kennedy's path to the White House."
—*The Wall Street Journal*

"The book is most impressive for its meticulously detailed approach to the
fierce Kennedy drive toward the ultimate goal of the presidency."
—*The Washington Times*

"Excellent."
—*Dallas Morning News*

"A fresh and fascinating account."
—*Richmond Times-Dispatch*

"An important work for any JFK student or fan. . . . Put this one on your
bookshelf—you'll want to return to it often."
—*The Buffalo News*

"The two former *Boston Globe* reporters argue that JFK's campaign was
much more than the year-long affair depicted in Teddy White's *The Making
of the President 1960*."
—*CNN*

"An excellent chronicle of JFK's innovations, his true personality, and how
close he came to losing."
—*Kirkus Reviews*, starred review

"The exciting and illuminating tale of John F. Kennedy's calculated run for the presidency . . . a very compelling account of a landmark election."
—*Booklist*, starred review

"An in-depth narrative based on oral histories, personal interviews, and secondary sources. . . . The authors add a new perspective to literature on Kennedy by focusing on his electioneering efforts rather than his persona and policy outcomes."
—*Library Journal*

"Oliphant and Wilkie's evocative, behind-the-scenes account goes beyond what we knew from Teddy White and others about how a youthful senator beat the political establishment and won the presidency. Their portrait of Kennedy shows him to be 'part gambler but also part cold realist' whose political instincts served him well and broke new ground in presidential campaigns that his successors have followed."
—Susan Page, Washington bureau chief, *USA TODAY*

"*The Road to Camelot* grabs you on the first page and never lets go. Two of our country's finest journalists take us deep inside John F. Kennedy's at once old-fashioned and brilliantly innovative political operation and show how it made him president. Along the way, they teach us a lot about our country. This book is a gift to history, to all who love politics, and to anyone who likes a good story, brilliantly told."
—E.J. Dionne Jr., author of the *New York Times* bestseller
Why the Right Went Wrong

"A spellbinding story of the brash young scion of a wealthy Catholic family plotting his way to the presidency. Kennedy created the modern campaign while cajoling the canny and still-controlling party bosses. Though we know the ending, it's a nail-biting and well-told tale."
—Cokie Roberts, author and political commentator for
ABC News and NPR

"Two of the best political reporters around tell the story of an ambitious young senator who would not wait his turn and changed all the old rules to become our thirty-fifth president. *The Road to Camelot* is a wonderful narrative of the self-driven campaign of the man who became President Kennedy. An exciting time. A great read."
—Richard Reeves, author of *President Kennedy: Profile of Power* and
President Reagan: The Triumph of Imagination

ALSO BY THOMAS OLIPHANT

Baseball as a Road to God: Seeing Beyond the Game
(with John Sexton and Peter J. Schwartz)

Utter Incompetents: Ego and Ideology in the Age of Bush

*Praying for Gil Hodges: A Memoir of the 1955 World Series
and One Family's Love of the Brooklyn Dodgers*

All by Myself: The Unmaking of a Presidential Campaign
(with Christine Mary Black)

ALSO BY CURTIS WILKIE

*Assassins, Eccentrics, Politicians and Other Persons of Interest:
Fifty Pieces from the Road*

*The Fall of the House of Zeus:
The Rise and Ruin of America's Most Powerful Trial Lawyer*

Dixie: A Personal Odyssey Through Events That Shaped the Modern South

Arkansas Mischief: The Birth of a National Scandal (with Jim McDougal)

THOMAS OLIPHANT

and

CURTIS WILKIE

THE
ROAD
TO
CAMELOT

Inside JFK's
Five-Year Campaign

SIMON & SCHUSTER PAPERBACKS

NEW YORK   LONDON   TORONTO   SYDNEY   NEW DELHI

Simon & Schuster Paperbacks
An Imprint of Simon & Schuster, Inc.
1230 Avenue of the Americas
New York, NY 10020

First Simon & Schuster paperback edition May 2018

SIMON & SCHUSTER PAPERBACKS and colophon are registered trademarks of Simon & Schuster, Inc.

For information about special discounts for bulk purchases, please contact Simon & Schuster Special Sales at 1-866-506-1949 or business@simonandschuster.com.

The Simon & Schuster Speakers Bureau can bring authors to your live event. For more information or to book an event contact the Simon & Schuster Speakers Bureau at 1-866-248-3049 or visit our website at www.simonspeakers.com.

Interior design by Joy O'Meara

Manufactured in the United States of America

10 9 8 7 6 5 4 3 2 1

The Library of Congress has cataloged the hardcover edition as follows:
Names: Oliphant, Thomas, author. | Wilkie, Curtis, co-author.
Title: The road to Camelot : inside JFK's five-year campaign / Thomas Oliphant and Curtis Wilkie.
Description: First Simon & Schuster hardcover edition. | New York : Simon & Schuster, 2017. | "Simon & Schuster nonfiction original hardcover"—Title page verso. | Includes bibliographical references and index.
Identifiers: LCCN 2016050682 (print) | LCCN 2017000324 (ebook) | ISBN 9781501105562 (hardback) | ISBN 9781501105579 (trade paperback) | ISBN 9781501105586 (ebook)
Subjects: LCSH: Presidents—United States—Election—1960. | Kennedy, John F. (John Fitzgerald), 1917–1963. | Presidential candidates—United States—Biography. | Political campaigns—United States—History—20th century. | United States—Politics and government—1953–1961. | BISAC: HISTORY / United States / 20th Century. | POLITICAL SCIENCE / Political Process / Elections. | POLITICAL SCIENCE / Political Process / General.
Classification: LCC E837.7 .O45 2017 (print) | LCC E837.7 (ebook) | DDC 973.922092—dc23
LC record available at https://lccn.loc.gov/2016050682

ISBN 978-1-5011-0556-2
ISBN 978-1-5011-0557-9 (pbk)
ISBN 978-1-5011-0558-6 (ebook)

In loving memory of Nancy Roberson Wilkie

1944–2016

CONTENTS

THE
ROAD
TO
CAMELOT

CHAPTER ONE

The Spark

Senator Lyndon B. Johnson's heart attack hit him on July 2, 1955, while he was visiting a businessman friend and benefactor in the Virginia horse and estate country west of Washington.

President Dwight D. Eisenhower's came barely ten weeks later, on a late September evening while he was visiting his in-laws near Denver.

This unprecedented cardiac double-header was medically no minor event. Johnson was kept in the U.S. Naval Hospital just outside Washington for seven weeks and didn't resume his frenetic work schedule until December. Eisenhower remained in Fitzsimons Army Hospital in nearby Aurora, Colorado, for seven weeks and wasn't working at his accustomed pace until after the New Year.

The shock to the country's governance and politics was similarly severe. Eisenhower was felled as he was beginning to gear up for what most observers assumed would be a relatively easy run for reelection in 1956. The war hero and America's thirty-fourth president was popular and not without major successes in his first term. Now, suddenly, his future was in doubt.

Johnson was a rookie, having become the Senate's majority leader only that January, after the Democratic Party regained control of the Senate in the previous year's elections, but he had been learning the ropes of leadership for nearly twenty years. His dreams of the presidency were only dreams; first he had a Senate to run. But now his doctors kept him from the work he loved.

In the twenty-first century it is commonplace for heart patients to be up, active, and working within weeks, often days. This wasn't the case in 1955, when long recuperations predicted long-term disability. In his forties and clearly recovering, Johnson was still robust, but doubts about the health of the sixty-five-year-old Eisenhower persisted for months.

One man among the millions concerned about Eisenhower's health and future was Joseph Patrick Kennedy, no ordinary man and no ordinary superrich tycoon. He had been around big-time politics for more than twenty years and involved in local politics in his native Massachusetts all his life. Holding the loftiest of ambitions for his second son, then a freshman senator with no national standing whatsoever—yet blessed by his family name, wealth, and nearly a decade of political success—Kennedy saw opportunity in Eisenhower's misfortune. Being a man of bold action, often rash, he hatched a plan and set out to make it happen.

With the agreement of his son John Fitzgerald and the knowledge of other members of his large family, Kennedy approached Johnson. He knew Johnson well and had supported him financially as he rose to the apex of the Senate. To underline his seriousness, Kennedy enlisted as an emissary one of Washington's most effective lobbyists, Thomas G. Corcoran, comfortably ensconced in his second career after service as one of the important members of Franklin D. Roosevelt's White House staff.

Kennedy's message was simple and over-the-top presumptuous: *With Eisenhower hospitalized, the architecture of the 1956 election has been changed. You should run for president. I will make sure your campaign never lacks for lavish financing. And my son will be your running mate.*

There is no evidence that Johnson seriously considered Kennedy's offer and no plausible argument that he should have. To Corcoran and to Kennedy, Johnson simply said he wasn't interested, that he wasn't running. There is also no evidence that Kennedy and his son did anything more than let the matter drop quietly, though according to Corcoran there was an outburst from younger brother Robert Francis—still evolving as a young adult but already known for his temper and grudges—over Johnson's quick dismissal of his father's overture.

Nevertheless the episode reverberated, though not in the way Joseph Kennedy had intended. It represented a spark, the first time national office was the subject of something other than formless ambition and hope and talk, and it ignited a five-year quest that culminated in Jack Kennedy's transformative election as the country's thirty-fifth president at the young age of forty-three.

After that October, every time there was an option on the table involving national office—the vice presidency over the next ten months, the presidency immediately thereafter—Kennedy chose to move forward. His campaign was not a scripted operation but a long, continuous pursuit. At first it was tentative, with Kennedy appearing detached, even doubtful. But by the end of the summer of 1956 Kennedy felt the presidency was staring him in the face. On Thanksgiving that year he made the commitment to start running.

One reason Kennedy decided to move forward is that it was the only direction his fortunes could go. In the mid-1950s he was not a consequential figure in national politics. Even after nearly a decade in Congress he was considered more of a socialite and a war hero than a political leader. He had no developed philosophy or ideology, and his Senate contemporaries considered him an indifferent Democrat with occasionally independent tendencies. He was not involved prominently in any great cause or issue and enjoyed no real standing inside the Senate. He was not even the undisputed master of politics in his home state. He was nowhere near the top of any list of Democrats to watch. When assessing him as a politician, the word commentators used most frequently was *potential*, not *power*.

"Kennedy was then really in the second rank even of Democratic politicians," explained Abram Chayes, a Harvard Law School professor and early supporter who eventually made it to the top of the Kennedy State Department. "He was not by any means thought of as a guy with a real chance even for the vice presidency."

Senator Joseph Clark, a liberal icon from Pennsylvania who was never particularly close to Kennedy, later acknowledged, "We all underestimated Kennedy. Nobody paid an awful lot of attention to him except as a brash young man who wanted to be President and who would never make it."

Kennedy had prepped for his presidential campaign with a bid to get on the 1956 Democratic ticket with Adlai Stevenson. Amid the first stirrings of that race, others were more seriously considered as running mates for Stevenson. Among the more prominent were Senator Estes Kefauver of Tennessee, who had briefly run for president in 1952 and was known nationally for his investigations of organized crime and the drug industry; young Hubert Humphrey, a senator from Minnesota, who had electrified the national convention in 1948 with his fiery attack on Jim Crow while forever antagonizing the Deep South; and there were others.

As names began to circulate, Kennedy's interest grew, stimulated by his father's short-lived initiative. It flowed as much from his bemused, flattered ambition and his long-standing enjoyment of challenges as from any realistic intention to seek higher office. Still, his interest was genuine. And he had someone close enough to his substantive and political life to meaningfully assist him.

Theodore C. Sorensen, then all of twenty-seven, had been a top aide for two years when the two famous heart attacks occurred. A Nebraskan with deep progressive family roots, Sorensen was that rarest of political species: someone who could work on the development of policy and ideas while helping shape them into speeches and articles, often with simple eloquence. "The Senator's own interest in the nomination was growing, more out of a sense of competition than of conviction," Sorensen recalled years later. But Kennedy regularly approved his aide's suggestions to advance his position, albeit with "skeptical encouragement."

An even closer, more intimate participant, Kennedy's brother Robert said, "I think he just wanted to see what it looked like, to put his foot in the water and see how cold it was, but he hadn't made up his mind to swim by any means."

One of the very first articles that referred to Kennedy by name as a vice presidential possibility appeared in the fall of 1955 in *Newsweek* magazine's Periscope column, a weekly compilation of rumors, gossip, and occasionally hard information that many politicians read closely.

Kennedy was curious enough to personally call the page's editor in New York, Debs Myers, to ask who was doing the mentioning.

"Me," Myers replied, introducing Kennedy to one of the many ways reporters manage to insert their own hunches and views into stories.

But the mentions continued, and reporters increasingly began attributing them to unnamed supporters of Stevenson himself, signaling that the topic was alive for real. Kennedy continued to listen and, whenever an option was on the table, to be proactive. (One exception was an earlier Sorensen memorandum, in November 1955, citing public speculation about Kennedy's health. The senator was less than a year removed from two major spinal surgeries involving a long recuperation during which he nearly died. He had also started a steroid regimen to treat a form of Addison's disease. Sorensen had suggested that he prepare a report on Kennedy's health to deal with any questions. Kennedy simply said no, possibly to avoid attracting more attention to the subject; possibly because it would be too obvious an effort to affect Stevenson's choice of a running mate; possibly for both reasons.)

At the end of 1955, according to Sorensen, Kennedy was thinking of entering the New Hampshire primary three months hence as a New England "favorite son"—a gambit to gain prominence for himself and to hold the delegation for Stevenson. (Kefauver had famously beaten Stevenson there in 1952 and figured to do so again.) However, that idea was dropped after Stevenson's campaign manager, a veteran politician from Pennsylvania named James Finnegan, made it clear that he favored an actual endorsement instead, which Kennedy promptly delivered once it was certain that his Senate leader, Lyndon Johnson, had no interest in running for president.

But as 1956 began, Kennedy was openly in the mix. He occasionally referred to the situation in public, typically with one of his increasingly notable attributes, his wit. Appearing in January at a testimonial for Senator George Smathers of Florida, a personal friend, Kennedy told a hoary joke about how the Senate held a secret ballot to choose the next president and each senator wound up with one vote.

"We all know that all 96 Senators"—Alaska and Hawaii were not yet states—"do not consider themselves potential candidates for President," Kennedy said. "Some are only candidates for vice president."

President Eisenhower's serious heart attack inaugurated a months-long period of doubt about his future as well as his health. He was in the hospital in Colorado for nearly two months and rested at Key West in Florida afterward. Like Johnson, the president was essentially out of commission until the end of the year. What is more, Eisenhower publicly confessed his reservations about seeking a second term, a topic that divided his physicians. It wasn't until mid-January 1956 that signs of a budding reelection effort began to appear, and it wasn't until the end of February that the president formally announced that he would run again.

In short, Joe Kennedy's timing was poor. Regardless of Eisenhower's intentions, the elder Kennedy had hardly offered Johnson an easy road to nomination, much less election. Jack Kennedy's acquiescence in his father's plan, moreover, proved to be ill-considered in such an uncertain atmosphere. Eventually his father would turn as sharply negative about his son's presence on the 1956 Democratic ticket as he had once been ebulliently positive. He now argued, by letter and telephone, that Eisenhower would most likely win and that taking the second spot on Stevenson's slate would wind up being a career failure for his son.

Yet by then Jack Kennedy was comfortable with his own views and prepared to ignore his father's frequently overstated advice. His competitive family members were accustomed to making their own decisions.

CHAPTER TWO

Mating Game

By tradition, national politicians do not run for vice presidential nominations. Instead they try to attract an invitation to join a presidential nominee's ticket, always aware that their fate ultimately is not in their hands.

In 1956, the year Jack Kennedy became a national political presence, he followed that tradition—though he walked right up to the edge of violating it. Barely behind the scenes he courted the attention he had begun to receive. He labored to become the dominant figure in his home state. He confronted obstacles that might augur against his selection by Stevenson. And he pushed back against arguments from his father that he was seeking fools' gold on a ticket doomed to defeat by President Eisenhower.

Kennedy was flattered by the growing interest, but also diffident, displaying elements of his trademark dispassion when analyzing himself. Contrary to myth, he wasn't privately pining for the presidency from the moment he returned from his celebrated service in World War II, having just lost his older brother—the more natural politician—in a dangerous combat mission over the English Channel. Nor was he simply an agent of the wishes of his father. Joseph Kennedy meddled, kibitzed, and provided money, especially at the beginning of his son's career. But the old man was also knee-jerk opinionated, overbearing, and imperious. Jack and his siblings loved their father, but they were inclined to take or leave his advice as they saw fit.

The force behind Kennedy's ambition was Kennedy himself. "Sometimes you read that he was a reluctant figure being dragooned into politics by his father. I didn't get that impression at all. I gathered that it was a wholesome, full-blown wish on his part," recalled Charles Bartlett, a close friend and contemporary who became a syndicated newspaper columnist. Bartlett first met Kennedy in The Patio, a popular Palm Beach nightclub, just after the war ended, a time when Kennedy was moving away from a fledgling writing career to try politics. Bartlett, who later introduced Kennedy to Jacqueline Bouvier, knew him and his instincts very well.

From the outset of Kennedy's first congressional campaign in 1946, there is other testimony that he—not his father—determined his political future. According to James G. Colbert, a veteran political reporter for the old *Boston Post* who knew the father long before he met the son, it was a "mistaken impression" that Joe Kennedy—or Jack's locally famous grandfather, John "Honey Fitz" Fitzgerald, a former mayor of Boston— were able to run either Jack's public or private life. "I want to tell you the one who ran it was John F. Kennedy. He made the decisions. He listened to the ideas of his father and I think probably to a lesser extent to his grandfather and the advice that I know about his getting he disregarded. He made his own decisions which as I say were frequently contrary to what older people thought he should do."

Andrew Dazzi, a circulation manager for the *Boston Globe* who was extremely close to Joe Kennedy and aided him as well as his son during a period of primitive press ethics, had this observation: "It's often been said that his father swayed him. I never believed he could sway him. His father, with all due respect to him, was a politician of the old school. We were now coming into a new era. We had to do different things. . . . I used to see him [Jack Kennedy] stand right up to him. He really let him have it. And I admired him for it because I think it showed he had courage of his own."

Long before there was a Ted Sorensen on the staff or a loyal "Irish Mafia" composed of men named O'Brien, O'Donnell, Powers, Donahue, and others, Kennedy had assistance from some of his father's retainers, but he quickly established his own independence.

To the extent Kennedy had a campaign manager for his first congressional campaign in 1946 it was a young man from an advertising and public relations firm that Joe Kennedy used, the Dowd Agency. Mark Dalton worked with Jack Kennedy on politics as well as writing on major issues over the next six years in a role that anticipated Sorensen's. Dalton was crudely elbowed aside at the beginning of Kennedy's 1952 campaign for the Senate, but he left with strong memories of his association with the family.

Dalton called the father "the essential campaign manager." In the beginning he talked to Joe Kennedy on the phone daily. But according to Dalton, his task was to keep the father in the campaign loop rather than to follow his orders.

The father's immense wealth was certainly a factor in the victory. According to Dalton, the total cost—perhaps $250,000, mostly for billboard and radio advertising—seemed high but was "not exorbitant" for the times. Jack Kennedy himself liked to joke that his famously tightwad father was happy to underwrite a win but refused to pay for a landslide. He knew he was indebted to his father. But he believed that he benefited from name recognition far more than from his father's money. The fact that most people in the district knew what his name represented was his initial leg up on a crowded field. He had his mother's father, Honey Fitz, a living political legend in Massachusetts, as well as his own father, one of the country's best-known and most successful businessmen, who had served as President Franklin D. Roosevelt's ambassador to Britain before they split over Joseph's isolationist views just before World War II began.

Fitzgerald and Joseph P. Kennedy represented the polar opposites of the Irish American experience in their immense local celebrity, one the flamboyant politician and the other the overbearing titan of wealth and influence. Honey Fitz became Boston's mayor at the turn of the century, after serving as a congressman and champion of immigrants. He was gregarious and jovial; his trademark was his habit of singing "Sweet Adeline" whenever the spirit, as opposed to spirits, moved him.

As mayor his rise was meteoric, as he put his stamp on a major expansion of the city's port, its first-in-the-nation subway, and even the construction of a home for the Babe Ruth–led Boston Red Sox called Fenway Park. There were even a few "mentions" of him as vice presidential material for the Democrats in 1912.

Then his political life disintegrated. The corruption in his city administration was as widespread as its successes. Running for reelection in 1913 against an upstart named James Michael Curley, he suddenly quit the race. Only much later did the real reason emerge: a blackmail letter Curley had delivered to Fitzgerald's wife, threatening to reveal what would have been a gigantic scandal. Curley claimed to have witnesses who saw Fitzgerald kissing a young woman at a roadhouse in the town of Middleton. Her name was Elizabeth Ryan, but she became part of local lore by her nickname, "Toodles."

After Fitzgerald's withdrawal from the mayoral race, he came close (within 30,000 votes) in a Senate race with Henry Cabot Lodge Sr. Then came the career-crushing defeats—for mayor, for governor, and in a final indignity, for the Democratic Senate nomination in 1942.

But four years later, introducing his young grandson around the district, Fitzgerald was still personally revered in his hometown. This was the district from which Curley had just resigned after being elected to another term as mayor, though he was already under federal investigation for corruption that would send him to prison while Jack Kennedy was campaigning.

In the early years Fitzgerald had been a rival of Joe Kennedy's father, P.J., the proprietor of a tavern and a ward heeler with clout in the family's adopted base of East Boston. But they had become allies after Fitzgerald's election as mayor. The marriage of P.J.'s son in 1914 to Fitzgerald's daughter and well-known political surrogate, Rose, was as much a political merger as a love affair.

But Joe Kennedy chose a different path after graduating from Harvard. With local banking, manufacturing, the stock market, the movies, and real estate he had amassed a fortune by the time he started dabbling in high-stakes politics to help Franklin Roosevelt get elected president in 1932. His reward—first chairman of the new, post-Crash Securities and

Exchange Commission—may have seemed odd, but his record as a rare fox who actually guarded the chicken coop was widely praised.

In 1938 his appointment as ambassador to Britain seemed to take him even higher until, like his father-in-law, he ended his own career. The issue was not a woman, though his private life was notoriously messy, but his fervent isolationism and then passivity in the face of Nazi Germany's advances. The break with Roosevelt was ugly, but he remained a prominent figure in Massachusetts with considerable influence and respect who had lost one son in the war and raised another who had distinguished himself in combat.

This was the history and name recognition from which Jack Kennedy benefited when he began his own political career and which set him apart from the large field of two-dimensional pols who opposed him. Boston's political tradition is not uniquely tribal, but the ironies in this saga are exquisite: Jack ran for the seat left vacant by the man who had blackmailed his grandfather and then refused to sign a petition calling for the man's pardon. This helped him in his 1952 race for the Senate to defeat the man whose father had put another nail in his grandfather's political coffin. Jack's superwealthy father married Fitzgerald's beloved daughter, and his most trusted assistant was one Edward Moore, who had been the top aide not only to Fitzgerald but to Mayor Curley as well; Joe even named his youngest son after Moore. Not even Chicago or New York could top that tale.

Early in his career Jack Kennedy barely looked beyond his congressional seat. He later insisted that when he first ran for Congress—and for years afterward—he never (he repeated the word three times) thought about running for president. "I thought I might be governor of Massachusetts someday," he confessed.

According to Sorensen, their first actual conversation about higher office took place roughly a year into his first Senate term, probably in 1954. Kennedy, he said, was mostly negative about the prospect, citing his relative youth, inexperience, and spotty record. Sorensen didn't disagree, but assessing the country's mood as the Eisenhower period drew toward a close, they both felt youth could be made into an asset. After the episode with his father and Lyndon Johnson, followed by casual references in the press about him as a potential Democratic running mate in 1956, Kennedy began to drop his pessimism. He became interested, if not fully persuaded. At one point that pivotal winter he referred to the vice presidential speculation as "the only game in town."

As was his habit, Sorensen served as a more positive, assertive, and forward-looking voice in the office. In addition to making the obvious point that an impressive performance in 1956 would be its own reward, Sorensen was the first to point to the elephant in Kennedy's room: his religion. "As I told JFK," he said much later, "I believed that the nomination, to say nothing of the Vice Presidency itself, could be a first step to overcome the religious obstacle to his becoming President."

By the beginning of 1956 Kennedy had begun to make the transition from a promising freshman senator to a prospective vice presidential nominee. The first words of encouragement came right after the year began, in the form of a letter from a prominent state senator saying he wanted to start contacting Democrats nationally to urge Kennedy's consideration as running-mate material. This was no ordinary state senator, some local tub-thumper whose zeal exceeded his judgment. Andrew Quigley *was* Chelsea, one of the older blue-collar communities that bordered Boston; in addition to being its most important political leader, Quigley published the local newspaper and had been a Kennedy ally for years. Within a week Kennedy replied. He suggested to Quigley that the timing was off but said he would stay in touch.

Another sign of interest appeared in the form of reporters trooping to Kennedy's Senate office to take his measure. The parade started immediately after the holidays. Kennedy was one of several Democrats deemed worthy of consideration for a place on the ticket, so it was only natural that reporters would want to visit, exchange gossip, and trade bits of information.

The crowd in Kennedy's office reflected the mutual regard between reporters and the freshman senator. They enjoyed each other's company. Kennedy had several personal friends within the Washington writing corps, especially among syndicated columnists, then a genuine influence in those days before television covered political news and events.

At first there was nothing special about most of the visits, but a change in the content of what he was hearing caught Kennedy's attention. It was no longer simple "mentions" in political gossip but intelligence that Kennedy's name was being dropped by people high in the camp of Stevenson, the front-runner for the presidential nomination, should he decide to run again against Eisenhower.

One of the first to employ this tidbit was a writer better known for his foreign affairs reporting. Theodore H. White was working on a piece for *Collier's* magazine, one of the mass-circulation picture-and-prose stalwarts of that era. White told Kennedy that Stevenson's people were touting him; he also supplied a list of the other names being discussed: the popular mayor of New York, Robert Wagner, and two Tennessee politicians, Frank Clement, the young governor with a reputation for oratorical excellence who would wind up giving the keynote speech at the national convention, and the state's widely admired other senator, Albert Gore.

This was flattering and contributed to the increasingly heady atmosphere in Kennedy's bustling office. At the same time, however, his supporters couldn't avoid some prudent conspiracy-theorizing. This kind of speculation, so the reasoning went, would benefit Stevenson as well as Kennedy because it undercut the presidential aspirations of other Democratic figures thinking about running: Governor W. Averell Harriman of New York, another scion of great wealth who had been a New Deal diplomat before winning office two years earlier; and Estes Kefauver, who had come out of nowhere to win the New Hampshire primary in 1952 and was likely to mount a better-organized challenge in 1956. For Stevenson's people to be touting the likes of Kennedy and Wagner of the East Coast as well as two Tennesseans could be a sly way of undercutting both Harriman and Kefauver.

Events, however, quickly overshadowed possible conspiracies, both on Kennedy's New England turf and nationally. He got a boost from Governor Luther Hodges of North Carolina, a moderate leader who emphasized economic development rather than race. Hodges declared that having Kennedy on the ticket would be acceptable in the South. In New England the new year brought public support from two governors, Abraham Ribicoff of Connecticut and Dennis Roberts of Rhode Island. But most important, Kennedy got the backing of the region's foremost figure in national party politics, John Bailey of Connecticut. With New Deal roots, the state party chairman dominated his own turf and exerted influence far beyond Connecticut's borders. Bailey had a reputation as a coalition builder rather than an iron-fisted boss. As the 1956 campaign year began, he led his state party establishment into an early endorsement of a second Stevenson candidacy, and he used his clout to arrange a regional Democratic event, a dinner in Hartford, with Stevenson as the main attraction. Bailey's second goal was to increase the luster around Kennedy, whom he had known since he ran for the Senate. Kennedy was on the dais at the dinner when Bailey, in a rare burst of enthusiasm, said in his introduction of Stevenson, "We have at the banquet table tonight not only the candidate for President but also the candidate for Vice President."

Yet privately Bailey harbored no such illusions. "You have to remember," he later recalled, "that nobody really thought Jack Kennedy was going to be nominated for Vice President. . . . It was quite something to think of a Catholic even aspiring to run for Vice President."

Into this dynamic walked another writer whom Kennedy used to take his most important step to signal interest in the vice presidential nomination. Fletcher Knebel was a Cowles Publications columnist and writer, representing a mini media empire consisting of *Look* magazine and the *Des Moines Register* and *Minneapolis Star-Tribune* newspapers. Acerbic and witty, he was the kind of journalist Kennedy enjoyed. (Knebel wrote novels on the side. After Kennedy became president, one of them, written with fellow Cowles man Charles Bailey, was made into a popular movie, *Seven Days in May*, about a fictional attempted military coup in the United States.)

"Early in '56, I was just chewing the rug with him one day," Knebel recalled, "and he just kind of casually says, 'You know, you guys have this Catholic thing all wrong.' He says, 'I think a Catholic would run better for Vice President, maybe not President. He would run better for Vice President than a Protestant would on the Democratic ticket.' I said, 'Oh is that right, do you have the figures?' 'No,' but he said, 'Let's get some up. Let's research it.' So he called Ted Sorensen in."

This little dance had about as much spontaneity as a Latin Mass. Sorensen, believing that the "Kennedy for Vice President" boomlet would help combat the bigotry facing American Catholics and make it easier to elect one president someday, had already begun looking into data about Catholic voting patterns. He was far from finished with his research, but he brought in some of what he'd found. Knebel reacted by suggesting a piece for *Look*, including quotes from Kennedy himself. Since Kennedy had been hoping to prompt exactly that response, he replied with a single word: "Sure."

Knebel's visit motivated Sorensen to finish his study. The result, completed in the spring of 1956, shortly before Knebel's article was published, was a sixteen-page report loaded with numbers on the Catholic vote in postwar presidential elections. Kennedy decided to distribute the document quietly to a limited number of people to promote public discussion among Democratic Party leaders and selected newspaper columnists. That required a separate decision: What to call it? Kennedy did not want to be linked directly to the self-serving paper. Thus the "Bailey Report" was born.

"I got the credit but Sorensen did the work," the Connecticut boss chuckled later.

Critics later dismissed Sorensen's document as propaganda by a cheerleader. In fact it was accurate, thorough, and prescient.

In Bailey's words, the document "caused many people to think." Sorensen himself said, "The widespread attention accorded its contents at least reopened the previously closed assumption that a Catholic on the ticket spelled defeat."

It is impossible to overstate just how "closed" that assumption had been ever since New York's governor Al Smith was trounced by Republican Herbert Hoover in the 1928 presidential election. Objective analysis of those results has long since confirmed that Smith's religion, while a factor, was far from the major reason he lost badly in the last national contest before the American economy crashed. But the assumption that Catholicism cost the Democrat became unchallenged "fact" almost immediately and lasted nearly thirty years without being refuted.

The "Bailey Report" contained no theology-based discussion of bigotry. Instead it was a dry study of election returns linked to the argument that a national candidate's Catholicism could be a benefit as well as a hindrance. It advanced the idea that a Catholic on the ticket in 1956 could help turn around serious problems for the Democratic Party that were visible in Eisenhower's first victory over Stevenson. This point of view would become central to Kennedy's political strategy. From his flirtation for a place on the 1956 ticket to his election in 1960, he would defend himself vigorously against the notion that Catholic politicians were susceptible to clerical influence. He would also use his own experience dealing with prejudice to mobilize his fellow Catholics. He came to view his religion as a two-edged sword, at least as capable of helping as of hurting.

Sorensen began his report by asking whether there existed, in fact, a bloc of voters who voted as Catholics rather than as Republicans or Democrats. Citing a considerable body of research from prominent sociologists and pioneering pollsters such as Paul Lazarsfeld, Louis Bean, Samuel Lubell, George Gallup, and Angus Campbell, Sorensen was able to answer yes. "All indicate that there is, or can be such a thing as a 'Catholic' vote, whereby a high proportion of Catholics of all ages, residences, occupations and economic status vote for a well-known Catholic candidate or a ticket with special Catholic appeal," Sorensen wrote.

He quoted Lubell: "Catholic voting strength is currently at its peak, in view of the maturing of the offspring of the Italians, Czechs and other former immigrant elements." Sorensen also cited the work of Gallup and Campbell in noting that Catholics consistently turned out to vote in greater proportions than non-Catholics. Examining the raw numbers in the polls, he suggested that because of the large concentration of Catholics in fourteen pivotal states with 261 votes in the Electoral College (five fewer than needed in those days to win the presidency), Catholics were even more important than their overall share of the electorate indicated, then about 25 percent.

Moreover Sorensen argued that anti-Catholic sentiment was concentrated in the South, where Reconstruction lore still made the Republican Party largely anathema and Democrats dominated. National polls were finding that 25 percent of voters were "concerned" about a Catholic candidate; that adverse number was closer to 33 percent in the South. But Sorensen's arithmetic showed that if even a third of those Dixie Democrats stayed home or voted Republican, the "Solid South" that monolithically supported Democratic candidates would still rule and "few if any Southern electoral votes would be lost."

Sorensen understated the opposition among prominent Democrats to nominating a Catholic for national office, a group including House Speaker Sam Rayburn and former president Harry Truman as well as some Catholic Democrats, among them David Lawrence, the mayor of Pittsburgh, who was destined to become a powerful governor, and a former national party chairman, Frank McKinney.

Opponents invariably cited one date, 1928, the year Hoover defeated Smith, as if that ended the argument. Sorensen confronted it by writing, "The 'Al Smith myth' is one of the falsest myths in politics." He embraced the work of a Columbia sociologist, William F. Ogburn, on an issue that had almost been forgotten: Prohibition. Smith had opposed Prohibition, and after studying the returns in 173 counties in northern states Ogburn concluded, "Prohibition sentiment was three times more decisive an influence in the election than the religious issue."

Sorensen also claimed that 1928 was a Republican year anyway, the fruit of eight years of GOP dominance in a period of general prosperity, while Smith was painted as "a Tammany product from the streets of New York, a portly, cigar-smoking stereotype of the immigrant-based political boss." The country had changed since then, Sorensen argued, especially in its view of Catholics as increasingly mainstream. As evidence, one 1956 Gallup poll was headlined "Qualified Catholic Could Be President."

Finally, Sorensen used voting statistics and his gaggle of experts to argue that the famed New Deal coalition of voters began developing in

1928, four years before Franklin D. Roosevelt's election. He employed statistics from urban counties in New Jersey and Ohio with big Catholic constituencies demonstrating that the Democratic vote skyrocketed in 1928, when Smith was a candidate. He invoked a claim made by Lubell, one of the first American pollsters, that the Republican hold on the cities was broken not by Roosevelt but by Smith. And Sorensen quoted a young pollster with the Roper Organization, Louis Harris, who claimed, "Al Smith marked the beginning of the Democratic era which ended in 1952."

With memories of Eisenhower's 1952 election still fresh, Sorensen considered the impact of the Catholic vote. He found that Eisenhower had enjoyed strong support from Catholics who seemed to be moving away from the Democratic base. The shift threatened the party's national interests. Truman's winning margins in four heavily Catholic cities (Chicago, Los Angeles, Cleveland, and Providence) had led to victories in Illinois, California, Ohio, and Rhode Island in 1948. Without the Electoral College votes of those four states, Truman would have lost. Four years later all four states went to Eisenhower.

The ultimate prize in the coming election, in Sorensen's view, was winning those fourteen states where swing-vote Catholics could hold the balance of power and deliver 261 electoral votes to the Democrats, almost enough to triumph

Kennedy had already identified two distinct problems: his age—he was only thirty-nine—and his comparative inexperience in national and international affairs, not to mention politics. He had left few footprints in his first Washington decade. No legislation bore his name, nor was he identified with any significant issue or cause. He had no close allies in Congress, and in the Democratic Party he had a reputation for being an occasional maverick not always amenable to party discipline, much less loyalty.

As spring arrived in 1956, the principal competitors for the second spot on a national ticket headed by Stevenson continued to be Estes Kefauver and Hubert Humphrey. In fact Kefauver was still a presidential candidate; he and Stevenson faced decisive primary contests in Florida and California after the Tennessee senator's early victories in New Hampshire and Minnesota. Meanwhile Stevenson made a weak showing in Massachusetts, where a write-in campaign for House Majority Leader John McCormack, who was assumed to be for Averell Harriman, succeeded.

But Stevenson held the upper hand, and Kennedy knew that both of his potential rivals to join Stevenson on the ticket had regional flaws. If Stevenson chose Kefauver, he would have to confront the powers in the southern Democratic Party, who despised Kefauver for his refusal to play the role of a diehard segregationist. With Humphrey, who had combined traditional liberalism with passionate attacks on racial segregation for nearly a decade, there was an equally stark problem in the South. He too would be looked upon with disfavor by the vital southern bloc.

Kennedy contemplated an opening for himself. Perhaps he might be selected to deliver the keynote speech at the national convention, a job often given to promising fresh faces in the party. But another Massachusetts man, Governor Paul Dever, had been given the honor in 1952, and it turned out badly. Dever, an occasional competitor of Kennedy's back home, gave a lackluster address and wound up losing his bid for reelection. In 1956 the keynote speech was ultimately given to another young and up-and-coming figure, Governor Frank Clement of Tennessee. The "boy orator" was also considered a vice presidential possibility, but the two other Tennesseans, Kefauver and Gore, were thought to outrank Clement on Stevenson's short list.

Even though he was passed over, Kennedy continued to hold out hope of a breakthrough.

That was not his father's attitude. With Eisenhower no longer vulnerable, a place on a losing Democratic ticket would tarnish his son's image—and Catholicism would be blamed for defeat.

In a rare written response to his father, Kennedy downplayed the likelihood of his nomination. He said the attention he was getting would someday be worth his backstage effort, pointing out, "While I think the prospects are rather limited, it does seem of some use to have all this churning up."

Apart from his father's disapproval, Kennedy faced opposition to his selection from two factions in the party that were important to Stevenson: agriculture interests centered in the Midwest and liberals in love with both FDR's legacy and Stevenson's record as an ideological purist.

Almost from the moment he arrived in the Senate, Kennedy had acquired a reputation for being an Eisenhower ally on agriculture. He had cheered the president's proposal to make vital government programs supporting crop prices "flexible": higher in bad times, but lower when prices were producing relative prosperity. But ever since the New Deal, Democrats were advocates of fixed support levels. Their allies on small and medium-size farms were in favor of keeping the price support programs stable, based on a fixed percentage of past levels, a concept known as "parity." Most midwestern Democrats opposed the flexible support idea—not to mention its hard-line and controversial advocate, Agriculture Secretary Ezra Taft Benson.

In the face of mixed conditions in rural America, Kennedy eventually saw the error in his past advocacy and changed his mind, but Democrats from the Farm Belt were not inclined to forget. They generally embraced Kennedy's competitor for Stevenson's attention, Hubert Humphrey. As the vice presidential maneuvering increased in 1956, one of Humphrey's most vocal surrogates, another attractive young governor, Orville Freeman of Minnesota, pronounced Kennedy "unacceptable" in the region.

The misgivings of many liberals were no less formidable. Their doubts primarily concerned Kennedy's record regarding one of their most emotional issues: the activities of Senator Joseph McCarthy of Wisconsin and the practice of communist witch-hunting that became known as McCarthyism in the 1950s.

McCarthy had been elected to the Senate in 1946 as another veteran who had Joseph Kennedy's financial support. No matter that McCarthy was Republican, he was an Irish Catholic and friendly with the family. He had visited the compound on Cape Cod and expressed interest in dating Jack's sister, Eunice. The elder Kennedy continued to support him even after McCarthy emerged as a demagogue who indiscriminately branded blameless Americans as dangerous communists. Joe Kennedy was not his only patron. In the Catholic hierarchy and the more conservative elements of the laity, anticommunism was almost gospel. McCarthy was able to elicit strong support in heavily Catholic Massachusetts, where the most conservative newspaper back then, the *Boston Post*, was often rabidly in his corner.

Further complicating the McCarthy-Kennedy relationship, the senator's younger brother Robert had worked for McCarthy. Just out of law school and after a brief stint in the Justice Department, Robert took a job on his committee as the Democrats' staff director. He was loyal to his party, even joining a walkout they staged over their representation on the committee and its staff. But according to McCarthy's top aide throughout this period, the infamous lawyer Roy Cohn, Robert had no role in the seemingly endless investigations of alleged communist influence in and outside the government. Instead he asked for and got the assignment to look into the practices of Greek shipowners who regularly transported American products to Iron Curtain countries. The trade would have been illegal if direct. Cohn emphasized that Kennedy "had one principal investigation. And he ran that all his way. I had nothing to do with it and he had nothing to do with anything I did. . . . I saw him almost never."

His older brother was not involved in any of McCarthy's activities and never made any statement as a senator supporting him—or condemning him. He did oppose McCarthy on a handful of political matters involving appointments. As a congressman Kennedy had joined McCarthy in pursuing a labor leader from Wisconsin who organized a strike at a factory during World War II and subsequently went to jail for perjury regarding his communist ties. But as a senator Kennedy had stayed silent.

When McCarthy's excesses finally went way too far—involving alleged communist influence in the army—a move to censure him unfolded in the Senate in early 1954. A vote was scheduled, and Sorensen prepared a long statement for Kennedy, justifying a planned Yes vote. But after the Senate decided that it should further investigate the charges, Kennedy canceled its release at the last minute. By the time the probe was completed Kennedy was in a New York hospital after the first of his two surgeries.

When the roll-call vote that destroyed McCarthy came in December 1954, Kennedy was still in the hospital, in serious condition. The reason for his absence has been largely accepted. However, there was another option open that day, involving a Senate procedure known as a "pair," in which two absent senators announce positions on opposite sides of a question. Sorensen was on the Senate floor that day, authorized to pair Kennedy with another senator. Sorensen always insisted it was his own decision not to make the move because he was not then in communication with his ailing boss. He preferred to let Kennedy be recorded as absent on the grounds that it would be wrong for him to take a position on a grave matter he had not studied.

As a result Kennedy's record during the McCarthy period became the subject of much criticism. In a sarcastic reference to his Pulitzer Prize–winning book, *Profiles in Courage*, about eight senators who braved political retribution on principle, Eleanor Roosevelt wisecracked that she wished Kennedy had shown "less profile and more courage."

(The last word, ironically, may have been prepared by Kennedy himself, when there was a stirring of the old embers in 1959, with his presidential campaign already well under way. In elite circles it was triggered by the first major book about the period, by the *New Yorker*'s Richard Rovere. Kennedy arranged to review *Senator Joe McCarthy* for the *Washington Post*. He consulted with several supporters on his draft, including Harvard professor and former Stevenson confidante Arthur Schlesinger Jr. and Edwin O'Connor, author of a best-selling novel about Boston politics, *The Last Hurrah*. At his request they submitted a small number of paragraphs for inclusion in Kennedy's broader, if belated condemnation of McCarthyism, including the following: "In the early 1950s many Americans in Congress and out failed to respond to a sustained series of damaging and irresponsible assaults made in the Senate of the United States against innocent American citizens and against every principle of liberty itself. . . . They were wrong to keep silent. And I was wrong in keeping silent." Kennedy thanked them for their help but never delivered the statement, saying he would keep it "in reserve.")

Farmers, liberals, and his father aside, Kennedy's sub rosa campaign for Stevenson's attention never stalled. It included contacts between Kennedy allies and Stevenson intimates. John Bailey and Sorensen, in particular, tried to stay in touch. At one point in the spring Bailey saw Stevenson himself in Chicago. According to a note Abe Ribicoff wrote to Kennedy, Bailey reported, "Adlai is giving considerable thought to you for the second spot."

Throughout that fateful spring there was one additional Kennedy project, conceived in secret but executed in public with bizarre fanfare. From the time he went to Washington a decade earlier, Kennedy had been slow in accumulating power in his home state. He won his House seat as an outsider; he was elected to the Senate as an outsider. It had been an article of faith in Kennedy's world that Massachusetts's grubby politics were to be shunned.

But by 1956 his lack of clout in the state was a source of concern among an Irish American coterie of his close aides who were steeped in Massachusetts politics. They recognized that Majority Leader McCormack, another Bostonian, had a hold over the state Democratic Party and that his power posed a threat to Kennedy's interests. If he wanted to begin maneuvering for national office, they argued, it was time to challenge McCormack and erase the impression that Kennedy was powerless on his own turf.

CHAPTER THREE

Ousting Onions

Even as Kennedy wrestled with strategy to build national strength and recognition before the 1956 Democratic convention, several of his wily associates pushed on him a less lofty project. They urged him to plunge into the rawest form of politics, to seize control of the Massachusetts state Democratic Party apparatus by overthrowing its chairman in a daring coup d'état.

The move would not only put Kennedy into open conflict with the venerable John W. McCormack, who controlled the party establishment in the state; it would also force Kennedy to engage in the sort of Pier Six brawl with cantankerous county chairmen and committeemen that he had been avoiding since he first became a congressional candidate ten years earlier. His target would ostensibly be the chairman of the party's eighty-member executive committee, William H. Burke, an obscure tavern owner and farmer from western Massachusetts known as "Onions" for one of the crops he raised. But the public fight would be with Burke's patron. And in the words of John E. Powers, a veteran of the Boston political scene, Burke "was controlled wholly by John McCormack. As chairman of the state committee, he operated that just as a subsidiary to John McCormack's office."

McCormack was a native of South Boston, a working-class, Irish Catholic neighborhood justly famous for its insularity and suspicion of outsiders that produced an inordinate number of successful politicians throughout the twentieth century. A generation older than Kennedy, McCormack enjoyed status and seniority on Capitol Hill. He had been a member of the state legislature before Kennedy was in kindergarten and won election to Congress in 1928. He had been the number two Democrat since 1940. As the chief lieutenant for Sam Rayburn of Texas, the speaker of the House, McCormack served as the New England half of the very first "Austin-Boston axis," a reference to the marriages of convenience that were made in Washington between crafty leaders from Texas and Massachusetts.

Though they were fellow Democrats from Massachusetts, Kennedy and McCormack had never been close. In private conversations with friends the young senator spoke guardedly about the older man but made it clear that he did not consider McCormack a role model. At the same time Kennedy knew that seniority delivered authority and license in Congress, and it had been necessary to show deference to the House leader. By undertaking the challenge, Kennedy knew he risked antagonizing not only McCormack but also Rayburn, one of the most durable and influential figures in the capital.

Kennedy would be creating trouble back home as well. He would be battling McCormack loyalists in the party, a cast of characters that seemed to have spilled from the pages of *The Last Hurrah*, published that very year. The book was a colorful fictionalized account of the all-too real career of James Michael Curley, a quintessential Boston politician whose corruption was as famous as the power he accumulated over the years as mayor, governor, and member of Congress—and as inmate at the Federal Correctional Institution in Danbury, Connecticut. Curley had won a full pardon from President Truman in 1950. A few years earlier McCormack had circulated a petition to win Curley's release from prison, and Kennedy had refused to sign it—the only member of the state's delegation to Congress to do so. Kennedy was settling an ancient score. His mother, Rose, had passed on a bit of family history: it was Curley who undermined her father, John Fitzgerald, and helped drive him from office as mayor of Boston in 1913. So the grandson of Honey Fitz turned his back on Curley decades later, and Curley would not forget the slight. Now Curley was out of prison and had two years left to live. He too would be sure to fight Kennedy.

McCormack's South Boston and other ethnic communities in the city were regular battlegrounds, their disputes often over petty issues of patronage; they seemed foreign to Kennedy. Though a descendant of Irish Catholic politicians himself, Kennedy was a son of Harvard and privilege. He did not grow up in "the neighborhoods"; he never lived in "the projects."

Kenny O'Donnell and Dave Powers, two early political allies of Kennedy's, began encouraging him to take over the state party organization after he won his Senate seat in 1952. They argued that the committee was full of hacks, and being veteran Massachusetts Democrats by then, they were familiar with hacks.

O'Donnell had become a loyal member of the Kennedy team in 1946, when Robert Kennedy, his football teammate at Harvard, enlisted him in his brother's first congressional campaign. Ten years later O'Donnell, by this time a corporate public relations man, had become one of Kennedy's most valuable—and unpaid—political advisors in the state. Powers was more than a decade older, and though he lacked an Ivy League degree he was no less vigilant about Kennedy's interests. The son of Irish immigrants in the gritty Boston neighborhood of Charlestown, he evolved into one of Kennedy's closest friends.

Both O'Donnell and Powers studied local politics and fully understood that the tavern owner Burke was indebted to McCormack for his position as collector of the Port of Boston, and they knew that during Democratic administrations the state committee was filled with others who held patronage jobs that could be traced to McCormack. The senator's advisors insisted that the committee was weak and ripe for picking by energetic activists tied to Kennedy. Originally he was not inclined to take that step. But by the spring of 1956 he saw that if he could take charge of the state party he would be in a position to control the state's delegation to the national convention that summer. When his aides renewed their appeal, Kennedy showed interest.

It would require him again to ignore the advice of his father. According to O'Donnell, the elder Kennedy told his son, "Leave it alone and don't get in the gutter with those bums up there in Boston." The fight promised to be the Irish equivalent of a Tong war, and Joe Kennedy complained that O'Donnell and Larry O'Brien, another leader of his son's Irish Mafia, were advocating action "to feather their own nest" in the seedy politics of Massachusetts, an especially ridiculous example of the elder Kennedy's hyperbole habit.

O'Brien, for example, was an attorney with deep roots in the state Democratic Party. His father had been a player in Springfield politics; the son had labored for other Democratic officials before serving as director of Kennedy's 1952 Senate campaign.

There were several subplots in the developing drama.

Kennedy supported Adlai Stevenson in the contest for the Democratic presidential nomination and wanted to arrange for as many Stevenson votes as possible on the Massachusetts delegation. McCormack, on the other hand, was working with Rayburn and former president Truman— who favored New York's governor and former prominent New Deal diplomat Averell Harriman— to deny Stevenson the nomination.

Kennedy was joined by an unlikely ally, former Massachusetts governor Paul Dever. Relations were cool between the two men. Kennedy was on the rise, while Dever had been out of office for four years, powerless and recovering from a heart attack. Onions Burke served as a mutual enemy. Dever was still annoyed that after his loss of the governor's office in 1952 his own man had been replaced as committee chairman. Dever hoped that Burke's overthrow might restore some of his influence while also serving as a measure of revenge. Besides, Dever, like Kennedy, supported Stevenson.

Without revealing that he planned to strip Burke of his chairmanship, Kennedy approached him and McCormack prior to the April primary, ostensibly in the interests of Stevenson's presidential campaign. He told them he was prepared to run as a favorite son himself against McCormack unless they agreed to give him and Dever a hand in selecting convention delegates. If they made that concession, Kennedy said, McCormack could run unopposed as a favorite son—and Burke would be able to continue as chairman.

The deal was struck, and McCormack shared the selection of the delegate slate with Kennedy and Dever. But Kennedy betrayed the second part of the bargain when he set out to find enough fresh candidates to run for seats on the state Democratic committee in the primary in order to stack the organization with his own followers, who would then vote out Burke. Kennedy instructed his staff, "We can't let Burke or McCormack know that we're trying to get our people on the state committee. Keep working on it, but don't let Burke know about it, and don't mention my name to anybody."

The brewing struggle also broke up a tenuous relationship between John Fox, the temperamental publisher of the *Boston Post*, and the equally headstrong Kennedy family.

In 1952 the elder Kennedy loaned Fox $500,000 that the publisher desperately needed to keep his newspaper afloat. The *Post* had been re- liably Republican; now it endorsed young John F. Kennedy, who was opposing incumbent Republican senator Henry Cabot Lodge that year. Though there were suspicions that the father had bought his son the *Post*'s support, the link between the loan and the endorsement did not become known for several years.

But Fox broke with the Kennedys in 1956, when his newspaper began championing McCormack's favorite-son campaign in editorials that ap- peared almost daily. Fox's broadsides were aimed at Stevenson, who was depicted as soft on communism; the editorials implied that Senator Ken- nedy's colors too had turned pinkish. Fox, a Harvard man, had sought Kennedy's support for an alumni committee that would discourage fi- nancial gifts to the school until it purged the faculty of leftists. Kennedy refused to participate and fell from Fox's favor less than two years after the *Post*'s endorsement.

The skirmish over control of the state committee widened as liber- als, who abhorred McCarthyism and Fox, rallied to Kennedy's side. Stal- warts of Americans for Democratic Action (ADA) such as Samuel Beer, a renowned Harvard professor who later became the national chairman of the liberal organization, joined in the putsch against Onions Burke. According to Joseph Rauh, a leading ADA figure who was constantly pushing the national Democratic Party to the left, Kennedy was sud- denly perceived as "a young liberal against the machine."

The morning after the primary Kennedy asked his aides for a head count. Of the eighty committee members who had been chosen, they figured that no more than thirty were loyal to Burke. Twenty were considered friendly to Kennedy. That meant the fight would be decided by the thirty committee members who had not pledged loyalty to either side. Kennedy asked for a list of their names and all the information that could be gathered about each one. He said he intended to visit personally with each of them.

The following day Kennedy drove to the western part of the state to begin canvassing the committee members; he astonished his aides by calling Burke and making an appointment to have breakfast with him in Northampton. The meeting did not go well. Kennedy told Burke he would be voted out of office and suggested that he resign gracefully to save face. Instead of surrendering, Burke warned Kennedy that he would suffer a humiliating defeat if he tried to unseat him. As soon as the breakfast was over, the normally diplomatic senator surprised a local reporter by vowing to remove Burke as chairman. A feud that had been mostly confined to Democratic politicians burst into a public donnybrook, dominating the front pages of newspapers across Massachusetts.

Burke provoked one story with the accusation that Kennedy had offered him Curley's seat on the Democratic National Committee if Burke would step down from the state committee. Curley, an enemy of the Kennedys and a master at assuming the posture of a man unfairly wounded by political calumny, corroborated the story, claiming that Kennedy had tried to bribe him into retiring. "He hasn't got enough money to buy me. I never took any money from him, or from his family, and I never will," declared the legendary Bostonian, who had twice served time for fraud, in state prison in 1904 and in a federal penitentiary in the late 1940s.

The situation degenerated into just the kind of spectacle Joe Kennedy had predicted.

Kennedy had been so preoccupied with dethroning Onions that he failed to tap an alternate candidate. When his aides reminded him to do so, he thought of two Irishmen with whom he felt comfortable: O'Donnell, his brother Robert's roommate at Harvard, and an impressive young man named Dick Donahue, who had a Dartmouth degree and was beginning to attract notice in the party.

O'Donnell argued that the new committee members would reject either one of Kennedy's well-educated friends. "They want an old familiar face," he insisted. He suggested John M. "Pat" Lynch, an old-shoe Irish Democrat who for years had been mayor of Somerville, a Boston suburb. O'Donnell padded Lynch's résumé by pointing out that he had played football at Holy Cross. But when he brought Lynch to meet the senator, Kennedy seemed appalled by Lynch's appearance. He was small, bald, and fit the image of a Boston pol. O'Donnell reasoned that Kennedy "was probably expecting somebody tall and distinguished looking—like Henry Fonda. Instead, I had brought him a leprechaun."

Mired in the ferocious culture of Boston politics, where practitioners joked about "Irish Alzheimer's," a mythical malady causing one to forget everything but a grudge, Kennedy agreed to settle on Lynch as his candidate.

The dispute headed for a showdown, but the two sides could not even agree upon a venue. Burke's forces planned a committee meeting for Saturday, May 19, at a hotel in Springfield, close to Burke's Connecticut Valley home. Lynch's backers called for the meeting to be held at the Hotel Bradford in Boston. When Burke yielded, he said he did so to avoid "further disruption of the Democratic Party."

The day before the gathering, the *Boston Globe*'s front-page headline was "McCormack Rebukes Kennedy, Dever." The paper reported the majority leader saying "he [would] consider it a personal repudiation" if Burke was not reelected chairman. McCormack then implied that Kennedy's failure to support a former Massachusetts congressman, Foster Furcolo, in his Senate race in 1954 had cost the Democratic candidate the election. He also complained that Kennedy seemed to have forgotten how McCormack came to his aid in his 1952 Senate race. (Republican senator Jacob Javits of New York campaigned for Henry Cabot Lodge in a predominantly Jewish neighborhood in Boston, reminding the audience that Kennedy, the Democratic candidate, was the son of a man many believed to be anti-Semitic. McCormack, who represented two of the Jewish wards and was so popular there that he was called "Rabbi," came to Kennedy's defense, ripping Javits in a speech on Blue Hill Avenue in the Roxbury section of Boston.)

The Hotel Bradford, a traditional meeting place off Boston Common, was conducive to Kennedy's interests, but the date was not. His sister Jean was being married that Saturday, and he was expected to be an usher with his brothers Robert and Ted at the ceremony at St. Patrick's Cathedral in Midtown Manhattan. One of the most prominent Catholic clergymen in the land, Francis Cardinal Spellman, was to officiate.

Kennedy flew to New York for the wedding, then quickly caught a shuttle back to Boston. Because McCormack had chosen to stay in Washington, Kennedy's advisors insisted that his presence was vital at the Hotel Bradford that afternoon as the committee members began arriving for the meeting. Kennedy disliked the ritual of glad-handing the small-time politicians, but he made the concession, standing in the lobby, smiling and greeting each committee member with a hearty handshake, a personal word, and an assurance that he stood behind Lynch.

The Kennedy team believed they had 47 votes lined up, enough to defeat Burke. But they were fighting rumors that Joe Kennedy was paying $500 for each one, and some of the Kennedy delegates who had not gotten $500 were left wondering if they had missed out on a deal. Meanwhile McCormack's men were said to be dangling promises of lush patronage jobs before wavering committee members. One member was prepared to switch from Lynch to Burke after he was offered a job as bartender at Otis Air Force Base on Cape Cod. He tearfully switched back to Lynch after Kennedy confronted him.

While Kennedy worked the crowd, he drew glares and boos from Burke's followers. He astonished everyone by approaching the majority leader's brother, Edward "Knocko" McCormack, at three hundred pounds a menacing, intimidating figure. Each year at the rowdy St. Patrick's Day Parade in South Boston, Knocko rode an enormous white horse down Broadway to drunken cheers. Like a pair of prizefighters at the start of a bout, Kennedy and Knocko shook hands. It would be the last gracious gesture of the afternoon.

Kennedy prudently retired to a private room, leaving his political fate in the hands of his aides, who had always been more enthusiastic about the enterprise than he. For their first maneuver, they hired two plainclothes policemen to keep everyone but committee members from the ballroom where the meeting would take place. Although Burke served as chairman of the state committee, he was not a formal member, so the policemen were prepared to stop him from entering. However, Burke was as big and brawny as the guards, and he was accompanied by three of his followers on the committee. Bellowing that Democrats, not the police, would determine who could attend the meeting, Burke and his crew pushed past the officers. Once the doorway was breached, dozens of reporters, photographers, and curious spectators poured into the room. There were cries to expel the press. Amid the commotion, a scuffle broke out between another pair of Irishmen, a pro-Burke committeeman named Cleary and a former Boston election commissioner allied with Kennedy named Connors. When Connors put his nose within an inch of Cleary's face and demanded to know "What right has Burke or the press in here?," Cleary responded by shoving him out the door and a dozen feet down the hallway.

Inside the ballroom the two candidates for chairman exchanged insults. Burke, a hundred pounds heavier than his adversary, told Lynch, "Paddy, I ought to knock you right on your ass." Rising to his full height of five feet, six inches, Lynch the leprechaun replied, "Here's my card, Bill. You know where you can find me."

Meanwhile Knocko McCormack looked as ominous as an aggravated bull. Larry O'Brien, one of Kennedy's top aides, thought it would help to reinforce the two plainclothesmen by calling Boston Police Commissioner Thomas F. Sullivan to the scene. But Sullivan turned out to be a disciple of John McCormack's, and he threatened to arrest O'Brien.

The room teetered toward riot, with shouts and taunts and threats, until Ida Lyons, the committee secretary, called the meeting to order. Kennedy's forces objected to her as an officer on the grounds that she was a member of the committee that was being replaced. There were also arguments over the credentials of new members and whether the chairman's election should be held by secret ballot. But finally, a semblance of order was restored. Assured that the proceedings would remain public, Burke retreated to his private room to await the vote.

In the end it wasn't close. Pat Lynch took 47 votes to 31 for Burke. Reporters found Burke huddled in his room with several of his supporters who had brought him news of his defeat. He was defiant, declaring that he would run against Kennedy in 1958 for the Senate seat. "The junior senator may be able to buy a majority of the members of the state committee at the last hour," he snarled, "but I will face him on his record two years from now. . . . The multi-millionaire senator will be asked by me to place his record before the Democratic voters."

Kennedy ignored Burke's blast. In a statement he called the outcome "the beginning of a new era for Massachusetts Democrats" and insisted that the action was not directed at John McCormack. Then he rushed back to New York, where his sister's wedding reception at the stately Plaza Hotel was still lively.

The next day the Boston Globe described the event at the Hotel Bradford: "The will of United States Senator John F. Kennedy prevailed last night as his choice for chairman of the Democratic State Committee won election at a stormy meeting marked by scuffles, name-calling and booing."

A month later Kennedy met with McCormack in Washington to settle the aftermath of their confrontation over the state committee. The senator was able to bargain from strength. McCormack conceded that it would be "satisfactory" for Kennedy to be elected chairman of the Massachusetts delegation to the Democratic National Convention. Kennedy acceded to McCormack's request that the delegation support him unanimously as a favorite son on the first ballot, and McCormack agreed to release the delegates after one ballot. When McCormack asked for "some position" for Burke, Kennedy told him, "It would be difficult for me to accept Burke because of what he had said."

The victory put Kennedy in a commanding position as the Massachusetts delegation prepared to go to Chicago for the convention. Although he privately held out the hope that he would be chosen as Stevenson's running mate, he continued to deny that this had been the motivation for his move on McCormack and Onions Burke. "I was not fighting for the Massachusetts delegation in order to have 'chips' for the vice presidential race," he wrote in a memo to Ted Sorensen. "I was fighting for it because I had publicly endorsed Stevenson and I wanted to make good on my commitment."

One of the first phone calls Kennedy made after the riotous affair had ended and before he dashed back to New York was to James Finnegan, Stevenson's campaign manager. Still involved in their own tussle with Kefauver, the Stevenson people were pleased.

In retrospect Kennedy's closest advisors were split in their judgment about the wisdom of his fighting for the state party chairmanship. Sorensen believed that Kennedy had "plunged into the fray" against his own instincts. O'Brien felt it had been a mistake, that the battle had not been necessary. But to Kenny O'Donnell and Dave Powers, who had egged on Kennedy to seize control of the state committee, it was a "turning point in his career." Sixteen years later they would write of the Kennedy years, "Those of us who were closely associated with Kennedy regard his fight with Burke and McCormack as his coming of age as a party politician. . . . Kennedy arrived in Chicago as a new figure of stature in the party because he had beaten the Old Guard's John McCormack, a crony of Harry Truman and Sam Rayburn in a power struggle in McCormack's own state." Kennedy's "rise to prominence at the 1956 convention," they wrote, "was entirely due to his hard fight against an onion farmer back in Massachusetts a few months earlier."

CHAPTER FOUR

Winning by Losing

By the middle of 1956 Kennedy had many reasons to be encouraged. He had proved to be the master of politics back home. His cultivation of the press resulted in favorable national coverage; his face was being splashed on the covers of popular magazines. In the "Bailey Report" his Catholicism was portrayed as a plus rather than a minus. And the appearance of his own book, *Profiles in Courage*, added gravitas to his résumé. The thin, 164-page volume paid tribute to a bipartisan handful of men who served in the Senate, from John Quincy Adams shortly after the birth of the nation to Robert A. Taft, a modern conservative from Ohio. Following its publication in the spring of 1956, *Profiles in Courage* quickly made its way to the best-seller list.

With the approach of the Democratic National Convention, to be held in August in Chicago, things seemed to be breaking his way. Now that Stevenson had the presidential nomination in his grasp again, Kennedy felt that he should be included in any group of candidates being considered as Stevenson's running mate. Before leaving for the convention he confided to his secretary, Evelyn Lincoln, "I think I have the best chance with Stevenson."

Kennedy had been an early supporter and had ensured that a majority of the Massachusetts delegation would wind up in Stevenson's column. His family had already laid the foundation for a strong relationship with the former Illinois governor. His father owned Chicago's enormous Merchandise Mart commercial building, and his sister Eunice and her husband, Sargent Shriver, who ran the business for Joe Kennedy, were personal friends of Stevenson. In conversations with members of the Kennedy family, Stevenson talked of his fondness for Jack. Kennedy had his own allies among Stevenson's close advisors, especially Arthur Schlesinger Jr., a leading liberal, and Newton Minow, a partner in Stevenson's law firm.

Even before he took out Onions Burke at the gathering of state Democrats, Kennedy had been making moves to strengthen his influence at the convention. He called Congressman Thomas P. "Tip" O'Neill Jr., a friend who held his old U.S. House seat, to ask if his brother Robert could be appointed as a delegate from the state. No matter that Robert lived in Virginia; he was registered to vote at 108 Bowdoin in Boston, an address, O'Neill once said, that "all the family at one time or other" used as everything but an actual residence. Since most of the elected officials in Massachusetts named themselves delegates, O'Neill doubted there would be room for Kennedy's younger brother. "We kind of looked at Bobby as a kid in those days," he said. But Kennedy was insistent. "Tip, listen," he begged. "The reason I want Bob in there, in my opinion he's the smartest politician I've ever met in my life, and if lightning strikes, I'd like to have him on the floor with the credentials so he can be a real worker for me." O'Neill agreed to give up his own convention seat and allow Robert to serve as his substitute, loyally putting aside a personal dislike for the brash younger Kennedy that he never got over.

Meanwhile Sarge Shriver stayed close to the Stevenson operation and regularly passed on intelligence from Chicago. In July he telegrammed that the *Chicago Sun-Times* had just reported that Stevenson liked either Kennedy or Humphrey as a running mate. The newspaper preferred Kennedy. The Kennedy interests kept up the drumbeat. "We were lobbied to death," one Stevenson aide complained. After hearing from Schlesinger, who was inside the Stevenson circle, that "things looked good," Kennedy finally told Sorensen that he was prepared to make a serious bid for the spot.

He was anything but passive in his backstage activity. At one point in the spring he called a family friend and supporter, Robert Troutman, a politically active lawyer in Georgia, to request help in promoting him for the vice presidential nomination. Troutman, a Kennedy supporter but not a civil rights proponent, mentioned opposition in the region to the liberal Humphrey and the apostate Kefauver; on Kennedy's behalf he contacted Democrats in Georgia and South Carolina and reported a friendly reaction.

Kennedy was already certain of a place center stage at the convention. After the first choice for an early speaking role, Maine's new governor, Edmund Muskie, declined for local political reasons, Paul Butler, the national Democratic chairman, arranged for the ambitious senator to attract some of the spotlight. He asked the filmmaker Dore Schary to include Kennedy in his plans for *The Pursuit of Happiness*, a documentary extolling the party's history that would be shown to the delegates—and a nationwide television audience—on the first night of the convention. While visiting the California home of his brother-in-law, the actor Peter Lawford, Kennedy watched footage of the documentary with Schary. He liked what he saw and even offered some of his own language for the script he would read. Schary found Kennedy "so quick and so charming" when he dubbed his voice onto the film that he suggested to Stevenson that Kennedy would make an excellent partner in the general election.

Kennedy learned a week before he left for the convention that he might also be asked to deliver the speech nominating Stevenson. The two high-profile assignments would make him one of the most visible figures at the convention. But Kennedy began to fear that they might be consolation prizes. It seemed unlikely, he thought, that the man who nominated Stevenson would also be picked as his running mate.

Kennedy remained publicly coy. Landing in Chicago he told reporters, "I am not a candidate, and I am not campaigning for the office." But the activity of his followers said otherwise. The Kennedy organization had been preparing for the convention for weeks. They had been privy to inside information that there was a good chance Stevenson would throw the choice of his running mate to the delegates rather than make the decision himself.

The idea of an open convention had first been floated to Stevenson's high command in February in a memo from John Sharon, a former congressional aide who now worked for Stevenson. Sharon admitted that it was audacious of him to suggest such a departure from tradition, but he felt it could symbolize the democracy of the party, in contrast to a fixed Republican convention, and he argued that it would introduce an element of excitement to the proceedings.

Sharon had gotten to know Kennedy when he worked for a congressman with an office adjacent to Kennedy's, at the time a freshman in the House. He and Kennedy occasionally had lunch together and actually double-dated a few times. He admired Kennedy, but when he wrote the memo he was promoting a concept, not a man. Sharon met resistance from several of Stevenson's key advisors, but he continued to advocate an open selection of the vice presidential nominee in staff discussions and in conversations with political leaders friendly to other potential candidates.

Eventually speculation that Stevenson might turn the selection of his running mate over to the convention appeared in press reports. Through his backchannel contact with allies in the Stevenson campaign— corroborated by inside information conveyed by Sarge Shriver—Kennedy knew an open convention was a distinct possibility. He had come to Chicago hoping that Stevenson would pick him. But if the vice presidential nominee was to be chosen by the delegates, he was prepared to fight for it.

Over the summer political commentators had compiled a growing list of candidates. The nationally syndicated political columnist Doris Fleeson wrote that the Democrats enjoyed "an embarrassment of riches in vice presidential timber" and mentioned Senators Kennedy, Humphrey, and Kefauver.

Because Kefauver had served as chairman of a Senate committee whose investigation of organized crime in America had attracted national television coverage of its hearings, he was better known than his colleague Albert Gore. He added to his name recognition with arduous campaigns in 1952 and 1956 for the Democratic presidential nomination. Sometimes donning a coonskin cap for effect, Kefauver barnstormed across the country and proved to be Stevenson's principal opponent. When he withdrew from his failing campaign before the convention and endorsed Stevenson, Kefauver felt he had earned a favor from the nominee, and as soon as he got to Chicago he announced that he would accept the vice presidential spot if it became available. His supporters opened a "Kefauver for Vice President" headquarters in a ballroom of the Conrad Hilton. Kefauver met with Stevenson and asked him directly if he was in line to become his running mate. Stevenson was non-committal.

Stevenson disliked Kefauver, who had a reputation for excessive drinking and reckless extramarital affairs. Some of his colleagues in the Senate, where he was not very popular, found him crude and conniving. But Kefauver had built considerable strength at the convention by winning delegates during the primary season.

If not as well known as Kefauver, Gore was considered more respectable. He had a following among some fellow senators and members of the party establishment. If Stevenson intended to balance his ticket with a southerner, then Gore might be a safer choice.

The third Tennessean said to be under consideration was Frank Clement, who had visions that his keynote address on the first night of the convention might propel him to heights once reached by William Jennings Bryan, whose "Cross of Gold" speech at the 1896 convention created a delegate stampede that gave Bryan the presidential nomination. (In his address Clement criticized President Eisenhower, a golfer, for gazing down "the green fairways of indifference." He cried, repeatedly, "How long, America, oh how long" would the nation suffer a Republican administration? But the speech was so lengthy and florid that he never materialized as a candidate for the vice presidential nomination. One irreverent journalist composed a mock biblical beginning for his account of the speech: "The Democrats last night smote President Eisenhower with the jawbone of an ass.")

There were others eager to serve with Stevenson. Among them the most prominent was Humphrey, who arrived at the convention believing he would be chosen. The Minnesota senator had made a name for himself at the 1948 convention. As a youthful mayor of Minneapolis his famous speech on behalf of a strong civil rights plank led to a walkout by some Deep South delegations and the formation of a segregationist

Dixiecrat ticket in the general election that year. Humphrey became a bête noire among conservative elements of the party as a result of his outspoken views on race and his progressive record in the Senate. Yet for those very reasons he was embraced as a darling by liberals generally allied with Stevenson.

After a private conversation in late July with Stevenson, Humphrey was convinced he would be chosen. In their talk the prospective presidential nominee had been blunt about his reluctance to choose Kefauver. He had mused openly about Gore, Senator Stuart Symington of Missouri, and Mayor Robert Wagner of New York. After leading Humphrey through a discussion of the strengths and weaknesses of these men, Stevenson asked, "Well, Hubert, why don't you think about it yourself?"

Humphrey had already been thinking about it for weeks. He believed he would be supported by southern leaders in Congress such as the two powerful Texans, Senate Majority Leader Lyndon Johnson and House Speaker Sam Rayburn, as well as Senator Richard Russell of Georgia. Humphrey was so confident he would be Stevenson's choice that he announced in early August that he would be a formal candidate for the vice presidential nomination, a rare break with tradition.

But Stevenson had been put off by a meeting with party elders in late July, when former president Truman dismissed Humphrey as "too radical." The leaders warned Stevenson that Kefauver would be unacceptable and that Catholicism probably ruled out Kennedy. Rayburn was particularly contemptuous of Kennedy. "If we have to have a Catholic," he told Stevenson, "I hope we don't have to take that little pissant Kennedy."

The convention began on August 13 with both Kefauver and Humphrey satisfied they would be on the Democratic ticket before the week was out, while Kennedy had great hope for himself. During opening night ceremonies Kennedy received a resounding ovation from the delegates for narrating *The Pursuit of Happiness*. The Massachusetts delegation staged the first favorite-son demonstration of the week with a noisy parade around the floor, and the cheers for Kennedy when he appeared on stage to take a bow were louder than those for Clement after his keynote address.

The next morning, however, Kennedy had his spirits dampened. A mutual friend, Washington lawyer Abba Schwarz, arranged a meeting between Kennedy and Eleanor Roosevelt, the doyenne of the Democratic Party, in the hope that he might win her favor. The widow of Franklin Roosevelt was known to be cool toward Kennedy. She had disliked his father for years, from the time he served as ambassador to London, when his tolerance of the Nazis had been an embarrassment to her husband. And she felt that Jack Kennedy had been cowardly when the Senate grappled with the zealous anticommunist Joe McCarthy earlier in the decade.

The meeting took place at the Blackstone Hotel, scene of the infamous "smoke-filled room" where Republican satraps chose Warren G. Harding as their party's nominee for president in 1920. When Kennedy arrived, he found Mrs. Roosevelt's suite filled with two of her sons, a daughter-in-law, and a secretary typing in the corner. The noise of telephones constantly ringing was disconcerting, and the disorder grew when several of the Roosevelt grandchildren arrived to pick up their convention tickets. Rather than arranging a private space to talk with her visitor, Mrs. Roosevelt told her grandchildren, "Just sit on the beds. I'm busy."

She was brutally brusque with Kennedy, asking one question: "Why did you not stand up against McCarthyism?"

"That was so long ago," he fumbled, and he gave a rambling account of Senate procedure. But he had been the only senator who did not vote, and though he had a legitimate reason for his absence, he had failed to take a public stand against McCarthy. Mrs. Roosevelt was not satisfied with his explanation and dismissed him.

It was a humiliating experience, and Kennedy was further discomforted later in the day during a private meeting with Stevenson. As he had anticipated, he was asked to deliver the nominating speech. Kennedy asked flatly whether that meant he had been disqualified as a candidate for the vice presidential nomination. "No," Stevenson answered. "Not necessarily." But Kennedy had begun to develop strong doubts. He even recommended Humphrey for the position.

Later in the day Kennedy told his friend Schlesinger, "I think I should know whether or not I've been eliminated before I make the nominating speech." Schlesinger assured him that no decision had been made yet.

In this atmosphere of uncertainty Kennedy tackled his latest high-priority assignment. When first approached about the speech, he and Sorensen had been assured by Stevenson's staff that they would have plenty of time to work on it. Now he was told by a Stevenson aide that the speech was being written by the Stevenson campaign. Less than twenty-four hours before Kennedy would go on national television again, a draft was delivered to Sorensen. He thought it terrible. He found Kennedy on the convention floor and showed him the draft. Kennedy was appalled by the collection of clichés and boring tropes produced by the Stevenson staff.

They went to work on their own version. Kennedy dictated the opening lines and suggested some general ideas, and Sorensen labored through the night. At 7 a.m. he rushed a copy to Kennedy at his hotel. The senator excised some passages and added others. A secretary retyped the new draft, and a copy was sent to the TelePrompTer booth at the convention.

Kennedy would be speaking at 11 a.m., so he and Sorensen boarded a taxi and set off on the long drive to the Chicago Amphitheater, the convention site adjacent to the vast stockyards on the far south side of the city. En route Kennedy looked at his copy of the speech and realized that parts of it were illegible. Oaths reminiscent of his navy days spilled from his mouth. It was a fuck-up of major proportions. As the cab sped down Michigan Avenue, Kennedy saw a familiar face trying to hail a taxi: Tom Winship, a reporter for the *Boston Globe*. The senator commanded the driver to stop and pick up Winship, then he enlisted the journalist's help. As soon as they reached the Amphitheater, Winship went to the press room and typed two clear pages. Kennedy got the refreshed copy to the TelePrompTer fifteen minutes before he would go before the cameras.

Kennedy delivered the address flawlessly, and for the second time that week applause washed over him. At this point he had done all he could do to make himself irresistible as a vice presidential nominee. He didn't know that Stevenson had conducted two private meetings that would turn the convention's orderly process into a night and day of frenetic activity.

In a session with his closest advisors it became clear Stevenson was lean-ing toward an open convention. Some big-city bosses, such as Jake Arvey of Chicago and David Lawrence of Pittsburgh, had come around on the subject, and the only major holdout was Stevenson's campaign manager, James Finnegan. The candidate instructed the group to "thrash it out." Realizing that he alone still opposed the idea, Finnegan gave in.

Fortified by the unanimity among his advisors, Stevenson summoned the party's top leadership to a room at the Stock Yard Inn, adjacent to the Amphitheater, where he told them of his decision. Rayburn, who presided over the convention, and Butler, the Democratic national chair-man, strongly opposed holding an open convention. They felt it reflected Stevenson's indecisive nature, a terminal weakness among politicians. But for once Stevenson's mind was set.

Encountering John Sharon, who had first suggested an open conven-tion, Stevenson said, "John, I have either done the smartest thing in my life or I've done the dumbest thing." Lyndon Johnson, who had attended the meeting, afterward pronounced it "the goddamndest, stupidest move a politician could make."

Near midnight, after formally accepting the nomination, Stevenson shocked the delegates by announcing, "I have decided that the selection of the vice presidential nominee should be made through the free pro-cesses of the convention, so that the Democratic Party's candidate for this office may join me before the nation, not as one man's selection, but as one chosen by our great party, even as I have been chosen."

This triggered a frantic rush involving most of the leading figures of the party as well as men who would dominate American politics for the coming decades, and it set the stage for an afternoon of drama the next day. No modern convention since then has matched the suspense, intrigue, deal making, and high-stakes pressure it produced over an eighteen-hour period.

Kefauver felt betrayed. He called New York's Liberal Party leader, Alex Rose, one of his most prominent supporters, and told him, "I'm packing up and I'm leaving Chicago with a blast. They double-crossed me." Rose pleaded with him not to do anything intemperate, then hurried to Kefauver's suite, where others were counseling him to stay and make a run for the second place on the ticket. "At least talk to Adlai before you leave town," suggested the pollster Elmo Roper.

Kefauver agreed to accompany Roper to a private visit with Stevenson. Mollified by their conversation, he then agreed to have his name put in nomination, and his forces began an all-night effort to track down delegates who had supported his presidential campaign.

However, the Tennessee delegation refused to endorse Kefauver. He was so unpopular among most of his fellow Tennesseans that they had intended to vote for Clement as an alternative. Then, when Clement's speech failed to generate momentum, the delegation turned to Gore, using the unit rule to ensure that he would get all 32 of the state's votes. (For the states that used it, a simple majority could command an entire delegation.)

A similar situation prevailed in the Texas delegation, which had been prepared to support Clement in an effort to block Kefauver, who was detested by both Rayburn and Johnson. A short-lived Gore campaign, which attracted scattered southern votes, materialized among other foes of Kefauver.

Sure that he would be chosen, Humphrey was actually writing his acceptance speech when he heard of Stevenson's decision. He and his team also scurried to round up delegates.

A cross-current of machinations occurred within the New York delegation, where the rivalry between Governor Harriman and Mayor Wagner resulted in Wagner's decision to make a largely symbolic run for the vice presidential nomination. (This was after a feeble effort by Harriman to mount a challenge for the presidential nomination ended in a first-ballot landslide for Stevenson.)

Following his unplanned meeting with Kefauver, Stevenson felt it was necessary to invite all of the prospective running mates to come see him to demonstrate that he had not intended to show favoritism to Kefauver. When he arrived, Kennedy grumbled to members of Stevenson's operation that it seemed to be "a fixed convention."

While he waited in Stevenson's suite, Kennedy had a short, private talk with Wagner in a bathroom. Wagner assured him that the New York delegation—the convention's largest, with 98 votes—would support Wagner on the first ballot, then rally behind Kennedy on the second. The warring New Yorkers agreed on one thing: it would be helpful to have a Catholic on the ticket.

While Kennedy dealt with party power brokers, his team gathered in a suite at the Conrad Hilton to plot their course. Most of his family was there as well, but it was Robert Kennedy who tackled the unpleasant duty of calling his father on a transatlantic telephone line to announce that Jack was making a run for the ticket. Robert winced as his father unleashed from overseas what Kenny O'Donnell described as "blue language." Joe Kennedy called his oldest surviving son an "idiot" and predicted that he was destroying his political career. At the end of the conversation, overheard by others in the room, Robert looked around with a wan smile and said simply, "Whew."

Despite their father's outburst, the Kennedys worked through the night. Armed with a pen and a legal pad, Robert began a haphazard tally of friendly delegates in various states. John Bailey, the party boss from Connecticut, spoke up: "This isn't the way to do this thing." He suggested assigning specific supporters to contact each delegation to plead Kennedy's case in individual caucuses before balloting began at noon.

The Kennedy advisors were relative novices in the exercise of power. When Carmine DeSapio, the head of New York City's Tammany Hall political organization, came to the Kennedy suite, he was kept waiting for a half hour. No one knew who he was or that he was prepared to help deliver his delegation to Kennedy.

After daybreak Kennedy spoke at several caucuses and met with many key people. He was pleased to learn that the Georgia delegation planned to give all its votes to him on the first ballot. His efforts to build a political alliance in Dixie—something that would prove impossible in a few years—began that day. He knew that some of the durable old bulls in the Senate, committee chairmen such as Jim Eastland and John Stennis of Mississippi, might be open to courtship. These men personally liked the young senator from Massachusetts, and they loathed Kefauver. Terry Sanford, a future governor and senator from North Carolina, said Kennedy's support among his state's delegates was "a way of knocking down Kefauver, whom they considered a traitor to the South."

When the afternoon session began, Kennedy asked Abe Ribicoff to give his nominating speech. Ribicoff noted the irony of a Jew advocating a Catholic for the ticket. To display southern support, Kennedy arranged for his good friend Senator George Smathers of Florida to second the nomination. Midway through his speech Smathers felt a sharp pain in his back and feared he was being seized by a heart attack, but the discomfort was caused by a gavel wielded by Sam Rayburn. He hissed for Smathers to yield for a surprising endorsement from John McCormack. In the hubbub on the floor, Robert Kennedy had approached his brother's rival in the Bay State delegation to ask if he would speak on Jack's behalf. "I guess so," McCormack said unenthusiastically. Standing at the rostrum he called for the convention to "go East for a vice presidential candidate," but he did not mention Kennedy's name until the final sentence.

This was the first convention to have a wide television audience. Coverage was gavel-to-gavel, so cameras were on hand to capture all of the excitement. The unfolding scene was described the next day in the *New York Times* by Russell Baker as "a spectacle that might have confounded all Christendom in the old days," a political struggle in an atmosphere shaken by "a shrieking pandemonium with 11,000 people on their feet and howling."

Given space to watch the proceedings on television in the Stock Yard Inn, a few steps from the convention hall, Kennedy huddled inside Room 104 with only Sorensen and a Chicago plainclothes officer, assigned as a guard, as companions. There was a knock on the door. Tom Winship, the *Globe* reporter, had tracked down the senator. He asked, "Any chance of coming in to watch the balloting on TV?"

"Sure," said Kennedy. "Come on in." After several nights with little sleep and days filled with activity, he was visibly exhausted, lying on a bed in his undershorts. He liked to bathe to relax and soothe his aching back, and was waiting for the tub to fill.

Kennedy enjoyed the company of Winship, a colorful, uninhibited personality whose years at Harvard had overlapped his own. While the candidate soaked in the tub, Winship sat on the closed toilet seat and they chatted.

After the preliminaries and nominating speeches, the first roll-call vote began shortly after 2:30 p.m. and proceeded along fairly predictable lines. Kefauver did well in the states where he had won delegates in the primaries. Gore's strength was confined to the South. Humphrey collected scattered votes from delegations with pockets of liberals, but he trailed almost everywhere but in his home state. Wagner got all of New York's 98 votes, but other than two nearby states on the eastern seaboard, New Jersey and Delaware, he was shut out. The biggest surprise came from Kennedy's strong showing; he took all the votes in the southern states of Georgia, Louisiana, and Virginia to build on his support in the Northeast.

At the end of the balloting an organist played "Linger Awhile" as officials double-checked the numbers: Kefauver 483½; Kennedy 304; Gore 178; Wagner 162½; Humphrey 134½. No one was close to the 687 votes needed to win the nomination. Officials prepared for round two. (Prolonged balloting once seemed pro forma at Democratic conventions. While it had taken Bryan only five ballots to win the 1896 nomination, John Davis struggled through 103 ballots before he was nominated in 1924.) It would have seemed inconceivable in Chicago that afternoon, but since that time no national political convention has been forced to a second ballot.

Calculations were difficult because no competitive roll calls had been expected after Stevenson secured the presidential nomination. The Amphitheater's engineers had taken down the Totalizer—a device similar to a basketball scoreboard—leaving delegates to keep track of the voting on the backs of envelopes and loose sheets of paper. Although the television networks were able to maintain an unofficial running count for the nationwide audience, it became almost impossible to get an accurate figure on the floor.

The little group in Room 104 watched developments on TV with the rest of the country. Kennedy seemed serene. He expressed delight over the unanimous vote from Georgia and attributed Virginia's support to the fact that he had served on navy PT boats during World War II with the son of Virginia's former governor, John S. Battle. But he knew that he needed more votes, and he was not sure where to turn.

After his second-place finish on the first ballot, Kennedy was moved to a larger room to accommodate a growing group of followers. On the convention floor the scene became chaotic. While conventioneers paraded up and down the aisles, bearing placards for their favorites and tooting horns, others stood on chairs, clamoring for attention. Kennedy partisans roamed the Amphitheater, looking for anyone who might help. "Bobby and I ran around the floor like a couple of nuts," said Kenny O'Donnell. "We didn't know two people in the place."

In a desperate attempt to arrest Kefauver's advantage, Robert Kennedy grabbed at the arm of Michigan's governor, G. Mennen "Soapy" Williams, as he moved off the floor. Forty of Michigan's 44 votes had gone for Kefauver on the first ballot. "Why are you against my brother?" Robert demanded. Williams, a leader of liberal forces in the party, was "flabbergasted" by the confrontation and shook himself free from the young man. Williams had a more important mission. He headed toward a room behind the rostrum where Humphrey was cloistered with a few advisors.

Humphrey had watched the first roll-call vote with dismay. He already felt deceived by Stevenson; now he was rejected by 90 percent of the delegates. He knew political jackals would be coming to ask him to give his votes to another. Never a man to hide his emotions, he began to cry softly.

Learning that Kefauver himself was on his way to meet with Humphrey, Kennedy dispatched Sorensen to see if he could arrange his own meeting with Humphrey. It was a daunting assignment for the twenty-eight-year-old aide, and his naïveté quickly showed. He couldn't locate

Humphrey, but he encountered, by chance, Humphrey's campaign manager, a sardonic congressman from Minnesota named Eugene McCarthy. When Sorensen suggested a parlay between Kennedy and Humphrey, McCarthy brushed him aside. "Forget it," he told Sorensen. "All we have are farmers and Protestants," making a reference to Kennedy's Catholicism and his recent votes—unpopular in the farm states—on agriculture bills.*

While Sorensen was turned back, Kefauver succeeded in finding Humphrey's hideout, where Soapy Williams and Michigan's Democratic party chairman Neil Staebler were already imploring the Minnesota senator to yield his support. Kefauver embraced the weeping Humphrey and appeared close to tears himself. "Hubert, I've just got to have those delegates," he pleaded. "Hubert, you've just got to help me."

Humphrey croaked instructions to an aide: Go tell Senators Stuart Symington of Missouri and J. William Fulbright of Arkansas, "I'm for Kefauver."

As the second ballot moved alphabetically through the states, Missouri switched. After giving Humphrey 34½ votes on the first ballot, the state now threw 36 of its 38 votes to Kefauver.

But the move barely slowed Kennedy's building momentum. At this point he led Kefauver 256½ to 196.

Across the convention floor delegates were baying to be heard. California had passed on its turn, unable to get a firm tally on a delegation divided between 37 for Kefauver and 25 for Kennedy. James Roosevelt, Eleanor's son, wrestled with another Californian for control of the state's standard, a post marking the location of the state's delegation on the floor.

From the podium the acting convention chairman, Senator Warren Magnuson, peered into the confusion and called on other states. Nevada gave Kennedy 13½ of its 14 votes. New Jersey, which earlier had supported Wagner, awarded Kennedy 30 of its 36 votes.

---

* There were untold ironies to the exchange. Twelve years later McCarthy, once a Catholic seminarian himself, would run for the Democratic presidential nomination as an opponent of the Vietnam War. The antiwar movement would drive President Johnson from office and help defeat his vice president, Humphrey, in the general election. But the turbulent 1968 campaign would also claim the life of Robert Kennedy, who entered the contest for the Democratic nomination. After Johnson dropped out, Kennedy was assassinated on the night he defeated McCarthy in the California primary.

New York, the giant, was next. The Tammany chieftain Carmine DeSapio, inscrutable behind tinted glasses, announced, "New York gives one and a half votes for Kefauver; ninety-six and a half votes for the next vice president of the United States, John Kennedy."

The Amphitheater shook with roars.

A more stunning report came from Texas. Though Johnson had lobbied for Humphrey, and Rayburn's dislike of Kennedy was known, the two leaders' antipathy toward Kefauver moved them to swing the state from its support of Gore. Bound by a unit rule, Texas switched to Kennedy. Never one to shy from a dramatic moment, Johnson gripped the microphone and shouted, "Texas proudly casts its fifty-six votes for the fighting sailor who wears the scars of battle, that fearless senator, the next vice president of the United States, John Kennedy of Massachusetts."

The Texas vote pushed Kennedy's lead over Kefauver to 504 to 395. He appeared to be approaching a majority. Robert Kennedy could be seen on the convention floor, flashing two fingers in a "V for victory" salute. Sarge Shriver burst into Kennedy's hotel room, yelling, "Jack, you've got it!"

Kennedy, however, counseled his team to restrain themselves. Kefauver was not yet beaten.

After all of the states were recorded at the conclusion of the roll call, Kennedy held 613½ votes to 551½ for Kefauver. Instead of moving automatically to a third ballot, officials on the rostrum recognized Kentucky for a switch. The state moved its 30 votes from Gore's column to Kennedy. The senator from Massachusetts reached his high-water mark of 643½ votes—only 43½ from winning.

New drama was taking place off-stage involving the Tennessee delegation. Many in the state party had never forgiven Kefauver for breaking the political machine that once ruled the state, the organization of Ed "Boss" Crump of Memphis. Rather than rally behind him, the delegation was prepared to stick with Gore, even though he had fallen to only 110½ votes during the second ballot.

Gore had retreated from the floor to follow the events on television in the Railroad Room, a free watering spot for delegates and reporters that the railroad industry regularly sponsored at the conventions. It was there that Silliman Evans Jr., publisher of the *Tennessean*, an influential Nashville newspaper, found him. Like most publishers, Evans acted as a booster for his home state. He loved the idea of having a Tennessee man on the ticket, but it seemed obvious that Gore could not be that man. He lacked the delegates.

Now Evans reminded Gore that his career had been nourished by the editorial support of his father, Silliman Evans Sr., and the *Tennessean*. Gore's career would be ended, promised Evans, if he didn't get out of the race and yield his votes to Kefauver. Clutching Gore's lapels, Evans warned him, "You'll never get the Tennessean's support for anything again, not even dogcatcher."

Chastened by the newspaper publisher and pressured by events, Gore returned to the floor. Only minutes after his state had cast all 32 of its votes for him on the second ballot, he got recognition to speak. He was brief: "Mr. Chairman, with thanks to this great, free Democratic convention, I request that my name be withdrawn in favor of my colleague, Senator Estes Kefauver."

The hall erupted into new roars. Wildly waving their standards, delegations from several states sought recognition. One of those states was South Carolina, which was ready to throw all 20 of its votes to Kennedy, which might have checked Kefauver's sudden momentum. But Rayburn chose to recognize Oklahoma, which moved its 28 votes from Gore to Kefauver. Then Minnesota gave all 30 of its votes to Kefauver. Missouri followed with 37 votes for Kefauver, putting him slightly ahead of Kennedy. The trend became irreversible.

Afterward some of Kennedy's advisors privately complained that Rayburn had recognized the pro-Kefauver delegations as payback to Kennedy for the embarrassment he had caused Rayburn's ally John McCormack at the state convention in the spring.

But Kennedy was magnanimous in defeat. Seeing from the televised proceedings that a succession of states was falling for Kefauver, he looked at Sorensen and simply said, "Let's go." The pair hurried from the hotel room to an unguarded back door to the Amphitheater and made their way to the rear of the platform. Kennedy took a seat behind Rayburn, who was trying to restore order in the raucous arena. Someone whispered to the convention chairman that Kennedy was there.

The Virgin Islands had just changed its 3 votes to Kefauver. Rayburn pounded the gavel, shouting, "Will the convention be in order?" He paused as the noise subsided. "If there is no objection, the chair will recognize Senator John Kennedy of Massachusetts."

For the third time that week the spotlight fell on Kennedy. He smiled and waved at friends. His eyes appeared to be glistening. Then, speaking without notes, he expressed appreciation "to Democrats from all parts of the country, north and south, east and west, who have been so generous and kind to me this afternoon." He said the outcome "bears out the good judgment of our Governor Stevenson in deciding that this issue should be taken to the floor of the convention," and he closed his brief remarks by saying the convention "has selected a man who has campaigned in all parts of the country, who has worked untiringly for the party, who will serve as an admirable running mate to Governor Stevenson." He asked that the convention "make Estes Kefauver's nomination unanimous."

There were final, thunderous shouts from the floor and the spectators gallery, and it was over.

Stevenson had been watching the event on television with several advisors in his suite at the Blackstone. When it was clear that Kefauver would be his running mate, he perceptibly slumped, as if he himself had been defeated.

CHAPTER FIVE

The Decision

Kennedy had won the respect of the Democratic delegates as well as the adoration of many in the national television audience. Even the most vociferous critic of his bid for a place on the ticket—his father—had called from overseas to praise him for his performance and to declare that the convention could not have gone better. Kennedy had gained prominence but would not be saddled with a formal spot on Stevenson's doomed ticket. He seemed to have a limitless future that could include a serious push for the presidency in 1960.

Though he had been optimistic during his race for the vice presidential nomination, Kennedy had always been philosophical about his chances. Weeks before the convention he had mused privately with Ted Sorensen about his prospects. He hoped to be chosen in Chicago, but doubted he would be. Asked if he would be disappointed if the exercise failed, he was characteristically dispassionate. "Yes," he told Sorensen. "And that disappointment would be deep enough to last from the day they ballot on the vice presidential nomination until I leave for Europe two days later."

Kennedy departed for Europe almost immediately following the convention, leaving his very pregnant wife with her mother in Rhode Island. He stopped by his father's luxurious hangout in France before going sailing and partying in the Mediterranean with an entourage that included his brother Ted and a Harvard buddy who had been elected to Congress from Massachusetts in 1954, Torbert Macdonald. Kennedy was at sea when he got word that Jacqueline had gone prematurely into a difficult labor, producing a stillborn daughter they would name Arabella. He didn't abandon his pals and return home right away, however, but left it to his brother Robert to be in Jacqueline's hospital room when she awoke from her ordeal. It was an example of Kennedy's feckless relationship with his wife, a faithlessness that went largely unreported in his lifetime. Once he returned, he tried to make amends by spending the next two weeks with her before returning to Washington.

Instead of plunging back into Senate business, Kennedy developed a role for himself in the six weeks left until the November election. Well aware of what a valuable commodity he had become, the Stevenson campaign initially suggested that he campaign for the ticket in the Northeast, where Stevenson had done poorly in 1952. Kennedy had other plans. He didn't bother rejecting the Stevenson organization's casual suggestion; he simply drew up a national campaign schedule for himself designed to maximize his exposure during a period that would extend a few months past the election.

According to John Sharon, the Stevenson aide, Kennedy's attitude frustrated the nominee's campaign. "We tried to get Kennedy to speak in those states where he was most effective, particularly in Massachusetts," Sharon recalled. "Jack had his own invitations to speak around the country. He pretty much ran his own campaign. There was a lot of mumbling about that."

Kennedy was a hot property that fall. Sorensen remembered going to Kennedy's home in the tony Washington suburb of McLean, Virginia, early one September evening: "I took over a briefcase filled with speaking invitations that had poured in from all over the country. I placed on his dining room table those I thought were of serious interest, arranging them by geography and date, trying to form a rough speaking schedule for the next several months, arranging them also in terms of priority and category—including political gatherings, universities and civic organizations. After a long night working out a tentative schedule, he casually uttered seven fateful words, 'You may as well come with me.'"

This was the beginning of an intimate association that would last another seven years and hundreds of thousands of miles, fusing Kennedy's fresh political mind with Sorensen's, the man he called his "intellectual blood bank." But in the autumn of 1956 what they mapped out on that dining-room table would produce in barely six weeks more than 150 separate appearances in twenty-four states covering at least thirty thousand miles. Only Stevenson and Kefauver campaigned harder or more visibly.

At nearly all of his appearances, Kennedy was a vigorous partisan—but far more on behalf of the Democratic Party than on behalf of Adlai Stevenson. He was crafty enough to be supportive, avoiding any accusation that he was ignoring the nominee. But his focus dealt more often with party differences than candidate differences. As he put it in Winston-Salem, North Carolina, in early October, "Perhaps the most striking contrast between our party leadership and that of the Republicans . . . is the predominance of young leadership in the Democratic Party and the absence of that leadership on the Republican side." To make his point, a cascade of names rolled from his tongue: Albert Gore, Hubert Humphrey, Russell Long (son of the legendary Huey Long and by then a young Louisiana senator), Mike Mansfield, Lyndon Johnson, Estes Kefauver, and several governors: Edmund Muskie of Maine, Robert Meyner of New Jersey, G. Mennen Williams of Michigan, Abraham Ribicoff of Connecticut, Orville Freeman of Minnesota, and LeRoy Collins of Florida. The name he didn't mention was his own, though it had now become arguably better known than any of the others.

Compared to this roster of promising Democrats, Kennedy concluded, the Republicans had only Dwight D. Eisenhower and, for the future, Richard Nixon. Case closed, he would add to cheers.

That was Kennedy in public. Behind the scenes his political activity was much less subtle. Even before he hit the road he was parceling out political assignments to his intimates. On September 5, his brother-in-law Sargent Shriver sent a note to Kennedy's secretary, Evelyn Lincoln: "Sen. Kennedy asked me to obtain for him a complete list of all the delegates and alternate delegates to the Democratic National Convention together with their home addresses." The delivery date was set for the next day; if past conventions served as any guide, the vast majority of the delegates would return in 1960.

Once on the road Kennedy made more than one stop in New York City, usually in the company of Mayor Wagner, who was running an uphill race for the Senate against the popular liberal Republican Jacob Javits. In addition to speaking, Kennedy took extra time to make radio and television commercials for Wagner.

"We were conscious that he was going to run for a number of years," Wagner said later, "especially after the '56 convention. It was obvious Jack Kennedy had some plan in mind because he was moving around upstate and in New York City. He was meeting with the leaders."

Kennedy's plans were even more explicit next door, in New Jersey. That fall he cemented friendships with two Democratic congressmen who became close personal friends, Frank Thompson and Harrison Williams, who would later be elected senator. Thompson, who had not attended the Chicago convention, asked Kennedy to be the main attraction for a party dinner that fall. While they were together Kennedy brought up 1960 and sought Thompson's help.

"He wasn't quite that definite about it," Thompson remembered. "He said, 'I have some hopes for 1960.' I wasn't sure at the time whether it was vice president again or President. But he asked if I would do whatever I could to help him in New Jersey between then, 1956, and 1960."

For Kennedy the highlight of his grueling national tour may have been an October foray into Louisiana. This was one of the Deep South states that had given his vice presidential chances surprising support at the Chicago convention. The Louisiana delegation had been seated across from Massachusetts on the floor, and several of the delegates, seeing Kennedy as an attractive young politician with a future, voted for him. That fall the attraction deepened.

Kennedy's hosts were a collection of Democrats who were considered racial moderates by the southern standards of the day. Unlike their counterparts elsewhere in the region, they sought closer ties to the national party, could see the handwriting on the wall about the future of official segregation, and wanted to nudge their poverty-plagued state further into the twentieth century. The group included Camille Gravel, the state representative on the Democratic National Committee and an ally of the national chairman, Paul Butler of Indiana; a state party colleague, Philip Desmarais; and a popular local figure, Edmund Reggie from the Cajun country town of Crowley.*

Stevenson's earlier appearance in the state had been borderline perfunctory; for Kennedy, though, they pulled out all the stops. During the day he was escorted to a raucous Yambalaya Festival in Opelousas, where he was featured in the parade, took time to crown the festival queen, and briefly addressed a party rally. In the evening he was taken to New Orleans, where he appeared at the season's major Democratic Party dinner—an occasion for the first statewide broadcast on live television. He was still telling tales about the day months later.

Kennedy's appearance also helped solidify the ties among these moderate, mostly Catholic Democrats in a state that was one-third Catholic. Along with some labor union leaders, they put together an organization after the election, the United Democrats of Louisiana, that became the nucleus of Kennedy's presidential campaign in the state.

Kennedy was not the only member of his family hitting the road that September to experience the maelstrom of a presidential campaign for the first time. While he and Sorensen endured the logistical nightmare of travel by themselves, his brother Robert joined Stevenson's traveling staff for the stretch drive. According to Schlesinger, the request came from Stevenson to Jack, who volunteered his brother. Robert's job was to connect with Democratic politicians, especially Catholics, as the entourage moved around the country. His presence was noticed but not widely publicized. To more than one Stevenson aide it was apparent that Robert was there to learn as much as help.

Sharon said the idea of enlisting Robert originated with James Finnegan, the campaign manager, who was both sensitive to Steven-

---

* Reggie's daughter, Victoria, would one day marry Ted Kennedy.

son's need to attract more Catholics and eager to show Democrats that the suddenly very popular Jack Kennedy was on their team. The actual appearance of the younger Kennedy, however, drew mixed internal reviews. "I thought it was sort of a tragic sight," Sharon recalled, "because whenever the governor would appear, Bobby would stand up and take a bow to the cheers of the crowd. But he never did anything. If I had been Bobby I would have been frustrated as well if all I did was sitting around, traveling, standing up and taking bows."

As Schlesinger put it, "From my own viewpoint on Stevenson's staff, Robert Kennedy seemed an alien presence, sullen and rather ominous, saying little, looking grim and exuding an atmosphere of bleak disapproval. . . . Robert Kennedy seemed uncomfortable with the rest of us. One's memory was of Bobby making notes, always making notes."

There were no complaints about his performance from Stevenson's top aide, William McCormick Blair Jr.: "I know he felt that we made lots of mistakes, and of course we did. But he was always nice about it."

According to Robert's roommate on the campaign trail, Stevenson's law partner Newton Minow, "Bob learned what not to do. Adlai spent too much time writing his own speeches and not meeting people. Bob didn't like Adlai and he made no attempt to hide it."

What bothered the young and impatient Kennedy was the campaign's chronic indecision. It seemed to start with the candidate, and to the thirty-year-old it was maddening. He collected all the notes he made in the back of buses, trains, and planes that fall and used the material in a lengthy report that was closely held within his family after the election. The document amounted to his treatise on what a bad campaign looked like.

Much of the report was devoted to relatively minor gripes about scheduling, speaking style, and shoddy advance work. But the younger Kennedy made it clear the indecision really bothered him. His feelings were crystallized by an all-day conference Stevenson held with his senior staff at his home north of Chicago in Libertyville with just a few weeks left in his campaign. At the time Stevenson trailed Eisenhower in public polls by more than 20 percentage points. "He spent all day long discussing matters that should have taken, at the most, a half-hour," Robert wrote.

Robert called the day "a real eye-opener for me. It was a conference that really disturbed me as far as thinking that he should be president of the United States. . . . Stevenson just did not seem to be able to make any kind of decision. . . . Stevenson was just not a man of action at all."

Years later Robert confessed an amazing secret to John Bartlow Martin, one of Stevenson's speechwriters, who went on to become an experienced diplomat in the Kennedy administration: on Election Day he voted for Eisenhower.

Despite his brother's skepticism, Jack Kennedy did not share the view of most observers, that Stevenson didn't have a chance of being elected president. "Well, in September, I thought he might [win]," he later recalled. "I thought he had a pretty good chance. At the end of the convention we all got excited. Well, for a little while there. Stevenson was awfully active and Eisenhower wasn't. I was just talking to Democrats."

By October, however, the Eisenhower victory appeared imminent, though Kennedy gamely soldiered on to the end. In addition to getting yet another shot at a national television audience as the host of the Democrats' telethon on the eve of the election, Kennedy was also chosen as the Democratic representative on NBC's *Meet the Press* on the final Sunday in October. The popular program had been on the air since the late 1940s. Besides a moderator, its panel of newsmen included a permanent panelist whom Kennedy and his father knew well, the acerbic Lawrence Spivak, and three reporters who had plenty of time in a half-hour show to ask follow-up questions. (This was a long time ago in America: the sponsor was a company that plugged the virtues of its brake linings, which were made with asbestos.)

Like the scores of people who introduced him around the country that fall, the longtime moderator, Ned Brooks, referred to the drama of the national convention and presented Kennedy as someone with considerable "future possibilities."

In close-up this was the Kennedy Americans would gradually get to know well: loyally partisan but also cool, in what seemed effortless command of detail but also forceful; he had gained weight, his features were filled out, and at thirty-nine he no longer looked or sounded young. His words came directly from the campaign trail, emphasizing the differences between the parties more than the Stevenson-Eisenhower battle and arguing that the Democrats had the corner on youth and vigor and thus the future.

But he was also the same independent-minded Democrat who occasionally ruffled his more partisan colleagues. He spoke in depth about his past disagreements with other Democrats over farm policy. He disagreed with a Stevenson suggestion to end the military draft and was quizzed closely about the preponderance of southern votes he won during his brief pursuit of the vice presidential nomination. In all, his thirty minutes on *Meet the Press* did far more for Kennedy than for Stevenson.

The Eisenhower victory was definitive: 57 percent of the popular vote, forty-one states carried, 457 electoral votes in the last presidential election before Alaska and Hawaii became states and enlarged the Electoral College. But it was a lonely landslide, as the Democrats solidified their control of both houses of Congress. For the next four years Eisenhower would once again have to deal with two very closely allied Texans: Speaker Rayburn and Senate Majority Leader Johnson, whose presidential ambitions knew no bounds.

Inside Kennedy's Senate office Sorensen went to work almost immediately on a private update of all his information about Catholic voters that had been compiled as part of the "Bailey Report." What had been cited as very worrisome after the 1952 election was starting to look perilously like a realignment in 1956. Sorensen described "a steady turning of Catholic voters away from the Democratic Party, particularly in Presidential campaigns." In his analysis the significant voting bloc that was 66 percent Democratic for Truman in 1948 and just 50 percent in 1952 had sided with the Republican nominee in 1956 "for the first time in more than a generation." The list of states that went for Eisenhower (and their Catholic vote percentages) included Rhode Island (60), Massachusetts (50), New Jersey (39), Connecticut (49), Louisiana (34), and New Mexico (46). For good measure he threw in some major cities that flipped, including Chicago (49), Milwaukee (41), and Baltimore (31).

Kennedy himself supplied another hint of his interest, and in the oddest of venues: Boston's venerable, Brahmin-ruled social organization, the Tavern Club. Located off an alley in downtown's tiny theater district, it was a symbol of the blue-blooded aristocracy that had kept down Irish Americans like the Kennedys for decades; the club harbored members whom the rogue politician James Michael Curley enjoyed disparaging as "the people who part their names in the middle." Just two days after the election Kennedy showed up at the Tavern Club to make his first post-election appearance, or as he quipped, "my first major speech in many months that has not begun with those stirring and memorable words, 'Fellow Democrats.'"

Kennedy did not shy away from poking gentle fun at his august audience. He noted that his appearance was strictly off the record and said he appreciated their adherence to the ground rules of secrecy in order to secure his candor. But he couldn't resist adding, "This may be due in some measure to the fact that I have never confided in you."

His remarks had been prepared with obvious care, befitting a national player whom some of the club members would nonetheless have described as coming from the wrong side of the tracks. There was wry wit about his defeat in Chicago, as well as humor about the indignities of life on the road.

Kennedy also had a decent tidbit for his hosts. After recounting his experiences in Stevenson's presidential campaign he simply said, "Indeed there is always the danger that I may participate in another one myself." As hints go, that was fairly strong, even if confined to the club dining room.

What the public did not hear in 1956 were Kennedy's private discussions with his family about running for president in 1960. Kennedy listened to his sisters' concerns about his health, which had been a problem ever since he entered politics. It had been eighteen months since his convalescence after his two back surgeries and nearly fatal complications; his Addison's disease remained under tolerable control with the aid of steroids, and he had concluded a hyperactive political year in good condition and had not hesitated to plot an equally vigorous 1957.

The real problem was that his back remained a mess. Sixty years later his sister Jean could still mimic the grimace on his face as he bent to enter an automobile.

Religion was another topic of these family discussions. In the months before the Democratic convention, the public discussion of his Catholicism (much of it promoted by Kennedy himself) had been almost academic. While campaigning for Stevenson he had not faced any sustained, high-profile attacks based on his faith. Nevertheless inside his family there were fears of what anti-Catholic prejudice would actually look and feel like.

With this in mind, Kennedy addressed the issue during the fall campaign, under relatively safe conditions where his comments received no national attention that could have created controversy. During a speech on Columbus Day in Pittsburgh, for example, he said, "We tend to forget the moral and spiritual issues which inhere in the fateful encounter of which the physical war is but one manifestation," and he referred to "the ascendancy of moral issues which overshadow the East-West political and military struggles."

Kennedy encountered no adverse reaction from his immediate family to his interest in a presidential campaign, and nothing surfaced that made running for president objectively unwise. That left the decision up to him, and he was ready to decide.

The seminal event would be the family's traditional Thanksgiving gathering at Joe and Rose's house on Cape Cod. Located on the water at the end of a quiet street just minutes from the kitschy bustle of Hyannis, it was less a mansion and more a large, comfortable home just steps from the houses of other family members inside what became known as "the Kennedy compound." Off the living room was a small room that served as a study, and after the dishes were cleared following a typically lively dinner, it was to the study that Kennedy and his father repaired to talk about the future. In an interview she gave in 2015, Jean Kennedy Smith described the father-son meeting as the culmination of those family talks that had gone on since the summer.

Through the decades only two other accounts based on the memories of people who were there have survived. One appeared in Doris Kearns Goodwin's sweeping *The Fitzgeralds and the Kennedys* and is based on an interview with Rose Kennedy in the early 1980s. The other was from Ted Kennedy, a young law student at the time, which he included in his memoir *True Compass*, published just before his death in 2009.

In Rose's understanding of the tête-à-tête in that little room, she said, "I remember thinking it was like a minuet with each partner anticipating the steps of the other." To Ted the conversation "had apparently been a kind of moot court in reverse, Jack citing all the reasons why he should not run (he was Catholic, only thirty-nine, none of the party's leaders had indicated any support for such a move) and our father countering each one."

According to Rose, her husband's closing summary was positive and eloquent: "Just remember, this country is not a private preserve for Protestants. There's a whole new generation out there and it's filled with the sons and daughters of immigrants from all over the world and these people are going to be mighty proud that one of their own is running for President. And that pride will be your spur, it will give your campaign an intensity we've never seen in public life." She said her son grinned broadly and replied, "Well, Dad, I guess there's only one question left. When do we start?"

Both sources agree the two emerged from the study smiling, with their arms around each other. At the sight, wrote Ted, "a charge of energy ran through our family."

Kennedy himself didn't tell a soul what had happened in his father's study, with one exception: the witty Charlestown pol David Powers, whom he had recruited for his congressional campaign in 1946 and who became as regular a traveling companion as Sorensen. Kennedy told Powers, "If we work our asses off from now on, we'll pick up all the marbles next time."

Some people, of course, didn't need to be told. Having helped his boss plan most of the next six months of political travel, Sorensen gave him a revealing Christmas present a month later: a large map of the United States. Sorensen had colored in each state according to the percentage of its delegation that had supported Kennedy for vice president. "This was the guide," Sorensen later wrote, "often consulted for the next three years of traveling and strategizing."

Having made the decision to run, Kennedy wasted no time getting started. In fact the day before his Thanksgiving melodrama, he was in Baltimore performing a standard chore of Democratic politicians: supporting Israel at a conference linked to Histadrut, an Israeli labor organization. (He had attended a tribute in Boston for Foreign Minister Golda Meir two days before that.)

His first major date after Thanksgiving was in Miami Beach on December 12 before the conservative American Farm Bureau. Kennedy noted the irony up front: "My very appearance here is contrary to accepted practice. For in Washington, although senators from farm states may decide whether Boston should have an urban development program and what labor relations laws should govern our major cities, a city senator from an eastern state is not supposed to have any positive thoughts of his own on farm issues or have anything to say of interest to farmers."

But for a presidential candidate attempting to repair frayed relations with an important constituency it made perfect sense.

CHAPTER SIX

Starting Early

The telephone call came right after New Year's in 1957. The recipient in Atlanta, media mogul Leonard Reinsch, was the most knowledgeable source in the Democratic Party on the increasing ties between politics and a world of broadcasting undergoing upheaval because of the new power of television. For good measure Reinsch was the boss at Cox Broadcasting, an excellent example of this explosive growth.

Kennedy was calling to ask if he could send someone to talk with Reinsch about campaigning, appearing on television, and an American spectacle that seemed to hold considerable potential for televised impact: the national nominating convention. Reinsch quickly assented and within days Lynn Johnson, an executive from the Kennedy family–owned Merchandise Mart in Chicago, arrived in his office. What followed were roughly a half-dozen meetings between Reinsch and Kennedy in Washington that began a close relationship lasting through the 1960 campaign.

Reinsch's institutional memory was vast, extending from advice to Franklin D. Roosevelt during his final reelection campaign, in 1944, to Harry Truman in 1948 and Adlai Stevenson during both presidential elections in the 1950s. There was even more to his relevant background. Reinsch was a very big shot at Cox Broadcasting, founded by James M. Cox, the Democratic presidential nominee in 1920. Cox may have gotten thumped by Warren G. Harding in the "return to normalcy" election, but before he began expanding his media empire he had been a well-regarded governor of Ohio. Reinsch, in short, had a personal connection to the entire history of the modern Democratic Party as well as an understanding of the modern media, and in 1960 he would be the party's radio-television director—as well as a Kennedy man.

Reinsch represented just the tip of a growing assemblage of backstage activity as word seeped into the political world that Kennedy was up to something more than a repeat of Chicago with a different outcome. In the spring of 1957, at a party before the annual dinner of Washington's Gridiron Club, the premier example of the cozy relationship between self-important press figures and prominent politicians, Kennedy bumped into Newton Minow, Stevenson's law partner, who had been helpful in his vice presidential bid. Said Minow, "Jack, if you're still interested in the vice presidency you've got it next time."

Replied Kennedy, incredulously, "Vice president? Vice president? Newt, I'm going to run for president."

None of these statements was widely reported, however. Unlike today, the media waited for formal announcements rather than broadcast the slightest rumor. There was a great deal of running room backstage, and Kennedy took full advantage of it.

No one outside Kennedy's small inner circle noticed that at every appearance or speech either Sorensen or a secretary quietly collected the names and contact information of virtually everyone with whom he met. This would lead to further exchanges between the candidate and his prospective supporters. No candidate had ever used such a tactic. When a formal campaign was formed two years later the bulging files contained roughly thirty thousand names. An incipient organization was in place before Hubert Humphrey had even had his first meeting to discuss 1960 strategy, and Lyndon Johnson was still playing Hamlet on the Potomac, wondering whether to actually declare himself a candidate.

In the spring Kennedy was the commencement speaker at the University of Georgia. For this date family friend Robert Troutman organized a large reception to broaden Kennedy's exposure. More than a thousand invitations were sent out; according to Troutman, each name went into the swelling campaign files, and each person would get a Christmas card every year until Kennedy was in the White House.

Many noticed the continual bursts of favorable national publicity, largely attracted by the force of Kennedy's personality. But hardly anyone realized the impact of a steady accumulation in policy and scholarly journals of pieces written by Kennedy and Sorensen—the total would approach fifty—as well as speeches developing a detailed view on all the major foreign and domestic topics of the day, from the nuclear arms race to unemployment compensation. Kennedy was well aware that in addition to his religion, the major obstacles to his candidacy were his relative youth and the absence of a significant accomplishment in his congressional record. Speaking with authority on the major issues would, in time, mitigate those problems.

Kennedy also began trying to resolve political questions that were visible in the delegate votes for vice president at the 1956 convention. These were especially apparent in the western states. One of his office neighbors during his House days was a fellow World War II veteran, Wayne Aspinall of Colorado. From the outset of their friendship, Aspinall was aware of Kennedy's independent streak, notably as a fiscal conservative who occasionally opposed reclamation and other western projects advocates felt were important to the region's economic health.

Shortly after the 1956 election Kennedy invited Aspinall to lunch in his Senate office. After the dishes were cleared Kennedy asked why the western states hadn't voted for him; Aspinall, who had supported Kefauver, replied that Kennedy was simply not considered a friend of the West. They discussed development issues in depth. Kennedy listened and requested the names of western Democrats who knew the issues best. "And of course that was the time," Aspinall recalled, "when I knew that Senator Kennedy was running for the presidency of the United States." Over the coming months Kennedy developed more nuanced and detailed positions about a region that would supply his margin of nomination victory in Los Angeles three years later.

Aspinall was not the only westerner on Kennedy's radar. In 1957 Wyoming had a new party chairman, an energetic, convivial fellow named Teno Roncalio. Among the first phone calls he received from outside the

state was one from Sorensen, requesting a visit with Wyoming's prominent Democrats. Roncalio was happy to oblige because he had a request
of his own: getting Kennedy into the state in 1958 to stump for candidates
in local elections. Sorensen agreed to the deal and went to Wyoming to
plan his boss's schedule. He minced no words with Roncalio, telling him
Kennedy was planning to seek the presidency and was looking for early
supporters.

Beyond policy, basic questions still remained for Kennedy: How to
run, and against which likely opponents? The list of potential adversaries began with Stevenson. In 1957 an important source of information
about the two-time nominee's intentions was Hyman Raskin, another
of Stevenson's longtime advisors, who was well connected in the West
and with labor unions. A product of Sioux City, Iowa, Raskin had the
sharpest elbows in Stevenson's rarefied liberal world. After laboring at
the top of the campaigns in 1952 and 1956, he was now working privately
in Chicago.

Raskin was unusual in believing immediately after the 1956 election
that Kennedy would be a viable presidential candidate. Meeting with
Stevenson supporters and delegates in Florida during the holidays, he
was impressed by their great interest in Kennedy. Discussing Kennedy
with Stevenson himself, Raskin learned that the former nominee would
"definitely" not be a presidential candidate again and was happy that
virtually his entire Chicago-based high command—including William
Blair and Willard Wirtz as well as Minow—were big fans of Kennedy.
This still left open the question of what the widely beloved Stevenson
would do if the national convention opened without a clear first-ballot
choice.

Raskin's Kennedy connection became real after Florida's Senator
Smathers got them together later that year. Raskin appears to have been
the only person outside the immediate family who was invited to Joseph
Kennedy's estate in Palm Beach over the December 1957 holidays to talk
politics. With Kennedy, his father, and his brother Robert in attendance,
Raskin recalled, "I did most of the talking and Ambassador Kennedy
asked most of the questions."

The conversation revealed a difference of opinion and therefore of strategy. Raskin was in favor of what Kennedy was already doing: raising his profile both personally and politically, working on organization from outside the known political world while preparing to step up the pace after his presumed reelection in 1958. The candidate's father, however, believed the convention would remain the deliberative, brokered affair it had been for decades; making speeches and getting publicity was fine, but it was through private deals with the most powerful Democrats that success would come. It was a fact, after all, that even with sixteen primaries scheduled in 1960, roughly three-quarters of the delegates would be selected via long-established processes that fell short of real democracy. In theory all but a relative handful of delegates would arrive uncommitted in Los Angeles in 1960.

Kennedy had heard the essence of this point of view from his father throughout his decade in politics but had consistently gone another way.

Kennedy was determined to approach his campaign in a manner that, though new to presidential politics, he had already established in his previous campaigns: "Start early." In the story of how he harvested delegates for 1960 by making person-to-person connections rather than pandering to party bosses, the past truly serves as prologue.

During the formative stages of Kennedy's uphill battle against Henry Cabot Lodge in 1952, Joe Kennedy had let his imagination and ambition roam freely in front of his son and the former ambassador's day-to-day Massachusetts political operative, Francis X. Morrissey. "I will work out plans to elect you President," Morrissey recalled the father telling the son. "It will not be any more difficult for you to be elected President than it will be to win the Lodge fight. While it will require a tremendous amount of work on your part, you will need about twenty key men in the country to get the nomination, for it is these men who will control the nomination."

Joe's theory wasn't accurate in 1952, and it was far outdated four years later; for 1960 it was simply irrelevant. More important, Jack Kennedy had never thought about politics that way, not in his very first campaign for Congress in 1946, not in his upset of Lodge, and not now, in his coming campaign for the Democratic presidential nomination in 1960.

Instead he preferred to think of himself as a grassroots organizer who started well ahead of his opponents. He recognized his major assets—the family political connections to Grandfather Honey Fitz as well as his father's money, influence, and brokering skills. But he emphasized the importance of developing a ground-level organization of devoted followers.

On the cusp of his climactic campaign he said, "I started early, in my opinion the most important key to political success. . . . I worked really hard trying to get the support of the non-professionals who are much more ready to commit themselves early than the traditional politicians. . . . I did the same thing in '52 as I'm doing now, which may not be successful nationally. Start early."

Kennedy had jumped into his first congressional race in late 1945, almost immediately after James Michael Curley resigned his House seat following his election as mayor of Boston, even in the midst of a federal corruption investigation that would send him to jail the following year. The rest of the large field in the Democratic primary the following June would not be active until the spring. That late start would cost them when Kennedy's preparation months earlier helped earn him victory. Six years later he employed the same tactic—"Start early"—against a napping Senator Lodge.

"In 1952," Kennedy recalled, "I worked a year and a half ahead of the November election, a year and a half before Senator Lodge did. I believe most aspirants for public office start much too late. . . . For the politician to make a dent in the consciousness of the great majority of the people is a long and laborious job."

Along the way Kennedy employed several other innovations. Before the Democratic congressional primary in 1946 one of his young campaign workers in Cambridge came up with the idea of hosting a huge tea party for women in the district, lured by engraved invitations and the prospect of meeting an attractive candidate and members of his large and well-known family. Kennedy pulled off the famous event at the staid Hotel Commander just off Harvard Square when hundreds of women with little history in politics came to mingle with the Kennedys. In 1952 Kennedy hosted more than thirty of these events, shaking hands with at least seventy-five thousand people.

There was more. In 1951, when he decided to run for the Senate, his state party appeared preoccupied with the reelection of its popular governor, Paul Dever. So Kennedy organized every one of the more than 350 cities and towns in Massachusetts, installing someone in each operation whose first loyalty was to Kennedy. They were called "secretaries," a title chosen to avoid any whiff of the old-time party bosses.*

When Kennedy first ran for the Senate, he had more than twenty thousand volunteers. They were overseen by a new face in the Kennedy command group, Lawrence O'Brien, a Springfield native who had previously served on Foster Furcolo's congressional staff in Washington. The son of Irish immigrants, O'Brien was more analytic in his approach to politics than the brawling style favored by so many of the Irish pols in Massachusetts. His beginnings were modest; his father owned a tavern-restaurant that had been crushed by the Depression but struggled back at least to solvency as his boy grew up. O'Brien had a law degree, six years of experience as an aide to Furcolo, and a deserved reputation for meticulous work; his reserved, formal manner obscured the private delight of an immigrant's son every time politicians like Curley (whom he otherwise detested) stuck a thumb in the eyes of the ruling Brahmins. He easily won the trust of Kennedy, his elder by two months.

The first thing O'Brien did was use the signatures on Kennedy's nominating petitions to build the organization. Back then, some 2,500 verified signatures were required to get on the primary ballot; by O'Brien's typically meticulous count, Kennedy turned in no fewer than 232,324. Each individual got a thank-you note. The thirty teas the following year were very important as well, but equally so was O'Brien's insistence that everyone who attended must sign in with contact information. Each of them also got a thank-you note with a plea to volunteer. Soon O'Brien had some seventy-five thousand names. And there were "coffees" as well as "teas"; when Kennedy and his siblings and mother were featured on a morning television program, neighbors at some five thousand prearranged house parties watched the show together.

---

* The Kennedy family's political base in the state would be maintained without interruption all the way through his brother Ted's long political career.

Even then it was O'Brien's unshaken conviction that as a supplement to Kennedy's public campaigning, diligent organizational work was worth 3 to 5 percentage points in the final balloting. That grassroots strategy was in place four years later, when Kennedy began his run for president.

Late in his first congressional primary campaign, in 1946, Kennedy distributed an eight-page "newspaper" with photos and text about his life, war record, and issue positions. It was delivered to every household in his sprawling district. Six years later the Kennedy campaign papered the entire state with what they called "the tabloid." The tabloids would go out by the millions to key states in 1960.

In 1946, by the time serious Kennedy money was being spent on radio advertisements and billboards, Kennedy may have already come close to nailing the election for his congressional seat. More than a month from the June primary the *Boston Post* published a survey indicating he was poised to get roughly as much support as all the other candidates combined. Not believing it, Joe Kennedy quietly paid for another poll, by a firm used by the *New York Daily News*. It reported the same result, which accurately predicted the outcome on primary day.

The past was indeed prologue—with one major exception. When his presidential campaign began, Kennedy had to deal with the task not only of introducing himself to the country but also of reassuring a national Democratic Party that didn't know him very well and didn't especially trust him.

Hence the frenetic campaigning. He made more than 140 appearances in 1957 alone, after sorting through some 2,500 invitations. A dozen seemed to arrive daily. There were hundreds of phone calls and numerous meetings with Reinsch and others. Kennedy enjoyed a sudden ramping up of his exposure in mass-market media outlets, particularly in popular magazines, on a scale that no one else in the mix for the presidential nomination could match. All this activity increased his reputation as a thoughtful participant in the major domestic and foreign policy issues of the day, making it harder for skeptics and critics to paint him as too young and too green. He also began an effort to woo the national press, especially writers who focused on politics, to convince them to take him seriously as a national figure, even if most of them accepted the conventional wisdom that his winning the Democratic nomination was a bridge too far.

Kennedy may have been a novice in big-time politics, but not where celebrity was concerned. From the day he entered school in the 1920s to the moment he decided to run for president, an aura of fame and family fortune had surrounded him. It suffused his adolescent experiences in this country and abroad. His wedding in Newport, Rhode Island, and the enormous reception afterward was the subject of a photo spread and story in *Life* magazine. That fall the newlyweds were visited on prime-time television by Edward R. Murrow for his popular interview show, *Person to Person*. Kennedy and his parents had always courted the large magazines that served as the important media outlets when television was just beginning to expand its reach into American culture. And editors and television producers knew the handsome young senator produced sales and ratings that a Johnson or Humphrey could only dream—and complain—about.

Even before CBS set up its cameras for the *Person to Person* interview, the *Saturday Evening Post* was burnishing Kennedy's fame. The middlebrow magazine was locked with another popular weekly, *Look*, in a circulation war with the powerhouse *Life*, which at its height sold 13.5 million copies a week. The *Saturday Evening Post* weighed in with a gushing cover story titled "The Amazing Kennedys," which declared that they embodied "the flowering of another great political family, such as the Adamses, the Lodges and the La Follettes," a twentieth-century progressive Wisconsin clan. Not to be outdone, *Look* followed that summer with an eight-page spread built around a fresh angle: the rising brother-stars, Jack and Robert.

But in that first year of Kennedy's shadow campaign the love affair between the Kennedys and Henry Luce's Time-Life empire throbbed most passionately. Luce and Joe Kennedy knew each other very well, and both understood that in a general election the publisher's Republican beliefs would overrule their friendship. But before then Luce was only too happy to help Jack Kennedy at every turn, with the added benefit that the Kennedy features always sold. *Life's* first major investment of space as Kennedy started running in 1957 was a piece in March titled "Where the Democrats Go from Here." The author was John F. Kennedy, who dared to urge his party to embrace working families. It was a bland prescription, but it got his name in print. The joke in Kennedy's world was that someone in the office should be fired for not exploiting the access further by selling an athletic angle, like touch football or sailing, for Luce's latest successful creation, *Sports Illustrated*.

Yet nothing topped Kennedy's exposure in the country's most important newsweekly, *Time*. In the fall the magazine followed him on a legitimate story, a visit to Jackson, Mississippi, to urge obedience to federal court desegregation orders, even as the embers of the fire in Little Rock, Arkansas, were still glowing. That was followed, on November 18, by a brief but glowing account of one of Kennedy's scores of successful political jaunts, this one in Kansas. Then, on December 2, came the ultimate: a cover story.

The long piece made a few stabs at thoroughness (religion, age, and résumé) and mentioned the other likely candidates in 1960: Humphrey, Stevenson, Johnson, and Kefauver, as well as a few dark horses—the freshly elected governor of New Jersey, Robert Meyner; G. Mennen Williams, governor of Michigan; and Senator Wayne Morse of Oregon. But there was no mistaking the true focus of the story, which was an excellent example of what people in the news and political trades would call a "puff piece," a flattering account of a fresh personality on the national scene willing to take on the obstacles facing him. Consider one of Kennedy's quotes in the article: "Nobody is going to hand me the nomination. If I were governor of a large state, Protestant, and fifty-five, I could sit back and let it come to me. But if I'm going to get it I'll have to work for it, and damn hard."

Time clumsily referred to Kennedy's political fortunes as "a soaring satellite." That term appears to have been a partial steal from yet another cover story that year, in *Esquire*, which served up yet another marvelous example of the hyper-prose Kennedy evoked. Reaching back to the Chicago convention for its liftoff, the story, "Who Will Win in 1960?," reported, "He reached the publicity stratosphere with one rocket burst of television and stays there, floating effortless like a satellite, worrying the Hell out of other earthly and Democratic hopefuls."

In one of its very few cautionary notes, the *Time* cover story wondered if Kennedy's political emergence represented a case of "too far too fast." There was no indication that Kennedy himself agreed with that assessment. He and Sorensen did agree, however, that it was extremely important that he project seriousness where the key issues of the day were concerned, that his exposure not be designed solely to raise his profile nationally as something akin to an entertainment figure. More than a few eyebrows twitched, for example, when the *Time* cover story described the enraptured reaction to his public appearance by two women, with not a syllable of reference to anything Kennedy had said. Far more than religion or age or résumé, Kennedy and Sorensen feared the sobriquet "lightweight."

They worked hard to avoid it. As his campaign began, Kennedy's byline appeared in the first of more than three dozen journals and magazines—many of them decidedly on the highbrow side—unveiling positions and commentary on a host of domestic and foreign policy matters. Yes, he wrote "Young Men in Politics" for the magazine *Living for Young Homemakers*, but he also offered an early sample of his views on the growing number of "neutral" nations in the cold war, penning "If India Falls" for the *Progressive*. His increasingly liberal views on immigration got an airing in the newsletter of the American Committee on Italian Immigration, and he shared an award with the Washington newsletter of the Delta Zeta sorority for a piece on the role of education in the struggle against communism. An updated version of the "Bailey Report" on Catholic and non-Catholic voting trends appeared in *Jubilee*, and he contributed an essay for *Everywoman* titled "Would You Want Your Daughter to Be President?" The pre-feminist-era piece was optimistic, but he emphasized the importance of sound qualifications. For the National Education Association's magazine he advocated federal aid to local school districts to help pay teachers' salaries, and he came through on an offer from *McCall's* to produce a female version of *Profiles in Courage*, focusing on the stories of the maverick congresswoman Jeannette Rankin, the seventeenth-century religious freedom pioneer Anne Hutchinson, and Prudence Crandall, a nineteenth-century trailblazer in integrated education.

At first Kennedy's speaking schedule did not contribute much to this transformation. By 1957 he had been in the political business for a decade, and it was second nature for him to follow a politician's ritual in his rhetoric—to sound eloquent and erudite without saying anything particularly important or controversial. He had a standing instruction for Sorensen—"I can't afford to sound just like any senator"—but that was more for his own comfort because he hated repeating himself. Speechwriter Sorensen prepared what he called "sections," short bursts on different topics that could be plugged into Kennedy's remarks to create the illusion of variety.

This emphasis on making a good impression rather than making waves tended to highlight the few occasions when Kennedy actively sought headlines. There were primarily two areas that prompted him to speak out: foreign policy, and corruption and racketeering in the labor union movement. Each case was connected to changes in Kennedy's Senate life that proved important when he formally became a presidential candidate.

As 1957 began, Kennedy finally succeeded, after years of pleading, in getting a seat on the prestigious Senate Foreign Relations Committee. At the same time he decided to take a Democratic slot on a special committee being established to investigate "improper activities in labor and management." It would become popularly known as the Senate Rackets Committee, and its hearings provided daytime television viewing for a vast national audience. It was no coincidence that the committee's staff director was Robert Kennedy. John Kennedy's position on the investigative panel proved helpful. His Rackets Committee work inspired invitations to speak beginning in March 1957 and continually thereafter, especially in the South, where suspicions about union activism were historically greater than in the rest of the country.

In Washington—and among the political cognoscenti around the country—Kennedy's early activity was seen as a harbinger for 1960, though more often as a play for the second place on a Democratic ticket instead of a bid for the presidential nomination As he began to deal more and more with reporters and columnists, Kennedy strove to be taken seriously and not casually dismissed. In this he was enormously successful.

By the spring the commentators impressed by Kennedy included Marquis Childs, a prolific writer, correspondent, and eventually syndicated columnist whose home base was the *St. Louis Post-Dispatch*. "Seldom in the annals of this political capital," he wrote that May, "has anyone risen as rapidly and as steadily as Sen. John F. Kennedy in the ten years since he came to the House from Massachusetts."

The implications for 1960 were noted, even while Kennedy's prospects were discounted. The press has always had an enormous bias toward the conventional, and in the 1950s the status quo did not seem favorable for a relative newcomer who could crash the party only by winning primaries. Instead the press continued to focus on the future national convention as a deliberative body composed of party chieftains who would make decisions independent of mere voters' views in primaries in a minority of the states. That meant Lyndon Johnson had to be ruled in as a major force and that Adlai Stevenson couldn't be ruled out for a third candidacy.

Against that consensus Kennedy labored with writers in his private dealings to make sure they understood he was running and to appreciate there was a method to his madness.

"Most people didn't take Kennedy very seriously early on," recalled Robert Donovan, an influential correspondent at the *New York Herald Tribune* and later the *Los Angeles Times*.* "It just seemed unlikely and [yet] you knew that he thought very seriously that he was going to be the nominee of that party."

For years it has been a practice in Washington that political figures meet with small groups of writers to exchange gossip and size each other up. These sessions, over lunch, cocktails, or dinner, are almost always ei-

---

* Donovan eventually wrote the book that became the movie *PT109*, about Kennedy's wartime heroism.

ther off the record or on what is known as "deep background," meaning no quotation or attribution of any kind is allowed. These ground rules allow for more candor and more vigor in the conversations. In accounts of Kennedy's meetings with the journalists, he made no attempt to disguise his efforts to win the Democratic nomination; still, there were no headlines blaring "Kennedy Is Running." Typically he tried to make it clear that his activity was more a campaign of personal ambition than a gesture on behalf of some issue-oriented cause.

At one gathering in the staid Metropolitan Club, around the corner from the White House, Kennedy was pushed on why he thought he should be president. His reply: "It's not that I have some burning thing to take to the nation. It's just, 'Why not me?'" At a meeting early in 1957 the discussion turned to Stevenson's prospects. After Kennedy got an earful of positive assessments from the writers about the two-time nominee, he replied sharply, "How can you say a thing like that? Adlai Stevenson is the most embittered human being I know. He's been embittered by these two defeats and just wouldn't be worth another run at this thing."

More often Kennedy was able to discuss the merits of possible candidacies, including his own, methodically. Recalled Peter Lisagor, a widely admired scribe for the *Chicago Daily News*, "He went over Symington and Humphrey as I recall it, and Adlai, pointing up their liabilities and their assets. And then he went over himself and this is where he won the whole group with this totally detached, cool, candid evaluation of himself—the fact that he was a man of relative youth, Catholic, inexperienced in the Senate and no administrative experience, all the rest of it— and came out with the conclusion that he was at least as well qualified as any of the others and made a good case for it."

The attraction between Kennedy and the writers was mutual, and genuine—even if somewhat overblown as the years passed. He had some very close friends in the business—Charles Bartlett, Joseph Alsop, and, especially as 1960 neared, Ben Bradlee. But his growing favorable image was more the result of his own quotable accessibility than of friendly reporters anxious to promote him—and to cover up the indiscretions in his private life.

On a few occasions reporters operated as Kennedy's political eyes and ears and shared material with him—sometimes handing over their own stories before publication. For example, Sorensen had in his possession several pages of Fletcher Knebel's copy headed for his Cowles Publications outlets in Des Moines and Minneapolis. Jerry Landay, a Westinghouse Broadcasting newscaster on his way to stints at ABC and CBS, gave Kennedy the benefit of his considerable knowledge of world affairs in a memorandum on important issues addressed "to the hosts of becalmed voters of the country who seem to find solace in the optimistic readings of Nixon."

Probably the most eyebrow-raising example of ethically questionable dialogue between Kennedy and a journalist involved regular memoranda, crammed with political information, sent to Kennedy by columnist Bruce Biossat. If there was a dean of political writing in the 1950s, it was Biossat. His résumé dated from Franklin Roosevelt's third term, and he had a sterling reputation for detailed, shrewd reporting among his colleagues. Syndicated by the North American Newspaper Alliance, Biossat's commentary was for years must reading in the political world. But long before the primaries began—and up until the election in 1960—Biossat had an exclusive audience of top Kennedy aides who studied his memos regularly.

More significant, Kennedy's dealings with the press revealed a campaign behind the scenes that could not have been more proactive. If a columnist or editorial writer had something complimentary to say, he could be assured of getting a note expressing gratitude. Critical articles were just as likely to get a response, usually mild-mannered but pointed. Kennedy's attentive attitude extended to situations that could have become serious but wound up barely qualifying as bumps in the road.

The first important instance of damage control occurred about nine months into Kennedy's campaign in 1957, when he slipped into New York Hospital for surgery on the area where his two major back operations in 1954–55 had concentrated. The procedure was neither dangerous nor particularly serious, but it was needed to drain a soft-tissue abscess around the original incision. Kennedy was off the road just briefly, but his hospitalization did serve as an opportunity to gauge how, if at all, his health would be handled as his drive for the nomination proceeded.

Nearly a decade earlier, while in Britain, Kennedy had been formally, and secretly, diagnosed with Addison's disease, a condition in which the adrenal glands do not produce enough steroid hormones. It is a chronic condition and was generally considered quite serious, until steroid medicines were found that could control it. Kennedy had been taking them orally for years, successfully.

Nevertheless his health was something of a mess. He had lousy digestion, was prone to frequent infections, and the back surgeries only marginally improved his chronic pain. He took several medicines regularly to alleviate his problems, including continual injections of procaine to deaden his back pain when it became severe.

Aware of the political ramifications of a serious illness, Kennedy and those close to him who knew his condition lied from the outset about the Addison's disease. And in the years before detailed medical histories became de rigueur for national politicians his full health profile, including his sickly childhood, was consistently masked. The lie was assisted by the fact that when he was feeling well he was photographed as an active, athletic adult—playing golf (he was very good), tossing a football around in vigorous games with family and friends on Cape Cod, and keeping to a trying schedule that had been his hallmark since his first race for Congress.

When Fletcher Knebel prepared the first article about his health, Kennedy's staff came up with a statement that dodged the larger truth but was at least medically accurate as far as it went. Versions of the explanation were used throughout the presidential campaign. To wit: "I contracted malaria during the war and had a series of fevers. Diagnosis showed that the malaria had caused a malfunctioning of the adrenal glands. From 1946 through 1949 I underwent treatment for this malfunctioning and the glands were restored to their full use. I have received no treatment for it since that time and had no recurrence of the trouble."

As it turned out, no one really noticed. As far as is known, after his New York Hospital stay, Kennedy never spent another day in a hospital until he died six years later. The brief hospitalization was the occasion for some rethinking of his overall health and some understandable second thoughts from his father. However, his new doctor, Janet Travell, looked at him and his upcoming, busy schedule and advised no changes.

Three months later there was a second incident, which could have been much more serious. Kennedy had received a publicity boost and commercial success for *Profiles in Courage*. In the spring of 1957 the book's run was crowned with a Pulitzer Prize for history. As soon as the award was announced, there was immediate, jealous speculation behind the scenes in Washington and New York and insinuations that Kennedy's authorship could be suspect.

The rumors remained just that until Saturday evening, December 7, on an ABC show hosted by a young broadcaster named Mike Wallace. Television was just beginning to put more edge and controversy into its discussion programs, and Wallace was an early practitioner. One of his guests that evening was the syndicated columnist Drew Pearson, whose "Washington Merry-Go-Round" made him the capital's premier scandalmonger.

Wallace provoked the incident when the subject of the book came up by asking Pearson, "Who wrote the book for him?" Pearson didn't offer a name, but he remarked that Kennedy had "won a Pulitzer Prize on a book that was ghostwritten for him. . . . The book 'Profiles in Courage' was written for Senator Kennedy by somebody else and he has never acknowledged that fact."

Joseph Kennedy hit the roof, and his son was no less angry and concerned. Joe acted first, calling Clark Clifford, the onetime Truman aide who had become a legendary lawyer and Washington insider. Clifford recalled the father's outburst and demands that ABC and Pearson be sued: "I waited until he finished this long tirade over the telephone, to which I said, 'Well it all depends on what you want to accomplish; if you want to drag the matter out for possibly two or three years without getting a conclusion then that's exactly the best way to do it and get occasional publicity about it and all. If, on the other hand you would like to get a retraction—which is what we ought to go with—which would clear it up, then I think we ought to get in touch with them and let's don't talk about suing any more at all."

Clifford didn't earn top dollar for nothing. Joe quickly quieted down and agreed. After meeting with his son and Sorensen, Clifford and they went to New York with voluminous files on the book from both the senator and Sorensen. The father wanted to send someone down from Boston as well, but a storm blocked him. That left Kennedy, Sorensen, and Clifford to spend two days with ABC boss Leonard Goldenson and a vice president.

The truth is that the book was a genuine collaboration with Sorensen, with some additional material in the form of certain chapter drafts by Jules David, a Georgetown University professor whom Jacqueline Kennedy knew. The material, which survives, demonstrates that the idea and form of the volume were Kennedy's alone. Shaped in 1955 during his long recuperation in Florida from his back surgeries, the manuscript has Kennedy's handwriting all over it, from beginning to end.

The ABC executives had nothing to counter the Kennedy offensive. Over the telephone Pearson himself acknowledged having no relevant evidence. The full retraction was on the air by the next broadcast of the Wallace program. Ironically the statement was ghostwritten—by Sorensen. The Kennedy office stayed on the alert for any other charges that someone other than the senator had been the author, but there were none during the course of his campaign.

At the close of the year the family gathered for the holidays—along with their invited political guest, Hy Raskin—still unsure and divided over campaign strategy but satisfied at how the first year had gone for the candidate. Kennedy had a head start on his potential rivals and had managed to create far more interest than controversy.

For perspective, Sorensen said, he found insight in a historian friend's odd linkage of Kennedy's approach to Mao Zedong's strategy in his successful revolution in China—to encircle the major cities from the outside, patiently waiting for them to crumble—with the British political practice of focusing on "rotten boroughs," the out-of-the-way constituencies where organizational work could proceed successfully without attracting much attention from opponents. The analogies seemed to fit.

But the campaign Sorensen was in effect managing at this point was also pure Kennedy, based on the assumption he had treated as gospel ever since his first campaign for Congress in 1946: Start very, very early, and work first from outside formal party structures. In a meeting with Democrats in the Midwest, Sorensen summarized his boss's firm belief: "One hour of work in 1957 is worth two hours of work in 1958."

Sorensen also recalled Kennedy saying, "In every campaign I've ever been in, they've said I was starting too early—that I would peak too soon or get too much exposure or run out of gas or be too easy a target. I would never have won any race following that advice."

CHAPTER SEVEN

Defying the Idea of Empire

From the moment Kennedy won election to the Senate, he coveted a seat on the Foreign Relations Committee. Foreign policy was his main interest, and in order to keep the option open he initially took a relatively light committee burden as a freshman. He also deflected strenuous efforts by his father to get him on the business-oriented Commerce Committee, providing another glimpse into their complex relationship as well as a window on Lyndon Johnson's solicitous treatment of his junior colleague during the 1950s.

Joseph Kennedy felt so strongly about his son's status in the Senate that he enlisted two friends on the U.S. Supreme Court, Chief Justice Fred Vinson and Justice William O. Douglas, along with a handful of high-powered lawyer-lobbyists, to add their influence to his efforts. According to Johnson confidante Horace Busby, Johnson instructed one of the lobbyists, Wallace M. "Bim" Cohen, to tell the elder Kennedy he was "dumb as hell" to keep pushing the idea. "If we put him on the Commerce Committee, the press, and especially the liberal press, will immediately identify that the reason he is there is to tend to [Joe's] interests, to serve [Joe's] financial interests. . . . Tell him that if I put Jack Kennedy on the committee he will never be President of the United States; he has no hope of being President of the United States."

Senator Kennedy appreciated his father's advice but never let up on his own campaign to get on his preferred committee. He was aware that Estes Kefauver, who also coveted the assignment, had been told to his face by Johnson that he would never be picked. Johnson informed Kefauver that assignments to the committee went to "team players" and that Kefauver didn't qualify as one.

In the spring of 1955 Kennedy wrote to Johnson privately, reminding him that they had discussed his future on several occasions. As Kennedy put it to his leader, "No other Democratic Senator has such limited committee assignments. . . . Moreover, every other Democrat who entered the Senate in January of 1953 with me has substantially improved his committee status since assignments were made at the time. . . . I have not." Still, Kennedy's status languished.

But after Kennedy's dramatic rise to prominence in 1956 everything changed. As 1957 began, Kennedy was on the Foreign Relations Committee. There is no evidence that at this point Johnson saw him as a likely rival for his own presidential ambitions. But it is clear that Johnson was thinking of the merits of earning Joseph Kennedy's gratitude (and perhaps a contribution or two), not his son's. As he told the historian Doris Kearns Goodwin, "I kept picturing old Joe Kennedy sitting there with all that power and wealth feeling indebted to me for the rest of his life, and I sure liked that picture."

For presidential candidate Kennedy, the Foreign Relations Committee represented a public platform for his ideas, far more than an opportunity for legislative accomplishment. It was a place to change the image some detractors had of him as a young, inexperienced lightweight with little substance. Almost immediately upon obtaining his committee seat, he rushed to occupy it, producing a torrent of articles and speeches addressing cold war problems and targeting several other issues. He studied and spoke about the country's relations with the "captive nations" inside the Soviet Bloc and gave consideration to U.S. policy toward countries that chose neutrality in the struggle. And he joined a respectable group who concluded the country was in danger of losing its superiority in nuclear weaponry and missiles. What gradually developed out of Kennedy's activity was a portrait of a somewhat different Democrat—loudly anticommunist but loudly anticolonial too. He proved to be more activist than diplomat, suspicious of U.S. military involvement abroad but increasingly worried about the state of America's preparedness. With some of his unorthodox initiatives Kennedy created a persona that columnist and friend Joseph Alsop summarized as "a Stevenson with balls."

Politically Kennedy designed his rhetoric to address what he recognized as his personal vulnerabilities. At the same time he tackled what he felt were the two major vulnerabilities of his party: it was too naïve about the Soviet Union and not tough enough in confronting communism.

Kennedy's venture into foreign policy was the result of years of maneuvering; his plunge the same year into the risky territory of Senator John McClellan's investigation of labor union corruption was something of a surprise. In this his brother Robert preceded him by taking the job of the Rackets Committee's chief counsel. Once again both Kennedys ignored the loud opposition of their father, who worried that their involvement in the probe into unions would needlessly antagonize the labor movement. Indeed more than one Senate Democrat with 1960 ambitions (Hubert Humphrey and Stuart Symington being the best examples) gave the Rackets Committee, a wide berth. By contrast, the Kennedy brothers saw more opportunity than peril. To them it was a chance to have high-profile roles in nationally televised congressional hearings. They realized that the investigation would focus on a virulent form of corruption that was largely confined to the Teamsters Union and did not threaten the mainstream unions that were a part of the old Democratic Party coalition.

Gradually Kennedy's work on that committee moved him closer to what would become his most significant accomplishment as a legislator: he assumed the lead role in crafting a statutory response to the wrongdoing the Rackets Committee so dramatically exposed. In fashioning the most far-reaching labor legislation since the Taft-Hartley Act a decade before, Kennedy would display an ability in domestic policy and legislating that he could cite as a presidential candidate. But he also knew that he had to show an understanding of foreign affairs that were often tangled by unpredictable events.

As 1957 began, the world was catching its breath after two crises in the Middle East and in Eastern Europe the previous fall that reflected the tensions of the cold war. At the same time, in hot spots around the globe, incipient revolutions were building strength in colonies in Africa and Asia held by American allies France, England, Belgium, and Portugal.

Even though the Suez Crisis took place in the Middle East, it had origins in the conflict between the Soviet Union and Western democracies. The United States was alert to any signs of Soviet encroachment in the unstable and oil-rich Middle East. When it appeared that President Gamal Abdel Nasser of Egypt was moving toward a closer relationship with the Soviets, the United States and England retaliated by refusing to finance the construction of a major Egyptian dam on the Nile River at Aswan. Their decision provoked Nasser to nationalize the Suez Canal Company, which was controlled by the French and British and regulated the flow of ships and goods through the vital waterway connecting the Mediterranean with the Red Sea. Nasser declared martial law in the canal zone and said he intended to collect tolls to pay for the construction of the Aswan Dam.

Nasser's action was an insult as well as an economic blow to the two European powers, so France and England secretly worked out a plot to regain control of the canal by drawing Israel into an unusual alliance that would lead to a military strike on Egypt and an effort to depose Nasser. The moves created a diplomatic emergency and threatened to touch off a wider war. To avoid Soviet intervention, the United States turned against its historic allies and sponsored UN resolutions demanding that the British, French, and Israeli troops withdraw from the region. Abandoned by the United States and confronted with adverse world opinion, the three countries pulled out of Suez.

The incident embarrassed Israel and destroyed British and French influence in the Middle East, leaving Nasser the ultimate victor—a heroic figure in an Arab world that so desperately needed one.

While the Suez affair boiled, Eastern Europe was shaken by another conflict involving the Soviet Union, this time in Hungary. For nearly three weeks in late October and early November thousands of Hungarians revolted against a government that took its orders from Moscow. For a few days it appeared that the Soviet Union might bow to the movement in Hungary that demanded independence, a democratically elected government, and a formal break with the Warsaw Pact. Instead the Soviets struck back with crushing force. Led by hundreds of tanks, the Soviet Army moved on the capital, Budapest, and set up a military occupation in other parts of the country. Outmanned and overwhelmed by the Soviet might, the Hungarian resistance crumbled within days. It was one of the most brutal examples of Soviet power in the cold war. The Hungarian freedom fighters were seen as heroes in the West, but in their own country they were reduced to their former status as powerless people paying fealty to Moscow.

Hungary was not an isolated crisis. There were conflagrations as well in Algeria and Southeast Asia and sub-Saharan Africa. At the time they seemed like brushfires compared to the thundering collisions in Egypt and Hungary, but the liberation movements in the scattered colonies would grow into confrontations that would soon change the complexion of the world.

The events would prove a challenge to the United States, still feeling its way as a superpower following World War II. But the instability overseas gave an ambitious young senator from Massachusetts a chance to demonstrate that he was capable of creative thinking in a critical area where he had not been tested. It was easy, and politically safe, to take a hard line against the Soviet Union and communism. Kennedy did that. But he also recognized that by expressing an understanding of injustices that fueled liberation movements—even some driven by Marxist elements—he might appeal to a constituency of voters who believed U.S. foreign policy had been calcified by the cold war. Just as important, he might show the foreign policy establishment and the Democratic Party that he was ready to be president.

When Kennedy joined the committee its members, with a couple of exceptions, were thoughtful and sophisticated students of foreign affairs. As the committee's junior member, Kennedy found himself surrounded by more experienced elders. But in many ways he was far more worldly and well-traveled. During his childhood he had vacationed abroad with his family. While a student at Harvard he had spent months living in London while his father served as U.S. ambassador to England, exposing him to high-stakes diplomacy. The experience helped shape his 1940 senior thesis, which he originally called "Appeasement at Munich," a paper that explored British policy toward Nazi Germany as Europe lurched toward World War II. The thesis, which carried a turgid subtitle—"The Inevitable Result of the Slowness of Conversion of the British Democracy from a Disarmament to a Rearmament Policy"—was published in book form later that year with the help of his father and two faithful family friends. Henry Luce wrote an introduction, and Arthur Krock, a *New York Times* columnist and Joe Kennedy retainer, was recruited to refine the writing. The title became *Why England Slept*, a play on an earlier Winston Churchill volume, *While England Slept*. It became a best-seller.

Even as war in Europe approached, young Kennedy had embarked on visits to danger zones, usually accompanied by a couple of friends; on one jaunt his companion was young Byron "Whizzer" White from Colorado, who would later play a major role in Kennedy's war service and presidential campaign.*

Kennedy visited Hitler's strongholds in Munich and Berlin. His 1939 itinerary included Danzig, the disputed Baltic seaport claimed by both Poland and Germany, as well as Moscow, Leningrad, and Kiev in the Soviet Union. He later traveled to Hungary, Lithuania, Latvia, Estonia, Romania, Turkey, and Egypt. While in the Middle East he toured Palestine, then under a British mandate. In many cases his trips were facilitated by American foreign service officers acting on the instructions of Ambassador Kennedy. Along the way he wrote detailed reports to his father that were sometimes at odds with U.S. policy and somewhat discomforting to the old man.

But in his first years in the House, Kennedy seemed reluctant to take daring positions on foreign policy. For a Democrat from the Northeast his voting record appeared doctrinaire. He was not a rabid red-baiter, but

---

* As a young navy lawyer Byron White would conveniently chair the official investigation into the loss of Kennedy's PT boat and ended up with a seat on the U.S. Supreme Court.

he came close a few times. As a freshman, years before Joe McCarthy surfaced, he had participated in the inquisition into one leftist labor official's
involvement in a World War II strike. He had also joined in the "Who
lost China?" contretemps after Mao's revolution succeeded, singling out
President Truman as well as Harvard faculty members John Fairbank
and Owen Lattimore. He faulted their judgment but stopped well short
of questioning their loyalty.

His friend John Sharon remembered that when the Korean War
began to fester, Kennedy believed that Truman's secretary of state Dean
Acheson should be sacked. In those days, Sharon said, "everybody was
demanding that Dean Acheson be fired." Acheson quickly returned the
contempt, even before Kennedy began running for president, disparaging both his qualifications and his views.

Sharon had the impression that Kennedy "was more parroting his
father's view than he was expressing his own independent judgment. His
father, I know, did call him quite frequently when he was a congressman.
And I think his father's influence—to the extent that he had any—was
probably more pronounced then than it was later on."

In 1951, during his third term in the House, Kennedy decided that he
wanted to be able to talk more intelligently about foreign policy as he
pondered a campaign for Henry Cabot Lodge's Senate seat, so he set out
with his brother Robert and sister Pat on a long and prophetic trip that
covered nearly twenty-five thousand miles in seven weeks. Traveling as
part of a congressional group, they toured Israel—the country that replaced most of old Palestine on the Middle East map—where Kennedy
was treated like a nobody. Franklin D. Roosevelt Jr., who led the visitors
to various appointments, attracted most of the attention. Afterward they
pushed on to Iran, Pakistan, and India, where Kennedy had an audience
with Prime Minister Jawaharlal Nehru. He was annoyed there too, because the Indian leader took little interest in him and directed his comments to his attractive sister. Kennedy developed a lasting antipathy for
Nehru. "He didn't like him much," recalled Robert Kennedy, "because
he was so superior, and his personality was rather offensive."

From the Subcontinent it was on to the Far East, to Singapore, Thailand, and Korea, where American troops were at war with communist forces from the North. That was exciting. But it was a stop in French Indochina that would be particularly memorable. It was a historic period for the colony soon to be known as Vietnam. Faced with a growing liberation movement, the French military and their puppet government were barely clinging to control. Kennedy arrived with the impression that U.S. policy in support of the French was wrong, that the French would ultimately lose their war and the country. He left convinced of that assessment. Though the young congressman was spoon-fed positive claims at official briefings by French and American officials, he did not accept their intelligence. He flew to Hanoi with the French general Jean de Lattre de Tassigny to see firsthand the area where Foreign Legion forces were fighting an indigenous guerrilla army led by Ho Chi Minh, who had declared an independent Democratic Republic of Vietnam. Kennedy admired the aging French general as a noble, patriotic soldier but thought he was locked into a hopeless assignment.

Although the three Kennedy siblings were treated royally in Saigon at the palace of Bao Dai, the emperor who was basically a figurehead installed by the French, the hospitality failed to convert Kennedy. Nor did a lecture by the American ambassador Donald R. Heath, who strongly favored the French. Kennedy was more impressed by a private conversation with another American, Edmund Gullion, a career foreign service officer who sounded wise and expressed skepticism about the Franco-American position. While in Saigon, Kennedy also sought out the views of Western journalists posted in the region and found that they too believed French colonialism would soon fall in Southeast Asia.

Kennedy's experience in Indochina near the end of the long trip played into his departure from American political dogma concerning colonies held by its allies. When he returned home, he delivered a radio speech sharply critical of Western determination to fight communism "by merely the force of arms." Saying that he had traveled over territory "in which the fires of nationalism so long dormant have been kindled and are now ablaze," Kennedy called for the United States "to build strong native non-communist sentiments within these areas." He was scathing in his comments about U.S. policy in French Indochina: "We have allied ourselves to the desperate efforts of a French regime to hang on to the remnants of empire." He also made a rare attempt at legislating, at one point offering a proposal in the House to tie U.S. aid to progress in diplomacy to resolve the conflict. He lost badly.

The speech marked the beginning of another rupture between Kennedy and his father, this time on foreign policy. A month later Joe Kennedy was given a spot on the same radio network, and he used his time to ridicule his son's theories. He dismissed the idea of building "unnecessary" new alliances. "Perhaps," he mused, "our next effort will be to ally to ourselves the Eskimos of the North Pole and the Penguins of the Antarctic."

A year later Joe admitted, "I couldn't possibly have a worse argument with anyone about foreign policy than I have had with my son." The estrangement was mutual. Jack said he and his father no longer discussed foreign policy: "We're just so far part, there's just no point to it. I've given up arguing with him."

After the collapse of French colonial rule in Indochina, the liberation struggle shifted to Algeria, where the French were being challenged by the National Liberation Front (FLN), a revolutionary movement representing Arab Muslims, who made up the majority of the population in the North African state. The situation was complicated by the presence of thousands of white French settlers, known as *pieds noirs*, who considered themselves bona fide citizens of France and were prepared to go to war against their fellow Algerians.

The FLN objected to France's claim that Algeria, colonized by the French in 1834, was now a formal appendage of France, with the old colony divided into three departments belonging to the French federation, whose capital was Paris. In a move by the FLN that coincided with the Battle of Dien Bien Phu in Indochina, hostilities began in Algeria in 1954 and soared after two years to an intense level, with urban guerrilla warfare lacerating the streets and casbahs of the city of Algiers. There were acts of terrorism and counterterrorism, and both sides used torture to extract information. The Battle of Algiers gained worldwide attention, and nearly a half million French troops were deployed to put down the rebellion.

Earlier in 1957 the "Eisenhower Doctrine" was adopted as the Middle East policy of the United States. It promised military and economic aid to any Middle East country confronted with a communist threat. The policy supplemented the ten-year-old "Truman Doctrine" that offered American aid to Greece and Turkey to resist communist aggression. The new doctrine was being applied in Algeria, where military equipment sold by the United States to France was being employed against the FLN partisans.

Kennedy had been looking for a moment to break from convention, to move dramatically away from the Senate fold, where it was comfortable to be a vigorous supporter of American allies, to offer routine condemnations of communism, and to be suspicious of insurrections overseas. It was not difficult for him to speak out against the primary voices of the administration's policy, Secretary of State John Foster Dulles and U.S. ambassador to the United Nations, Henry Cabot Lodge. Kennedy was privately contemptuous of Dulles, he believed him a pious relic of American triumphalism who talked too much of "godless communism." Kennedy complained that "public thinking is still being bullied by slogans which are either false in context or irrelevant to the new phase of competitive coexistence in which we live." And Lodge, who expressed support of the French position in a February 1957 speech to the UN, was an old political rival, the man whose Senate seat Kennedy had taken.

Like so many of the liberation movements of the period, the FLN had ideologues who were intellectually linked to Marxism. But a spirit of Arab nationalism seemed to be a stronger force behind the Algerian rebels, and in Kennedy's mind their desire for independence dovetailed with his strong aversion to colonialism. He had seen French colonialism, and disliked it, in Indochina. So he chose Algeria to serve as the subject for his first major foreign policy speech, knowing that it would be controversial and anger many members of the nation's foreign policy establishment. But he also knew that a bold and reasoned statement on behalf of freedom for people half a world away would win headlines and, importantly, respect from liberal intellectuals he had trouble reaching in his campaign for political recognition.

From the outset of his congressional career Kennedy had called upon the considerable academic community in Boston and, across the Charles River, in Cambridge. But for this initiative he sought sources with personal knowledge of the region and an appreciation of the reasons behind the upheaval. His friend John Kenneth Galbraith, a noted Harvard economist, introduced him to two representatives of the FLN in Washington, Abdelkader Chanderli, who had an important role in winning Western sympathy for the movement, and Chanderli's associate Mohammed Yazid. Kennedy also met leaders from Tunisia, which had recently won independence from France and shared a border with Algeria. His Tunisian contacts included the son of Habib Bourguiba, a leading figure in the struggle for independence who was now president of Tunisia, and Mongi Slim, the Tunisian ambassador to Washington.

Kennedy's approach fit a pattern. In foreign affairs he was more of a shopper than he was beholden to a single policy expert. He employed a research assistant in his Boston office, Deirdre Henderson, who typically collected memoranda and speech drafts from noted academics, depending on the topic. She occasionally contributed papers herself, especially on the expanding military budget.

Professors are always pleased to be asked, and Kennedy's office was aggressive in asking. When a Senate resolution on Eisenhower's Middle East policy started to advance toward the floor, Sorensen sent a letter to at least a dozen wise men based on questions that have provoked years of debate: "Does the president have authority to use American troops abroad where American nationals, bases, treaties or other direct interests are not endangered or involved in the absence of a congressional declaration of war? Is a mere declaration of national interest or danger to national security sufficient?"

As time passed, Kennedy came to admire and depend on the work of one young academic, Fred Holborn, who from early 1957 on was his principal aide working on Algeria and whose role expanded almost exponentially as a full-time staff member. The child of early refugees from Nazi Germany, the highly educated Holborn was a Harvard teaching assistant in a course presided over by McGeorge Bundy, a scholar with CIA ties who had a future in government. One of the students in his class was a young Ted Kennedy. Later, in the mid-1950s, Ted joined Holborn during a tour of Northern Africa—ostensibly as a stringer for the International News Service—and told his brother Jack about him. The younger Kennedy had a letter from his senator-brother that got them access into the more sensitive parts of Algeria, where a closer study of the situation was possible.

The Algeria speech became a major production for the Kennedy office. A draft outline, which incorporated a variety of ideas, was prepared by Holborn. Another Harvard expert, Arthur Holcombe, provided valuable research material. Knowing that the issue would be especially sensitive regarding the French, Kennedy even drew upon the knowledge of his wife, Jacqueline. Her family, the Bouviers, had French roots, and she was both fluent in the language and knowledgeable about the country's rich culture. While the speech was being prepared she spent weeks in her husband's office, translating French diplomatic cables. Sorensen too had his hands in the speechwriting.

Until his Algeria speech Kennedy had not been known as a politician who courted controversy. Holborn recalled, "He had handled relatively safe subjects. . . . He had been handling . . . subjects that didn't create storms generally." This speech would challenge the Washington consensus that allies, especially NATO allies, should not be criticized for policies within their own spheres of influence because of the overriding importance of cold war unity.

Kennedy's office made sure that an advance copy of the speech was personally delivered to every reporter in Washington accredited by the Senate press gallery. A messenger even took copies to journalists' homes. By orchestrating the extraordinary delivery Kennedy ensured that the speech would be noticed by important opinion makers in the capital. It was another sign of the presidential campaign to come.

Kennedy delivered the speech on the Senate floor on July 2, 1957. His opening line set the tone: "The most powerful single force in the world today is neither communism nor capitalism, neither the H-bomb nor the guided missile—it is man's eternal desire to be free and independent."

Kennedy faulted Eisenhower's foreign policy team for failing to deal with the Algerian question effectively, and after saying he was "reluctant to appear critical of our oldest and first ally," he lashed out at France for treating Algerians as second-class citizens—if citizens at all. Although the French claimed Algeria as an "integral part" of France, he said, they "never truly recognized Algerians as French citizens," denying them proper representation in the French Assembly and "the social, political and economic benefits" enjoyed by other French citizens. Instead of cultivating leaders in Algeria, France "deliberately stifled educational opportunities for Algerian natives, jailed, exiled or executed their leaders, and outlawed their political parties and activities."

He was equally critical of the United States, which had tried to block discussion of the situation in the United Nations. "Instead of contributing our efforts to a cease-fire and settlement," the United States had armed the French with helicopters, "which the natives especially fear and hate" because the equipment had been used against Algerian rebels.

Drawing a grim parallel to events in Indochina, Kennedy asked, "Did that tragic episode not teach us that, whether France likes it or not, admits it or not, or has our support or not, their overseas territories are sooner or later, one by one, inevitably going to break free and look with suspicion on the Western nations who impeded their steps to independence?"

The speech triggered more reaction than any Kennedy had previously delivered. The New York Times called it "perhaps the most comprehensive and outspoken arraignment of Western policy toward Algeria yet presented by an American in public office." A columnist in the Christian Science Monitor complimented Kennedy for raising American consciousness, noting than an ordinary citizen "may not at this moment be too interested in the issue of independence for Algeria raised in the U.S. Senate by the young Democratic senator from Massachusetts, John F., Kennedy, but if he understands the 'whys' and 'wherefores' he may become deeply interested." Gilbert Harrison, editor and publisher of the New Republic, a liberal weekly, wrote Kennedy an approving letter.

But Kennedy was rebuked by many others. Friends told him that Stevenson was upset by the speech. Another prominent Democrat, former secretary of state Acheson, went public with his criticism. In a speech in Massachusetts he implied that Kennedy did not understand "the humiliating agony of the loss of power" and warned that a French withdrawal from Algeria would be "followed by chaos." The French Foreign Ministry expressed shock at the American senator's gall to intrude on a French concern. Alistair Cooke, the American-centric British commentator, wrote in the *Manchester Guardian Weekly* that Kennedy's speech served no other purpose than "pitching him into center stage." Joe himself had an interesting reaction. After his son wondered whether he had been too forceful, the elder Kennedy told him, "For years the political sharpshooters have raised hell with me because I wanted to keep the United States out of all countries except South America. Now they are raising hell with you because you want the United States in. I don't think they hurt me, and I'm sure they won't hurt you."

Kennedy also got an encouraging letter from Chester Bowles, a former governor of Connecticut who had served as U.S. ambassador to India earlier in the decade. Bowles, who would shortly become a Kennedy supporter, told the senator, "[You are] dead right in the position you have taken" and offered some political advice: "This is one kind of foreign policy issue that the American people can understand. And unless we Democrats can find such ways to discuss what is really going on abroad in terms that fit the experience and beliefs of the average citizen, we will continue to find ourselves at a disadvantage every time the president tells a press conference that he thinks that peace is a good thing."

Writing in response Kennedy reaffirmed his belief that colonialism was ending and that the United States should recognize that fact. "I do not see that anything is to be gained by trying to stonewall the irreversible trends which are running through the uncommitted parts of the world."

Within a year Kennedy could claim vindication when French voters turned out their Fourth Republic leaders and elevated the World War II hero General Charles de Gaulle, who considered Algeria an anachronistic burden. Kennedy's reaction was undisguised joy, calling de Gaulle's election as president "one of the historic events of post-war Europe." He compared the significance of France's release of Algeria to the breakaway moves of Yugoslavia out of the Soviet military alliance in the previous decade, the development of the Marshall Plan, and the death of Josef Stalin.

With his Algeria speech Kennedy had crossed a political Rubicon.

Before the year was out he would make several other carefully modulated speeches. He would return to the Senate floor to defend his position on Algeria, but he would also use the august chamber to attack the Soviet Union for the Iron Curtain it kept around Eastern Europe. There was consistency to his messages. The freedoms that he advocated for colonized people were the same freedoms he asked for those living in Soviet satellite nations.

Within a month of his Algeria speech he launched his initiative on Poland, arguing that the United States should be prepared to assist countries in the Soviet Bloc the instant they showed clear signs of seeking more independence, as Yugoslavia had. And with the aid of an important Republican on the Foreign Relations Committee, John Sherman Cooper of Kentucky, he called for assistance for India's fledgling democracy, insisting that the United States should not see neutrality in the cold war as opposition. At first he had some success working privately with Eisenhower administration officials, but when the White House abruptly reversed gear and opposed both initiatives, Kennedy suspected politics. The issues would have to wait, but it was a clear sign that his increasing prominence had been noticed from on high.

All this activity attracted the attention of the editors of *Foreign Affairs*, a highbrow journal published by the Council on Foreign Relations and read by virtually every foreign policy maven in America. For its October 1957 issue Kennedy was asked to contribute the lead article, a seventeen-page tour d'horizon titled "A Democrat Looks at Foreign Policy."

The piece, which covered a "geopolitical map of the world," appeared to be the handiwork of an informal cadre of foreign policy advisors Kennedy was assembling, with specialists for Asia, Africa, Western Europe, the Soviet Bloc, and the Middle East. But in places it reeked of raw partisanship, as if Kennedy were already warming up for the general election in 1960. He charged that the Republican administration had failed to adjust its policies to keep up with international upheavals that were changing the world's landscape. There existed a "lack of decision and conviction in our leadership," a leadership "which seeks too often to substitute slogans for solutions, which at times has even taken pride in the timidity of its ideas."

Kennedy also managed to become a major, visible figure in a serious debate about U.S. nuclear forces. Throughout the 1950s, the first full cold war decade, there had been discussions in think tanks, in Congress, and within the Eisenhower administration about improvement in Soviet missile capabilities and whether a credible first-strike capability would be achieved within a decade. It was a complex issue with a catchy name: "the missile gap." Kennedy plunged into the debate, and he had good company, including a possible rival in 1960, Senator Stuart Symington of Missouri, who was known for his defense expertise and had served as secretary of the air force in the Truman administration.

Kennedy made a major speech in the Senate at the height of the national debate in August 1958, and the following year made a series of proposals to improve U.S. defenses, contending that "it is no longer true that the best defense is a good offense; there is no point in merely multiplying sitting ducks." The speech caused a considerable stir. It was praised, for example, by Joseph Alsop as "one of the most remarkable speeches on American defense and national strategy since the end of the last war."

The performance offered another glimpse into the incestuous ties between writers and politicians in Washington. Alsop had actually encouraged Kennedy to deliver the speech he praised so fulsomely. A powerful figure in Washington and a Georgetown neighbor of the Kennedys, Alsop wrote on July 30, 1958, that the Kremlin was on its way "to gain an almost unchallengeable superiority in the nuclear striking power that was once our speciality." The column revealed classified information about Soviet missile production. Kennedy inserted the column into the daily *Congressional Record*. Pleased, Alsop told Kennedy he should make a speech, which he did, parroting the same classified information Alsop had used in his column. Alsop responded with not just one column but two praising Kennedy and citing the statistics Kennedy had used— which had come from his own column.

CHAPTER EIGHT

Beyond the New Deal

At the end of 1958, just as Kennedy was winning reelection in Massachusetts in a landslide that surprised many, a book was published by a moderately well-known MIT professor who had a more than casual relationship with him. The title, *The Stages of Economic Growth: A Non-Communist Manifesto*, sounded like a textbook, but it was really a long essay. Instead of offering untested revolutionary theory, it dealt with how developing countries become developed and how developed societies try to maintain their vigor. The author, Walt Whitman Rostow, had been kibitzing on issues with Kennedy for a year. He was a source for an unusual blend of economic as well as foreign policy material, reflecting his interests as well as his expertise. He influenced Kennedy's thinking about subjects as wide-ranging as developing countries like India and advanced nations such as the slow-growing United States of the late 1950s. With government experience during World War II and consultant duties afterward—including time with the Eisenhower administration—Rostow was an excellent example of the kind of activist intellectual that Kennedy attracted.

Rostow discussed his book often with Kennedy while he was writing it. He tackled the process of development—a hot academic as well as political topic in the 1950s as new countries emerged from crumbling empires in Asia and Africa. The birth of these states raised cold war tensions. The book had special relevance to ideas in Kennedy's nascent campaign in its discussion of more advanced societies, from the United States to the Soviet Union.

Of the United States Rostow wrote in professorial patois, "The automobile–durable consumers' goods–suburbia sectoral complex had lost in the 1950s the capacity to drive forward American growth." This description related to an economic statistic much discussed at that time: the decline to roughly 2.5 percent annually in the rate of growth of the economy's output of goods and services (the gross domestic product) from rates nearly double that in the period following World War II.

In a subsequent edition of the book Rostow posed his fundamental question about advanced societies: "Will man fall into secular, spiritual stagnation, finding no worthy outlet for the expression of his energies, talents and instinct to reach for immortality?"

In comments destined to be associated with Kennedy, Rostow emphasized the importance of his questions to countries like the United States "as they turned to explore new frontiers." He went on to describe a "great struggle to find new, peaceful frontiers for the human experience." And he used another phrase that became equally well-known, though it would prove to be more appropriate to the campaign trail than academic discourse. He summed up the purpose of the activism he advocated by saying that he wanted to "get this country moving again." As the primaries approached, Kennedy began invoking the words on the stump. (But he resisted Rostow's entreaty to make it the opening sentence of his acceptance speech after winning the nomination at the Democratic convention.)

Kennedy's intellectual exercise with Rostow represented his maturation as a full-blown public figure.

As a presidential candidate Kennedy advocated activism over agenda. He had often expressed his desire to be in Theodore Roosevelt's "arena," where the stakes were high and power politics mattered more than ideology. He would produce his share of "ten-point plans," all of them left of center. But he preferred his policy statements to be "new" rather than simply "liberal," and he clearly enjoyed the challenge of addressing specific issues in depth. The bulk of his rhetoric and eloquence was focused on ideas to tackle major problems with zest, because he believed the nation was gripped by intellectual stagnation. His quarrel was more with the America of the 1950s—a sleepy decade—than with the policies of the Eisenhower administration, and he knew that taking on the popular war-hero president was a campaign no-no from the beginning. As a Democratic candidate Kennedy wanted to present himself as an impatient agent for change rather than a programmatic partisan.

Kennedy was introduced to Rostow by foreign policy coordinator Fred Holborn in 1957, when Kennedy was looking for help in developing an aid package for neutral India. Rostow had consulted on the same issue for Eisenhower, who appreciated his ideas but never became personally close to him. The Walt Rostow of the 1950s was a good fit for Kennedy; he had wide-ranging interests and expertise on foreign as well as domestic challenges, and he had an ability to write clearly.* He was genuinely attracted to what he called Kennedy's "remarkable computer of a mind," which made room for Rostow's own long menu of ideas.

Walt and Eugene Rostow represented one of two formidable brother acts that made strong contributions to Kennedy's quest for intellectual answers. Eugene V. Debs Rostow was dean of the Yale Law School at the time. The Rostows were often paired with McGeorge Bundy, dean of the Faculty of Arts and Sciences at Harvard, and his brother, William Bundy, who had worked as an analyst for the CIA. The four were more or less contemporaries of Kennedy and highly regarded on matters of intelligence and foreign policy.

In an interview shortly after his close call for a place on the ticket at the 1956 convention—before the rest of the political world knew he was actually running for president—Kennedy was asked to describe himself. "I like to think of myself as a practical liberal," he replied. The descrip-

---

* In 1960 Rostow would be one of a dozen people Sorensen asked to submit language for Kennedy's acceptance speech. Rostow's anticommunism back then matched Kennedy's in vigor, and he was able to provide new ideas for combating Moscow before his activist mind plunged into the quagmire of Vietnam after Kennedy's death. The Johnson administration Americanized the war and Rostow became one of its most recognizable hawks.

tion was not accurate. In national affairs Kennedy took risks, and many of them were calculated. He began to develop a new image for himself in a country that had known him in the mid-1950s as a celebrity.

In his most visible role in domestic policymaking, Kennedy in 1957 ventured where many of his colleagues—including some aspiring presidential candidates—did not dare to go. At a time when organized labor represented one of the strongest forces in the Democratic Party, Kennedy ended nearly a decade of political silence on an issue that affected virtually every American: health care. Sticking his neck out on an issue where the opposition—the insurance industry and the conservative world of physicians—had been brutally effective since the 1930s, he embellished on an idea initially advanced by Aime Forand, a relatively obscure, labor-oriented congressman from Rhode Island. Forand had proposed universal hospital insurance coverage financed through the Social Security system's payroll tax, but it was Kennedy who brought it to center stage, targeted initially on the elderly.

He did the same with public schools, another pressing issue. Education in America suddenly became a focal point following the Soviet Union's 1957 launch of *Sputnik*, the first satellite to orbit the planet. Kennedy decided to challenge a multitude of determined opponents who felt the schools should be the exclusive concern of local governments. He defied convention by proposing that the federal government send money directly to local school districts to help fund operating costs. By doing so he resolved a debate that had taken place in his own mind since the 1940s; he concluded that federal dollars should not go directly to parochial schools—a position that put him in conflict with the Catholic Church.

When he started his covert run for president in 1956, Kennedy was essentially a blank slate on the principal questions of the day. He was the spokesman for no issue and had no legislative achievement. He might have had bright promise, but he had only the barest bones of a record. Simple political calculation required that the blank slate be filled. There was little time as Kennedy began traveling and subtly campaigning in 1957, but he plunged into a couple of politically perilous areas—labor unions and social programs—during his four-year effort to establish a stronger record in Congress. The work was methodical. At first his most significant moves to attract attention were in foreign affairs. His rhetoric on domestic issues was boilerplate and partisan; gradually, however, that began to change in the sensitive world of labor unions, where substance and politics were joined at the hip.

"The base of support for President Kennedy was labor," recalled Meyer "Mike" Feldman, an experienced policy specialist and lawyer who joined the staff during 1958 to work with Sorensen, researching major issues and helping develop ideas and proposals. "In order to have solid labor support, he had to have the liberal community support him. I think there were a great many liberal pressures on him. Up until 1958 his coloration was a pretty conservative coloration; beginning around the time I came to work he became more and more liberal."

In part this was pure politics. Early on, Kennedy understood that Johnson was his most formidable potential opponent. Kennedy was still trying to woo southern Democrats, but always with the recognition that he might not succeed because he favored civil rights. But it was also a given around Kennedy that Johnson, as the Democrat closest to the southern establishment in Congress, would face enormous obstacles winning support in northern states. "Now if he couldn't get the south, which was the center of conservatism, he had to get the north in order to get the votes to be nominated," Feldman explained. "So taking one step at a time in the effort to get the nomination he had to have a liberal image."

On paper Kennedy could never be Humphrey. There was not a cause involving civil rights or labor that the Minnesota senator and likely presidential candidate had not supported, usually with full-throated eloquence. All of the leading unions and civil rights organizations anticipated supporting him in 1960, and even Kennedy himself acknowledged Humphrey's influence on his own views, especially civil rights.

Some Democrats suspected the influence went even further. James Rowe, who was close to both Johnson and Humphrey, liked to joke that on many major issues Humphrey usually controlled three votes: his own, Kennedy's, and that of the famously cautious Stuart Symington.

As events unfolded, a leadership route opened for Kennedy, and he jumped at the opportunity. In the beginning of 1957 he and his brother Robert took assignments on the Rackets Committee—over the strenuous objections of their father—that put them squarely in the midst of a national discussion about organized labor. Unions were nearing the zenith of their membership numbers and had the ability to influence any legislative threats to their existence.

As nationally televised hearings by the committee increasingly regaled—and repelled—much of the country with lurid tales of gangsters, rigged union elections, and personal profiteering, Kennedy became the principal Democrat overseeing the legislative response to the outrages.

As 1957 wore on, Kennedy's decision to get involved in the investigation appeared almost prescient. The principal target of the hearing was the large and swaggering Teamsters Union, led by the shadowy Dave Beck and his Mussolini-like leader-in-waiting Jimmy Hoffa, who had already made a Faustian bargain with organized crime. Television audiences loved the show almost as much as they had been fascinated by Kefauver's hearings six years earlier, which introduced the country to the Mafia's national tentacles.

Kennedy was not the star of the show; his relentless brother was, compiling an encyclopedic record of wrongdoing by the Teamsters. Robert also bored into the vulnerable witnesses, especially Beck and Hoffa, with withering questions. While he destroyed the Teamsters' credibility, he compiled material for a best-selling book about the mess, *The Enemy Within*, which was released near the eve of the 1960 campaign. But while Robert controlled the drama, Jack was a prominent presence in the hearings, despite his constant travels on the campaign trail. He always seemed to enter the set at critical moments to deliver penetrating observations. The well-known liberal lawyer Joseph Rauh said Kennedy's timing was so fortuitous that he assumed Robert tipped him off about what was on the agenda.

Slowly the hearings began to produce material for Kennedy's speeches as his campaign gathered momentum. He made the argument that no Democrat could tolerate corruption in a movement whose fundamental purpose was to represent workers' rights and their economic health. But he also deftly used his position on the committee to push back against business and conservative interests that sought to attack labor's organizing and collective bargaining role, which included the use of strikes.

During the hearings Kennedy's three major opponents on the committee were very conservative Republicans: Barry Goldwater of Arizona, Karl Mundt of South Dakota, and Carl Curtis of Nebraska. In 1957 the trio focused on a long, bitter strike led by the United Auto Workers against Wisconsin's Kohler Company, the bathroom fixtures giant. From the company and its political allies came angry charges of coercive activity, and Robert Kennedy accommodated them by sending investigators. Jack meanwhile arranged the UAW's response to the accusations. No evidence of illegal conduct was found in Wisconsin, and the strike was actually settled while the committee hearings were still going on.

Over the course of Kennedy's work on the committee, union leadership took notice and slowly began to change its view of Joe Kennedy's son, a man they had viewed with suspicion ever since his arrival in Congress a decade earlier. Rauh, the UAW's counsel during the investigation, said later, "Whenever the UAW needed John Kennedy, he was there. . . . He was very warm and sympathetic about our problem and very derogatory about Goldwater, Mundt and Curtis. He just felt they were beneath contempt, the three of them. He was very interested in being helpful and he was very helpful."

Thanks to the hearings and his membership on the Senate Labor Committee, Kennedy became the key Democrat involved in drafting legislative solutions to labor corruption. The effort—shunned by more senior colleagues—would occupy the bulk of his time in Washington over the next two years. Substantively the risk was that the rights workers had won over the preceding generation would be eroded even more than they had been in the Taft-Hartley Act of the late 1940s; politically for Kennedy there was the danger of provoking angry opposition from unions wanting no legislation at all.

Kennedy saw it as an opportunity to demonstrate to his colleagues and other political insiders that he was capable of major legislative achievement on a high-profile issue. It was also a chance to show nearly 20 million labor union members that he could be an effective friend. Most important, the voting public would learn that he was a serious national player and no lightweight.

But the cost was steep: months of laborious work crafting a bill in the Senate, dealing with an antagonistic House of Representatives, searching for a way to reconcile the two branches' differing approaches, watching the clock run out on Congress at the end of 1958, and then having to slog through the entire process all over again in 1959 before legislation could be agreed upon.

As the Senate lawmaking process began after the dramatic hearings wound down, Kennedy imported Archibald Cox, one of the country's top labor law experts and a Harvard Law School professor, to advise him every step of the way. Cox quickly convened his own group of experts to help Kennedy pull together a legislative proposal that was ready by the end of the year.*

Watching him up close for the next two years Cox observed a mix of politician and independent intellectual, eventually sharing Walt Rostow's view of his policymaking mind. "Unlike so many public figures," Cox later recalled, "especially in the legislative branch, he had tremendous interest in the substance, the merits of these problems, even down to rather small details, and he really did seem to be interested in getting to the bottom of it. . . . I suppose I might say that it was an intellectual interest."

After working at close quarters with important staff members, especially Sorensen and Ralph Dungan, the Kennedy aide who most often dealt with the unions, Cox was certain Kennedy appreciated the gamble as he oversaw the legislative process. "There had been the feeling that this pretty nearly would make or break him. To get the nomination and get the election he had to get a bill through. On the other hand it was a tightrope. If the bill that went through was too restrictive that would be death."

---

* Cox, a lanky, avuncular, Central Casting version of a professor, would head a committee of academics that Kennedy formed in 1959 to churn out position papers for his campaign. It was an operation Cox himself said never produced anything of much value to Kennedy. But it was an early clue that many prominent liberal minds had moved on from Stevenson. Cox would later be tapped as the Kennedy administration's solicitor general on his way to fame as the Watergate special prosecutor fired by President Nixon in the "Saturday Night Massacre" that helped drive Nixon from office in disgrace.

The challenge was to focus as much of the legislative product as possible on the union abuses the hearings had dramatized, with new regulations promoting reforms to ban election chicanery and tighten financial rules to combat corruption. At the same time Kennedy worked to block moves by influential members of the business community and some Republicans who sought to limit the ability of unions to organize membership drives, call strikes, and stage consumer boycotts. In the Senate he succeeded with the assistance of Republicans like Irving Ives of New York, his cosponsor, and John Sherman Cooper of Kentucky, his colleague on the Labor Committee. The Senate votes in 1958 were nearly unanimous.

There was, however, a close call, which Cox admitted "caught us entirely off balance." An effort to expand on the restrictions in Taft-Hartley was packaged under the tempting title of a "labor bill of rights" and pushed as an amendment by the Labor Committee chairman, Democrat John McClellan, who had also chaired the investigative committee hearings. McClellan was content to lurk in the background and leave the job of crafting the legislation to Kennedy. When the tough version favored by McClellan narrowly passed the Senate, Majority Leader Johnson helped Kennedy and his allies plot a parliamentary maneuver that made reconsideration possible. A second, less onerous proposal prevailed that nearly all the unions said they could live with.

Slowly Kennedy and Cox, with diplomatic assistance from Arthur Goldberg, another highly regarded labor lawyer, had nudged the labor movement from almost violent opposition to any legislation to acceptance of Kennedy's argument that something had to be enacted. Kennedy wanted labor to help shape it.* At the beginning of 1958, when Kennedy opened hearings on his proposal by observing that many "friends" of the movement had helped assemble it, AFL-CIO chief George Meany grumbled into his microphone, "God save us from our friends." By the

---

* Goldberg, who was especially close to the Steelworkers union, was the first secretary of labor in the Kennedy administration. Kennedy later named him to the Supreme Court, but Johnson persuaded him to step down to become ambassador to the United Nations upon the death of Adlai Stevenson.

end of the year Meany and other major union leaders were working daily with Kennedy and Cox.

The real problem was the House of Representatives. It was an election year, and the Democrats were poised to capitalize on soft economic conditions to win more seats, but the House remained in the firm grip of a coalition of southern Democrats and conservative Republicans. It produced what Kennedy supporter and prominent Williams College professor James MacGregor Burns would describe in his best-seller as "the deadlock of democracy." In the judgment of Speaker Rayburn, the choice was between a measure most Democrats and unions would see as hideous and impossible to reconcile with the Senate bill, and no action at all. To complicate the situation, the Eisenhower administration, guided by Labor Secretary James Mitchell, began to weigh in on the side of the conservatives. With grumbling all around, the legislation died with the close of the session.

But Kennedy did it all over again in 1959. With far more Democratic members after the off-year elections, the House was able to pass a bill, albeit with more restrictions than either Kennedy or the labor movement could tolerate. That meant Kennedy would have to shoulder responsibility for hammering out a final version between the two branches. He and Cox now went to work on House Democrats, none more important than a young congressman from Arizona, Stewart Udall, like Kennedy an activist by nature but not a knee-jerk partisan.

"When we came back in '59," Udall recalled, "many of us felt that this issue was absolutely crucial to the future of the Democratic Party and the politics of the 1960 campaign because we controlled the Congress, and if we couldn't write some kind of labor legislation, the Republicans would quite rightly make a major point to the American people that we were too close to the labor organizations, that we were, in effect, too tightly controlled by them."

During House consideration and the ensuing negotiations with the Senate, Cox and Kennedy helped Udall run what he called his "school" for interested members, mostly young first- and second-termers who frequently held the balance of power on important votes. "We fought violently in committee, page by page on various amendments," said Udall.

"We'd fight over amendments and fight over amendments to amendments."

But Kennedy's allies largely prevailed in the House and in the conference committee with the Senate that Kennedy oversaw. The final legislation confronted the abuses publicized in the Rackets Committee hearings, but its regulations promoting more fair play in union elections and more transparency in union finances were soft enough to win the acquiescence of the major unions, with the exception of the ever-angry Machinists.

The bill ultimately bore the names of the bipartisan sponsors of the House version, Democrat Phil Landrum of Georgia and Republican Robert Griffin of Michigan. According to Cox, Kennedy had no objection to the absence of his name from the legislative marquee. He preferred the fact that he had won respect in vital circles for his long months of work.

When Kennedy's presidential campaign began in earnest, volunteers at virtually every union-dominated event in the primary states of Wisconsin and West Virginia distributed flyers listing fifteen examples of his work on the bill that protected unions.

Because of the tedious and grubby ritual of legislating and power-brokering, there simply wasn't time in the late 1950s for Kennedy to develop any more major examples of his capabilities as a senator. So to be taken seriously as a candidate, he turned to the advocacy of innovative big ideas to fill out his political portrait.

One issue that steadily percolated in the 1950s involved America's elderly citizens. As one of his Massachusetts allies, Congressman Thomas P. O'Neill Jr., was fond of saying, there was no elderly middle class back then; you were either very comfortable or barely surviving. The poorer group, getting by with puny Social Security benefits, had no access to any kind of health care outside of charity hospitals. In 1958, at Kennedy's request, Sorensen and Mike Feldman recruited a University of Michigan professor with both past government experience in Washington and political connections from his support of Stevenson earlier in the decade.

Wilbur Cohen was another liberal academic who gravitated toward Kennedy as the decade drew to a close. His first job was to develop what Kennedy would call a bill of rights for the elderly, with adequate health care among its tenets.*

In the process Kennedy knowingly walked into a political minefield that ambitious men had avoided for a decade. The idea for some form of a national insurance program to help finance health care had been around ever since Theodore Roosevelt borrowed it from Europe to be part of his Bull Moose platform in 1912. During the Depression Franklin Roosevelt had seriously considered adding it to his proposal for what became Social Security but decided health care would be a political bridge too far.

Harry Truman labored mightily to get traction for a proposal in the late 1940s, but by then powerful opposition had been organized among doctors through their American Medical Association and the insurance lobby. They pushed the politically successful argument that this would constitute "socialized medicine." In the cold war *socialized* was a buzz word. Truman's idea went nowhere. But by the time Kennedy was running for president the concept was being revived on the fringes of the political world.

Kennedy developed his own approach to the subject. His vehicle had its origin in academic circles in the 1930s, where it was argued that using a small premium on the fledgling Social Security system's payroll tax as a funding source could generate enough dollars to make a national hospital insurance program feasible. In the 1950s the idea was grabbed by Aime Forand, a solid labor Democrat from New England, who put together legislation focusing initially on the elderly; if that could be accomplished, wider coverage would come incrementally. By the end of the decade the Forand proposal had revived the policy argument and awakened all the well-organized opponents. Their ranks included a movie actor and for-

---

* Cohen, then only in his forties, actually went on the letterhead of "Senior Citizens for Kennedy" in 1960, but the chuckles this evoked in the campaign were more than matched by the respect Cohen commanded for his policy work. In the Kennedy administration he began as No. 2 in the old Department of Health, Education and Welfare. After Kennedy's death Johnson made him secretary. It was he who implemented the Kennedy proposal known as Medicare after its enactment in 1965.

mer Democrat who was shilling for big business on the radio, Ronald Reagan.

The debate was loud enough to generate a conservative counterproposal, which was enacted and named after its conservative Democratic cosponsors, the mighty Senator Bob Kerr of Oklahoma and the chairman of the House Ways and Means Committee, Wilbur Mills of Arkansas. It brought some relief to the poorest of the elderly but was limited in its reach. The program was widely derided for its requirement that prospective beneficiaries sign a statement declaring themselves destitute. Kennedy condemned the humiliating, bureaucratic demand, calling it a "pauper's oath."

Kennedy seized on the Forand proposal. Less than three weeks after officially declaring his candidacy he was ready with speeches, background material, and advocates to promote the idea throughout the campaign. His effort attracted fervent opposition on the familiar grounds of Big Government, "socialized medicine," and other right-wing cold war themes. But on balance the initiative gave Kennedy national standing as a legitimate player in an important debate over a domestic issue.

That was equally true for another debate he became engaged in, a heated national argument over the future and financing of public schools. The topic had grown increasingly prominent in public affairs after World War II as a swelling population spilled out of cities and rural areas into new communities called suburbs. Many jurisdictions—the old cities as well as the new suburbs—struggled to finance their schools on inadequate property tax bases. The inequity produced wide disparities between a few superrich, world-class districts and communities that lacked enough classrooms and textbooks. The shock delivered by the Soviet Union's leap into space heightened the serious nature of the national conversation. It was complicated by a powerful tradition that local schools should be managed locally, free of "outside" control, a belief made even more intense by the growing national argument over segregated public schools.

This was one of the few issues Kennedy had taken on at the beginning of his political career. His first proposal was made as a second-term congressman, and he updated it regularly in legislation and speeches as his career advanced. He called for direct federal assistance to local districts to help pay for operating expenses. In 1949 he joined a small group of congressional supporters seeking $300 million in annual aid; the figure was periodically raised over the years to account for inflation and a growing population of Baby Boomers.

Once again Kennedy faced the counterargument against Big Government, made more intense by racial strife. Federal aid to education also forced him, for the first time in his political career, to confront his religion. As the national debate intensified, the hierarchy of the Catholic Church clamored to get some of the proposed aid for its parochial schools, arguing that they often served needy communities and took fiscal pressure off the public schools. But Kennedy pushed back—on solid constitutional grounds. In the dispute he invited considerable criticism from his Church. Instead of sending him into retreat, however, the clash gave him an early opportunity to demonstrate his independence.

In the early years of Kennedy's consideration of the touchy issue, he opposed general-purpose aid for church-run schools but supported specific appropriations to help buy school buses and textbooks and pay for school nurses and other services. As time passed and his candidacy loomed, he took a harder line on the subject.

Kennedy did not campaign as an issues-based candidate, throwing detailed plans and proposals at audiences. Instead he attempted to awaken voters to a domestic landscape littered with unmet needs and festering problems that demanded attention. Rather than push programs, he urged personal involvement.

Walt Rostow was not the only person influencing Kennedy's spirited activism. In early 1959 still another onetime Stevenson supporter and speechwriter, Harvard's Arthur Schlesinger Jr., was comfortably aboard Kennedy's campaign. It was an easy transition for the Pulitzer Prize–winning historian, who had urged Stevenson to pick Kennedy as his running mate in 1956.

While Kennedy's brother-in-law Stephen Smith was establishing a covert campaign office at the foot of Capitol Hill, Schlesinger was circulating a twenty-three-page memorandum to Kennedy and a few top aides. The document was labeled "Confidential" in the senator's files, and it made the case for a campaign "to get the country moving again." In Schlesinger's view it was the natural order of things for a country that historically moved in cycles between relative activism and relative passivity, a view for which his equally illustrious father, Arthur Schlesinger Sr., was already known.

Writing that "there is an inherent cyclical rhythm in our national affairs," Schlesinger said he sensed "a growing desire to start moving forward as a nation again" after a decade of relative quiescence. After years marked by the Depression and world war, it made historical sense that there was "a condition of national weariness produced by two decades of unrelenting crises." Referring specifically to President Eisenhower, Schlesinger sneered that "his particular contribution to the art of politics was to make politics boring at a time when the American people wanted any excuse to forget public policy."

No more, Schlesinger argued. To emphasize the nation's underlying discontent and desire for change, he appealed to Kennedy's intellectual side by citing not opinion polls but cultural indicators: the rise of the Beat generation of popular writers like Jack Kerouac and even "sick" comics like Mort Sahl and Lenny Bruce. He mentioned the popularity of a novel by the Russian Boris Pasternak, *Doctor Zhivago*, and noted the enthusiastic reception accorded the newly installed Cuban leader, Fidel Castro, on his recent official visit to the United States, where he drew ten thousand people in little Cambridge and forty thousand to New York's Central Park. The interest in new and revolutionary figures represented, he said, a mixture of anxiety and yearning.

Schlesinger did not propose another New Deal; instead he saw an analogy with the Progressive Era at the turn of the century, particularly in "the concept of the public interest, the general welfare and the national interest." Americans, he said, wanted a leader pushing for unified purpose, even sacrifice.

CHAPTER NINE

Playing Dixie

Even before he left Chicago after the 1956 Democratic convention Kennedy had recognized the potential for an unusual alliance. Nine of the southern delegations had given him support during the decisive second ballot for vice president. He was under no illusion that this represented a firm commitment in the future; he knew their votes were driven by their hatred of Kefauver and that their attraction to him was more personal than substantive. Still, he marveled that those states where fundamentalist Protestant faiths were dominant and ministers inveighed against the dangers of Catholicism loyal to Rome had been willing to side with him. Talking with a family friend, the *New York Times* columnist Arthur Krock, at the Drake Hotel hours after he failed to get the vice presidential nomination, Kennedy made a wry remark: "I'll be singing Dixie the rest of my life."

When he began his undeclared presidential campaign in 1957, there was reason to hope that the South might form a significant part of his base in reaching for the nomination. There was precedent for southern support of an eastern Catholic in a national election. In 1928 Al Smith carried six of the eleven states of the old Confederacy. While being swept away by Herbert Hoover in more heavily populated and cosmopolitan states, the New York governor nonetheless won Alabama, Arkansas, Georgia, Louisiana, Mississippi, and South Carolina.

Like the embrace of Kennedy at the convention, the southern show-ing for Smith did not reflect a bond between the New Yorker and Dixie but rather a deep southern antipathy for his opponent's party. The re-gion had been hostile to the Republican Party for decades following the Civil War and Reconstruction. The party of Lincoln—and the home of ardent abolitionists who had been punitive in victory—was held respon-sible for the humiliation of the South. Politically the former Confederate states morphed into the "Solid South," a powerful bloc that voted almost monolithically for Democrats. In some states the Republican Party did not exist beyond a few newly enfranchised blacks and a handful of way-ward whites. As a result the Catholic Smith won 91 percent of the vote in South Carolina and 81 percent in Mississippi, an amazing outcome in two of the most rigidly right-wing states in the Union.

Into the 1950s Democrats ruled the region as governors and mayors. Congressional delegations from the South were exclusively Democratic. Because the same men were repeatedly sent to Washington they accu-mulated power through seniority. And with a notable exception or two, they not only practiced segregation at home but defended it ruthlessly as committee chairmen on Capitol Hill.

Young Senator Kennedy found it necessary to pay fealty to the old southern bulls who controlled the place, following the recommendation of an old aphorism, "Go along to get along." He understood the impor-tance of obeying the dictates of the Texan Lyndon Johnson, the Senate majority leader. He knew to join James Eastland of Mississippi, chairman of the Judiciary Committee, for evening cocktails in his office; to show deference to Richard Russell of Georgia, who controlled the Armed Ser-vices Committee; to cultivate his contemporary, Russell Long of Louisi-ana, an emerging force on the Finance Committee; and to appreciate the value of a genuine friendship with George Smathers of Florida.

Kennedy believed he had a viable relationship with southern leaders that he could build upon. But it would require an extraordinary exercise, a tightrope walk between the southern forces and a civil rights move-ment beginning to gather momentum.

In 1957 the nation was awakening to the demand by blacks—buttressed by a chorus of sympathetic whites—to strike down segregation. Kennedy was not part of this awakening. He was a reliable northern Democratic politician on civil rights issues, but by background, temperament, and political calculation he was not a strong voice on the subject. Not until later did he come to appreciate the brutal oppression of the Jim Crow system and the moral force of the movement for equality. In addition to his privileged upbringing, he was shielded from direct experience with the privations of African American reality as well as from the deeply segregated South, and his primary interest when he entered politics was foreign affairs.

At the same time he touched all the issues of the day—opposing the poll tax, supporting efforts to confront open discrimination in hiring practices, and advocating a quicker end to colonialism—from his very first campaign for Congress through his election to the Senate in 1952. Missing were his voice and leadership in the broader struggle for civil rights; his was a meek stance similar to his muted position on McCarthy's witch hunts.

In its historic *Brown v. Board of Education* decision in 1954 the U.S. Supreme Court had outlawed segregation in public schools—yet ruled that recalcitrant school districts could move with "deliberate speed" to integrate their facilities. They moved grudgingly, if at all. Kennedy's reluctance to push harder for quicker action was apparent in his opposition to an amendment to a 1956 bill that would have blocked federal aid to segregated schools, foreshadowing more, higher-profile trimming the following year. Asked about his positions in an appearance on CBS's *Face the Nation*, Kennedy explained that if the amendment were attached to a broader federal aid bill the measure would not pass. The segregation issue, he said, was being "dealt with very satisfactorily by the Supreme Court." Pressed about the slow enforcement of the *Brown* ruling, he replied, "They came to a decision in 1954. It was unanimous and it is the law. . . . As I understand, the Supreme Court used the words 'deliberate speed,' which may sound like a paradox but isn't, I don't think, and left it to the judgment of the lower federal courts as to when it should be carried out, and I think that is a satisfactory arrangement."

Civil rights activists found the refusal of the southern schools to comply with the *Brown* decision unacceptable, and the question of racial equality moved rapidly from the courts and classrooms into the streets of America.

Public consciousness had been jarred by two fateful incidents in 1955. In the late summer Emmett Till, a fourteen-year-old black boy from Chicago visiting relatives in rural Mississippi, had been abducted, brutalized, and murdered, accused of having the temerity to whistle at a white woman. That December the grievance of black passengers weary of being ordered to yield their seats to whites on crowded buses boiled over into a massive protest in Montgomery, Alabama. When Rosa Parks refused to give up her bus seat and was arrested, she became a symbol for a new phase of the movement that triggered a bus boycott and the establishment of the Montgomery Improvement Association, an organization echoing with demands for justice for local blacks and headed by a young minister named Martin Luther King Jr.

Two months later, upstate in Tuscaloosa, white mobs thwarted the *Brown* decision by creating so much campus turmoil that Autherine Lucy, the first black student to enroll, under a court order, at the University of Alabama, was forced out of school. Following a riot, the university trustees suspended Lucy on the grounds that they were protecting her safety.

Fury was building on many fronts. By 1957 the two sides were digging in for a bitter, protracted battle, and it would become increasingly difficult to compromise.

Civil rights was terra incognito to the young senator from Massachusetts. With the pressures of the cold war intensifying, Kennedy seemed more intrigued by foreign policy questions than the racial struggle at home. Blacks composed less than 2 percent of his state's population and commanded little political clout. When he campaigned for the Senate in 1952, he ventured into a few black wards, but their votes were not much of a consideration.

Kennedy had grown up versed in the discrimination against the Irish in America. His parents' generation remembered the nineteenth-century "help wanted" advertisements in newspapers that included the condition "No Irish need apply," barely camouflaged by the widely used initials NINA. The Kennedy children learned that the world was full of disadvantaged people who suffered from bigotry. But no special concern was shown for blacks.

Kennedy was educated at elite schools and served in a segregated navy. No black with any influence had been a member of his congressional staff or was among his inner circle of friends. It was not that he was a bigot, but simply that his social and political life kept blacks at a distance.

By comparison Kennedy's supporters at the Chicago convention included an interesting assortment of segregationist leaders and virulent racists who either favored him personally or were bound to him by their delegation's unit rule. From South Carolina, Senator Strom Thurmond, who led the breakaway Dixiecrats in 1948, was counted in Kennedy's column. From Arkansas, he had the support of Governor Orval E. Faubus, who within a year would embroil President Eisenhower and the federal government in a major racial conflict. From Alabama, two figures on the threshold of infamy were also in Kennedy's ranks: Eugene "Bull" Connor, the Birmingham police commissioner who would unleash attack dogs and fire hoses on youthful black demonstrators, and a local judge named George C. Wallace, who became the face of southern resistance to black aspirations. From Georgia, he enjoyed the support of a pair of newspaper publishers who were well-known segregationist voices: James Gray, who would push back the followers of Dr. King in a confrontation in Gray's hometown of Albany, and Roy Harris, who used his *Augusta Courier* editorials to promote the idea that blacks were an inferior race. From Mississippi, he claimed the votes of Jim Eastland, a notorious champion of segregation, and Eastland's key ally back home, the obdurate speaker of the state's House of Representatives, Walter Sillers.

After Chicago, Kennedy courted some of them. In a letter to a hardline Mississippi segregationist, Congressman John Bell Williams, with whom he had served in the House, he wrote, "I appreciated the help and support which you gave my candidacy at the convention. Certainly the unanimous action of the Mississippi delegation on the second ballot, which I am sure was done in large measure to your efforts, was most helpful in making the run as close as it was."*

Kennedy also exchanged friendly letters with George Wallace, offering help, if needed, in his coming campaign for governor in 1958, and sending his "highest regards and best wishes for your success." Wallace, who would complain he was "outniggered" in the Democratic primary that year, responded that he intended to be a delegate to the 1960 convention. He told Kennedy, "I have always been interested in you and want you to know that I shall continue to be so."

Kennedy showered the 1956 convention delegates with copies of *Profiles in Courage*. The Pulitzer Prize–winning book included a chapter saluting Mississippi's L. Q. C. Lamar, a secessionist and Confederate veteran who changed his stripes after the Civil War in order to gain the reputation of a statesman. One of eight men cited by Kennedy, Lamar won the author's praise for delivering a touching eulogy for Charles Sumner, a senator from Massachusetts who had been one of the most vocal critics of the South in the run-up to the Civil War. In his remarks on the Senate floor, Lamar appealed for national unity: "My countrymen! Know one another and you will love one another." By including Lamar in his pantheon of American heroes, Kennedy stroked southern pride and revealed a desire for their favorable recognition.

Surveying the current political landscape, Kennedy felt encouraged not only by his madcap, enthusiastic reception in Louisiana during the Stevenson campaign but by the stature he seemed to have among the state's party elders. One Louisiana leader, Edmund Reggie, already promoting him for president, believed Kennedy could become "the darling of the South."

Kennedy also heard from William Winter, a young Mississippi delegate.† Although Kennedy had served as the anti-Kefauver candidate supported by southerners in Chicago, Winter wrote, "Let me assure you

---

* Williams was stripped of his Democratic seniority after supporting Barry Goldwater in 1964. He went home to be elected governor in 1967 and led segregationist forces in their long battle against school desegregation in the state.

† Winter would rise from the state's racial quagmire to become a progressive governor a quarter-century later.

that my vote, and I believe that most of the delegation was an affirmative vote for you and not just a vote against somebody else."

Within months of the Chicago convention Kennedy would have his developing friendship with the South tested by the votes he would be forced to cast on the first major civil rights bill to be debated in Congress in the twentieth century. The measure was originally drafted to protect voting rights, but it was actually a fig leaf to cover a more ambitious assault on "the southern way of life." The bill would easily clear the House, but once it went to the Senate in early 1957, it took on new dimensions as liberals vowed their strong commitment even as the formidable southern bloc worked to gut it.

Kennedy was not the only senator squeezed by the legislation. The bill represented a far bigger quandary for the man he expected to be one of his chief rivals for the Democratic presidential nomination in 1960, Lyndon Johnson, who was charged with steering the bill to passage. With his Texas background, Johnson appeared to be a natural political fit with his fellow southerners, but he knew that blind adherence to southern values would cost him elsewhere. Shepherding a civil rights bill might act as an antidote to liberal Democrats' suspicions that he was just another wheeler-dealer from Dixie. Yet Johnson risked alienating his base of support in the South if he were held responsible for a strong civil rights bill. It presented a tantalizing conundrum. With Texas-size determination he took up the burden of moving the legislation through the contentious shoals to craft something that might ultimately appease both sides. His tactics created dilemmas for other Democrats, and the Massachusetts senator would be bruised by the process.

Kennedy's first ticklish moment came when liberals attempted to keep the bill from being assigned to the Judiciary Committee, whose chairman was Eastland, the very man whose trust Kennedy had been pursuing. The Sphinx-like Eastland was a quiet killer of any legislation remotely tied to civil rights. His home was a Mississippi Delta plantation where his wealth had been built on the backs of poor black farm laborers. He rarely gave speeches, but in the Senate he was a ringleader of forces that defeated any bill designed to aid voting rights by eliminating poll taxes and literacy tests and any legislation that would have made lynching a federal crime. Since the end of World War II, dozens of bills had been buried in Eastland's committee. Johnson, who would use all of his legislative legerdemain during the struggle over the civil rights bill, believed that by sending it to the Judiciary Committee it would be weakened by concessions to the South but would emerge as something that could win final passage. With Johnson manipulating the measure's path, a motion to divert the bill away from the Judiciary Committee failed. To the consternation of civil rights lobbyists and many of his friends, Kennedy voted with the majority to keep the bill in Eastland's hands.

A second critical roll-call vote settled the most significant fight. The bill's Title III would have given the federal government increased power to take civil and criminal action against anyone accused of violating the civil rights—and not merely the voting rights—of others. During the debate Richard Russell of Georgia—another of the southern leaders Kennedy had targeted as a potential source of support—vehemently attacked the provision. Invoking the troubled history of Reconstruction, he warned that federal military forces could be used again against the South. Moreover, he said, "under this bill, if the attorney general should contend that separate eating places, places of amusement and the like in the South" were deemed guilty of discrimination, then "white people who operated the place of amusement could be jailed without benefit of jury trial and kept in jail until they either rotted or until they conformed to the edict to integrate their place of business."

Title III represented the heart of the bill, and Kennedy was vigorously lobbied by such advocates as Joseph Rauh, the point man for the liberal Americans for Democratic Action, who concluded that the senator "wanted to be on both sides." It seemed to be a period in his life, Rauh said later, "when the civil rights thing wasn't quite clear to him."

Under pressure from liberals in Washington as well as back home in Boston, Kennedy voted for Title III, but it was defeated on the Senate floor.

This left a third controversial amendment, another sop to the South. It would require that any criminal contempt cases involving voting rights would be tried by juries rather than heard by judges. The language sounded as if it ensured basic freedoms for the accused; in fact it assured that any defendant would be acquitted by all-white juries, which were the norm in the South.

Kennedy was ambivalent and sought help from several legal scholars, most notably Paul Freund of Harvard Law School, whose advice was mixed. Freund said he would oppose the measure himself but told Kennedy that voting for the jury trial amendment would not "constitute a betrayal of principle." Kennedy shared Freund's letter with Rauh, who felt Kennedy "misused the letter a little bit."

The floor fight was critical because if a simple amendment was defeated the result would be a southern filibuster to block the entire legislative package. At nearly the last minute a rescuer entered the picture in the person of a freshman senator from the West at the dawn of a distinguished career, Frank Church of Idaho, for whom Kennedy had campaigned in 1956. Church's proposal forbade discrimination in the selection of juries in federal trials; it would have required diligent enforcement, but it was more than a token. It was enough to attract several northern and western Democrats, including Kennedy; it also got the vital backing of Johnson, eager to protect his standing with northern Democrats after the defeat of Title III.

On his way out of the Senate chamber after the successful vote, Kennedy literally bumped into Church's wife, Bethine, and told her, "Frank did a great thing today; he enabled me, he made it possible for me to vote for the jury trial."

Kennedy voted for the amendment, siding again with the southern bloc.

During the battle Kennedy encountered for the first time a black leader named Roy Wilkins, the executive secretary of the National Association for the Advancement of Colored People. They met in the Senate dining room, where Kennedy spoke at length during a late lunch about his decision to support the amendment. "It appeared to me that the senator might have been inclined to vote otherwise had someone talked to him beforehand and with some of the background material I was able to give him," Wilkins said later. He decided that Kennedy knew little about civil rights, and his unfavorable impression would lead to explosive criticism of him the following year.

But Kennedy escaped the debate with some standing among his southern colleagues, just as he had intended. And Johnson, the engineer of the bill, was able to claim credit for the passage of the first civil rights legislation since 1875 while at the same time watering it down to the satisfaction of the South.

The political games-playing was obvious to anyone following the struggle on Capitol Hill. Tom Wicker, a young reporter covering the story for a North Carolina newspaper, remembered, "The feeling in Washington at the time was that Kennedy had somewhat straddled the issue." Wicker, who became a distinguished columnist for the *New York Times*, figured Kennedy "was hoping to have quite a bit of Southern support in the convention in 1960."

In all the legislative maneuvering and positioning the question for Jack and Robert Kennedy was how to effectively achieve civil rights progress while showing a willingness to compromise. The jury trial amendment was an obstacle, to be sure, but there was a constitutional case to be made for it; furthermore its defeat could torpedo the bill itself. That made it acceptable, especially after Church helped change it.

To Robert these episodes illustrated his problem with liberals, who, he once said in exasperation, "are in love with death." He often used extreme imagery, including this passage: "You showed you were for civil rights by sending up legislation whether the legislation passed or not and made a speech. It didn't matter what you did for the Negro as long as you had these outward manifestations of being interested. Well, my brother and I thought that really didn't make any sense and what mattered was doing something."

Before President Eisenhower could sign the Civil Rights Act of 1957 in early September, a new drama began unfolding with the start of school in Little Rock, Arkansas. Nine black students had been selected to integrate Central High School, a popular, previously all-white facility just blocks from the state capitol. But the night before they arrived for the first day of classes, Governor Orval E. Faubus delivered a televised address to announce that he was sending units of the Arkansas National Guard to do the work that segregationist groups were promising to do: block the students from attending. Faubus couched his action as a move to ensure peace and preserve the status quo. Instead he created havoc and made an early entry for himself in the ledger of southern governors determined to use all their power to prevent the desegregation of their schools.

Faubus was an unlikely obstructionist. The son of a fiery socialist, he had been given his middle name, Eugene, in honor of Eugene Debs, the national leader of the Socialist Party. He had even attended Commonwealth College, a left-leaning institution that was shut down in 1940 because of charges that it sponsored subversive activities. As a product of the northwestern part of the state, which had relatively few blacks and escaped racial conflict, Faubus had been elected as a moderate who used Arkansas Power & Light Company as his whipping boy instead of the U.S. Supreme Court.

It seemed logical for Kennedy to consider him a prospective supporter. However, Faubus became another example of a southern politician infected by the toxin of race. It was assumed that he deployed the National Guard out of fear that he would be defeated for reelection in 1958 if he acquiesced in school integration. Arkansas governors had two-year terms at the time, and Faubus had been challenged in 1956 by a demagogic segregationist named Jim Johnson riding the rabid support of the Citizens Councils, a network of local organizations set up across the South to fight the *Brown* decision. A Council publication called "Arkansas Faith" branded Faubus as a politician "who would trade your daughter for a mess of nigger votes." With another election coming in less than a year, Faubus withered in the face of the racist onslaught. Little Rock was bristling with threats of a human blockade of Central High School by fanatics who would be coming out of the woods with guns drawn. By stopping the black students with the National Guard, Faubus co-opted his critics.

Eisenhower could be pushed, as he was during the debate over the civil rights bill, and he was sometimes slow to react. After nearly three weeks of negotiation with Faubus failed to resolve the situation, a federal judge enjoined the governor from employing the National Guard to keep out the black students. But when the "Little Rock Nine" reappeared at the school, they were met by hundreds of whites shouting insults. After the students were slipped through a side door and were safely inside the building, the crowd transferred their anger to journalists covering the story. White toughs pounced on four representatives of the black press, while others encouraged the violence with shrieks of "Anyone got a rope? We'll hang 'em." Police failed to intervene on the black reporters' behalf, but eventually moved in, clubbing members of the crowd. With the capital of Arkansas gripped by pandemonium, the terrorized students were dismissed—for their own safety—from Central High before noon.

Eisenhower had seen enough. He ordered a thousand paratroopers from the 101st Airborne Division of the U.S. Army into Little Rock and, for good measure, federalized the National Guard to take them out of Faubus's hands. The president's use of force ensured that the nine students could attend the school and served as emphatic proof that the *Brown* decision could be implemented in the South.

But it revived a political nightmare that had colored debate in the Senate a few weeks earlier: the specter of federal troops sent to beat down the South. Faubus called the arrival of the 101st Airborne an "occupation." To other southerners it seemed like the coming of a second Reconstruction.

In this unsettled environment Kennedy had the audacity to make a political appearance the next month in the stronghold of segregation, Mississippi. As many as two thousand Mississippians attended the $5-a-plate dinner at the Heidelberg Hotel on Capitol Street to listen to the visitor from Massachusetts. Shortly before the event began, Kennedy learned of a taunting quote from Wirt Yerger, the state chairman of a Republican Party that was in its infancy. In an article in that day's Jackson newspaper, Yerger challenged Kennedy to state his views on integration. "Is it not a fact," Yerger asked, "that he voted for the infamous Section Three of the so-called Civil Rights Bill?"

Kennedy had planned to again laud the career of L. Q. C. Lamar and to talk of the benefits of party loyalty. But instead of delivering the toothless words that had been prepared for him, he took a pen to his speech and made several revisions. At the outset he observed that it should be possible for Democrats to disagree on some subjects without causing a major schism in the party. The all-white audience, composed almost exclusively of segregationists, gave him a pattering of applause but appeared suspicious. Kennedy then veered from his prepared remarks to say that he had read Yerger's comment and announced, "I accept the challenge."

"You who have been gracious enough to invite me here realize that we do not see eye to eye on all national issues," he continued. "I have no hesitancy in telling the Republican chairman the same thing I said in my own city of Boston: that I accept the Supreme Court decision as the supreme law of the land. I know that we do not all agree on that issue, but I think most of us do agree on the necessity to uphold law and order in every part of the land."

Then, his voice rising, Kennedy had a retort for a party led by a president who had just sent troops to Arkansas: "I challenge the Republican chairman to tell us where he stands on President Eisenhower and Vice President Nixon." The crowd rose to its feet, clapping and cheering. One spectator spoke afterward of his wonder at seeing someone speak approvingly of integration and getting a standing ovation in Mississippi.

Following the dinner Kennedy was an overnight guest at the governor's mansion, where he talked until 2 a.m. with Governor J. P. Coleman, considered a racial moderate; the state's two senators, Jim Eastland and John Stennis, who were among segregation's strongest advocates in Washington; and members of the House delegation. Kennedy's early interest in pursuing the Democratic presidential nomination was implicit, but there was a more explicit subject on the minds of his hosts: Little Rock. The group sought to explain the peculiar problems of Mississippi, ensnared in its racial issues, to the visitor from New England. They spoke approvingly of the Supreme Court's mention of "deliberate speed." Pointing out that the history of segregation was older than the 140-year-old state, they warned that it could not be reversed overnight. They hoped Mississippians would be allowed to determine their own schedule for desegregation. It was also clear that they wanted no federal troops in the state. Coleman came away from the conversation with the belief that Kennedy, if elected president, would try every way possible to avoid dispatching troops to enforce a desegregation order. After Kennedy left Mississippi, Coleman was effusive in his praise. "I think he is our best presidential prospect for 1960, and I am all for him."

Jackson was just one of several stops in the region as Kennedy stepped through treacherous political territory, careful not to offend southerners yet, at the same time, holding on to his credentials as a national candidate. It required a delicate balance. One southern commentator, John Temple Graves, wrote approvingly of Kennedy's courtship of Dixie: "He is too intelligent to be making the advances without some sort of marriage in mind." Graves even predicted that Kennedy could become the "living antithesis of Earl Warren," the chief justice of the Supreme Court that had handed down the *Brown* decision.

CHAPTER TEN

Going National

At the beginning of 1958 Bernard Boutin was a young mayor of Laconia, New Hampshire, as well as the state's representative on the Democratic National Committee. He was also part of an impatient collection of up-and-coming Democrats working to end New Hampshire's decades-long domination by the Republicans in a state that traditionally conducted the first presidential primary. In Washington on party business one day, Boutin got a call from Ted Sorensen on behalf of sub rosa presidential candidate John Kennedy, asking if he had time to stop by the senator's office for a chat.

Kennedy got right to the point. First, he questioned Boutin closely on everything he knew about the New Hampshire primary and what it takes to win it. He also wanted a detailed report from the thirty-seven-year-old mayor on the party-building efforts he and his pals had undertaken. And he told Boutin that he was very seriously thinking about running in 1960.

"He just asked for my help and from then on I was a captive audience," Boutin recalled.

For the rest of that year and well into 1959, Kennedy's presidential campaign in the state was indistinguishable from Boutin's reform effort. Kennedy money poured into the state, as did his political allies, accompanied, eventually, by Kennedy himself. The senator was well aware that New Hampshire was an unpredictable place and that his status as a neighbor from Massachusetts meant essentially nothing. In the past two Democratic presidential primaries, New Hampshire had gone to the quirky liberal outsider Kefauver of Tennessee. The state tended to reward campaigning effort rather than respect candidates' geographic proximity.

Democrats in New Hampshire were not only outnumbered; they had to face a regular pummeling by the only statewide newspaper, the *Manchester Union Leader*, which featured strident right-wing editorials on its front page to supplement "news stories" so biased they seemed comical to national journalists who followed events in the first primary state.

"Let us face it frankly," Kennedy told a gathering of Boutin's game subversives in June 1958, "the minority party in a one-party state always suffers. Younger leaders are discouraged. National candidates and administrations of both parties ignore the one-party state and its problems."

The young Democrats, whose ranks included a future U.S. senator, Tom McIntyre, and one of the scions of a successful hotel-chain family, Bill Dunfey, were getting closer to their goal. After their Democratic candidate for governor in 1952 won only 36 percent of the vote, a Democrat carried 46 percent four years later. Their short-term goal was the 1958 election, when Boutin would come within 6,500 votes of winning the governor's office. But their efforts were moving toward a grander objective. By supporting the insurgency Kennedy was able to steer the group into a seamless transition to his own presidential campaign.

Kennedy knew of the brief inspection trips to New Hampshire made by representatives of such likely opponents as Lyndon Johnson, Stuart Symington, and Hubert Humphrey. He hardly needed an education on the obvious fact that his national candidacy could not survive a defeat next door to Massachusetts. This knowledge influenced his judgments about another state with a possibly pivotal primary in 1960, Wisconsin, a neighbor of Humphrey's adopted Minnesota.

New Hampshire, of course, was just the beginning. As he embarked on yet another year of punishing travel, Kennedy did not need polling data to understand the challenge. But he had begun to believe that data from the still-developing science of opinion sampling could help him pick his spots as he made plans to navigate an expanded landscape of sixteen scheduled primaries in 1960. He wanted informed evaluations of his emergence as a national figure. Accordingly, at the end of 1957 he did something no candidate for president had ever done before: he retained the services of a professional to monitor public opinion continually throughout his campaign.

During the first week of 1958 Kennedy sent a note along with a personal check for $5,000 to thirty-six-year-old Louis Harris at his new office in New York's Empire State Building. The meaning of his message to Harris was clear and succinct regarding 1960: "It is my hope, as I indicated over the telephone, that the contractual relationship established by this letter will be drawn upon frequently during the next three years." Kennedy emphasized that the first check was for national work "in the area of issues and personalities opinion research." An arrangement for his Senate reelection campaign would be made later.

Harris had spent a decade as an assistant to a pioneer in the polling business, Elmo Roper, before starting his own firm two years before. Already he was beginning to attract attention in Democratic Party circles for his work for Mayor Robert Wagner of New York and Senators Joseph Clark of Pennsylvania and Frank Church of Idaho. Harris was fresh off the triumph in New Jersey of Governor Robert Meyner, whom Kennedy knew had more than idle thoughts about 1960.

In a five-page memorandum to Sorensen pitching his service at the end of 1957, Harris wrote that from his "research comes the sound basis on which to assess where Senator Kennedy stands today, where his sources of strength and weakness are, and how he can maximize his margin of victory. . . . While we are Democrats we can assure you that we will not let our partisanship blind us from leveling and calling the facts as we find them."

Harris also reflected an awareness of Kennedy's broader view of the utility of polls in the context of his campaign strategy for both the primary states and the larger number of national convention delegates who would be chosen by other means. "While the degree to which these primaries are binding will vary," he wrote in a memorandum dated December 29, 1957, "there is an overall impressiveness we find in the total number of convention votes affected by primary elections. Together, the primaries represent over 40 percent of the delegate count at the Democratic convention. Any candidate who won them all would automatically become a serious contender; and a candidate who stayed out of them all would appear to have a hard, uphill, late-ballot fight to make."

Both Harris and his client saw that polls could be used as important leverage with the powerful party leaders in places where delegate selection was more of a backroom affair. Good research, Harris said, "can also be used as an effective piece of information with the leaders of many non-primary states." His theory anticipated the Kennedy methods used in major prizes like New York, California, and Ohio.

By February 1958 Sorensen was setting the early parameters on his boss's behalf; they chose not to review Oregon or Kentucky but commissioned a survey in California for $1,500 and allotted $7,500 for a more comprehensive look at Massachusetts. The California survey was taken during a two-day visit there by Kennedy in March. Harris noted that economic difficulties made the state an ideal Democratic target. He did not test Kennedy against other Democrats but conducted a mock heat against Richard Nixon, who had a strong California background. Kennedy wound up ahead 55 to 45 percent. Harris's data also provided the first hard evidence of the two-edged sword of Kennedy's Catholicism. In a state that was nearly one-fifth Catholic, Harris found Kennedy and Nixon splitting the votes of Protestants but Kennedy leading among Catholics by an overwhelming margin: 68 to 32 percent.

Harris's poll was taken before a political earthquake in the state that fall. In a maneuver that backfired spectacularly, with Nixon pulling the levers, the incumbent Republican governor, Goodwin Knight, ran for the Senate and the incumbent Republican senator, Minority Leader William Knowland, ran for governor. They both got crushed, ushering into the governor's mansion in Sacramento Edmund "Pat" Brown, who in short order would become a legend.

Democratic presidential candidates had often passed up California, which tended to divide its faction-ridden delegation among candidates rather than uniting behind a favorite son. Kennedy remained undecided about competing in California. The California survey showed he could be a credible national candidate, but it provided no data that could inform a decision on whether to enter the state's primary.

Kennedy kept testing the market in large states where entering primaries was at least an option. The Harris results were mixed, indicating neither an adoring electorate eager to vote for him nor a hostile public whose opinions constituted a hopeless obstacle. In August, based on nearly six hundred interviews in four eastern Pennsylvania counties, a survey showed Stevenson ahead in a three-way matchup with 37 percent, followed by Kennedy with 27 percent, and Meyner close with 24 percent. That was also the case, Harris found, in the important state of Ohio, which had an early filing deadline for its 1960 primary. One month after the Pennsylvania poll Harris found more evidence that Kennedy's campaigning, which had included more than one Ohio stop, was beginning to pay off. This time Harris sampled what he called a "laundry list" of possible candidates. The results: Kennedy 35 percent, Stevenson 30, and G. Mennen Williams of Michigan, Symington, and Humphrey all in single digits.

The poll put two factors in play that would remain important: religion and gender. Using Stevenson as the theoretical primary opponent, the two split the preferences of Protestants, but Kennedy was ahead by 20 percentage points among Catholics. Regarding gender, Kennedy and Stevenson were even among men, but Kennedy had a 10-percentage-point advantage among women.

These three surveys of major states, which supplied roughly a third of the delegates needed to win the nomination, still left Kennedy unconvinced about entering their primaries. But they gave him information about where he stood eighteen months before the actual voting and delegate selection would begin. And by using polling data Kennedy would have a chance to base his decisions on something more than hunches.

The smaller primary states also involved critical decisions. Two of them, Wisconsin and West Virginia, loomed especially large for a candidate who had to demonstrate an ability to win in order to have a prayer of clawing his way to nomination. Kennedy campaigned in each in 1958, and Lou Harris was very active in them as well, but his first polling results were inconclusive.

The results from Harris's initial survey were surprising. In the case of Wisconsin, his findings seemed counterintuitive. Humphrey was more than a neighbor; he had visited the state frequently for more than a decade and was always available to headline an event, always helpful on legislation, especially farm bills. But Kennedy was obviously stronger. In more than six hundred interviews conducted in late May, Harris didn't test the less well-known Kennedy against Humphrey directly. Instead he tested Nixon against Humphrey, Kennedy, and Symington. The results found Nixon comfortably ahead of Humphrey and Symington by double-digit margins. Yet Kennedy ran ahead of Nixon, though just barely.

The pattern was distinctly geographic. Kennedy did best in the city of Milwaukee and in other industrial communities; Nixon was strong in the more rural and small-town interior. Kennedy didn't need a trial heat to tell him the early advantage was his. The pollster's one cautionary note concerned religion, which Harris called "the largest single handicap he has in Wisconsin." His survey found 13 percent of the respondents saying that a candidate's religion mattered; half of these said they wouldn't vote for a Catholic. Dispensing with political correctness, Harris concluded, "The origins of this stem from the powerful Lutheran influence which is especially intolerant of other faiths."

The figures for a Catholic candidate were even more disturbing in West Virginia. The same month, Harris finished a poll of more than 450 potential voters and found 31 percent saying flatly that religion mattered to them; of these, 23 percent were anti-Catholic and 13 percent spoke negatively about Jews. Harris concluded, "When one out of every four voters is anti-Catholic it represents a serious issue of important dimensions."

In both states Harris's analysis of undecided voters discovered that the more people knew about Kennedy, the better he performed in the surveys. This insight led to a recommendation for more campaigning, especially in the rapidly growing suburbs around major cities, where younger families were flocking and partisan ties were looser. That was precisely how Kennedy proceeded in his second year of virtually nonstop travel.

By the standards of the day Kennedy would have been considered extremely active if people knew he was conducting opinion surveys on an unprecedented scale in states holding primaries. In fact he was doing much more than that. In addition to the constant traveling and speaking, he was beginning to organize, both in preparation for primary campaigns and to get such a jump on his competitors that their opposition in certain primaries might never materialize.

A classic example was Nebraska, which would hold a primary in May 1960 as part of a cluster that included Indiana, Maryland, Ohio, and West Virginia. There was no way of knowing which candidate might prove formidable. Nebraska could have been prime real estate for Humphrey or Symington, but Kennedy's preemptive actions took the state off the board.

In early 1958 he knew who would be the most important Democrat in the state. Bernard Boyle was not an elected official but the state's member of the Democratic National Committee. He had considerable political experience and clout and had known Kennedy since the craziness in Chicago two years before. During a visit to Washington he arranged to see the senator and heard him make two points: he was thinking of running for president, and he wanted Boyle to agree to host one of his famous backyard parties at his Omaha home. The core of the guest list would be made up of people who had been convention delegates in 1956 and planned on being in the Nebraska contingent again in 1960. Kennedy, well briefed as usual, pointed out that Boyle had hosted similar gatherings in the past for Averell Harriman, Adlai Stevenson, and the powerful Oklahoma senator Robert Kerr, an ally of Lyndon Johnson.

Boyle agreed, giving Kennedy the inside track to a statewide organization. Eventually Kennedy organizers made a half-dozen trips to the state to help put the event together. By the time Humphrey, Symington, and Johnson started prospecting for help more than a year later, Boyle had to tell them they were too late.

The same was true in several states that would not hold primaries but instead selected delegates in a variety of arcane procedures that essentially began with local caucuses and culminated in state conventions. Especially in the West these affairs were not run by "bosses" who could deliver significant blocs of votes; they were dominated by activists and veterans of local politics who took the trouble to show up at the caucuses. Colorado was typical, except that Colorado had Joe Dolan.

The young Denver lawyer with Capitol Hill experience showed up in Kennedy's office in 1957 to offer temporary help on legislative issues. Almost at once Kennedy and Sorensen began using Dolan to advance his frequent trips to the state. Dolan's work consisted of little more than placing a short notice that local papers ran in the women's pages. But in early 1958, when Kennedy arrived for a speaking engagement in Denver, Dolan took him to a spacious auditorium where more than eight thousand people were waiting.

"I felt that night for the first time," Dolan recalled, "he was going to be elected president. Anyone that can pull eighty-three hundred people who have to send in self-addressed stamped envelopes in the city of Denver in February is going to be president."

The public response to Kennedy impressed the activists and political veterans who dominated Colorado's caucus process. Dolan and his allies proceeded cautiously but methodically from that encouraging event. Along the way Dolan suggested one addition to the team, Byron "Whizzer" White, a lawyer and legendary Colorado athlete Kennedy had known since they toured European cities together before World War II. He would run Kennedy "clubs" outside the party machinery in the state. Eventually the concept would go national under White's guidance, following the model of Kennedy's "secretaries" system in Massachusetts.

Kennedy's strength in Colorado represented a breakthrough—like those in Nebraska and other unlikely states—made possible by his activity in 1958, when no one was looking, including his rivals.

His opposition continued to be blind as Kennedy made his first moves into Wisconsin and West Virginia, the two problematic states whose primaries appeared inviting.

West Virginia presented at least two issues for Kennedy to consider. By law, its primary indicated voters' preferences for candidates, but they actually chose convention delegates from various congressional districts. In addition the state was about 95 percent non-Catholic—and in some areas audibly anti-Catholic. But it also presented a grand opportunity: victory in seemingly hostile territory could finally put the vulnerability of Kennedy's Catholicism to rest.

According to one committed Kennedy supporter in the state, Robert P. McDonough, "the consensus . . . of the working politicians was that the West Virginia primary was a hazard in that if you won it you didn't get anything because the delegates by law were not committed, and if you lost it you had a black mark against you." McDonough, a businessman and political dabbler, became an early, unofficial leader of Kennedy's campaign in West Virginia. In Chicago in 1956 he had been a lonely Kennedy supporter in the state's delegation, which was dominated by Kefauver partisans, and he simply never stopped being supportive. McDonough was part of a tiny local network that imported Kennedy in 1958 to provide some stimulus to the Democratic Party's efforts. The group was based in Parkersburg, the state's fourth largest city, located on the Ohio River north of Charleston. McDonough hosted a luncheon for the senator and his wife at the Chancellor Hotel, which sold out. "We broke the record for a high-priced luncheon," McDonough recalled. "Got five dollars a head."

On the way to the airport afterward Kennedy asked McDonough what his plans were after the off-year election. Learning that he had none, the senator had Sorensen call him with an invitation to chat. It produced a meeting in due course at which McDonough got what he called "the treatment." "He put you in a chair and pulled up his chair opposite you and by the time he got through with you, you were convinced someone had put a hypodermic in you."

After McDonough pledged support for 1960, Kennedy asked him to work with Sorensen and Bob Wallace, who was in charge of the candidate's organizing efforts in those early days. This team was the genesis of "West Virginians for Kennedy" that operated outside normal Democratic Party channels.

Another example of the success of Kennedy's early toil was Harvey Bailey, who met the senator for the first time that day in Parkersburg. In addition to being an active Democrat, Bailey was also a Baptist minister with a radio program of his own. Before the luncheon he joined Kennedy in a parade down Market Street featuring local candidates. He rode in a convertible with his two daughters and was totally smitten, more by Kennedy's affability than his command of the issues of the day.

In the 1950s anti-Catholic prejudice was always present, but its impact varied widely. McDonough sensed the same phenomenon, and it was buttressed by Harris's polling data. McDonough had two additional insights: that anti-Catholic sentiment, like prejudice in general, was more emotional than rational and unsupported by any respected body of theological thought, and that Kennedy was comfortable answering questions about his religion. McDonough believed the opposition at this stage was limited to an occasional crude pamphlet. Kennedy, meanwhile, met the issue "head on. He brought the question up because early in the game he sensed that it was on people's minds."

Kennedy was learning that all the travel, speaking, and political labor worked. As Harris's polls kept telling him, he was one of those politicians who did better the more people came to see and hear him. "It isn't duplication," explained McDonough, "it's multiplication, it's persistence. . . . You deliberately set out to do everything you're going to do as many times as you can do it. It's selling by exposure."

As 1958 wore on, Kennedy believed his quiet work would clear the field in New Hampshire, so he was more easily tempted to create mischief in Wisconsin, the state bordering Humphrey's Minnesota.

"I think the most remarkable thing about Kennedy . . . was his ability to be objective about his own campaign," said Patrick Lucey, the state party chairman, who then stood on the threshold of a long political career. "He just seemed to be able to stand off, as though he were another person, totally disinterested in what was going on, and assess the effect of various elements of the campaign and make studious judgments about what they ought to do next."

While Kennedy temporized about entering the state's primary, there was no reason not to build local support that could sustain a Wisconsin campaign if he launched one. So he worked the state as if he had already made the decision. Keeping to his maxim about starting early, his first major opportunity came in 1957, with a special election in August to finish the term of the infamous Joseph McCarthy, who had died that spring. Kennedy seized the moment, with crucial ramifications.

Since Wisconsin was still essentially a Republican state, the GOP leaders planned to retain the seat by scheduling a very short campaign. But they hadn't reckoned on the Democratic nominee being William Proxmire, a delightfully exasperating, independent, onetime reporter who had served briefly in the state legislature. Proxmire had become a chronic candidate, defeated in races for governor three times. He was so politically incorrect that just a few months after McCarthy's death he continued to denounce him as a "disgrace." Hardly anyone in Wisconsin or Washington gave him a chance, and he knew he needed help.

"Senator Kennedy came out to Wisconsin at our request and was tremendously helpful," Proxmire said years later. That is putting it mildly. Kennedy not only campaigned for Proxmire in Milwaukee; he also stood at plant gates with him and stumped for him as far north as Green Bay, in industrial towns with large collections of his fellow Catholics. Proxmire stunned the political world by winning easily, a harbinger of the Democratic tide that would roll in the following year. He never forgot who had rallied to his side. Proxmire's memory and gratitude would produce possibly the single most important opening for Kennedy to compete in the Wisconsin primary.

One of the big Democratic winners in 1958 was Gaylord Nelson, who was elected governor of Wisconsin. A proud liberal and famous environmentalist, Nelson was an admirer of Humphrey. As a veteran state legislator he was also grateful for all of Humphrey's services to the state when the Democrats had no governor and no senator. When Humphrey began thinking about the presidency himself, one tactic he pursued was to persuade the new governor to run as a favorite son who could deliver the state's delegation to him. Nelson even announced at one point that he would do it. But Proxmire quickly provided resistance. "When I heard about this," he said, "I had been talking with some of the Kennedy people. I announced that if Nelson ran as a favorite son candidate I would run against him as a favorite son candidate. So he soon abandoned that."

Kennedy profited from his work on Proxmire's behalf in another way. It put him in touch with someone who became a legend in national politics and a cog in his Wisconsin primary campaign. Jerry Bruno, an Italian immigrant's son who never got past the ninth grade, was driving a forklift in the early 1950s at the large American Motors plant in his native Kenosha, when one evening he wandered upstairs in Pete's Bar to listen to Proxmire speak. Completely hooked, he began doing chores for the perennial candidate, honing skills in the arcane art of arranging events, doing what politicians call "advance."

Kennedy spotted him in 1957 and again the following year, when Proxmire had to run a second time for a full Senate term. After Prox-mire won again, he took Bruno to Washington. Within weeks Kennedy had invited Bruno to his Georgetown home to offer him a job back in Wisconsin. Proxmire did not object. The match-up with Kennedy was important because Bruno was far more than an advance man; he was an organizer, with deep ties to fellow unionists, and a major reason Kennedy was able to exploit the information in Harris's surveys that showed a division between rank-and-file union members and their Humphrey-oriented leaders. Patrick Lucey observed that the "union leaders knew in many instances that the rank-and-file were not with them." One state union official, Harvey Kitzman, "not only was unable to take . . . his largest local in the state [Bruno's own UAW No. 72 in Kenosha] away from Kennedy, but he finally just accepted this as an established fact and did not try to make inroads there because I think he felt that it would endanger his own position in the union."

The jockeying with labor unions illustrated a critical tactic of Kennedy's campaign: his emphasis on organizing at local levels outside the formal party and labor union structures. This was in contrast to the approach Humphrey would use. "Humphrey did conduct more of a traditional campaign in appealing to voting blocs [via their nominal leaders]," recalled Lucey. "The Kennedy campaign was, for a very large part, just an effective presentation of a celebrity."

Marguerite Benson would not have objected to that remark. A fervent Kennedy supporter from the time she first saw him at the 1956 convention, she was vice chair of the Wisconsin Democratic Party in 1958 and already beginning to put together the nucleus of organizations ready to do the grunt work whenever Kennedy came into the state. She planned to have a network ready to promote his candidacy. Based in Milwaukee, Benson joined two successful labor lawyers and the party leader in a state senate district. She called it "the itty bitty group" before adding, "But like many of these things it does mushroom." It was the equivalent of a Kennedy "club" even before Bruno took on the task of organizing the state.

By the time Kennedy arrived in Wisconsin in May 1958 to serve as the main attraction at the state party's annual fund-raising dinner, the state seemed to be primed to support him as soon as he announced his candidacy

The scope of Kennedy's campaign work two years ahead of the election year was unprecedented. But for someone attempting to break into prominence it was essential to plant seeds early, just as it made sense in 1946 for a young war veteran trying to beat the party regulars for a House seat or to topple an incumbent U.S. senator six years later. The gush of national publicity he created was one thing. Just as important was the fact that his voice on national and international issues now had more weight. In his second full year as an undeclared candidate, he was putting his much larger profile to work building a campaign in the states.

With exposure and backstage politics, however, came the inevitable criticism and opposition. During Kennedy's rise to renown, he became even more alert to any significant attacks. In his handling of the quarrel with ABC, Drew Pearson, and Mike Wallace over his authorship of *Profiles in Courage* he had demonstrated that he would not let stand false allegations against him. He understood the importance of "rapid response" long before the term became a part of the political lexicon.

A new attack came in late April 1958. Since the previous year's ordeal over the passage of the first civil rights legislation since Reconstruction, the head of the NAACP, Roy Wilkins, had kept to himself his disagreements with some of Kennedy's votes. But during an appearance in western Massachusetts Wilkins unloaded publicly.

"A man's record is a man's record . . . and when Kennedy voted, he was wrong," Wilkins's calculated assault began.

He got more personal, slamming Kennedy for consorting with such segregationists as Senator Herman Talmadge of Georgia and the state's governor, Marvin Griffin. Wilkins claimed newspapers had carried pictures of a beaming Kennedy with his arm around Griffin. "No pal of Griffin's can possibly be a pal of mine," he declared. "Griffin thinks I'm an animal."

Kennedy chose not to respond in public in order to avoid inflaming the situation. But within a week Wilkins had a personal letter from the senator, who said he was "somewhat surprised" to learn of the attack, noting that Wilkins had chosen not to criticize his Republican colleague from Massachusetts, Leverett Saltonstall, "whose voting record on civil rights over the years has certainly been far less friendly." Kennedy also pointed out that Wilkins's remarks had been made in Kennedy's home state while he was in the midst of a reelection campaign.

Kennedy repeated the substantive arguments he had made the year before to justify his votes on amendments to the bill, but he used most of his letter to forcefully make two other points. First, he wondered how, "in all seriousness," Wilkins could have said what he said in the context of Kennedy's twelve-year congressional record on civil rights. Second, he zeroed in on a factual error in Wilkins's remarks—his claim that Kennedy had appeared in a photograph with his arm around Governor Griffin. It never happened, Kennedy averred, and further suggested that Wilkins was alleging "guilt by association." Kennedy's use of the phrase awakened memories of Joe McCarthy's tactics. The "association" with Griffin never existed, Kennedy said, except for two formal appearances at large events.

It took Wilkins nearly a month to reply. His letter too was private, reflecting his own wish that the quarrel not become public. But while his tone was milder, it was not apologetic. His one concession was a claim that he had meant the reference to Griffin only "figuratively" and knew of no actual photograph of the two. Otherwise he remained critical of

Kennedy and implied harmful political consequences from his black constituency. Wilkins warned, "You have disturbed them because, while they know that logic and tradition would seem to dictate that you could not be in the Dixiecrat camp, you are hailed by the Dixiecrat leaders of South Carolina, Georgia and Mississippi, which, with Alabama are the 'worst' states on the Negro question. . . . I do know something of how they feel, and they feel uneasy over this apparent entente cordiale between Kennedy of Massachusetts and Griffin, [. . . George Bell] Timmerman, . . . Talmadge, . . . Eastland, et al., of Dixie."

Give or take a nuance, some of Kennedy's anger at Wilkins flowed from the fact that he was being called out for what he was actually doing—courting southern politicians with 1960 in mind. It was one of the few occasions someone criticized Kennedy's behavior in racial politics, an indication that he could not proceed with impunity. Nonwhite voters could provide the margin of victory or defeat in several large northern states; a public spat with one of the civil rights movement's most important leaders threatened real harm to both sides.

For the moment Kennedy preferred to let his anger guide his responses. Wilkins fell silent, but Kennedy struck with two more letters in early June and mid July, again focusing on Wilkins's inaccuracy concerning the nonexistent photo with Griffin and on what he insisted were factual errors in Wilkins's description of his votes on amendments to the civil rights legislation.

In his July 18 letter he got as overtly political as a national politician dares. "I think the time has come for you and me to have a personal conversation about future relations," he began ominously. He expanded his grievance to include recent comments about him by Wilkins's chief Washington representative, Clarence Mitchell, an NAACP lobbyist believed to be friendly with Republicans. Kennedy complained that Mitchell had been "quite outspoken against me" and observed pointedly that Mitchell's "close association with Mr. Nixon is well known in Washington." In closing, Kennedy couldn't resist sticking in the needle one more time: "I am somewhat saddened that, when speaking of pictures, you emphasized one which did not exist instead of the picture of you and me which does exist, taken at the NAACP banquet last fall."

But Kennedy did not stop there. For weeks he pestered aides and friends who knew people on the NAACP's board to intercede to keep Wilkins's antagonism from growing into a destructive feud. Their efforts appeared to pay off. On November 1, just before his reelection, Kennedy was honored at a large dinner by the Massachusetts Citizens Committee for Minority Rights. Wilkins did not attend, but a message from him was read to the six hundred guests. Their dispute seemed forgotten; Wilkins saluted Kennedy as having "one of the best voting records on civil rights and related issues of any senator in the Congress."

There was one more instructive example that year of Kennedy's tendency to react strongly to criticism. Eleanor Roosevelt was much more than the widely beloved widow of FDR; she was also a vigorous advocate of liberal causes and positions, in public appearances, on television, and in her widely circulated newspaper column, "My Day." She had also been an occasional thorn in Kennedy's side ever since his absence from the struggle against Joseph McCarthy.

In March, in one of five issues the *Saturday Evening Post* devoted to serializing her memoir, she spent considerable space on McCarthyism, writing that she had never heard Kennedy express himself on the topic and adding pointedly, "I can't be sure of the political future of anyone who does not willingly state where he stands on that issue."

In December, in her column as well as in a television appearance, Mrs. Roosevelt criticized him again. She said flatly that Kennedy's father "has been spending oodles of money all over the country and probably has a paid representative in every state by now." When asked on an ABC weekend show called *College News Conference* about a hypothetical race between a "conservative Democrat" and Nelson Rockefeller, a Republican fresh from his gubernatorial triumph over Averell Harriman in New York, she said, "I would not know at all; and I would hope very much that that particular problem would not come up. I would do all I possibly could, I think, to have us nominate someone, at least for President, who did not have any of the difficulties that might come up if Senator Kennedy were nominated. . . . I would hesitate to face the difficult decisions that have to be taken by the next President of the United States with someone who understands what courage is and admires it, but has not quite the independence to have it."

That same month there was a suspiciously similar message from the respected theologian and liberal Reinhold Niebuhr, commenting in the important journal of the political left, the *New Leader*, after a visit to Moscow by Hubert Humphrey. The Minnesota senator was already drawing favorable comment from liberals as it became increasingly clear that Stevenson would not campaign again in 1960. Niebuhr called Kennedy "charming" but cited two problems: first, his father "is spending too much money to satisfy his paternal love and ambition," which he called "not quite cricket"; second, Kennedy "hasn't given any vivid proof of political courage."

Kennedy chose to reply to Mrs. Roosevelt, sliding past the fact that his travels and grassroots organizing were indeed expensive, to insist there was much inaccuracy in the critique from the left. In letters he pressed her to name even one of these paid workers—or even one example of a dollar spent by Joe Kennedy on his son's current ambitions. Her reply was frosty: "Many people as I travel tell me of money spent by him in your behalf; this seems commonly accepted as fact."

Not by Kennedy. His reply to her latest charge contained an unequivocal denial: "My father has not spent any money around the country and has NO paid representatives for this purpose in ANY state of the union." For good measure he sent copies of the correspondence to his friend Philip Graham, the publisher of the *Washington Post* and a significant person in high-level Democratic politics.

That did it. Mrs. Roosevelt's January 6 column included a long Kennedy denial without comment. She later added that she had his "assurance" that the "rumors" were not true. Kennedy quickly sent her a thank-you note.

The disagreement with Mrs. Roosevelt served as a mildly sour end to a successful political year. Kennedy's 1958 reelection campaign had been a long anticlimax. Locally there was never doubt about the outcome.

For national consumption his interest was his winning margin. For an opponent, he drew a popular Boston lawyer, Vincent Celeste, who had trounced a blue blood for the nomination against the wishes of senior party officials. He had a solid law practice; former heavyweight champion Rocky Marciano of nearby Brockton was a client. Celeste had other business interests and had made a respectable showing against Kennedy in 1950, when Kennedy was winning his final reelection to the House. This time, however, Celeste made little headway railing against Kennedy's wealth. Following the national GOP's plan to target Walter Reuther of the UAW for character assassination, Celeste railed against Reuther too, but it did no good.

Kennedy took the campaign seriously and worked diligently for someone who didn't really need to do so. After Labor Day he budgeted more than three weeks for appearances around the state. And he kept his senior political operatives on local rather than national duty until his reelection was complete. Larry O'Brien, Kenny O'Donnell, and Dick Donahue all stayed in Massachusetts through November. At the end the numbers astonished everyone, attracting national notice as Kennedy won by the largest margin of any Senate candidate that year. The 1.3 million votes he won, his 360,000-vote advantage, and his 73 percent share of the vote exceeded even his own expectations.

As important as those numbers were to Kennedy, he and his party enjoyed some unexpected good fortune from the national results. With the added burden of economic difficulties during the sixth year of a presidency—a traditional problem for an incumbent political party— the Democrats added significantly to their numbers in Congress in 1958, electing promising liberals from the Northeast, Midwest, and West. Democrats also elected nine new governors. The outcome embarrassed the Republicans' most visible surrogate campaigner that year, Vice President Nixon.

Kennedy was lucky; some of his possible rivals for the Democratic presidential nomination either lost or did poorly. They included "Soapy" Williams of Michigan, a passionate liberal who barely won reelection as governor because of state budget woes. Chester Bowles, another well-regarded liberal, failed to win his party's Senate nomination in Connecticut. These men's setbacks meant that Kennedy would begin 1959 as a fresh face whose potential rivals were Washington-based figures, with the lone exception of Governor Meyner of New Jersey.

Shortly after the 1958 election it became clear to Kennedy's senior aides that change was coming. What might have seemed like a guerrilla operation—starting with just Kennedy and Sorensen, a few key associates, and a growing file of names of people around the country ready to help at the precinct level—was about to become a formal campaign with many more individuals directly involved. One man in particular began to appear with increasing frequency. He was lean, almost ascetic, handsome, and married to the youngest Kennedy sibling, Jean. Importantly, he had valuable experience in business management through the family enterprise he had been brought up in; moreover he helped manage the Kennedy family's enormous holdings.

Stephen Smith was considered a very tough guy, especially when crossed, and his dedication to his brother-in-law was unquestioned. He shared a lack of national political experience with virtually everyone else who was working for Kennedy, but his business background, take-charge persona, and family ties gave him the natural authority to operate the fledgling political enterprise day to day.

As if there were any doubt that Kennedy's campaign was about to shed the freelancing informality of its first two years, a memo was distributed to the inner circle, which included Ted Kennedy, O'Brien, O'Donnell, and two new hires: press secretary Pierre Salinger and Bob Wallace, who was setting up Kennedy operations in the states. "In the interest of taking up as little of the Senator's time as possible," the memo instructed, "all requests that must be made from this office to the Senator should be directed through Steve Smith."

All that was missing was an uber-boss, and Robert Kennedy would arrive shortly. Already his influence was apparent in the presence of two names on that distribution list. One was Salinger's. Portly, wine-loving, and cigar-chomping, Salinger had emerged from the newspaper business in San Francisco. He had come to Kennedy's attention via his investigative work on corruption in the Teamsters union. Most fellow writers liked and trusted him, though there was never any mistaking his true allegiance.

By far the more important figure was O'Donnell. He had been a close friend of Robert Kennedy for a dozen years by then, a relationship forged on the Harvard football team after the war, on which O'Donnell was the star and captain and Robert the scrappy kid who fought his way onto the squad. He came from a football family, not a political one. His father, Cleo, was a legendary coach and then athletic director at Holy Cross in the tough, central Massachusetts city of Worcester; his older brother had preceded him on the Harvard team.

O'Donnell had a tough time in World War II, making constant bombing runs under extreme conditions in Europe. He didn't talk much about his experiences, but one tale he never denied had him climbing down into the bomb bay and literally kicking loose a stuck bomb to make it fall to its target. He often dealt with political obstacles in the same way.

Recruited by Robert Kennedy to help on his brother's first congressional race, O'Donnell then bounced around the private sector after law school but was back at Robert's elbow for the fight to unseat Lodge in 1952. He helped plot the demise of Onions Burke. And then, to Jack Kennedy's mild displeasure, Robert insisted on taking him along to work on the Senate Rackets Committee, though they made time after hours to do national political work as well, especially with labor unions.

O'Donnell personified the campaign's aversion to titles and fiefdoms. Jack Kennedy simply wanted him close—to go see someone, work out a deal, threaten a recalcitrant politician, and above all to give political advice in his direct, gruff, laconic manner. For the campaign to come, that would mean traveling with the candidate almost all the time. Like so many of Kennedy's more intimate associates, he was famously discreet— so much so that a saying used for years to describe members of what became known as the "well-oiled Kennedy machine" was said to have originated about him: "He wouldn't tell you if your pants were on fire."

After the 1958 elections there was a small dinner at Hickory Hill, Robert Kennedy's home in McLean, with the high command and the candidate. On these occasions there was often an outsider or two present.

This time it was Jack Conway, who handled important policy and political chores for the UAW's Reuther. Jack Kennedy had grown increasingly fond of Conway's brusque manner, as well as his political judgment, as he worked closely with the union leaders on legislative and political matters after the 1956 election.

It was understood that an endorsement by the union was out of the question. The UAW's heart was with Humphrey and Stevenson. But Reuther's neutrality gave individual union officials the freedom to do as they pleased. Conway knew Kennedy was running, and he wanted to support him personally.

No strategic decisions were made that evening, but Conway contributed to a consensus: the key to both nomination and eventual election would be winning majority support in at least ten of the fourteen largest states in the country. And as far as the first objective—the nomination—was concerned, the group reinforced Kennedy's feeling that the road to New York and California had to first go through primaries in Wisconsin and West Virginia.

CHAPTER ELEVEN

Challenging Favorite Sons

Discussions with Jack and Bobby have indicated a desire that I move quickly into the area of basic organization. . . . Such an organization would be effective in promoting Kennedy among party leaders, delegates, various groups, the press, and later, the voters. It could also keep us advised on the local political climate, where to concentrate, when to make candidate appearances, scheduling of speakers, etc."

This blueprint for a major part of Kennedy's campaign for the Democratic presidential nomination—its operation in the states, where the national convention delegates would be elected and selected—was prepared in March 1959 for the campaign's high command by a bookish but quick-witted fellow whose name has been largely lost over the ensuing decades.

Robert A. Wallace, four years younger than Kennedy, was from rural Oklahoma, but his PhD was from the University of Chicago and his mentor was one of midcentury liberalism's titans, Senator Paul Douglas of Illinois. He had known Kennedy casually since the early 1950s, but his real connection was through Ted Sorensen, whom he got to know working on obscure details of the railroad retirement system. Wallace and Douglas both were impressed by young Sorensen, and after Kennedy won election to the Senate they lobbied on his behalf with the new senator, who was hiring staff.

Wallace and Sorensen were close; they shared a preference for ideas and public policy over brass-tacks politics and talked frequently about the evolving presidential campaign. "I think your main problem is that you've got great strength in the big city organizations but you have no strength at all where Kefauver was strong—in the Midwest, the West and the Protestant areas," Wallace told his friend after the 1958 election. "All your strength with the Catholic-oriented groups won't mean anything unless you can show you've got strength outside that. You need to do that to win the nomination and the election."

Wallace explained how it could be done. "You can't work this through your big city organization. They are poison to this Kefauver-type politician. Instead you could work up a series of Kennedy for President clubs, stretch these kinds of clubs all over the country, especially the Midwest and West. It's only through these clubs that you can survive and demonstrate grass roots strength."

Sorensen, not surprisingly, asked for a memorandum. Wallace supplied it, and Kennedy invited him to his Georgetown home for further discussion. In effect Wallace had written his way into a job; Kennedy wanted him to actually do what he described—to establish a Kennedy presence in various states that would operate outside the formal Democratic Party channels.

At the time Wallace was running the staff of the Senate's Committee on Banking and Urban Affairs, which Douglas chaired. He quickly accepted Kennedy's offer, with Douglas's enthusiastic support. There was no pay cut; he continued to get $16,000, disbursed out of what he called "private" funds—almost certainly the Joseph P. Kennedy Foundation. Other Kennedy campaign workers were being paid from similar sources as the campaign slowly took formal shape under Steve Smith's daily direction in an office building at the foot of Capitol Hill.

O'Brien took charge of the Kennedy effort in states nationwide, concentrating on the largest states and the biggest of the big shots. Wallace dealt with the rest. The overlap was considerable. One of the more delightful aspects of the Kennedy campaign was that there were no titles in the national office, with just two exceptions: Robert Kennedy was the campaign manager, and, for the convenience of reporters, Pierre Salinger was called the press secretary.

One thing was decidedly different from Kennedy's 1952 Massachusetts campaign: the pace of activity in 1959. This time insider and outsider approaches were being taken simultaneously in both primary and nonprimary states. Iowa was an excellent example; it had no primary, and it became one of the places on Wallace's crammed itinerary. In the years before Iowa's precinct caucuses became famous in presidential politics, they were ignored nationally and were only faintly noticed inside the state. The "winner" was invariably a collection of uncommitted activists in a process repeated through counties and congressional districts to the state convention. Only then was serious thought given to which candidate for the presidential nomination to support to maximize Iowa's influence as an agricultural state.

In 1959 Iowa was on a short list of Kennedy targets. After close examination of his prospects, his goal was to take 18 of the state's 26 delegates. Linking Iowa with California, Nebraska, Alabama, Arizona, Colorado, and Utah, the Kennedy campaign originally targeted this collection of seven states to produce 194 delegates—more than 25 percent of what they would need to win the nomination.

Iowa's Democratic governor, Herschel Loveless, was on a list of politicians—mostly governors—considered likely to be nominated as candidates themselves as a way of holding together their uncommitted delegations. Loveless was a relatively conservative Democrat but above all a passionate advocate for small farm agriculture. He had supported Kefauver for vice president at the 1956 convention and recalled of Kennedy's candidacy, "I opposed him quite violently." The governor remembered telling Kennedy to his face in Chicago that he did not consider him knowledgeable about agriculture and thought his voting record on price supports was poor.

For the next four years, whenever Loveless was in Washington, Kennedy would be "one of the first people to catch me down at the hotel" to talk about agriculture. The visits were frequent, and as time passed, Loveless's view softened. Accompanying Kennedy on his visits to the state, he could tell that interest in the senator was increasing. On one visit to Iowa City, home of the state university, he took Kennedy to a football game against Notre Dame. The senator diplomatically vowed to "cheer for Iowa and pray for Notre Dame."

Loveless was genuinely neutral at this point. He encouraged all the likely candidates to visit Iowa and was willing to escort those who did. But he was still attracted to the idea of being a candidate himself for a ballot or two as a way of clinging to influence or perhaps even getting the vice presidential nomination. Yet he was well aware of the growing attraction to Kennedy among local officials and activists who were most likely to be chosen as delegates.

What the governor was not aware of was how well organized these Kennedy interests were. The key figure was a lawyer from heavily Catholic eastern Iowa named Ed McDermott. He had known Kennedy since a brief stint on Capitol Hill in 1950, longer than Loveless, and their relationship was personal and social. Geography was a principal reason, not just because of agricultural concerns but also because, except for Johnson, all of Kennedy's likely competitors came from states that border Iowa: Humphrey from Minnesota, Symington from Missouri, and Stevenson from Illinois. "Some early work would have to be done in Iowa," McDermott explained, "if we were going to overcome that natural tendency of the Democrats in that state to identify with someone who is geographically closer to them."

McDermott got the green light to start organizing in the spring of 1959. The result was Iowans for Kennedy, a prototype for the "clubs" Bob Wallace was talking about in his memorandum. Acutely aware that Kennedy's religion lurked in the background and was an unavoidable topic in Iowa—with Lutherans in the northern and more than a few Baptists in the southern part of the state—McDermott recruited as his organization's co-chairman a prominent lawyer from western Iowa, Lumond F. Wilcox, who happened to be a lay leader in the Methodist Church.

They quickly moved into open activity on Kennedy's behalf at local levels, with the caucus process uppermost in their minds. McDermott explained, "I thought that the best way to assure a favorable vote in the Iowa delegation for John Kennedy was to try and have individuals from the Democratic Party elected to the convention in Los Angeles that were predisposed, if not pre-committed to support [him]."

His approach was to scour the state for Democrats who had not previously been activists, similar to the Kennedy-backed search for new blood in New Hampshire in 1958. McDermott labored to get as many as possible enlisted before the state convention the following spring. His organization played a major role when Kennedy attended the Iowa–Notre Dame football game, sponsoring a reception for Kennedy at the student union that packed the hall.

By the late fall Kennedy's increasing national exposure and constant activity in the state were clearly paying off. A survey by the *Des Moines Register* of all ninety-nine county Democratic chairmen showed a clear preference for Kennedy inside the party establishment—by 3 to 2 over Symington and by 3 to 1 or better over Stevenson and Humphrey.

Stimulated and supervised by Wallace and Sorensen—and an increasingly active O'Brien—the Kennedy campaign was organizing all over the Midwest and West, from Arizona and Colorado to Idaho and Utah, even as Kennedy was developing a strong presence in the sixteen primary states. And all of this was going on in the absence of any activity by his rivals.

Humphrey had done no presidential campaign work during the roughly thirty months that Kennedy had already spent traveling and organizing. Humphrey's first political meeting did not take place until July 11, 1959, following ceremonies in Duluth, Minnesota, marking the opening of the St. Lawrence Seaway. The meeting involved a general discussion of the situation, had no agenda, and produced no strategic or tactical decisions. The most important Humphrey-related development at this point was the recruitment—by default—of one of Johnson's closest confidants, James Rowe, a prominent operator in Democratic politics since the days of the New Deal. Rowe had finally moved away from Johnson in despair after failing to convince him to be an active candidate in at least some of the 1960 primaries.

Kennedy's advisors did not believe Humphrey had a credible path to the presidential nomination, but because he seemed certain to fight in Wisconsin, and possibly elsewhere, they took him seriously. Concerned about Kennedy's own ability to reach out to liberal Democrats—a key Humphrey constituency—the Kennedy staff had done extensive research on Humphrey's record and found a potential weakness. Sorensen told an academic ally that summer that a "thorough check" of public records failed to turn up a single instance of Humphrey's ever having mentioned Joseph McCarthy in any statement, or of ever having condemned his red-baiting rhetoric or methods. There was no evidence Humphrey had participated in the debate before McCarthy's censure in 1954 or had voted to curtail the funding for his investigations. This absence of activity would mitigate Kennedy's own silence on McCarthy.

The news about Stevenson and Illinois was equally upbeat. No one was closer to the two-time nominee than J. Edward Day, who had begun practicing law with Stevenson in Chicago in the late 1930s and served in his gubernatorial administration. By the late 1950s Day was a major player in the insurance business on the West Coast and a key ally of Governor Pat Brown of California. Though Day's ties to Stevenson remained strong, he realized that his old friend was of two minds about 1960: he was adamant about not becoming a formal candidate and entering any primaries, but he still wanted the prize, making him an obvious figure of consequence if the nomination ended up being brokered at the convention. "He hoped to be nominated," recalled Day. "I had been through the reluctant candidate routine in 1952, and I knew that wasn't going to work again because there were so much better alternative candidates available than in 1952, especially Kennedy."

Another politically active Democrat with infinitely more power than Day had a similar view of Stevenson's prospects. Mayor Richard J. Daley of Chicago was nearing the end of his first term and focused primarily on his city. But already he was in command of the national convention delegation that would represent Chicago and its surrounding suburbs in Cook County. In 1959 Daley remained noncommittal and cagey, but Kennedy received indirect reports that the mayor was favorably disposed toward him. An important confirmation came that fall in a private report from Kennedy's political columnist friend, Bruce Biossat. After an off-the-record chat with the mayor, Biossat reported to Kennedy that Daley "indicated strong support," conditioned on Kennedy victories in the primaries. Daley was said "to still be wondering about Stevenson's plans." Biossat had also talked with Stevenson, who said he was looking only for a "real draft" and had no intention of running in any of the upcoming primaries.

Kennedy was even more encouraged by what he was hearing from Senator Douglas, in many ways the antithesis of Daley. A committed reformer and liberal, a wounded war hero, Douglas was also widely recognized as an economics scholar. He had been in the middle of efforts to support Sorensen's hiring by Kennedy in 1953, and in subsequent dealings with the younger senator he paid him the ultimate Douglas compliment, calling him "a first-rate intellect."

Above all, Kennedy had been Douglas's partner in pushing a major new idea: the targeting of more federal assistance to what were known then as "depressed areas," parts of the country suffering unusually severe economic hardships. Vetoed twice by President Eisenhower, the legislation was to become an issue in 1960.

Douglas would be running for reelection in 1960, and, like Daley, he preferred to stay out of presidential politics. However, he passed word to his state's Democratic leadership that he was for Kennedy. This inside information from Illinois raised the possibility that Kennedy could skip the state's primary. If he could succeed in other primaries, Kennedy was led to believe, Daley and Douglas would likely deliver to him most of the state's 69 convention delegates. With this assurance Kennedy withdrew his name from the Illinois ballot shortly after declaring his candidacy.

Stevenson was not the only national Democrat pinning his hopes on a brokered convention. After considerable effort testing his appeal in 1959, Stuart Symington decided against running in the primaries. He had traveled almost as much as Kennedy that year, logging thirty-one thousand miles and visiting twenty-two states. However, his advisors could not help but notice that most of the places had already been mined more than once by Kennedy. Even Symington's top aide in the Senate, Stanley Fike, had doubts about the intensity of the Missouri senator's desire.

As the political world prepared for the election year, the designated Symington scenario sketcher was his closest advisor, Washington attorney and power broker Clark Clifford. Far removed from his Missouri roots and his status as Truman's valuable White House aide, Clifford had come to epitomize Washington by the late 1950s. He had a malady common in the capital: a political conflict of interest. He served as a frequent Kennedy family attorney—notably in the flap over authorship of *Profiles in Courage*—but was siding with Symington and busy disparaging Kennedy's chances.

Clifford felt special dynamics were required for Symington to claim the nomination. Though Symington might go into the convention without a substantial bloc of voters, Clifford thought delegates would turn to him as a respectable alternative to such flawed candidates as the two-time loser Stevenson, the limited liberal Humphrey, the southerner Johnson, and the young, inexperienced, Catholic Kennedy.

"In the case of Kennedy," Clifford said before the campaign year began, "I do not believe he will get the nomination for a great many reasons. I know he will win primaries. I realize he will go into the convention with more votes than any other candidate. But despite his tremendous popularity and obvious appeal, when the time comes close, the people are going to look at him and they are not going to want that young man to sit at a table with Khrushchev.

"I believe the religious factor will also stop Kennedy. I deplore it, but it is there. I was brought up in a section of Missouri where anti-Catholicism is strong. I don't share it, but I know it is there and I can't ignore it."

It was a vintage Clifford argument—elegant, logical, and, plausible-sounding.

But the strategy meant that Symington would not contest the primaries, and that gave Kennedy an excellent chance of taking another midwestern primary state, Indiana, which was a genuine Missouri cousin.

Larry O'Brien's first official campaign trip in April 1959 was to Indiana. He spent five days in a state where he had never been before. After a methodical series of discussions with every politician he could find—a typical approach for O'Brien—he concluded that "there was no great groundswell for Kennedy." He got his first direct sense that religion could emerge as a problem, and there was some talk that a Hoosier might run in the primary to keep the convention delegation united and uncommitted. The name of freshman senator Vance Hartke was mentioned most often.

However, O'Brien detected no Symington activity or sympathy in the state. By announcing his intention to run in Indiana, Kennedy might actually rid the state of other contenders, giving him a shot at all 34 of the state's delegates. "The thing that amazes me," O'Brien said, "is that we had the field almost entirely to ourselves. . . . Kennedy was able to work unopposed toward the nomination for months, at least as far as grass-roots American politics was concerned. He was running free. . . . The Washington columnists kept writing about what a political genius Lyndon Johnson was, and we kept locking up delegates."

Just weeks before that jaunt O'Brien had participated in what Kennedy's personal assistant, Dave Powers, called the campaign's first "organizational meeting," held at Joseph Kennedy's mansion in Palm Beach on April Fools' Day; Sorensen called it "the Summit." In fact it appears to have been neither, but more of a show-and-tell session and an opportunity for the inner circle of the developing campaign to get together. They sat on the beach in lounge chairs arranged in a semicircle facing the water. Five of the ten participants were either family members or might as well have been: Joseph; his son Jack, the candidate; his son Robert, the campaign manager; his son-in-law Stephen Smith, who was running the day-to-day operations; and one of Jack's closest friends, Paul "Red" Fay, whom he had known since their PT boat days in the Pacific during the war. (The other Kennedy son, Ted, was at the University of Virginia Law School.) Four others had key political responsibilities: O'Brien, O'Donnell, pollster Louis Harris, and newcomer Bob Wallace, in his second month on the job.

And then there was Sorensen, well aware that his three-year mission as Kennedy's lone accomplice was about to be transformed. Sorensen was making his own transition, taking responsibility for the candidate's rhetoric and positions on the major issues, though he would continue to perform political tasks on the road.

Physically the expansion of the campaign was already palpable in

Washington. Smith and a handful of workers had moved into offices on the fifth floor of a building on the Senate side of Capitol Hill named for its major occupant, the oil giant Esso (eventually Exxon); instead of Kennedy's, Smith's name was discreetly posted on the list of tenants in the lobby and on the entrance door upstairs.

At this point the most valuable commodity in the operation was the information on potential supporters Sorensen and his assistant, Jean Lewis, had been collecting from the road for the past two years. There were seventy thousand names in the files, along with contact information and political intelligence.

The Palm Beach gathering required no important decisions. Before anyone could discuss finances or a budget, Joseph intervened to make clear that while spending needed to be policed, "Whatever it takes" would be the guiding principle. The financial commitment prompted his sons to feign fear for their inheritances.

More levity and eye-rolling followed after the campaign manager performed a classic "new guy" maneuver a bit too dramatically. Robert expressed alarm at taking over an operation that had done next to nothing and remained an organizational mess. Jack nudged Red Fay and muttered loudly so all could hear, "How would you like looking forward to that voice blasting in your ear for the next six months?" He then quipped, "All right, Bobby, we've been able to do a few things in your absence, but we're very appreciative of your support and intend to call on it extensively."

The great bulk of the time was occupied with a detailed exposition by Kennedy and Sorensen on the nomination battle in each of the states and other jurisdictions where convention delegates would be chosen. "Our main conclusion," O'Brien recalled, "was that America is one hell of a big country and no set of rules applied to all the states." There was consensus, though, that the essence of the approach Kennedy had followed ever since 1946 would apply to the presidential campaign: start very early, maintain high visibility, and work relentlessly to build support outside the power centers of the Democratic Party.

For all the bonhomie in Palm Beach, one ominous note lay in the details: a list of states that could easily coalesce to block Kennedy's nomination—not through a loss in primaries but by traditional backroom political maneuvers. The roll was long and, to Kennedy's shrewd eyes, frightening in its implications.

The states included—at a minimum—California, Michigan, New Jersey, Pennsylvania, Florida, Ohio, Maryland, North Carolina, Colorado, Kansas, and Iowa. Give or take an assumption, Illinois too probably belonged on the list. And attached to each state was a name—sometimes more than one—of a major Democratic Party figure with considerable influence who was far from ready to support Kennedy for president.

To make the situation worse, all these men were considering becoming presidential candidates themselves—at least in their home state—as a way of accumulating their own delegate blocs to affect the ultimate selection of the nominee. These pseudo-candidates were called "favorite sons," the men who had actually gone into the storied smoke-filled rooms to turn conventions into brokered affairs. What is more, their influence was often enhanced, especially in the South, by many state party rules that forced all of a state's votes to be cast for or against an issue or a candidate based only on a bare majority of its delegates—the so-called unit rule.

In Kennedy's reading of the arithmetic, there was no way he could win the presidential nomination if these states stayed with favorite sons in the initial stages of the national convention. And it was also his view, based on reality, that if he could not win the nomination on an early ballot, there was no way the powerful men in his party would favor the nomination of a young outsider. He could overwhelm them with victories in the primaries and superior polling numbers in their own states, but that was all the potential leverage he had.

Kennedy was no stranger to these rules and facts of political life. Even before the 1956 campaign was under way, he had considered running in New Hampshire as a favorite son to hold its delegation together for Stevenson. After 1956 he had briefly considered seeking the help of the Massachusetts legislature to give his home state the unit rule.

As he began the third full year of his quest for the presidency, whittling down the number of favorite sons became his highest priority. His frenetic campaigning would continue, but its purpose was now more than simply winning the states most likely to be contested in primaries; it was also to persuade potential favorite sons not to run—sometimes by employing Harris's poll numbers that favored Kennedy to demonstrate that he could embarrass them on their home turf if necessary.

Just as important, Kennedy could not afford to ignore the stark fact that while the sixteen primaries were crucial and were increasingly attractive to him, the overwhelming majority of national convention delegates would be selected in relative obscurity at local levels and at state party conventions. That is why presidential hopefuls in the past had largely ignored early groundwork in these states, relying on the support of the bosses at the national convention.

Kefauver had sprung to prominence by winning primaries, but Kennedy would be the first presidential candidate to attempt to dominate the delegate selection process from the precinct level. That accounted for the activities of Ed McDermott in Iowa and hundreds of people like him across America.

At Palm Beach the heart of Sorensen's presentation was a six-page summary of the national political situation. The intelligence became the basis for appearances Sorensen was making all over the country, often accompanied by Wallace, at small private gatherings of party officials and activists. The essence of their message boiled down to a standard pitch: the train is starting to leave the station, and you might want to consider hopping aboard. The outlook Sorensen had presented at Palm Beach was substantially informed by Harris's polls, though he did not quote from them, and his argument went beyond the numbers. Like his work three years earlier on religion with the "Bailey Report," Sorensen's latest paper was accurate and prescient, though not without holes. Above all, the assessment underscored the Kennedy strategy to curry favor rather than attack his party's establishment from the outside.

But Sorensen's statement didn't duck Kennedy's difficult path ahead: "He must work for the nomination if he is to get it; he cannot avoid primaries or taking controversial stands. He has supposed handicaps of age, religion and a Senate voting record and must prove his strength as the party's best vote getter. He must be their front-runner."

The state-to-state discussions conducted by Sorensen and Wallace emphasized Kennedy's strengths by using convention arithmetic. They made no reference to any substantive policy differences between Kennedy and his rivals, and they were careful to avoid any personal criticism of the other contenders.

At this early stage the biggest question inside the Kennedy inner circle was whether Johnson, generally seen as the most powerful potential opponent, would become a formal candidate and compete in primaries. Sorensen argued that Johnson's decision ultimately didn't matter because "the facts are that he cannot get 701 votes." (It was then thought that number was required for nomination; after party rules changes, the figure rose to 761.)

Johnson's political problem involved a post–Civil War reality, Sorensen explained: "It may not be a good thing but it is a fact—an historical, practical, mathematical fact—that no southerner can be nominated by a Democratic convention. . . . While not agreeing with all of the criticisms leveled at Johnson's leadership, the facts are that he cannot get 701 votes. Even if he were to be conceded every southern state, every border state and most of the moderate eastern and western states (such as Delaware, West Virginia, Kansas, Wyoming, etc.) there is still too large a bloc of states with liberal and minority votes that he cannot touch."

With no doubt that Humphrey would run, he was used as a bookend to Johnson—a northern liberal trapped by ideology and geography, with no hope in the South. Sorensen's assessment of Humphrey's chances: "Even if he won every primary, took all the farm states and all the more liberal states (Minnesota, Michigan, Wisconsin, Oregon, many in California and a few in New York) there would still be a large enough bloc he could not touch to prevent him from getting 701."

That left deadlocked convention scenarios—arguably the most threatening possibility. In addition to the specter of Johnson emerging in a brokered convention, Sorensen's presentation considered Stevenson and Symington. But Sorensen pointed out that there had been no true deadlocks since the 1924 catastrophe, when more than a hundred ballots were required to produce a losing nominee. Moreover, since a brief jockeying period before Franklin Roosevelt's first nomination in 1932, the party rules had changed. Instead of the old requirement of a two-thirds majority, a simple majority had been enough to secure the nomination since 1936.

Finally, Sorensen claimed, Kennedy's progress to this point indicated that the people who would make the decision in Los Angeles one year hence were already moving toward him. Press surveys of delegates were common in those days—both state by state and more broadly. One in 1959 that got widespread attention was a poll of delegates to the 1956 convention (most of whom could be expected back in 1960) by the *Chicago Daily News*. It found more than 420 favoring Kennedy, double the numbers for Stevenson and Symington, "and Johnson pretty well out of it in the 100s," as the Sorensen-Wallace argument put it.

For better—and for worse—that made Kennedy the front-runner, and the pitfalls were understood. After virtually nonstop campaigning since the 1956 convention adjourned, the Kennedy sales pitch was very hard but had the advantage of being accurate: "The amazing thing was that Jack Kennedy demonstrated dominant strength in every one of these (geographical) areas, that he was the only NATIONWIDE candidate the party had—that his appeal (at least in polls) cut across sectional, factional, economic, age, liberal-conservative and all other lines including religious." For good measure, Sorensen's presentation also noted that because of Kennedy's appeal in the increasingly populous suburbs—and even among nominal Republicans, especially Catholics—he consistently outperformed other Democrats against the nearly certain GOP nominee, Vice President Richard Nixon.

In the material he prepared for his forays across the country, Wallace was more dry and succinct. In a collection of thoughts on one page for the Palm Beach group, he simply referred to Johnson as a "southern candidate who did not play outside his native region" despite his enormous stature in Washington. Wallace's bottom line was this: "Adlai—wants it without taking a hand; Stu—wants it without taking a stand; and JFK— the front-runner who must work for it."

In the spring and summer of 1959 the campaign still needed a clear road map through the various states en route to the Democratic nomination. By the fall there was one, and it would be updated constantly through the primaries and beyond.

The headline over one memo dated November 4, two months before Kennedy formally announced, called the document "Kennedy Delegate Count (Confidential)." It was not the work of just one staff person; this was the campaign high command talking to itself. Naturally, with no results to cite yet, it was aspirational. But it was also an indication of priorities for candidate time and travel, political organizing, and expenditures.

With the latest convention rules from the Democratic National Committee now taken into account, Kennedy had to persuade at least 761 out of 1,521 delegates. The candidate's base of New England's six states would give him 114 votes. The count also assumed Kennedy's ability to win another six states holding primaries in 1960, based on data assembled by Harris. These states were Wisconsin, Oregon, Ohio (whether by outright Kennedy victory or a favorite son committed to putting his delegation behind Kennedy), Maryland, Nebraska, and Indiana. Together those primary states offered another 186 delegates. By this reckoning Kennedy still stood at a whisker under 40 percent of what he needed.

The most interesting primary state left out of this initial victory equation was West Virginia. No decision on Kennedy's participation in the primary had yet been made. The assessment noted that West Virginia's popular vote would be a nonbinding voter preference—called a "beauty contest." However, the calculations assumed that in the electoral contests for delegates Kennedy could count on getting 15 of the 25 at stake.

West Virginia was one of thirteen states where Kennedy had worked almost entirely behind the scenes for two years to assemble considerable strength. A few other states would conduct primaries (Illinois and Kentucky, for example), and two others (New Jersey and Florida) were almost certainly going for favorite sons on the first convention ballot, though Kennedy could expect large pockets of strength thereafter. But most of the states would be contested via the caucus–state convention process.

Leaving out the two states with favorite sons, that meant there were eleven states where Kennedy had information or commitments that gave him another 180 votes. That would give him 480. Nomination on the first ballot would require roughly 300 more delegate votes available in all but ten of the remaining states: Johnson's Texas, Symington's Missouri, Delaware, Arkansas, and six southern states operating under the unit rule (North Carolina, Georgia, Virginia, South Carolina, Mississippi, and Tennessee). The "Kennedy Delegate Count (Confidential)" described the southern states as "probably for Johnson."

The remaining 300 or so delegates needed to win the nomination would have to come from a pool of only 365 still believed to be available. Getting the nomination would be a very tight fit, but the road map was far from quixotic, and it was the best one around.

Kennedy had a relatively clear summary of the delegate road from Sorensen: "New England, plus the primaries, plus the big northern states, plus half of the west"—the rest of the sentence was revealing—"and scattered other votes to make up for a near shutout in the South." At no point in 1959 did Kennedy believe that his three-year campaign in the South would, in the end, help his chances. Despite all of his work, the region was failing to provide much support for his nomination.

Kennedy's courtship of the South probably reached its apogee at the beginning of the year, when he invited Governor John Patterson to his home while the Alabaman was visiting Washington. They had been friendly for some time, and Patterson would endorse Kennedy later in the year. In a reference to federal intervention in desegregation cases, Patterson stated, "If he had to put his foot on us it would be lightly." The endorsement didn't help Patterson among the diehard Jim Crow crowd, and it legitimately embarrassed Kennedy in the civil rights community—especially after it was learned that an Alabama party official who accompanied Patterson across Kennedy's Georgetown threshold had previously run the infamous White Citizens Councils in the state.

Throughout the region the civil rights movement was becoming increasingly organized, vocal, and litigious, and the segregationists were digging in. At the end of the year two gubernatorial elections symbolized the shift.

In Mississippi the relatively nonconfrontational J. P. Coleman was replaced by a bombastic trial lawyer and racist blowhard, Ross Barnett; in Louisiana a good ole boy, Jimmie Davis, succeeded the strange but populist "Uncle Earl" Long, brother to the slain "Kingfish," Huey P. Long. Davis too had an exotic reputation. He had written and crooned the country music standard "You Are My Sunshine" in the 1940s. Both Barnett and Davis could be expected to defend the South's white supremacist ways. And like so many white southern politicians, both men were hostile to any kind of racial dialogue as well as to Kennedy's candidacy.

CHAPTER TWELVE

The Shadow Campaign

In October 1959 Kennedy found himself in the lobby of the Daniel Boone Hotel, the place to be in Charleston, West Virginia. He was in the company of a widely known Democratic Party stalwart and supporter, Sidney L. Christie. Knowing that several moments of truth lay ahead, Kennedy was asking nearly every local person he encountered in those days whether he should enter the state's primary the following May.

Christie didn't hesitate before saying yes, and he told a story to illustrate his argument that Kennedy's religion need not be a significant obstacle to victory in West Virginia. Just that year, Christie said, his daughter had asked his blessing to marry a Catholic. Christie not only gave it with enthusiasm but also urged his daughter to convert, something his parents would never have done. For the primary, he said, the key fact would be whether Kennedy tried to hide his religion the way people remembered Al Smith doing in 1928. Kennedy should actually raise the matter himself and encourage people to ask him anything they wanted. That would attract far more voters than it would repel.

That was a common point of view but far from the only one in the state. Kennedy was also getting advice that West Virginia was too much of a risk to an outsider who could not afford to lose even one primary, that the primary itself did not commit the state's 25 delegates, and that

Kennedy could do better simply by having supporters working in the congressional districts.

As it was, Kennedy was already entrenched in the state, with local organizations outside regular party channels operating in each of West Virginia's fifty-five counties. Alfred Chapman, a businessman and veteran party man—he had been a delegate to every Democratic convention since 1944—felt the argument was a close one. Skeptics of a formal candidacy ranged from some of Kennedy's friends in the state to the top man in his national headquarters, Robert Kennedy. Chapman was in favor of filing, but he did not minimize the extent of anti-Catholic sentiment in the state. "In many counties we have run up against people very much against Kennedy," he said. "We had it here in our own Ohio County [its county seat was the steel town of Wheeling], very much opposed. We were smeared, we were laughed at, we were ridiculed that we didn't know what we were doing . . . that I ought to be ashamed of myself for pushing a Catholic."

The situation was similar in Wisconsin. Much progress had been made on the ground and Harris's polls were favorable, but no decision had been made on whether to file for the state's primary. Harris had already identified sentiment opposed to Kennedy in rural, mostly Lutheran parts of the state. But there was another element special to Wisconsin: residual affection for the party's 1952 and 1956 standard-bearer, Adlai Stevenson.

"My feeling that Stevenson should be the President was as strong then as it ever had been and the only question was, was there any practical possibility that it might occur," recalled a major Democrat in the state, James E. Doyle, a former party chairman who had been the head of Stevenson's national campaign in 1956. Stevenson allies in liberal areas of the state, especially Madison, the state capital and home of the state university, rejected overtures from both Kennedy and Humphrey, intending to support Stevenson if he should run again.

To boost his standing in Wisconsin, Kennedy's campaign scheduled a successful three-day tour of the state in September that included more than a dozen stops. This was an occasion when the Kennedy campaign got to showcase its premier organizer, Kenosha's own Jerry Bruno, who put together television-pleasing events and used them to expand a state-wide network of supporters. Starting three months ahead of time, Bruno's operation sent out well over thirty thousand pieces of mail and used the replies to build on a collection of ten thousand names of supporters in each of Wisconsin's thirty-two counties.

But Kennedy's religion was not ignored by the press covering his tour, nor by many of the citizens he encountered, to his occasional frustration. In one interview with a local news organization, Kennedy let that frustration show: "All these people who say I might be influenced by the Church, I'd like to ask them for specifics. What specific piece of legislation do they think I might vote with the Church instead of my conscience? On what possible point would Cardinal Spellman control me? Federal aid to education—I've proposed my own law; the Khrushchev visit—the Church hierarchy and I have differed. What specific legislation do they mean? If people would come out in the open with specifics then I can answer them point by point. But how can you answer a whispering campaign?"

Kennedy embraced his Catholicism, but religion had become just one source of political frustration. Another was the persistent refrain of *vice president* from both fellow politicians and journalists, which he suspected would continue until he started winning primaries. No matter how categorically he stated his intentions, Kennedy could not shake the speculation that after his very close call in 1956, he had the inside track to the second spot on the ticket in 1960. He was exasperated, and every so often he let it show.

He told Jack Bell, one of the Associated Press's senior correspondents, "As a matter of fact, you're correct about almost everything you write except one thing. You keep saying that, of course, Kennedy will wind up as the Vice Presidential nominee. I wish you'd get those goddam words out of your typewriter because I'm never going to take second place."

Despite his extensive organization, the goodwill he earned from his appearances, and consistently optimistic polling news during 1959, a final decision to actually enter the Wisconsin primary would be put off until the election year. The delay involved one of the most maddening aspects of nomination campaigning: the calendar. As the first candidate to think strategically about using the primaries as a wedge to woo and win the much larger pool of delegates from nonprimary states, Kennedy became the first candidate to have to think about how to campaign in one state after another.

In the past, only a tiny number of presidential primaries were actually contested, and campaigns typically arrived in a state and camped there for two weeks or so. For 1960 the logistics and the politics would be different. To put it simply, in the Kennedy campaign's judgment Wisconsin was hostage to Ohio. He could campaign vigorously in one or the other but not both.

The primary dates weighed on the Kennedy team as they plotted a course for the coming year. After the initial contest in New Hampshire in early March, there would be a break until the Wisconsin event on April 5. Then it would get ugly fast: a contest in Illinois the following week, then in New Jersey the week after that and Pennsylvania on April 26, before the Ohio primary on May 3, the same day as Indiana's. West Virginia's would come the following week, the same day as Nebraska's. Just one week later was the Maryland primary, followed quickly by Oregon's on May 20 and Florida's on May 24. The process would climax with the primaries in California and South Dakota on June 7.

For Kennedy time wasn't money; his father would take care of the money. Time, however, was priceless, and at first he doubted that he could parlay the primaries to create the perception that his momentum would lead inexorably to his nomination. But after study, the campaign tried to accomplish just that. So the high command turned its attention to four big and crucial states.

A key decision focused on Ohio, one of the largest states in play, with 64 convention delegates at stake. If someone like Governor Michael DiSalle could be persuaded or pressured into running as a favorite son and pledged to Kennedy ahead of time, his support—combined with allies elsewhere in Ohio—could effectively take the state off the contested primary table and give Kennedy his first victory before voting in the primaries even began.

Illinois involved an act of informed faith. With no other candidates competing in a nonbinding primary, a quiet Kennedy write-in campaign could produce a nice headline while the various local organizations—above all Mayor Daley's machine in Chicago—were electing their own people as delegates. Kennedy was told he could get them as his delegates if he won the genuinely contested primaries elsewhere.

A Kennedy decision about New Jersey made a mild virtue out of probable necessity. Robert Meyner, in his second successful term as governor, had national ambitions but little support outside his state. Believing the vice presidential nomination was possible for someone other than his fellow easterner Kennedy, Meyner was set to run in the primary as a favorite son. Kennedy decided to let him do so, confident that he would eventually get substantial support from the New Jersey delegation should the convention go to a second nomination ballot.

That left Pennsylvania, with 81 delegates at stake, the largest of the four potential roadblocks on the confused primary calendar. The state became the stage for a conflict between two powerful Catholics.

Pennsylvania was at least three states politically: in the east, the city of Philadelphia plus its sprawling suburbs; in the middle, a large collection of communities that included many steel-producing centers; and in the west, Pittsburgh and surrounding Allegheny County. In 1959 the state's Democrats were anything but Kennedy-oriented. The liberals were longtime Stevenson people, and in Philadelphia, where the head of the Democratic organization, William J. Green, reigned supreme, the initial flirtation was with Symington.

That all began to change as the year unfolded. After seeing Kennedy's potential in polls he was shown regularly, Green eventually cast his lot with him, as did several other county leaders. Senator Joseph Clark, a reliable liberal, was typical in letting it be known that Kennedy was at least his second choice, after Stevenson.

But not Governor David Lawrence. A genuinely major figure in twentieth-century American politics, he was an unusual combination of boss and passionate liberal, especially in his early advocacy of civil rights. He had been at every Democratic convention since 1912, when as a page he observed Woodrow Wilson's first nomination. At seventy, after holding numerous offices, including mayor of Pittsburgh through four terms, he was halfway through his one term as governor. He had been a key FDR man in the 1930s, an important Truman ally in the 1940s, and he adored Stevenson.

For the upcoming election Lawrence's ideological inclinations led him to want to hold out his state from early endorsements in the hope there might be a way to nominate Stevenson a third time. While his position involved no enmity toward Kennedy, Lawrence was the archetype of the older Catholic Democrat who felt strongly that the United States was not yet ready to elect one of their own as president, that a Catholic nominee would pose a political threat to the party. Lawrence not only believed that; he said so repeatedly and loudly, to Kennedy's intense displeasure.

If not contradicted, Lawrence's position could spread like a virus. So Kennedy contradicted it, just as repeatedly and loudly. Lawrence was the one major Democrat he quarreled with openly, demonstrating his determination to let no public challenge go unanswered. In his thinking, Exhibit A in the counterargument was Lawrence himself and his election in 1958.

Many others shared Lawrence's thinking about a Catholic running for president. Kennedy was asked about it by a college student during a stop on a three-day swing through Wisconsin. Using the case of a prominent Pennsylvania Democrat as rebuttal, Kennedy responded, "It would seem to me that the man who should complain in Pennsylvania is George Leader, who ran for the United States Senate on the same ticket with Lawrence and lost by 175,000 votes. Leader is not a Catholic and Lawrence is, and Lawrence won that election. And Catholics have won many other states around the country."

Back in his Washington office Kennedy had a statement prepared for whenever reporters called about Lawrence, saying he was "deeply disturbed" by Lawrence's repeated comments. Referring to Lawrence's solid victory the year before in the gubernatorial campaign, Kennedy insisted, "It ill behooves him now to be urging that this same opportunity should be denied to others."

That hardly won over the governor. Neither did the steady stream of Harris's polling data that Kennedy regularly sent to Harrisburg. One survey in particular stands out. As early as the fall of 1958, Harris had Kennedy beating Nixon in the state, with fully 57 percent of the likely voters, compared to Symington's 49 percent. Breaking it down, the survey showed Kennedy with 41 percent support among the state's Protestants, compared to Symington's 35 percent. In April 1959 Harris had Kennedy's margin holding at 57 to 43 percent over Nixon; among Democrats he thumped Humphrey by more than 8 to 1.

Kennedy's idea about Pennsylvania was to leave Lawrence largely alone but to keep crowding him by building support among Democrats east of Allegheny County. The primary would have no candidate names on the ballot, and the state's delegates would be directly elected. But nonbinding write-ins for president were not discouraged. In a note to Robert Kennedy in early January 1960 Sorensen wrote of a "non-partisan citizens committee" (the equivalent of one of Wallace's "clubs") to promote Kennedy in the state. To avoid a direct link to the Kennedy campaign, Sorensen said the group was operating "without any connection with this office."

In Kennedy's judgment nothing about Ohio could be left to chance. Logistically, however, the campaign did not see how he could compete adequately in the Ohio primary and still have time for Wisconsin. A fallback position involved collecting delegates by backing Kennedy surrogates in Wisconsin's congressional districts. On the other hand, Humphrey was virtually certain to compete in the state. Kennedy had gobs of polling data strongly suggesting his own frequent appearances in Wisconsin made it possible he could deal Humphrey a crippling blow there. If he dodged the preference primary in Wisconsin, Kennedy knew he would be undercutting his own strategy to leverage primary victories into convention delegate votes and the nomination.

As for Ohio, after more than two years of campaigning, the polling information was uniformly upbeat for Kennedy, with one exception: if a favorite son were to run in the state's primary it would matter greatly who it was. And the person the Kennedy campaign was most concerned about was Senator Frank Lausche.

Lausche would be sixty-five in 1960, after an extensive and successful career in politics as the quintessential ethnic Democrat. A World War I veteran from a Slovenian family, he had been mayor of Cleveland and a multiple-term governor of the state and had the distinction of having been considered a potential vice president by nominees in both parties— Truman in 1948 and Eisenhower in 1952 and briefly in 1956.

Known as an amiable grouch, Lausche was generally uninterested in national politics but a fiendish advocate for his state's interests and a master at navigating its political currents. He was moderate in ideology. Often conservative in his fiscal views, he voted with Republicans so often in the Senate that he was known in Ohio as "Frank the Fence" for the frequency of his vaults over it.

In November 1959 Harris's final survey of the state before the primary season showed Lausche statistically tied with Kennedy if he chose to run as a favorite son. By contrast, the survey had Kennedy easily defeating DiSalle, the state's Democratic governor, by 62 to 38 percent. Harris's latest polls also placed Kennedy well ahead of any legitimate opponent for the nomination, though Symington had more support as an also-ran than Humphrey.

Yet Kennedy's politicking in Ohio had been vigorous in 1959. Armed with the Harris polls, and after several appearances in the state, he had won the endorsement of the powerful Cuyahoga County party leader Raymond Miller as well as the more policy-oriented mayor of Cleveland Anthony Celebrezze. Meanwhile important inroads had been made in the southern part of the state, in Cincinnati and Columbus.

But a missing piece involved DiSalle, whose base was Toledo. He was barely fifty, and his career path had been bumpy. Though he had been mayor of the city where he was raised, he had been beaten in races for the U.S. House, for governor, and for senator before he was rescued by the national Democratic landslide of 1958. DiSalle had supported Kefauver over Kennedy for the vice presidential nomination in 1956. He had known the Tennessee senator for years, and in 1951 and 1955 he had turned aside Kefauver's entreaties to serve as national chairman of his long-shot presidential campaigns.

DiSalle was, in short, no boss like David Lawrence, though as governor his influence was considerable. Like Lawrence, he was not an actual Kennedy enemy, but the fact that he wanted to run as a favorite son in the primary put him in the way of Kennedy. Considering his polling numbers, Harris thought Kennedy should directly challenge DiSalle in the Ohio primary. In his visits to the state and in his telephone conversations with DiSalle, Kennedy not only shared the data with him but let him think the possibility of a challenge was real.

The contacts between Kennedy and DiSalle had begun early in 1959. In June Steve Smith called upon the perfect go-between and asked him to accompany Kennedy on a trip to Columbus. John Bailey, the Connecticut Democratic leader who had become a close Kennedy lieutenant, had known DiSalle for years. He and Kennedy had supper at the governor's mansion, and DiSalle spoke to Bailey privately the next day after a press conference. Bailey reported that the governor had been unequivocal. DiSalle had said, "Look, I'm going to be with this fellow. I don't know when, but I'm going to be for him—and that's between you and I."

Yet doubts lingered. That October, at a second "summit" of the Kennedy campaign, this one at Robert's house in the Hyannis Port compound, among Sorensen's marching orders from the candidate himself was an instruction to "see DiSalle and make sure he keeps his commitment." The day after New Year's had been fixed for Kennedy's formal announcement of his candidacy. He wanted to have the DiSalle endorsement in hand to demonstrate that he was a national, not simply a New England candidate. In December a Kennedy entourage descended on a neutral site, an airport hotel in Pittsburgh, for a clandestine meeting with DiSalle, who had slipped across the Ohio River after an engagement in Steubenville to meet with them. DiSalle agreed to make his own announcement on January 6. He would run in the Ohio primary as a Kennedy supporter as well as a favorite son, giving Kennedy a clear shot, with no opposition from any other candidate, at getting all of Ohio's 64 convention delegate votes.

Another major question facing Kennedy in 1959 was whether the governor of California could deliver delegates as faithfully as could the governor of Ohio. California was huge and growing exponentially, but the state's convention delegate total was the same as Pennsylvania's—81. It was a prize too big to ignore, but it posed unique problems for any candidate interested in its primary, which would end the voting season on the same day as the one in Humphrey's native South Dakota.

For a decade California had been led by relatively moderate Republican governors like Earl Warren and Goodwin Knight, but in the Democratic earthquake of 1958 Pat Brown had emerged.

Brown enjoyed national attention in his first year as governor and was interested in being chosen as the vice presidential nominee at the convention that would take place in his state's largest city the following July. Since a serious Catholic like Brown could not run in tandem with a serious Catholic like Kennedy, Brown was having discussions with other likely presidential candidates visiting the state at the time, notably Symington and Humphrey.

An important dynamic that complicated Kennedy's dealings with Brown stemmed from the fact that the Democrats in California were actually a shaky coalition of two parties, not always in harmony. There was the semblance of a regular organization representing local and Sacramento officials and basically loyal to Brown, and there was a powerful and vocal group of liberals under the umbrella of the California Democratic Council, earnestly pro-Stevenson and hoping to nominate him for a third attempt at the White House.

Thus Brown was at most a very dark horse and a very long shot for a place on the ticket, but only with someone other than Kennedy. Meanwhile Stevenson remained adamant about not campaigning in any primary, keeping himself a nonfactor until the convention itself. The one option that might keep both Democratic factions together was to make Brown an uncontested favorite son in the primary but committed to Kennedy as long as he won the other primaries.

To deal with this predicament, Kennedy dispatched Larry O'Brien, who had never been to the West Coast but was experienced in the delicate and occasionally hardball task of navigating among competing factions. His initial assignment was to go to Brown and suggest—not very subtly—that Kennedy was confident enough of potential support that he might simply enter the primary himself and win it, against Brown if necessary. "My hints were to keep him unsure about Kennedy's intentions. We had a pleasant talk, but we both were playing our own little games," O'Brien recalled.

O'Brien's best ammunition came from the arsenal of Harris polls. Shortly before primary season began Harris conducted a major survey of California based on nearly 1,600 interviews that reinforced Kennedy's confidence. It showed Kennedy beating Brown by 60 to 40 percent. With Humphrey thrown in to further test liberal sentiment, the figures gave Kennedy 47 percent, Brown 33, and Humphrey 20. The Democratic tradition in California was for their leaders—technically the party's executive committee, led by a governor if they had one—to go hide somewhere and handpick a delegation representative of all the foreseeable candidates and interests. Whom to support at the national convention would be effectively determined by the committee, with the expectation of minimal infighting.

With O'Brien monitoring the situation from a nearby hotel, the delegation was assembled in the coastal community of Carmel without incident. The night after they finished they met privately with Kennedy's senior aide and pledged to keep other candidates out of the primary if Kennedy did not enter it.

Joseph Cerrell, the state party's new executive director, explained, "They met to pledge to the Senator that if he would not enter the California primary the following June he would have the overwhelming support of the California delegation. I think they were all at that time very sincere and thought they could produce on it." But as it turned out, they couldn't. Don Bradley, a major party professional working northern California, stated, "It was a very hard delegation to control."

The crucial question Kennedy had to resolve was whether to let the process play out, leading to Brown's unchallenged position as the favorite son, or to intervene and run himself. The risk with the first course—Brown as an unopposed favorite son—was that without credible assurance of support after the primary Kennedy might have to face an unfriendly California delegation. But if Kennedy ran and defeated Brown, he would reap bruised egos and hurt feelings that might gravely harm his effort to carry the state against Nixon in the fall.

The critical assurance Kennedy wanted would have to come from Brown himself. With the clock ticking on California's filing deadline, the governor flew to Washington and visited Kennedy at his home. The stakes were as high as they get in national politics.

Kennedy confided to Red Fay, "I told Pat I had no desire to come into California and get into a fight with him in the primary. It would split the party and could lead to the Republicans regaining control. Besides, we took a poll in California which indicated I would beat Pat easily. I showed him the poll and he agreed to give his support."

The story was pretty much the same from Pat Brown's perspective. He said he knew all about Kennedy's polls but urged him to worry about being "divisive." Kennedy said he wanted a promise from Brown that he would not clamor to be the nominee for vice president. Attempting to bargain, Brown said he would make the promise—unless it became clear Kennedy was not going to get the presidential nomination. Kennedy insisted that the promise be unequivocal, so Brown obliged.

The climax came, according to Brown, when "Kennedy then said something else that I will never forget as long as I live. If he wins New Hampshire, Wisconsin, runs second in Oregon and is leading in the Gallup polls, he is entitled to the support of the governor of California." Brown replied, "I can assure you that the governor of the state of California will be for John F. Kennedy for the Presidency of the United States."

What made Kennedy's long campaign so unusual and astonishing is that even while he was engaging in high-stakes maneuvering and bargaining with major party figures behind the scenes in the largest states, his key aides were almost casually plucking delegates from numerous smaller delegations This effort, largely Bob Wallace's brainchild and essentially run by him from the road, was producing progress in surprising places— some in primary states, some not.

Almost from the beginning of the Kennedy-Sorensen journeys in 1957, the fledgling candidate had kept his eye on Oregon. Its primary came late, just before California's, making it a potential exclamation point after a successful season. And it had an extraordinary law: there was no such thing as candidates filing for themselves or organizing petition drives; Oregon's secretary of state had the power simply to put the name of anyone he considered to be a candidate on the ballot. In addition to exposing everyone to the prospect of victory or defeat, the state law made the primary attractive to serious candidates back then by awarding all its convention delegates to the winner.

After multiple appearances by Kennedy in the state, a Harris poll in the spring of 1959 that used his "laundry list" of candidates—including Johnson and Humphrey but not Stevenson—found Kennedy well ahead. In a crowded field he was getting 34 percent support among Protestants to go with 84 percent among Catholics.

A potential problem, as it developed later in the year, was likely to be the state's crusty senator Wayne Morse, running as a favorite son. In a long career Morse had been a Republican, a Democrat, and an Independent. He could be inspiringly principled, as he was on civil rights. Yet he could be as vicious as a viper when challenged. One constant for Morse was a deep commitment to the labor movement; that included some questionable ties to the Teamsters. He didn't dislike Kennedy, but he had attacked him furiously when Kennedy led the congressional effort to reform labor law in the wake of the Senate Rackets Committee's dramatic hearings exposing corruption nationally and on the West Coast in the Teamsters union.

On the other hand, Oregon had a long, progressive tradition, represented in the 1950s by the state's other senator, Richard Neuberger, and his wife, Maurine, who would succeed him after he succumbed to cancer in the spring of 1960. The ranks of Oregon's liberals also included a highly regarded member of Congress, Edith Green. All of the progressives had once worked fervently for Stevenson but were helping Kennedy behind the scenes by 1959.

Humphrey was the only other candidate likely to have a realistic

chance in Oregon, but to capitalize on his unimpeachably liberal background he would have to remain viable into late May, and the Kennedy
strategy was to eliminate him early. This would leave Kennedy basically
one-on-one against Morse. His friends in Oregon advised Kennedy that
a serious effort was likely to succeed. He decided to make one, the only
time in 1960 when he would directly challenge a favorite son in a primary.

Another improbable target of opportunity was Arizona, a place far removed from Kennedy's eastern comfort zone. The opportunity arose
because of the myopic thinking of "non-candidate" Lyndon Johnson.
Continuing to reject all pleas that he formally announce and enter at least
a primary or two to demonstrate popular appeal to go with his Washington backroom powers, Johnson insisted that he could rely on his mentor,
House Speaker Sam Rayburn, and a band of loyal senators to gain support
in their districts and states that could be deployed at a brokered national
convention. In Arizona that meant Johnson's strategy relied heavily on
the state's veteran senator, eighty-one-year-old Carl Hayden. But at this
twilight stage of his long career, Hayden would have had trouble fixing a
parking ticket in his rapidly changing and growing state.

Wallace and Sorensen—and Kennedy too—were amazed at how
walls in the state crumbled at the slightest nudge. Arizona traditionally operated under the unit rule at conventions, so if Kennedy could
get a majority of his supporters selected as delegates he could get all 17
votes.

Sorensen had discovered early that the state party chairman, Joseph
Walton, was more than willing to help behind the scenes. But the main
base for the effort was Pima County, which included Tucson. The mayor,
Don Hummel, was on board, and he had exactly the kind of grassroots
clout that a Washington politician like Hayden had relinquished years
earlier. The main producer, however, was the local congressman whose
district flowed south from Tucson toward the Mexican border. Stewart
Udall, a gunner on B-24s flying over Europe during the war, was in his

third term. Throughout the country Kennedy displayed a knack for finding committed supporters who were on the verge of blossoming into major political players. Udall was an excellent example; so was his law partner and brother, Morris K. Udall, a former county prosecutor.*

An unsigned note in Sorensen's files from early 1959 described the situation succinctly: "Kennedy has strong potential in Arizona." But the observation was accompanied by a plea "to get started soon."

Arizona was quietly added to the Kennedy campaign's growing list of priority targets.

As the year before *the* year neared its end, the now bustling offices on Constitution Avenue began preparing mass-mailings to announce Kennedy's formal candidacy to the more than seventy thousand names in the index card file. By then Johnson was regarded as Kennedy's most significant opponent. Like the rest of the political world, Kennedy and his aides had waited all year for a definitive statement of Johnson's plans. Declare candidacy? Run in one primary? Run in several primaries? Run in no primary? Be part of "Stop Kennedy" operations in key states with other candidates? Quietly collect delegates? Openly collect delegates?

Kennedy believed he needed to know something solid before 1960 began. So his brother Robert was dispatched to Texas. It was December and Congress was not in session; that meant Robert's destination was the LBJ Ranch, and that meant there was no way for him to brush off Johnson's insistence that they go deer hunting.

Accounts of that experience differ dramatically according to the loyalty of the source. The Johnson side claimed Robert was given a shotgun instead of a deer rifle, and the recoil from the first shot knocked him flat on his back. This gave Johnson a chance to help him back up and say, "Son, you've got to learn to handle a gun like a man." The Kennedy

---

* After Kennedy was elected president, Stewart Udall began a new life as secretary of the interior. His brother Morris had an equally illustrious career in the U.S. House and was runner-up to Jimmy Carter for the Democratic presidential nomination in 1976.

camp described vulgar Texas yahooism and accounts of standing around in a comfortable, specially constructed blind to take part in what seemed more like a slaughter than a sporting hunt.

The two men, who already hated each other irrationally, got the basic business done. Robert returned to tell his brother that Johnson would not campaign in a single primary. He did not get much information on how Johnson would behave as the date for the convention neared, but the path for Kennedy's goal of a first—or early—ballot nomination would be clear at least into May.

In O'Brien's files at the end of the year, as the words were being drafted for Kennedy's announcement of his candidacy, were summaries of the Gallup polls from the beginning and the end of 1959. They were as encouraging as Harris's in-house statistics. Gallup showed that Kennedy's number in the samplings of opinion about the most potentially plausible Democratic nominees had risen to 30 percent from 25; Stevenson's dropped to 26 from 29; Johnson fell to 10 from 17; and Symington and Humphrey remained in single digits, 5-ish, all year.

That made "front-runner" an accurate description of Kennedy. However, a campaign staff steeped in long years of Boston Red Sox futility knew the cliché about all the bold touting that accompanies spring training. In the end you still have to play the game.

CHAPTER THIRTEEN

Overconfidence in Wisconsin

Kennedy opened the election year with a formal announcement of his candidacy on January 2 in the Senate Caucus Room, whose marbled walls and soaring ceilings in a corner of the Old Senate Office Building had been the scene of historic hearings for much of the century. Despite the grandeur of the setting it was an anticlimactic event, for Kennedy had spent months building toward the moment. Now it was time to harvest enough delegates to the Democratic convention to deliver him the presidential nomination.

It was important to Kennedy that he make the strongest possible first impression before a still skeptical party—hence the push to get Ohio's governor DiSalle to publicly announce his unopposed favorite-son candidacy in the May primary and his pledge to swing his state's 61 convention votes to Kennedy. The announcement went off without a hitch.

The Kennedy campaign also had to assess the strength of potential rivals. Humphrey had made his intentions clear with his own announcement a few days earlier; he would be a formidable opponent in some of the primary states. Others delayed a decision. Symington dithered, still unsure whether to compete in the primaries. Truman, his principal supporter, warned against primaries; he had experienced defeat in the New Hampshire primary of 1952. Truman's nemesis that year, Estes Kefauver, had matured into a battle-scarred veteran of primaries in 1952 as well as 1956, but his course for 1960 was still unknown. And there was no assurance that Stevenson, the party's two-time nominee, would stay out of the race.

Nonetheless the year began with Humphrey as Kennedy's only known opponent in perhaps a few of the primaries and with the prospect that he would have no serious opponent in the important states of Maryland, Indiana, and Nebraska.

All of these men would have to be taken seriously, as well as others whose presidential dreams would never materialize. For all of the names being mentioned, Kennedy's inner circle believed that the greatest obstacle standing between Kennedy and the nomination would be Johnson. Though an unofficial "Johnson for President" organization had been operating out of Texas for several months, the Senate majority leader had no plans to enter the primaries. If he were going to claim the presidential nomination, he apparently planned do it the old-fashioned way—by calling in political IOUs and using his friendship with party bosses around the country as a fulcrum to exercise power at the convention from a base in the South. Johnson's plan represented the antithesis of Kennedy's campaign of political guerrilla warfare, designed to pick off delegates methodically, here and there, until he had won the countryside.

It was important that Kennedy not blunder in the primaries, so those he would enter were chosen with care. The District of Columbia, for example, was inconsequential because so few delegates were at stake. Washington was a city with a black majority, and Humphrey was very popular among blacks; the decision to cede it to him was easy. Kennedy had no plans to contest South Dakota either—Humphrey was a native of the state. Kennedy had no choice but to enter Oregon because the state listed all candidates on the ballot whether they liked it or not. Massachusetts was, of course, a lock for Kennedy. Yet his chances in the giant states of Pennsylvania, Illinois, and California depended on the blessings of powerful local leaders who often preferred to run as favorite sons in order to keep leverage at the convention. Kennedy could claim the support of DiSalle in Ohio, but Meyner of New Jersey still sounded as though he wanted to be a national candidate.

Before those primary dates in May, Wisconsin stood out as a place to deliver a mortal wound to Humphrey's chances in early April. Kennedy's polling data smelled of promise in Wisconsin. Likewise in West Virginia, where he had quietly assembled a network of local allies.

But no filing deadlines were imminent, so the Kennedy campaign put off final decisions. For a warm-up, Kennedy started his campaign in his native region.

New Hampshire represented unfriendly terrain for any Democrat. The state had a history of supporting Republicans, and its relatively small population had a surfeit of belligerent conservatives and expatriates from Massachusetts who had fled across the state line to escape sales taxes and income taxes, which were not imposed in New Hampshire. The state's two strongest voices belonged to the veteran Republican senator Styles Bridges, who was said to have a habit of co-opting nominal Democrats by placing them in jobs, and William Loeb, the obstreperous publisher of the *Manchester Union Leader*, who used his newspaper to savage Democrats almost daily.

But the beleaguered New Hampshire Democrats were stirring. Kennedy had begun enlisting their support as early as 1957, when he used his meeting with Bernie Boutin to turn the most important Democratic contact in the state into a devoted follower. Boutin wound up beaten in a race for governor in 1958, but he never stopped building a Kennedy organization in communities across New Hampshire. The work was so pervasive that no other serious candidate dared to challenge Kennedy there.

Though poised for an easy victory, Kennedy could not afford to finesse the March event without an effort. He realized that an impressive showing in New England, next door to Massachusetts, would establish a precedent Humphrey would need to follow in the Upper Midwest when the campaign moved to Wisconsin.

Kennedy spent a few days in New Hampshire, and members of his family pitched in. Brother Ted delivered a speech in halting French to an audience in Suncook, where many residents spoke the language naturally. Sisters Eunice, Jean, and Pat all made appearances in the state. His mother, Rose, spoke at a couple of colleges and even attended a bar mitzvah in Concord.

Neither the name of Humphrey nor that of any other credible rival would appear on the ballot in New Hampshire, yet it became obvious that the Kennedy campaign would brook no opposition there—not even by upstarts.

Like a Kentucky Derby once sprinkled with unworthy colts whose rich owners were willing to pay the entrance fee, the New Hampshire primary attracted egomaniacs who signed up as candidates for the splendor of seeing their name briefly in lights. In 1960 they came forth in New Hampshire: Elton Britt, a country singer whose recording of "There's a Star-Spangled Banner Waving Somewhere" was a wartime hit in 1944, and Lar "America First" Daly, who wore an Uncle Sam outfit and whose nickname bespoke his politics. The local Kennedy operation checked signatures on the pair's petitions to be on the ballot and found that many of the names were phony. Boutin called the senator to seek his approval of a plan to challenge the fringe candidates. Kennedy said he did not want to be seen as "strong-arming" the pair, but Boutin convinced him that the two men were merely trying to get publicity, and Kennedy agreed to the purge. In three days the names of Britt and Daly disappeared from the contest.

That left Paul Fisher, another eccentric character, as Kennedy's only active opponent. A ballpoint pen manufacturer, Fisher campaigned on a one-note issue: replacing sales and income taxes with a new system. Kennedy ignored him throughout the campaign, until Fisher showed up at the University of New Hampshire, where Kennedy had been invited to speak, to demand equal time. Kennedy said he had no objection but avoided sharing the stage. When Fisher finally took the podium to promote his tax plan the students booed.

Other attacks on Kennedy came from local Republicans. Loeb's newspaper, the largest in the state, hammered Kennedy almost every day, and Governor Wesley Powell, who had beaten Boutin two years earlier, accused Kennedy of being soft on communism. Kennedy was especially angered by the governor's remarks. Red-faced and pounding the rostrum for emphasis, he loudly condemned his critics in his final appearance before the polls opened.

Kennedy swamped his opposition in the Democratic primary with 43,372 votes to Fisher's 6,853 and a few hundred write-in votes.

Because of an irregular primary schedule that sometimes created long intervals between contests there were occasional respites from the intensity of the campaign. In Kennedy's case, there is evidence they provided time for dangerous liaisons. During one break, in Las Vegas, while the primaries were still being conducted, Sorensen was approached by a woman while he was lounging at a hotel swimming pool. She was aware of who he was, but he had "not the slightest idea who she was." Years later Sorensen said her appearance on national television gave him a name to go with the face he remembered. Back then it was Judith Campbell, eventually Judith Campbell Exner, who in her time cavorted with Frank Sinatra, Sam Giancana (the under boss of organized crime in Chicago), and Jack Kennedy.

After staying silent for more than forty years, especially while Jacqueline Kennedy was still alive, Sorensen, who was with Kennedy for the entire campaign, eventually discussed aspects of his boss's private life and the temptations that inevitably are offered an attractive, dynamic politician. "Like his father before him," Sorensen wrote in his memoir, "JFK did not resist those temptations when they became available."

Sorensen did not hide behind euphemisms. "It was self-indulgent," he wrote. "It does not reflect well on his attitude toward his public office, the sacred trust. It was wrong, and he knew it was wrong, which is why he went to great lengths to keep it hidden. . . . He should have known that ultimately the inevitable disclosure of his misconduct could diminish the moral force and credibility of all the good he was doing."

Sorensen stopped short of making a final point: that Kennedy's behavior threatened his campaign and the hopes of millions of people willing to support and believe in him.

There is a credible story that early on, Joseph Kennedy warned his son about this danger and threatened to appoint Sorensen his minder on the road. The source of the story was Kennedy himself.

During the campaign there was not a public hint about Judith Campbell. In those days an unwritten media consensus kept private lives private unless there was a public incident or a legal proceeding. There was also a general newspaper rule that rumors could not be the source of news stories.

In *The Dark Side of Camelot*, published in 1997, reporter Seymour Hersh wrote of a 1960 conversation between Kennedy and Maxwell Rabb, a wealthy Massachusetts attorney serving in the Eisenhower White House. According to Rabb, Kennedy asked him to tell Nixon and top Republican Party officials, "Stop spreading the word that I'm philandering." Rabb told him that Nixon denied personal involvement but that party chairman Leonard Hall was involved. Then Rabb assured Kennedy there would be no more such activity on any Republican official's part.

There were at least three situations that would have been very embarrassing and damaging if they had become public. One involved Kennedy's dalliances with Marilyn Monroe, which appeared to have begun during the 1960 campaign and included rendezvous at the home near Los Angeles of the actor Peter Lawford and his wife, Patricia, Kennedy's sister. At the time nothing resembling exposure occurred—an astonishing fact given the multiple reports in the gossipy movie industry following Monroe's death in 1962.

Another situation involved two men of great influence in the Washington of those days: the attorney and consummate insider Clark Clifford, and Johnson's top Senate aide, Bobby Baker. Each was aware of a matter involving a woman known then as Alicia Darr. Her real name was Barbara Maria Kopszynska, who came to the United States from Poland shortly after World War II. By the early 1950s she was known to the police to be operating a high-end brothel in New York. It has never been clear when she had a relationship with Kennedy or for how long. But references to her began to appear during a dispute she had with lawyers handling her messy divorce from a minor British actor and society figure named Edmund Purdom, and another clash with the family of a wealthy heir to the Singer sewing machine fortune, Alfred Corning Clark, who had a fatal heart attack just thirteen days after they were married. She prevailed against his family and lived out her days in luxury on New York's Fifth Avenue.

In the spring of 1960 Bobby Baker told John Kennedy of a New Jersey lawyer who claimed that, for $150,000, Darr was willing to give Johnson an affidavit disclosing her relationship with Kennedy. In an account in Hersh's book, Kennedy quickly penciled a two-page statement, had press secretary Pierre Salinger "countersign" it, and sealed it in an envelope. Hersh wrote that it was found still sealed among the papers of Kennedy's secretary, Evelyn Lincoln, when she died in 1995. Hersh did not quote the statement, except to say it states that "Baker said he thought it was blackmail and did not inform Johnson."

Around this time Kennedy approached Clark Clifford, who was still involved with Symington's presidential campaign. Sections of the attorney's oral history remain blacked out in 2017, but it is clear from the surrounding material that a sensitive matter was involved. Clifford would not discuss details with Hersh, but Hersh quotes him saying the matter involved somebody "who could destroy him [Kennedy]. I had a conversation with Jack Kennedy that was so dramatic that if I could live to be a million years old I could never forget it. Public knowledge could have blown the Kennedy nomination out of the water."

How Darr's life came to the attention of FBI agents is not known, though various legal proceedings involving her many disputes seem the likely source. In June 1963 FBI director J. Edgar Hoover summarized her file in a communication to Attorney General Robert Kennedy. Referring to material that had emerged in legal matters involving two of her former attorneys, Hoover brought up the Kennedy-Darr relationship and added that it alleged that Robert had gone to New York after the 1960 election to arrange a $500,000 settlement of a "case" involving President Kennedy.

There were problems with the material, made public in 1977. Darr flatly denied receiving a dime from the Kennedy family; there was no record of a case filed involving the two principals; and the allegation that Robert was somehow involved was supported by no evidence.

The third situation was different from the other two. In the spring of 1960 a brief item appeared in the *Washington Star*, the city's afternoon daily. In a blurry photograph a woman holding a picket sign is attempting to confront Kennedy during an appearance in Maryland. The woman was identified as Florence Kater, then living in Kennedy's Georgetown neighborhood with her husband, Leonard.

The previous spring Kater had mailed a letter and photographs to roughly fifty reporters, columnists, and editors alleging that after midnight on more than one occasion she had observed Kennedy arriving at and leaving the upstairs apartment of her tenant. In one version she said that after the tenant moved to another, nearby apartment, she had staked it out and taken the picture of the person she said was Kennedy as he left, again well after midnight.

When her story had no public effect, Kater's efforts became intense. She picketed over the next four years and wrote a longer account of what she said she saw to supplement the 1959 letter. Nothing came of her actions.

There were problems with her credibility. Her longer account appeared in 1963 in a newsletter that was published jointly by people active in both the American Nazi Party and the Ku Klux Klan. The blurry photograph was not dispositive. And in initial discussions (she said there were seven visits) with a representative of the Kennedy family (a Washington lawyer and former FBI and Justice Department official named James McInerney) the Katers told of their love of modern art and desire for an original painting by Modigliani.

Their tenant was Pamela Turnure, then in her early twenties. From a privileged background, she had begun work in Kennedy's Senate office, then in the campaign as the press aide to Jacqueline Kennedy, and she became Jacqueline's press secretary in the White House. She continued in that capacity after Jacqueline moved to New York. When Turnure married a Canadian investment executive in 1966, Jacqueline hosted her wedding reception. Turnure has never said a word about any of this; her oral history at the Kennedy Library is still closed in 2017.

These events make clear how reckless Kennedy's behavior was and how lucky he was that his career and candidacy were not ruined. In 1980, in an unnoticed speech, Sorensen made the best of an ugly situation by saying Kennedy "never permitted the pursuit of private pleasure to interfere with public duty."

In a private reply to Sorensen, Jacqueline wrote, "No one has ever so understood and so expressed all the facets of that unforgettable, elusive man."

Kennedy's extramarital interludes were diversions in a clearly compartmentalized life. Somehow he managed to elude scandal, even as he developed into one of the most recognizable figures in the nation in the early spring of 1960.

And as pace of the campaign picked up, Kennedy had to shift quickly from the friendly snows of New Hampshire to the equally wintry—but more hostile—landscape of Wisconsin, where he would be confronted with a critical four-week engagement with Humphrey, a man known as Wisconsin's "third senator" because of his labors in Washington on behalf of a neighboring, largely Republican constituency during a time when Joe McCarthy had been useless to his state.

Earlier in the year Kennedy mused about his problems in Wisconsin. In an off-the-record conversation following a Georgetown dinner with journalists Ben Bradlee and James Cannon and their wives, he told his friends, "An awful lot is fortune. Why is it that I have to run in Wisconsin, the one state where I have infinite troubles, when Hubert Humphrey has got nothing anyplace else? That's just a bad break."

In Wisconsin Kennedy would face questions about his votes on agricultural issues from residents of areas where dairy farming was as vital to economic health as heavy industry along the urban shores of Lake Michigan. Among the state's substantial Lutheran population there would also be skepticism over his Catholicism. (After a Harris survey of four rural congressional districts at the beginning of March, the pollster warned Kennedy to avoid any overt appeal to Catholics. When Kennedy appeared at a parochial school dedication in the area, Harris noted, "the Protestant vote immediately reacted.")

Humphrey meanwhile seemed at home in the state. He spoke with the distinctive accent and expressions of the region, punctuating his sentences with "You betcha!" or nodding in approval with a drawn-out "Yaahhh." Though a pharmacist before he entered politics, Humphrey could talk about agriculture with authority. As he toured the state by car, he could look out at the deep patches of white on the farmland and explain to a visitor how snow brought nitrogen to the soil and served as nature's fertilizer.

Kennedy knew Wisconsin would be a major test. In an appearance in New York before he ventured to the state, he wisecracked that Symington, who was still waiting to declare his candidacy, "is hoping Wisconsin will be a good clean fight—with no survivors."

The decision to challenge Humphrey actually came nearly three weeks before votes were cast in New Hampshire. Emboldened by the friends he had made in the state and encouraged by Harris surveys that showed him leading Humphrey, Kennedy took the plunge. (Extensive polling by Harris in December 1959 had found Kennedy ahead 54 to 46 in a head-on match with Humphrey that did not include undecided voters; Kennedy also led 40 to 34 in a sample that did take into account the undecided. However, the pollster added a prophetic warning: "A Kennedy-Humphrey race has all the earmarks of a close, hard-fought contest in Wisconsin.")

Robert Kennedy sent a detailed memo to thirteen members of his staff on February 19 making it clear that a commitment had been made to enter the Wisconsin primary, which would be held on April 5. He laid out plans for a statewide organization and the handling of five different pieces of campaign literature. Reprints of the *Reader's Digest* tale of Jack's "survival" in World War II and a separate "account of Senator Kennedy's record called 'A Time for Greatness'" were to be passed out across the state quickly. A "farm pamphlet" putting the best face on Kennedy's record on farm policy issues was prepared for limited distribution in rural areas, and a "labor pamphlet" would be "available in a short time," Robert promised. Most important, a "tabloid," a newspaper-like publication that had served Kennedy well in Massachusetts elections, would be ready for house-to-house distribution during the last two weeks of March. The timing for the tabloid, Robert wrote, would be "essential" for what he called "our most effective piece of literature." With his cold eye turned to the task ahead, Robert was attentive to every detail. Overruling an idea by Kennedy's followers in Wisconsin, he moved their state headquarters in Milwaukee far away from a Catholic cathedral.

From a political perspective, Wisconsin was a state divided by ideological and religious beliefs as well as farming and labor interests. Kennedy's strength would lie in Milwaukee, brimming with Catholics with Eastern European ancestry, and the industrialized cities of Kenosha and Racine. The territory to the north and west, bordering Minnesota, where the Protestant men wore the uniform of farmers—faded coveralls and brogans—looked to be more friendly to Humphrey.

The fight for delegates would be played out on this canvas. There would be a statewide popular vote, after which a "winner" would be declared. But the real contest was over delegates. Each of the state's ten congressional districts would elect two delegates to the national convention, and each region called for different tactics.

Seemingly benign, with its pastoral farms and city streets cleaned with German efficiency, Wisconsin proved to be turbulent and unpredictable politically. Once a reliably Republican state, it nurtured a wing of the party that grew into the Progressive Party, led by Robert La Follette earlier in the century. For a while the Progressives acted as a national force for reform; they eventually rejoined the Republican Party, but after an aberrant period when the state GOP was controlled by Joe McCarthy, many of its liberal members became Democrats. As a result the makeup of Wisconsin's Democratic Party bore a strong resemblance to Humphrey's Democratic-Farmer-Labor Party, which was forged from a vicious inner-party struggle in Minnesota. With the Progressives now in their ranks, Democrats in Wisconsin began to win major elections.

William Proxmire's election to fill McCarthy's unexpired Senate term was a breakthrough for the party—as well as for Kennedy, who was fondly remembered for coming to the state to campaign for Proxmire. The new senator became a valuable ally. Aside from his trips on behalf of Proxmire, Kennedy logged many more visits to reconnoiter Wisconsin between his original decision to run for president in 1956 and the 1960 primary—making at least three dozen stops. Along the way he and his

closest associates established lasting connections with a number of colorful political figures in the state, such as the advance man par excellence,
Jerry Bruno. But none was more memorable than a faux Irishman who
went by the name of Paul Corbin. He had been born in Canada with
the family name Kobinsky, and his personal history grew even murkier
after he moved to the United States and settled in the Wisconsin city of
Janesville.

Corbin hung around the fringes of the Democratic Party in the state
for years and was drawn into Kennedy's orbit after state party chairman
Pat Lucey asked him to organize a dinner for Kennedy in Janesville in
1958. To hear Corbin tell it, he employed the art of the con to turn the
event into a rollicking success. He oversold tickets, so he and Kennedy
found themselves confronted with the sight of several hundred people
locked out of the dinner, "milling outside and calling me a crook and
a thief." In a tale probably stuffed with blarney, Corbin claimed he was
prepared to set up a card table to offer refunds.

Thus Corbin's career with the Kennedys began—in spite of Corbin's
initial meeting with Robert Kennedy in a hotel in Wisconsin Rapids a
month before the primary. There Corbin claimed to have had an argument that ended with his telling Robert off. "I said he didn't know what
the hell the word 'civil' meant, and as far as he's concerned, he can go
to hell. I don't give a shit about him. He was just a young whippersnap-
per."

In fact Corbin wound up idolizing the Kennedy brothers and later
converted to Catholicism so that Robert and Ethel Kennedy could be his
godparents. But the Kennedys never wanted to know what the hyper-
loyal Corbin was doing to promote the campaign. At one point predominantly Catholic districts in Wisconsin were flooded with an anti-Catholic
mailing postmarked in Minnesota. Corbin was a logical suspect for what
appeared to be an attempt at reverse psychology; the five thousand crude
pamphlets lacked subtlety. After Wisconsin he joined the Kennedy entourage and became one of its unlikeliest associates. Of Corbin's contributions to the Kennedy operation, another member of the group, Arthur
Schlesinger Jr., wrote, "He took cheerful delight in causing trouble and
in reorganizing the truth."

For most of March Wisconsin occupied center stage in American politics. Against a stark backdrop of weather-beaten, remote towns emerging from another winter, Kennedy and Humphrey plowed the state in separate caravans, speaking at civic clubs and sparsely attended meetings in school gymnasiums. They stood at dawn at factory gates to greet the morning shift. It was there—in Milwaukee especially—where Kennedy found relief in beer halls crowded with hundreds of Catholic Polish Americans rounded up by his local connection, Congressman Clement Zablocki.

The tableau was preserved in a controversial documentary called *Primary*. Time-Life invested in the project, and producer Robert Drew had no trouble getting the telegenic Kennedy to agree to be followed around the state by handheld cameras and mobile microphones. Humphrey too went along with the concept rather than be left out. The fifty-five-minute film favored Kennedy, with scenes of adoring Milwaukee crowds surging to touch a sparkling Jacqueline. It was not so kind to Humphrey, who was often pictured in a dowdy milieu. But no network would air the film when it was completed later in the year, so it was reduced to twenty-six minutes and syndicated to local television stations owned by Time-Life.

The Kennedy campaign did not lack for sophistication or money. Harris was polling almost weekly, and Kennedy's team included early masters of the art of political commercials. Humphrey, on the other hand, suffered from a shortage of funds and disorganization. The TV time he paid for resulted in primitive productions, such as a tiresome call-in show where Humphrey sat at a desk and awkwardly wrestled with telephone cords as he tried to communicate with viewers. Yet there was something about Humphrey that resonated with the people, especially his ability to talk knowingly about farm production and price supports. When he criticized Kennedy for his ignorance on the subject, it nettled the New Englander.

For the second time in four years Kennedy found himself opposed not only by Humphrey, but by Humphrey's acidic colleague, Eugene Mc-

Carthy. In 1956 McCarthy had managed Humphrey's failed attempt to secure the vice presidential nomination. Now he too was a senator from Minnesota and involved in another effort to thwart Kennedy.

When Kennedy encountered McCarthy at a stop in Wisconsin, he snapped, "Tell Humphrey to lay off my farm voting record." McCarthy had a stinging riposte: "Jack, you've got looks, money and personality, and all Hubert's got is your voting record."

In the final days of the Wisconsin campaign the Kennedy operation allowed itself to be lulled into overconfidence. In the process it badly lost the battle over "expectations," which influence the interpretation of actual results and either establish or deny all-important momentum for the battles ahead. Polls uniformly indicated the Massachusetts senator would win the popular vote, and the Kennedy team boasted to reporters that it was possible he would win more than a simple majority in the important battle for delegates in the ten congressional districts. In one of his last surveys of the state, Harris helped set the tone. "The next two weeks of campaigning," he wrote, "are going to be critical in determining if Sen. Kennedy wins the state by a margin of between 8–2 (among Congressional districts) or 9–1 (where it stands now) or finds himself whittled down to a 6–4 squeak through."

According to Larry O'Brien, the campaign proceeded to "bungle" expectations in Wisconsin. One well-known player in the state, Edwin Bayley, later blamed himself for what happened. Bayley had been a senior reporter for the *Milwaukee Journal* but had changed sides and served as Governor Nelson's executive secretary during the primary campaign. He was one of those usually anonymous, knowledgeable local sources whom national reporters regularly consulted while making the rounds. Bayley's line down the stretch had been that Kennedy was clearly winning the popular vote and appeared to have a chance at taking seven, and possibly eight of the congressional districts. One of the reporters ended up quoting him by name and speculating in a "Periscope" item for *Newsweek* that Kennedy was trying for a sweep of the districts. The reporter, Ben Bradlee, was new to the presidential campaign trail, but because he was known to be a genuine Kennedy friend his item attracted much more than passing attention.

The confidence proved to be misplaced. As votes were counted on primary night, the early returns looked grim. Proxmire hosted a dinner party at his home and watched Sorensen's face turn "ashen." In his hotel suite Kennedy nervously smoked a cigar and paced the room, talking on the telephone from time to time to get updates. Though winning in most urban areas, he was losing the Protestant farmland, where he had hoped to do well, and a district including Madison, which he had expected to win.

Kennedy carried Wisconsin by more than 100,000 votes but ended in a "squeak-through" in the race for delegates. He carried only six congressional districts. It seemed like a rebuke.

Characteristically his brother Robert took the returns personally. When the state president of the Young Democrats, who had stayed neutral and tried to maintain good relations with both organizations, paid a courtesy call on his suite that night, Robert slammed the door in his face.

Kennedy was more verbal. His sister Eunice, seeing that he looked disappointed in spite of winning, asked, "What does it all mean, Johnny?"

"It means that we've got to go to West Virginia in the morning and do it all over again," he said. "And then we've got to go on to Maryland and Indiana and Oregon, and win all of them."

CHAPTER FOURTEEN

West Virginia Melodrama

In demographics and topography West Virginia looked like a foreign country to the group from Boston. It was a hardscrabble region beset in places by extreme poverty. The principal sources of commerce were the coal mines. The state was famous for deadly feuds between mountaineer families who occupied the hills and hollows. Few Catholics lived there, and fundamentalist denominations—Baptist and Pentecostal—outnumbered the more progressive Protestant congregations. West Virginia would be a tough challenge.

Kennedy believed he had an advantage in West Virginia, though it was a tenuous one. The question of whether he should have filed as a candidate in the state had been the subject of a spirited debate inside his operation for months. Kennedy leaned toward making a stand there. He had begun cultivating support in the state after developing his friendship with Robert McDonough, the businessman who hosted a packed event in Parkersburg that stimulated Kennedy's interest in the state two years earlier.

McDonough told him that West Virginia was a good place to test his ambitions. If he could win there, he could win across the country. But to Larry O'Brien, one of Kennedy's chief strategists, the state remained "low on our list of possible primaries."

Despite the candidate's interest in making West Virginia a target, there were arguments against it. At a 1959 strategy session Joseph Kennedy warned, "It's a nothing state, and they'll kill him over the Catholic thing."

Once again Jack disregarded his father's advice. He rose at the meeting and said, "Well, we've heard from the ambassador, and we're all very grateful, Dad, but I've got to run in West Virginia." It was almost as though he believed West Virginia was his kismet, a place of destiny.

Critical to understanding how he won there is Kennedy's character: part gambler but also part cold realist who understood that the alternative of not entering West Virginia involved jettisoning the essence of his campaign as the outsider trying to win over a reluctant party. Shortly after he made his decision he spent a long morning at his home in Washington with MIT professor Walt Rostow. Already an important domestic and foreign policy advisor, Rostow recalled Kennedy telling him that when he listened to advice he tried to focus on what his advisors were leaving out of their presentations.

"Take this decision about the West Virginia primary," Rostow remembered Kennedy saying. "All the experts have lined up for me why it is ridiculous for me to go into West Virginia. One: Hubert is to the left of me and these fellows are hungry and unemployed and New Dealish. Two: they are 95 percent Protestant. Three: if I get defeated there I am out. . . .

"But they are forgetting one simple, overriding point. I have no right to go before the Democratic convention and claim to be a candidate if I can only win primaries in states with 25 percent or more of Catholics. I must go in there. And I am going in."

Kennedy was heartened by a Harris poll taken in West Virginia in late 1959 that showed him beating Humphrey there 70 to 30 percent. Still, he put off a final decision. As the filing deadline of February 6 approached, Robert Kennedy made his own exploratory visit to West Virginia to meet with McDonough and about twenty-five other Kennedy supporters who had influence in different counties around the state. They gave him disturbing news: erstwhile supporters were now angered to learn that their candidate was Catholic. One man told him, "There's only one problem. . . . He's a Catholic. That's our goddamned problem." The group was divided.

McDonough remembered that some said Kennedy had "everything to lose and nothing to gain" by competing. But a couple of Democratic leaders made strong positive points, insisting that despite the hazards, West Virginia was a state where "you could bury the religious issue."

Robert left without making a commitment that his brother would stake out a political claim on the state. Instead he sought to avert a showdown with Humphrey. Kennedy was meeting in his Georgetown home with Arthur Goldberg and Alex Rose, two prominent liberals with critical connections to organized labor, when his younger brother called on the phone. Rose recalled that Robert was "hysterical" and cursing. Referring to Humphrey, Robert said, "Get that son of a bitch out of the primary in West Virginia. There's going to be a bloody religious war here."

Kennedy turned to Goldberg and Rose and asked if they felt he should enter West Virginia after hearing this "hot report from Bobby." Rose urged Kennedy to run. "If you make a good showing in a state where there are no Catholics, even if you get forty percent of the vote, it's a moral victory."

Kennedy waited. The next day Goldberg and Rose met with Humphrey, who was tense at the outset because he thought they were coming to advise him to stay out of West Virginia. Instead they told Humphrey he had "a perfect right to run," but warned that it would be destructive for "two leading liberals in the nation" to become engaged in a brutal campaign. They appealed to Humphrey to "conduct the kind of primary fight where you can shake hands after the primary and be friends." He said he would do so.

Goldberg and Rose were not Humphrey's only visitors following his Wisconsin defeat. His frequent ally and supporter throughout the 1950s, Walter Reuther, president of the United Auto Workers, urged him to avoid West Virginia. Along with his top political advisor, Jack Conway, they spent some three hours making the case that his defeat meant his nomination was a practical impossibility. Humphrey had no counterargument, but he wouldn't budge, talking generally of a more favorable, blue-collar electorate awaiting him in West Virginia.

———

His victory in Wisconsin reduced by his failure to reach expectations, Kennedy returned to Charleston for his first full day of campaigning in West Virginia. A troubling tone for the month ahead was set the night before he arrived, when the Rev. Norman Vincent Peale, one of America's best-known ministers, spoke at the city's Ancient Egyptian Arabic Order Nobles of the Mystic Shrine and disparaged the notion that a Catholic could be elected president and operate independently from dictates of the Vatican. Peale was a pioneer in the business of megachurches and televangelism. The pastor of a huge Reformed Church in New York, the star of radio and television programs on which he preached a fusion of religion and psychiatry, and the author of *The Power of Positive Thinking*—a best-seller for more than three years—Peale's following rivaled that of any minister in the country. His slap at Catholicism was broadcast statewide on radio and widely covered by newspapers.

When Kennedy spoke at a rally on the steps of Charleston's post office the next day, he was immediately hit with a Catholic question posed by a spectator in a gathering of several hundred. Kennedy paused for a moment, microphone in hand, then replied with a question of his own. "The fact that I was born a Catholic, does that mean that I can't be president of the United States? I'm able to serve in Congress, and my brother was able to give his life, but we can't be president?"

McDonough was with Kennedy, and he could sense a perceptible change in the crowd; they seemed to react favorably to Kennedy's response. After that speech, instead of skirting the Catholic issue he began to deal with it publicly, refining his remarks in Charleston into an assertive argument that Catholics seeking public office deserved to be treated like any other citizen.

More than McDonough's gut sense was involved. Robert Kennedy's view was also changing, his recent outburst notwithstanding. After Wisconsin he slipped into the state quietly and met William Battle, who had been a fellow PT boat commander with his brother and was now the attorney general of Virginia. Battle too had politics in his blood; his father had been governor of Virginia during the 1956 campaign. He and Robert rented a car and set off down the back roads of West Virginia.

An early stop was in Charleston, at the office of one of the state's lead-

202 THOMAS OLIPHANT AND CURTIS WILKIE

ing Protestants, Episcopal bishop Robert E. Lee Strider. Strider's daughter, who happened to work in Sargent Shriver's Chicago law office, had tipped off Robert that her father was ready to endorse his brother. Bishop Strider told the two men that as a lifelong Democrat he had ditched his party only once, to vote against Al Smith in 1928. The difference in 1960, he said, was Kennedy's willingness to discuss his religion openly, to answer questions about it and thus to allay fears and prejudice.

From there the pair headed south toward coal country, to Huntington, down through Logan, and then to Williamson in Mingo County. What they learned contributed to some campaign changes. For one, Jack Kennedy no longer waited for questions; he brought up the subject of religion briefly in his stump speeches. And at a brief detour to an American Society of Newspaper Editors convention in Washington he changed the topic from foreign affairs to religion. The message was indistinguishable from what he had been saying ever since the topic first emerged in 1956; the difference was that he became proactive, not passive, about discussing it.

In an echo of their 1956 study of Catholicism's impact on politics, Kennedy's advisors rediscovered that Catholicism was a double-edged sword, capable of cutting points both ways in West Virginia. Just as some voters sympathized with a candidate hamstrung by his religious beliefs, it was obvious that others were unwilling to tolerate the idea of a Catholic in the White House. When Ted Kennedy submitted to an interview by a man playing records and entertaining shoppers over a loudspeaker at a five-and-dime store in Williamson, he was grilled with questions about Rome's unhealthy influence. When a crowd gathered, the youngest Kennedy tried to respond, but his host played an Elvis record to drown out his answer. Ted learned later that the man was a Baptist minister.

Humphrey, sticking to his promise not to inflame the campaign, refused to exploit the religious issue in his own speeches. There was no need for him to do so. Simply by being Kennedy's opponent he became the beneficiary of a loud uprising against a Catholic candidate by wary Protestants driven by fiery sermons from the pulpits of fundamentalist churches.

Early in the primary Bob Wallace, the campaign's point man in developing "Kennedy clubs" around the country, counseled Kennedy to take two approaches: "Beat Humphrey over the head as a front man for Lyndon Johnson . . . [showing] that his whole candidacy is a sham. The second thing is to hit this Catholic thing head on and say 'I am a Catholic and I'm not going to turn the government over to the Pope.'"

Two weeks later Wallace had second thoughts after learning that Kennedy's West Virginia campaign—reeling from the assault by the religious right—had prepared a mass mailing to address the issue. In an April 23 memo to Robert Kennedy, Wallace wrote, "It was very courageous and probably necessary for JFK to raise the religious issue in what is probably the worst area of the country for him to do so, West Virginia. Having gotten into the ring with the bull however, I don't think he should wave a red flag at it. . . . Humphrey people could charge that we are the ones who are fanning it. . . . It could very likely stir up a rash of sermons and public statements by clergymen." The mailing was killed.

The marketing of Kennedy, religion and all, included one brand-new element: television commercials, typically running about thirty seconds. Until 1960 paid political television consisted almost entirely of longer blocks of time purchased very infrequently to showcase major speeches. (That was the case with the very first one, produced on behalf of Truman in 1948.) In the 1950s five-minute time purchases became relatively common, but television executives hated them and hectored campaign officials that they were upsetting viewers by cutting off the endings of their favorite programs.

Convinced that the rapidly expanding new medium was tailor-made for him, Kennedy was fishing around for fresh ideas when he got an unexpected assist from one of his sisters. Jean Kennedy Smith was an actress and had appeared in several television dramas. She was particularly fond of working with a producer named Jack Devine and encouraged her brother to talk to him.

Devine was quickly hired, and the first results of his work with Kennedy appeared just as the final month of the campaigning in West Virginia began. The productions are raw by twenty-first-century standards, but they were novel in 1960. Typically an announcer introduced a complimentary theme, like "The right way to run for president" or "Senator Kennedy goes to the people," and the rest of the commercial included footage of Kennedy speaking about issues such as education or unemployment.

A few were aimed at specific issues in the campaign. The closest thing to a negative ad bolstered the insistence that Humphrey's candidacy was really part of a "Stop Kennedy" movement designed to benefit others— the implication was Johnson and Symington—and that he himself was not really running in the state. In one spot the announcer warned, "Are you going to let yourself be used by the bosses, who in their smoke-filled rooms in Los Angeles, expect to handpick the next president of the United States? Well, they know they can't do it unless here in West Virginia they stop Kennedy." One of the commercials dealing with religion featured the campaign's most important surrogate in the state, Franklin D. Roosevelt Jr., whose father retained godlike status there.

No one measured frequency, spending, or impact with precision back then, but it is likely that any West Virginian who watched television in the evening, and most probably did, saw at least one Kennedy commercial before turning in.

To counter the religious debate Kennedy traveled the country like any other candidate, campaigning in small auditoriums filled with people curious to see the stranger from Massachusetts. He descended into coal mines—a tactic Humphrey failed to use—to seek support from the gritty rank and file of the United Mine Workers of America, a union whose leadership was unfriendly to Kennedy. Importantly, for the first time the son of Joe Kennedy—who had never known want—was exposed to extreme poverty among white people who dwelled in forlorn communities in the Appalachian foothills.

West Virginia represented a cultural gulf that Kennedy had to overcome. At one stop on the road an encounter between an Eastern sophisticate covering his campaign and a famous son of West Virginia demonstrated that gulf. At an eating place one night, Joseph Alsop, the respected columnist, regaled a group that included Robert Kennedy's

wife, Ethel, and a few other journalists with his report of interviewing a
mountain housewife during his door-to-door polling of local residents.
In his arch accent that could be mistaken for that of a British lord, Alsop
described the scene. The woman's hair was disheveled; she held a broom
and was accompanied by a child with mud on his feet and snot in his
nose. Alsop said he had been reduced to "polling a slab of pork."

During the long-winded account, Ted Kennedy arrived with Sam
Huff, one of the most revered figures in the state. Raised in the No. 9 coal
mining camp in Edna Gas, Huff had gone on to become an All-American
lineman at the University of West Virginia and an All-Pro with the New
York Giants. Leaning toward Ted, Huff whispered, "Who's the English-
man?"

Introductions were made, and Alsop asked, "What do you do, Sam?"

"I play football," he said.

"You play for a living, do you?"

"Yes, I do."

"I knew a fellow who played football once at Harvard," Alsop sniffed.
"No, maybe it was baseball. Hell, I don't know."

Alsop may have been out of touch, but the Kennedy campaign was
quickly learning about West Virginia. Matt Reese, a local political consultant, became a fixture on the Kennedy team. He rode with the candidate, introducing him to the unique mores of the state as Kennedy
moved tirelessly, speaking to any group that could be mustered. One day
the candidate developed laryngitis and pressed Reese into service as a
surrogate voice. Speaking in a familiar twang, Reese extolled Kennedy's
war record and his dedication to America. Fresh energy for the Kennedy
campaign seemed to be loose in the state. Before a reception for Kennedy
and his wife in Huntington, Reese predicted that six hundred to seven
hundred would attend. When several thousand pushed their way into
the hall, a fire marshal closed down access.

The apparent momentum infected even the normally cool candidate.
On a short plane ride during the final stretch, Kennedy was sitting with
his friend, the columnist Charles Bartlett. Under doctor's orders not to
speak between campaign stops, Kennedy passed him a note instead: "I'd
give my right testicle to win this one."

Besides visiting the mines, Kennedy had other ways to show affinity for the working class. During a televised debate with Humphrey, he relied on a gimmick. He concealed beneath the podium a ration of foodstuffs known as "government commodities," surplus products distributed by the U.S. Department of Agriculture to needy people—the precursor of food stamps. At a propitious moment he pulled into view an unappetizing dish—powdered eggs—declaring that this was the forced diet for West Virginia. It was his way of showing that he understood their hardship.

Meanwhile Kennedy's strategists began to appreciate that West Virginia was a confederation of political factions, where sheriffs—who collected taxes and political tribute and only nominally enforced the law—ruled their own counties. It was essential that the campaign penetrate these fiefdoms in order to win the sheriffs' endorsements and help in turning out supportive voters. Sometimes Kennedy did it with charm; more often he used money.

Humphrey found himself beset with several problems. To show his dedication as a senator, he rarely missed a roll call in Washington. Kennedy, on the other hand, spent most of his time campaigning in West Virginia rather than tend to duties on Capitol Hill. At the same time Humphrey was caught in a double bind by the religion issue. Even as he refused to address one of Kennedy's vulnerabilities, he was made to watch his rival gain momentum; yet if he spoke openly about Kennedy's Catholicism he knew he might be branded a bigot.

A damaging perception was also developing that Humphrey was no longer a credible candidate but was running in West Virginia to serve Johnson's interests in blocking Kennedy from the nomination. There was evidence to support that theory. Johnson actually went to West Virginia to deliver a speech that was clearly on Humphrey's behalf, and Johnson's close associate in the state, freshman Senator Robert Byrd, acted as Humphrey's chief agent there. Folksy when he chose to be, Byrd chose as the theme song for the primary campaign the country standard "Gimme That Old Time Religion." Strapped for funds to combat Kennedy's riches,

Humphrey accepted infusions of money from Johnson's Texas partisans. One of Humphrey's chief advisors was Jim Rowe, the Washington insider who made his bones during the New Deal and retained an intimate link to Johnson. Rowe acknowledged trying to raise money from supporters of Johnson and Symington to slow down the Kennedy movement in West Virginia. "We pointed out to them what seemed to me perfectly obvious. If Humphrey went down, they'd had it." Humphrey was unsuccessful in getting cooperation from Symington; money from Johnson was thrown into the battle, sometimes arriving in satchels of cash. But not nearly enough.

Then there was an ugly incident that questioned Humphrey's courage. But the controversy redounded against Kennedy too.

No greater political hero existed in West Virginia than Franklin D. Roosevelt. Memories of how his New Deal programs came to the aid of the impoverished state during the Depression were still vivid. So were recollections that the first lady went down into the mines herself to learn about the people's lives. Thus it was considered a masterstroke for the Kennedy campaign when they were able to bring the late president's namesake into the state to campaign.

The son seemed to enjoy the long hours, driven from one event to another in a car bearing a big sign proclaiming, "Franklin D. Roosevelt Jr. campaigning for his friend, John F. Kennedy, for president." He was escorted by a journeyman public relations specialist named Fred Forbes, who had first been hired by the Kennedy campaign as a $100-a-week worker in New Hampshire.

Forbes was carrying with him an explosive bit of opposition research—documents that had been passed on to the Kennedy campaign from Minnesota offering details of Humphrey's correspondence with his World War II draft board.

In the last days of the West Virginia effort, as innuendos about Humphrey's war record began to bubble to the surface, Robert Kennedy gave Forbes a folder with the draft board information to keep in a locked briefcase. Forbes was instructed to give the material to Roosevelt, to let him read it, then to retrieve the papers and lock them back into the briefcase. Under no circumstances was the information to be used without a command from Robert Kennedy or Kenny O'Donnell.

On Roosevelt's final day in West Virginia his schedule grew frazzled, and so did he and Forbes. An NBC crew insisted on getting the distinguished visitor into their oversized Lincoln to film an interview on the road. It was the only time Forbes let Roosevelt out of his sight during a week of travel. Isolated with the news team, Roosevelt was goaded into responding to a remark by the network reporter: "Mr. Roosevelt, they are saying that you have a lot of material on Mr. Humphrey's war record that you are afraid to talk about, and they say that you are just really scared to do this."

Fifteen minutes later Roosevelt returned to the campaign car. "Well, Freddie," he confessed, "I let it go."

"You let go of what?" asked Forbes.

"I told the Humphrey story. . . . This guy claimed I was yellow to talk about it."

Roosevelt had charged that Humphrey requested a number of deferments from military service and that letters had been written on his behalf vouching that his work was needed in Minnesota. He also said Humphrey had been turned down by the Naval Reserve in 1944, with no reason given. Later Humphrey was said to have appealed to the draft board on the grounds that he was involved in a war-essential industry with eighty-five workers. In 1945, Roosevelt reported, Humphrey was declared 4-F because of a hernia.

Asked if he was calling Humphrey a "draft dodger," Roosevelt replied, "I did not use that phrase. The record speaks for itself."

Instantaneously the Roosevelt incident took over the news in West Virginia on the last weekend of the campaign.

Kennedy quickly issued a statement: "Any discussion of the war record of Senator Humphrey was done without my knowledge and consent, and I disapprove of the injection of this issue into the campaign."

Humphrey refused to comment. But damage was done to both candidates.

Outspent and insulted by the Kennedy campaign, Humphrey began to lash out against the extravagant expenditures being made by his opponent with repeated references to bags filled with cash. In a speech to a small group at a courthouse in Martinsburg, Humphrey said, "I have no suitcase filled with money, and I have no open-end checkbook." In an apparent reference to the Kennedy style, he added, "If you are looking for someone for a lead part in a Hollywood extravaganza or for a television beauty, then don't take me." Bitterly he added that being born with "a silver spoon in one's mouth" and "graduating from a great university" were not qualifications to be president.

The image of suitcases carrying cash was the result of a change of mind by the Kennedy family patriarch. Though Joe Kennedy had once discouraged his son from running in West Virginia, the old man had also chortled of his determination to back his son at all costs, "By golly, we've come this far. We're not going to let money stand in our way now. We're going to get this thing, even if it takes every dime I've got."

It took tens of thousands of dollars, funneled to sheriffs in counties across the state who controlled powerful local organizations and had the ability to turn out votes. Larry O'Brien was given the task of overseeing these dealings. He assured them Kennedy would represent their best interests in Washington, then tried to settle on the price of their loyalty. Cash was handed out under the guise of "campaign expenses," ostensibly to be paid to Election Day workers. O'Brien's secretary, Phyllis Maddock, actually kept cash in a suitcase under her hotel bed to be doled out to the West Virginia politicians.

Another ranking member of the Massachusetts "Irish Mafia," Dick Donahue, did some firsthand negotiating and handed out the cash to cooperating local pols. The goal, he said, was to get the locals, usually sheriffs, to "slate" Kennedy on instruction cards handed out to voters indicating which candidates were officially preferred. West Virginia ballots were notoriously long—it seemed to outsiders that virtually every public job was elected—and this slating was a major advantage to Kennedy wherever he could arrange it. From the perspective of the local officials, their interest was in slating people who were popular and could help draw voters to support them and their local allies. During the final days of the campaign they were more than receptive to Kennedy's candidacy, sensing momentum. In fact Kennedy ended up getting slated statewide by each of the two Democrats vying for the nomination to take on the Republican governor Cecil Underwood.

There were denials when charges were made that Kennedy was buying the election. But in a postprimary memo to Robert Kennedy, Bob Wallace wrote, "The facts are that both sides bought votes."

Donahue was in West Virginia the entire, torturous month, working with O'Brien primarily out of Charleston. As he put it, "For West Virginia . . . nobody gives a damn who's president. As a matter of fact they have very little concern of who's governor. They're vitally concerned with who's assessor or sheriff."

Donahue claimed that on primary day the campaign spent about $36,000 in cash from O'Brien's hotel room, including $16,000 for the pro-Kennedy forces in Kanawha County. "There's no question in some of the counties they use some half-pints [of whiskey]," he added. "Some places they use a lot of two-dollar bills."

Most of Johnson's money arrived in the state through a local congressman and supporter, John Slack Jr. On primary day, Donahue recalled, Robert Kennedy screamed at him that the campaign had to match Johnson's outlays. Donahue quieted him by saying the campaign had done all it could already and it was too late for more.

(The question of where the cash for West Virginia came from has been the subject of rumors and speculation ever since, but very little hard evidence exists. One exception involves a man from New Jersey named Robert J. Burkhardt, who was a top political worker for Governor Meyner of New Jersey. Convinced that Kennedy was likely to win the nomination, Burkhardt broke with Meyner during the primaries on his way to running a Democratic voter registration drive in 1960 for one of Kennedy's friends, Congressman Frank Thompson of New Jersey. In a 1964 oral history interview for the Kennedy Library, one quotation from Burkhardt jumped off an otherwise drab page. Unprovoked he said, "I have heard also that during the West Virginia primary Angelo Malandra of Camden and Paul D'Amato of Atlantic City and others of Italian extraction were working with Frank Sinatra in influencing voters in the West Virginia campaign." There was no elaboration. Malandra and "Skinny" D'Amato had business interests that included nightclubs in

New Jersey and Nevada and personal connections to Mafia figures such as a major mobster in Chicago, Sam Giancana. The record is clear that Sinatra was actively helping Kennedy in his campaign. One of his hits, "High Hopes," was converted into an oft-played Kennedy campaign jingle. But there is no direct evidence about Mafia money, or the extent of Joe Kennedy's money or anything else of relevance beyond occasional, wiretapped, and unsupported boasts by gangsters and other hearsay without details or proof.)

After the primary the U.S. Justice Department sent FBI agents into the state, but Attorney General William Rogers called off the probe after several weeks without unearthing hard evidence from any side.

According to Robert Novak, a reporter for the *Wall Street Journal* at the time, the newspaper conducted a five-week investigation into the allegations. It resulted in the draft of a "carefully documented report of how a presidential nomination was purchased in West Virginia through illegal, clandestine payoffs to sheriffs who controlled the voting process." The story was never printed. Novak said the *Journal*'s in-house explanation blamed the unwillingness of sources to sign affidavits. But he believed the paper withheld the story, which was ready for print before the Democratic convention, because the editors believed "it was not the place of the *Wall Street Journal* to decide the presidential nominee."

Later Wallace acknowledged that Joe Kennedy had been the fount of much of the campaign's money. "I was paid out of private funds, and I'm sure others were," he said. "I think the financing for this came from the father's office in New York and I don't know the details of it. The credit cards that I had, the airline travel cards, were 'Joseph P. Kennedy.' "

It was invaluable to be able to tap an inexhaustible resource, he said. "Money was not a prime consideration. You had to be careful how you present it or you'd be criticized. But if I wanted to talk to a group of party leaders it was very simple for me to invite them out to dinner. And if I could have dinner with steak, I've often thought how much time people will give up for a five dollar steak dinner. It's incredible, but they will do it. Five bucks a throw for 50 or a hundred people."

In Wisconsin the Kennedy campaign had been overconfident. They were careful not to give the same signals in West Virginia. In conversations with reporters, campaign leaders lowered expectations and spoke of the possibility of defeat. Some even believed defeat was possible. At a gathering of Kennedy's high command on the eve of the primary, there was a discussion of how to handle a defeat, and it was decided that any respectable Kennedy vote in West Virginia could be described as "a moral victory" because of the overwhelming Protestant population.

Contingency planning may be wise, but there was no real reason for it in West Virginia in early May 1960. Over the years Kennedy's triumph in West Virginia has been romanticized. It became de rigueur to cite polls—occasionally by Louis Harris, usually without citation—supposedly showing that right after the Wisconsin vote Kennedy went into West Virginia trailing Humphrey by 60 to 40 percent.

In fact contemporary evidence suggests no such finding, certainly none by Harris. The *Charleston Daily Mail* carried a story by political editor Bob Mellace, claiming that "Sen. Hubert Humphrey has taken an impressive lead" over Kennedy. But the numbers were nowhere near 60 to 40 percent and were based on a very small and oddly spotty sample of 171 "employed residents of Chesapeake, Kanawha County and unemployed coal miners in a depressed area of Fayette County." Some cited Kennedy's religion; many did not. But the percentages come out to roughly 53 percent for Humphrey, 35 for Kennedy, and a rather high 12 percent undecided. The story said the survey was done by one of the paper's reporters along with Lou Harris himself and Joe Alsop, while a *Time* magazine correspondent observed. If so, the low figures for Kennedy may have been planted by his own partisans in a gullible newspaper.

Other than this one strange case, there is no evidence of elaborate manipulation by the Kennedy people to lower expectations in West Virginia. However, the evidence suggests that Kennedy's "precarious position" at the beginning of April was significantly exaggerated; he was actually building toward his impressive victory in early May.

According to Donahue, he gave one local official in the Charleston area a look at Harris's last poll on the final weekend—a 45–45 percent split with 10 percent undecided. Kennedy himself chose to spend the evening back in Washington. He invited his friends Ben Bradlee of *Newsweek* and his wife, Antonia, to join him and Jacqueline for dinner. The meal ended before any West Virginia returns had been reported. To kill time the Bradlees and Kennedys decided to go to a movie at a sleazy theater on the corner of New York Avenue and 14th Street to watch, as Bradlee recalled, "a nasty little thing called 'Private Property,' starring one Katie Manx as a horny housewife who kept getting raped and seduced by hoodlums." Kennedy kept leaving his seat to call his brother in West Virginia, but there was no definitive word.

Afterward the two couples returned to the Kennedy home on N Street in Georgetown to learn that victory was assured. They broke out champagne and rushed to the airport to board the campaign plane, the *Caroline*, named after Kennedy's daughter, and fly in triumph to Charleston. Kennedy won 61 percent of the popular vote, Humphrey only 39 percent.

The scene surrounding Humphrey was of political devastation. The senator from Minnesota, who had wept after being beaten by Kennedy and Kefauver at the 1956 convention, was again overcome by emotion. He had expected a whipping, confiding to his friend Joe Rauh on their flight into West Virginia earlier in the day that he would lose. But after walking from his hotel room to his headquarters to review a blackboard with each county's results, Humphrey looked distraught over the depth of his defeat. A banjo player who serenaded crowds at Humphrey events began to sob. The candidate comforted him before returning to his hotel suite. Inside the room a quarrel broke out among his close supporters over whether he should continue. Humphrey said he did not want to be part of a "Stop Kennedy" movement. At 12:08 a.m. the Associated Press moved a bulletin from Humphrey: "I am no longer a candidate for the Democratic nomination."

CHAPTER FIFTEEN

Cashing In

From the beginning Lyndon Johnson was a spectral presence in the 1960 campaign, undeclared as a candidate yet lurking in the wings as Kennedy's most formidable rival. Despite his assurances to Robert Kennedy at their awkward meeting the previous December that he had no intention of running in the primaries, Johnson always figured in the Kennedy campaign's long-range strategy. There seemed to be many signals that Johnson would have to be confronted at some point—if not in the primaries, then at the convention, where he could call in all of the IOUs he had collected in his years as Senate majority leader.

The year before, Johnson had already arranged for changes in Texas election laws that would enable him to run simultaneously for two offices in 1960: his own reelection to the Senate and as Democratic nominee for president or vice president. There was more evidence of his intentions in Austin: an office to promote an unofficial campaign, run by a Johnson protégé, an up-and-coming Texas politician named John Connally, who nursed a virulent hatred of Kennedy. Elsewhere another of the Texas senator's closest associates, Walter Jenkins, busied himself organizing "Johnson for President" clubs.

Then there were the whispers from Capitol Hill of efforts by Johnson and his associates to diminish Kennedy's image. Johnson was said to evoke belly laughs in the Senate cloakroom by telling of Joe Kennedy's pleas to put his son on the Foreign Relations Committee and by passing along unflattering descriptions of the young senator from Massachusetts as "a skinny little fellow that had all the diseases."

Standing at six feet, four inches, Johnson exuded power. Yet he had let Kennedy steal the march from him in the spring of 1960. Johnson's friends were puzzled by his absence in the primaries and wondered whether he worried that his heart might fail him again or that he harbored a psychological fear of defeat. More likely, it was thought, Johnson, believed that he need not bother with the primaries. Instead he could count on the influence of Senate committee chairmen he helped put in place. He could also draw upon the friendship of his legislative co-equal and personal mentor on the other side of the Hill, Sam Rayburn, to curry favor with party leaders and, if necessary, to intimidate young congressmen attracted to Kennedy.

A few days before the Arizona Democratic convention in April Congressman Stewart Udall was summoned to the speaker's rostrum in the House chamber. "I understand you're having a state convention," Rayburn said to Udall. "Are you right in the middle of this?"

Udall acknowledged that he was.

"Well, I have a candidate for the nomination," Rayburn growled. "My colleague from Texas. I don't want you to hurt him."

In an effort to soothe the old man, Udall replied, "Mr. Speaker, I'm not trying to hurt anybody. I committed myself several months ago to John Kennedy, and I'm going to do everything I can to help him. I am not trying to hurt your man. As a matter of fact, if Kennedy can't get the support in Arizona, your man obviously is the man who will. If I can't put Kennedy over, I'm not going to be against him."

Johnson had his partisans in Arizona. He was relying on the aging senator Carl Hayden and a former Arizona senator, Ernest McFarland, to carry the day for him in their state. But they proved to be spent forces, and after a series of acrimonious caucuses a different group, including people like Udall, bound to Kennedy, wound up winning two-thirds of the seats on the Arizona delegation to the national convention. With a unit rule in force, this put Kennedy in position to get all of the state's votes.

With Humphrey eliminated and the nation's political cognoscenti stunned by the size of Kennedy's victory in Protestant West Virginia, Kennedy began moving methodically through the remainder of the primary schedule with the goal of amassing as many delegates as possible toward the magic number of 761.

Unopposed, Kennedy won the Nebraska primary on the same night as his triumph in West Virginia, the result of his early groundwork in the state. He turned immediately to Maryland, which would hold its primary a week later. Even as he concentrated on West Virginia, the high command of his campaign staff had targeted Maryland as a fallback place to regain momentum if he lost in the Mountaineer State. However, they faced difficulties in Maryland from the start.

Governor J. Millard Tawes had planned to lead an uncommitted Maryland delegation to Los Angeles and was unhappy over Kennedy's decision to run in the state. Kennedy appeared briefly in Annapolis in February to file as a candidate; at the time this was considered a mere formality. But following Kennedy's impressive victories in the early primaries, his campaign asked Bernie Boutin, their erstwhile New Hampshire leader, to come south and help establish a beachhead in Maryland. He visited Tawes to tell him that Kennedy would compete in the state. "I am very sorry," Tawes told Boutin. "I wish the senator wouldn't come in."

"I'm very sorry to have troubled you, Governor," Boutin replied. "But we are in, and we're going to stay in."

The commitment had been made, but the execution was still lacking. There was inevitable friction in the Maryland organization between local leaders and out-of-state Kennedy men such as Boutin and Kennedy's close friend Congressman Torbert Macdonald of Massachusetts, who was supposed to set up an organization in Maryland but had little success. Democratic members of the state's congressional delegation were reluctant to get involved, and a well-known ward leader in Baltimore was demanding $12,000 from the campaign to deliver several precincts that were heavily Democratic.

When Boutin relayed word of the call for cash, Robert Kennedy instructed, "Tell him to go to hell." After Boutin passed on the message, the ward leader lowered his price to $3,000. Told of the markdown, Robert had the same reaction: "Tell him to go to hell."

Robert displayed bravado with the Baltimore politician, but he worried that the Maryland campaign was in a mess, wracked by backbiting and the refusal of the state's Democratic apparatus to get on board. And Kennedy faced a new candidate, Senator Wayne Morse of Oregon, who was using the Maryland primary to warm up for a test of Kennedy in Morse's state a few days later.

The day after West Virginia, Kennedy swept into Maryland. One of his friends, Joe Tydings, had taken unofficial charge of the effort there. The stepson of a former Maryland governor, Millard Tydings, the young legislator managed to enlist a couple of big names in Democratic circles: Baltimore's mayor Tommy D'Alesandro and Blair Lee. They set up a vigorous three-day tour of the state for Kennedy, which ranged from the suburbs outside Washington to Baltimore and on to several Eastern Shore communities. When Kennedy arrived as the victor in West Virginia, previously recalcitrant Maryland Democrats swarmed to be nearby. For style points Tydings commandeered a shiny convertible to ferry the candidate to an event in Havre de Grace, near Tydings's home. While on the Eastern Shore the Kennedy motorcade passed through a village called Kennedyville; there was regret afterward that the schedule had not included an event there.

By the time Kennedy finished the tour, the outcome in Maryland appeared to be a fait accompli. Governor Tawes did not need further persuasion; he made a public endorsement of Kennedy at the end of the week. He had been shown the results of a Harris survey in Maryland before the primary season that showed Kennedy whipping Symington—who grew up in Baltimore and whose family had developed an island in the Chesapeake Bay—by a whopping 56 to 11 percent. Matched against Tawes, once the putative favorite son, Kennedy led 54–20. Harris concluded, "Baltimore city looks solid as a rock. . . . No matter what combination of opponents is pitted against JFK in the Maryland primary, as of January, 1960, it now seems certain that the Massachusetts Democrats will emerge victorious and by a good margin."

Harris's prophecy played out four months later. Kennedy mauled his lone opponent, the maverick Senator Morse, by better than 4 to 1. He had already moved on to Oregon to challenge Morse on his home ground.

The Kennedy campaign had always viewed Oregon, one of the most independent and progressive of states, as problematic. There was no way to avoid the contest; the primary ballot would include the names of any candidate the secretary of state chose to list. At the first of the year Robert Kennedy had feared that Adlai Stevenson, another noncandidate who retained a strong liberal following in the state, might become a spoiler. In a January 20 memo to his brother, Robert wrote, "It is obviously important to try to keep Stevenson out of the Oregon primary." He proceeded to outline a Machiavellian way to do so.

Congressman Charles O. Porter would be behind any Stevenson initiative in the state, Robert said, adding that Porter "both dislikes and fears" Morse, who had become his political nemesis. "If you went to see Porter at a propitious moment and said that you were thinking of not actively running in Oregon if Stevenson was in the primary, then Porter might very well reconsider his efforts on behalf of Stevenson because the implication of your statement would be that the state would virtually be turned over to Wayne Morse."

Events over the next four months would make the suggestion unnecessary. Kennedy's string of primary wins had shaken out the field. Stevenson was no longer a threat in Oregon, and although Humphrey, Symington, and Johnson would all be on the ballot, the only active competitor would be Morse.

Described as "the loneliest man in Washington" because of his ornery manners and his refusal to follow the dictates of his party's leadership, Morse bolted from the Republican Party in 1955 to become a Democrat, but he regularly defied his new party too. When the Democratic national chairman Paul Butler criticized Morse earlier in the year, saying his favorite-son gambit would interfere "with bona fide candidates in presidential primaries," Morse declared himself a candidate in Maryland rather than dropping out in Oregon.

In spite of his embarrassing defeat in Maryland, Morse claimed he would get 60 percent of the vote in Oregon and turned his caustic tongue on Kennedy, calling him a "synthetic liberal," a "kiss the baby" type of candidate, and an "interloper" in Oregon affairs. No one knew whether his diatribes were the product of his cantankerous nature or provoked by some substantive policy differences. There had been at least one legislative dispute. As a strong ally of organized labor, Morse assailed Kennedy as an enemy of the labor movement because of his major role in the Landrum-Griffin union reform bill.

For all of Morse's criticism, Kennedy had been able to establish more than a mere foothold in Oregon's liberal community. With their old favorite, Stevenson, on the sidelines, many of the respected liberals in the state enlisted in the Kennedy campaign. Well before the primary date in May he had the backing of Edith Green, an imposing new voice for education and women's issues in Congress, as well as the friendship of the politically prominent Neuberger family.

For years Oregon's other Democratic senator, Richard Neuberger, had been engaged in a strange feud with Morse that could be traced to the time Neuberger was a law school student and Morse the dean of the University of Oregon Law School. Nearly three decades later the two men exchanged angry letters, delivered by messengers, to each other's Senate offices. Some of their correspondence was leaked to newspapers, and their longtime animosity went public. Two months before the Oregon primary the forty-seven-year-old Neuberger, suffering from cancer, died after a cerebral hemorrhage. His death sent his widow, Maurine, to his Senate seat and helped drive his mourning followers into the Kennedy camp.

Given the dynamics, it was not difficult for Kennedy to decide to compete in Oregon, the only primary where he would openly challenge a favorite son. He refused to be drawn into a personal fight with Morse and constantly lowballed his own chances, telling reporters that Morse should win.

Because the interval between the Maryland and Oregon primaries was less than a week, the state did not witness the marathon, two-man campaign that had characterized the struggle in West Virginia. But the

result was the same. Kennedy enjoyed another outstanding victory, getting 51 percent of the votes to Morse's 32 percent. The outcome served as
an exclamation point for Kennedy's spring offensive.

Kennedy did not contest the Florida primary, which came four days after
Oregon, for a very good reason. One of his best friends, George Smathers,
was running as a favorite son and could be relied upon to eventually add
his state's delegates to Kennedy's growing total. But there was a tale of
mutual mischief between the two men that preceded their agreement.

Kennedy had originally thought of entering the primary because he
felt Florida offered a chance for him to beat Johnson. Geographically
Florida extended farther south than other states in Dixie, but its demographics did not match its neighbors'. In the Miami–Fort Lauderdale
area, a substantial Jewish population was more likely to vote like New
York than like Georgia. Thousands of people had migrated to the sunny
state, bringing their moderate politics with them. In short, Florida had
pockets of hard-core conservatives who were raised there, but the state's
politics were more cosmopolitan than any other in the Deep South.

To preserve his own good relationship with his Senate majority
leader, Smathers thought he could head off a collision between Johnson and Kennedy by filing early as a favorite-son candidate. Johnson did
nothing.

Smathers was a dashing figure who won his Senate seat in 1950 in a
legendary campaign against the incumbent, a liberal Democrat named
Claude Pepper. With the cold war a major issue, Smathers branded his
opponent "Red Pepper" and a communist sympathizer. Stories that grew
out of the race may have been apocryphal, but they spread across the
region—accounts of Smathers speaking to dimwitted audiences, accus-
ing Pepper's sister of being a "thespian" in New York, and revealing that
Pepper once practiced "celibacy."

Smathers supported typical southern, conservative values, and was
a critic of the Supreme Court's historic desegregation decision in 1954.
But despite their differences, Smathers and Kennedy developed a close
friendship. Smathers was a member of Kennedy's wedding party and

later one of his companions on a stag sailing expedition in the Mediterranean in 1956, the time when Jackie Kennedy, back home in the United States, suffered a miscarriage. Roger Mudd, a familiar face on network television for decades, wrote that Kennedy and Smathers, "together or singly, were wolves on the prowl, always able to find or attract gorgeous prey."

On the morning of March 1, the filing deadline in Florida, Smathers got a call from Kennedy inviting him to breakfast at his office. Smathers thought it odd, even though they caroused together as playboys and shared many meals.

As they began eating, Kennedy looked at the clock and announced, "You've got two hours to withdraw."

"Two hours to withdraw from what?" asked Smathers.

"Withdraw from the race in Florida."

"Oh, my God," Smathers exclaimed. "Is today the day?"

"Yeah," Kennedy said, "today is the filing day, and you better get out because I'm going to run."

"Jack, I can't get out. The [state] Democratic Party has already nominated me. No way!"

"Well, you can always withdraw yourself," Kennedy said.

"No, I just simply can't do it. I can't let those people down. I've told them I was going to run and it's been in all the press and everyone knows it."

They continued their meal, and Kennedy seemed to be smirking. It was 11:30 a.m., and the minute hand was winding toward noon, the deadline, Kennedy claimed, for filing in Florida. He raised the subject again. "Come on!" he snapped. "You know damn well you're not going to run. It's just stupid. Get out!" He turned up the pressure. "I've got a guy down there in Tallahassee. He's got a check. He's going to file a check. And I'm going to be a candidate, and you have to run against me."

Smathers was adamant. "OK you're going to have to run against me. I don't think you can beat me down there."

Kennedy cited the case of a Maryland congressman who had entertained notions of running as a favorite son. "Look what I did to Danny Brewster in Maryland. He did the same thing, and I beat his ass." (Kennedy's staff was actually scaring off the competition in Maryland by showing polls to local politicians that demonstrated his strength there.)

"That's Danny Brewster in Maryland," Smathers retorted. "You haven't beaten Smathers in Florida yet."

Kennedy cursed and grinned again. "Look, you're my best friend. If I get this now, I can win the nomination down there. I'll just have the thing closed up. You just have to get out. You have only got five minutes." He said his secretary, Evelyn Lincoln, had an open telephone line to Florida to pass on the late decision.

"Jack, there's no use doing it. I am not going to get out. I cannot afford to. I told the people down there I'm going to run. You're going to get more than half the delegates anyway. What the hell are you worried about? You'll end up getting all of them. But they're all committed to me now. They have to stay with me through the first ballot."

At noon Kennedy declared, "Goddamnit. All right. Too late. OK, forget it." He leaned back in his chair, looked at his friend, and said, laughing, "You know, you're a son of a bitch."

"What are you so pissed off about?" Smathers asked. "This is a little ridiculous."

"I could have won," Kennedy said. "Now I have to go through this crap of courting all of you. . . . I wanted to win. I wanted to put it to Johnson, and that would have eliminated Johnson. That's the first good state in the South."

He called to his secretary, "Bring in the polls."

With the surveys laid out on his desk, Kennedy and Smathers studied the results. The numbers indicated that Kennedy ran ahead of Johnson in Florida—but not Smathers.

Smathers snorted in triumph and said to his buddy, "You dirty bastard. You would have run against me if it had looked like you could have won."

Smathers would run unopposed in the Florida primary, locking up the state's 30 votes. That would prevent any Kennedy rival—including Johnson—from getting support from a major state in the South on the critical first ballot and assure Kennedy of many Florida votes on any subsequent ballot.

While Kennedy was scoring impressive victories in the May primaries, the nation's attention was diverted by an international crisis that threw new foreign policy questions into the year's political equation. It was also the occasion for a rare but serious mistake by the front-runner.

On May 1 an American spy plane, flying at high altitude deep into the Soviet Union, was hit by a surface-to-air missile. Its CIA pilot, Francis Gary Powers, was captured after he bailed out as the secret aircraft, a U-2, plunged to earth. After the Soviets announced a mysterious crash, the U.S. government went into full denial, claiming that the plane went missing during a flight out of Turkey. The American reaction put President Eisenhower in the most embarrassing dilemma of his administration when the Soviets responded by parading the pilot, now a prisoner, and remains of the U-2 on television. Eisenhower was forced to admit that the United States had been engaged in an espionage mission in the skies over the communist superpower.

The U-2 incident set the scene for a second foreign policy disaster for the United States. In the middle of the month Soviet Premier Nikita Khrushchev abruptly walked out of a peace summit in Paris he was attending with the leaders of three Western governments: Eisenhower, Prime Minister Harold Macmillan of Great Britain, and President Charles de Gaulle of France.

The crisis not only begged for appropriate responses from the candidates to succeed Eisenhower; it also reintroduced the possibility that at the coming convention the Democrats might turn to Stevenson, considered a knowledgeable statesman well-seasoned in dealing with foreign policy issues; at least in terms of public perception, Kennedy was not.

Even as Kennedy overpowered his opponents on the primary ballots, his campaign now found itself fighting off the shadow candidacies of Stevenson as well as Johnson, especially after Kennedy flubbed a remark about the U-2 incident.

Although he had been beaten twice as the Democratic standard-bearer, Stevenson remained the darling of liberal purists, who constituted a considerable faction in the party. Eleanor Roosevelt had importuned him all year to run. The former first lady issued a public statement on June 10, endorsing Stevenson and recommending a Stevenson-Kennedy ticket. After agonizing over the proper wording for a response, Stevenson sent a wire to Mrs. Roosevelt the next day: "I do not now intend to try to influence the nomination in any way—by 'endorsing' anyone or trying to 'stop' anyone, or by seeking it myself. I have not made and will not make any 'deals' with anyone."

Intrigue was afoot, but the "Stop Kennedy" movement was uncoordinated. Only three days earlier, Stevenson had written privately to Humphrey, "You ask when I am 'going to make a direct move for the nomination.' I do not intend to make any 'move' at all, or to try to affect the nomination in any way. I don't think I have the right to interfere with the efforts of any who may, at this point, as citizens and Democrats, recommend my nomination; but I will do nothing to seek it myself."

All that would change.

His relationship with Kennedy had been unsettled since Kennedy's unsuccessful bid to get on his ticket in 1956 and Robert Kennedy's tour with Stevenson that fall as a campaign aide. Jack Kennedy felt that Stevenson's indecision in picking a running mate reflected a politician unable to make hard choices. His younger brother was more scathing in his critique of the 1956 Stevenson campaign effort; he later described Stevenson and his brother as "different types" who "never got along."

Stevenson was equally suspicious of the Kennedys. He withheld any endorsement of Kennedy during the primary season because he feared the country was not ready to embrace a Catholic candidate. He also told John Sharon, one of his closest associates, that he was troubled by Joe Kennedy. "I don't know myself what influence the old man has on Jack," he said. "I don't think the country has as short a memory as some people believe with respect to Ambassador Kennedy's views when he was ambassador."

According to Sharon, Stevenson felt "Bobby Kennedy was a fairly ruthless, though effective, schemer. He has some reservations in his own mind about how totally truthful Bobby was in his political maneuverings."

At one point in the spring of 1960, as Kennedy collected more and more delegates, Stevenson met secretly with Johnson in Washington, where they discussed a deal offered by Johnson that was designed to stop Kennedy short of the nomination. Johnson claimed to have more than 400 delegate votes sewed up at the convention. If he failed to crest beyond the 761 needed to win the nomination, he told Stevenson, he would throw them to the two-time nominee rather than see Kennedy win.

After their meeting Stevenson rode with Sharon to a luncheon meeting with another of his earnest liberal supporters in Washington, Agnes Meyer. He told Sharon he had just been privy to "the most anti-Kennedy diatribe he'd ever heard." Johnson had shown him polls displaying the public's resistance to a Catholic and had denigrated his fellow senator. Stevenson seemed stunned by the intensity of Johnson's attack. "I've heard a lot of anti-Kennedy talk from various people around the country," he told Sharon, "but never anything quite as vitriolic as that."

Johnson's loyalist in Texas, John Connally, piled on, telling Sharon that the Johnson camp was "convinced that the Kennedys could be proved to have bought the West Virginia primary."

Throughout the primaries Kennedy kept in touch with the Stevenson interests through frequent telephone conversations with his friend William Blair, who had been Stevenson's law partner. Stevenson was said to be irritated that Kennedy did not talk with him directly.

With Democratic liberals again looking toward Stevenson following the U-2 incident, middle men such as Blair and Sharon—who were friendly to both sides—concluded that the Kennedys believed Stevenson had joined a conspiracy to block them.

To discourage that belief, Stevenson sent a "Dear Jack" letter to the candidate on May 11, congratulating him on his success and declaring, "It reflects the confidence which you have earned through your campaign and your record." He said he would be willing to meet with Kennedy at any convenient time.

In a combustible political environment Kennedy traveled to Stevenson's country home in Libertyville outside Chicago the day after his triumph in Oregon. The meeting was arranged by Blair, who hoped it would lead to Stevenson's blessing Kennedy. The candidate and the former nominee met privately for less than an hour. Kennedy told Stevenson he felt he was within 80 to 100 delegate votes of winning the nomination and believed Stevenson's endorsement would put him over the top. The former Illinois governor said he was not ready to come out for anyone, but he assured his visitor he "would not be a party—overtly or covertly—to any 'stop Kennedy' movements." For the sake of party unity Stevenson stressed the importance of Kennedy's willingness, if nominated, to seek Johnson's cooperation. Kennedy said there was only one way to deal with Johnson: "beat him." He described Johnson as "a chronic liar": "He had been making all sorts of assurances to me for years and has lived up to none of them."

Less than an hour later Kennedy's anger at Johnson boiled over in a comment to Blair as he boarded his plane to Cape Cod: "Guess who the next person I see will be? The person who will say, 'I told you that son of a bitch has been running for president every moment since 1956'?" Blair immediately thought of the Kennedy family patriarch. He grinned and answered, "Daddy."

Afterward Stevenson told Arthur Schlesinger, who had a foot in both the Kennedy and the Stevenson camps, that he had made a "dire mistake" in mentioning Johnson to Kennedy; it had provoked him. Kennedy, in turn, told Schlesinger he believed Stevenson had been "snowed" by Johnson. Rather than bringing the two men together, the meeting further estranged them. Robert Kennedy said his brother regarded Stevenson as "a pain in the ass." He characterized the May negotiations between the Kennedys and Stevenson as having to deal with "the actions of an old woman."

His inability to extract an endorsement from Stevenson left Kennedy facing the possibility of a Stevenson uprising at the convention. But Kennedy moved to strengthen his foreign policy position with a speech in the Senate two weeks later that offered him some protection from complaints by Stevenson supporters that he was a naïf, out of his depths in foreign affairs, after he blundered badly in comments on the U-2 snafu.

Just before the Oregon primary, shortly after Khrushchev stalked out of the failed Paris summit, Kennedy was campaigning at a shopping center in Eugene when he got a press question about the crisis. Without preparation and obviously without thinking, he criticized the Eisenhower administration for what he called its "backing and filling" that month. Then he went further, saying he would have expressed "regret that the flight did take place . . . regret at the timing and give assurances that it would not happen again."

The eastern political establishment pounced on him. The Republican Senate leaders, Everett Dirksen of Illinois and Hugh Scott of Pennsylvania, raised the "suspicion of appeasement," and Nixon called the statement "naïve." More important, Johnson began to slam Kennedy. For days, as he made campaign-style trips around the country, he regularly shouted at the crowds, "I'm not prepared to apologize to Mr. Khrushchev! Are you?"

Kennedy did not respond immediately, and the attacks soon subsided. Instead he prepared a more comprehensive statement on the poor state of relations with the Soviet Union, and he delivered it on the Senate floor.

In the carefully constructed address Kennedy began by blaming Khrushchev for the collapse of the summit meeting: "The insults and distortions of Mr. Khrushchev—the violence of his attacks—shocked all Americans and united the country in admiration for the dignity and self-control of President Eisenhower."

But Kennedy quickly pivoted into sharp criticism of the Eisenhower administration's failure to develop a tough, constructive policy to confront the Soviet Union. "As a substitute for policy, Mr. Eisenhower has tried smiling at the Russians, our State Department has tried frowning at them, and Mr. Nixon has tried both. None have succeeded."

He outlined twelve points he intended to follow if elected president, ranging from an assurance that the nation would have invulnerable nuclear retaliatory power to a commitment to establish strong relationships with emerging nations in Africa, "to persuade them that they do not have to turn to Moscow for the guidance and friendship they so desperately need."

He described his position as "a challenging agenda" for himself and for the country. But for now he had to concentrate on more pressing political issues at home.

CHAPTER SIXTEEN

Tying Up Loose Ends

Kennedy and his staff were proud of a campaign that relentlessly pursued delegates while navigating past many of the big-city bosses and old-time Democratic power brokers who once were able to deliver delegations, en masse, to the candidate of their choice. But there were still influential figures in some states who had to be stroked.

In Illinois, which held a nonbinding preference primary on April 12, Kennedy developed a bond with Chicago's Mayor Daley, who had taken control of his city's fabled political machine by muscling aside the longtime party chairman, Jake Arvey. The mayor looked doughy, with pronounced jowls, and he had a gift for malapropism, yet he had managed to establish iron rule in the nation's second largest city. Kennedy took advantage of his important connections to Daley. Both men were Irish Catholics whose tribe had beaten the WASP establishment on its own turf. From his days in the Illinois legislature, Daley had known old Joe Kennedy, who was developing the massive Merchandise Mart on the Chicago River. The candidate's brother-in-law Sargent Shriver not only ran the Merchandise Mart; he served as chairman of the Chicago Board of Education. Most significant, Daley liked Kennedy's appeal to the ethnic and religious constituency of Cook County. He looked like the winner to serve at the top of a Democratic ticket, a national candidate who would help carry every local candidate on the machine slate to victory in the fall.

Winning elections meant winning power, which was essential to the reign of the Cook County Democratic Central Committee. Over the past thirty years the organization had built the most impressive political machine in American history. It was composed of men with Irish, Italian, Jewish, Polish, and other Eastern European backgrounds and filled with colorful characters, such as the saloonkeeper and Chicago alderman Paddy Bauler, who once famously declared, "Chicago ain't ready for reform." From the outside the machine had the odor of corruption, but inside it operated like an army, with unquestioned control flowing from the mayor's office to every ward leader and precinct captain in the giant city. The monstrous machine fed on patronage. Party loyalty meant employment for the faithful, and Daley controlled thousands of public jobs, ensuring that he would preside over an operation that could deliver practically every precinct in the city.

Upon Kennedy's formal announcement in January, Daley called him "highly qualified to lead our nation." It was a signal that he was ready to deal. Kennedy won 65 percent of the popular vote in the nonbinding primary, and with Daley's support—plus a quiet assist from Senator Paul Douglas in downstate Illinois—he would wind up with nearly 90 percent of the state's delegation.

Well in advance of the Ohio primary on May 3, Kennedy had obtained the endorsement of Governor Michael DiSalle and left him alone to win the primary as a favorite son, presiding over a delegation that would be unanimously committed to Kennedy.

Yet in New Jersey, another governor, Robert Meyner, had proved intractable. Meyner had been elected in 1954 as a reform candidate and enjoyed the backing of the new Hudson County chairman, John Kenny, who had ousted one of the most infamous political bosses in the land, Jersey City's Frank Hague. For six years Meyner prospered politically, building a strong statewide organization and marrying a cousin of Adlai Stevenson. Meyner thought he had potential to become a player on the national scene and planned to lead his own delegation to Los Angeles as a favorite son, a move that could deprive Kennedy of a first-ballot victory. (Serious allegations arose that Meyner had gone so far as to approve the hiring of a private investigator to link Kennedy to an illicit affair with a Radcliffe student, a plot that backfired when the detective tipped off the Kennedy campaign.) Kennedy decided to bypass the state. Later Rose Kennedy was struck by how he had been "particularly incensed" at Meyner during a Cape Cod break from campaigning.

Despite his problems in New Jersey, Kennedy won every primary where he competed, and by the end of May his position looked comfortable in the three vital industrial states of Illinois, Pennsylvania, and Ohio. Yet work remained in three other giant states: California, which would hold its primary on June 7; Michigan, where skeptical labor and civil rights forces controlled the state Democratic Party; and the faction-ridden state of New York, where a bizarre collection of local politicians was grappling for power.

Kennedy believed he had reached an understanding with California's governor, Pat Brown, who planned to run as a favorite son committed to Kennedy. However, the situation was roiled by a number of factors. There remained sentiment for Stevenson among members of the California Democratic Council, and Brown's allegiance to Kennedy appeared at times to be wavering.

On March 9, the day after Kennedy's first triumph in New Hampshire and the deadline for filing as a candidate in the California primary, the Kennedy organization surprised everyone by filing their own slate of prospective delegates to compete against Brown. The Humphrey campaign hurried to assemble its slate.

Brown was shocked. Fred Dutton, his chief aide, remembered, "We thought we had an arrangement with the Kennedy group and the Humphrey group, and everybody else, that nobody from the outside would come in, that the governor would be the only one on the ballot." He called Robert Kennedy and Humphrey as well, and the two outside candidates agreed to withdraw from the California race just before the Pacific Coast deadline that night.

Dutton described the threat by Kennedy to challenge the California

governor in his own state "a fairly good example of the hard-boiled game
the Kennedy group were playing. They were going to take no chances
that the Humphrey people might file a last minute delegation themselves, and they weren't going to take the word of the Humphrey people,
or us, or anybody else."

By June Humphrey had been eliminated, and Brown breezed to his
unopposed win. But it was clear that Brown could not control his delegation. There was an insurgency by members of the California Democratic Council who had never given up their affection for Stevenson, and
Brown continued to withhold public endorsement of Kennedy.

In the five weeks between the California primary and the convention,
the governor was subjected to intense efforts by Kennedy partisans. Dutton called it "an aggressive war of nerves." One of Kennedy's chief operatives in the state, Hyman Raskin, moved into a motel in Sacramento and
visited the governor's office at least twice a day. In an effort to reach out
to individual members of the delegation, Larry O'Brien met in Los Angeles with Jesse Unruh, a burly master of backroom politics who would
soon become speaker of the California Assembly. Unruh was helpful in
peeling away Brown delegates, converting them to Kennedy supporters.

Irritated by Brown's posture, Robert Kennedy traveled to the state
several times. "Bobby would call up and want to know why the hell the
Governor was vacillating," Dutton said. It turned out that Brown was
also dealing with a subterranean lobbying campaign by Stevenson interests. He faced resistance from the California Democratic Council, and
he heard from Stevenson himself. Brown was "torn apart" by the pressure, Dutton recalled. "Stevenson was working behind the scene, trying
to stir up support for himself, notwithstanding his public position of not
wanting to get involved." The former nominee called Sacramento several times from the Mount Kisco, New York, summer home of Agnes
Meyer, which had become Stevenson's preconvention retreat.

Ten days before the convention Brown got a message from another
powerful figure, Joseph P. Kennedy. The candidate's father was staying
nearby, at Lake Tahoe, and wanted to have dinner with the governor
that evening. He arrived at the governor's mansion at nightfall. Four
men would attend the secret meal. On one side, Pat Brown and his aide

Fred Dutton; on the other, Joe Kennedy and his son's deputy in California, Hy Raskin.

Although Brown was the host, Joe Kennedy was the dominant personality. The former ambassador delivered a forceful argument on behalf of his son. He noted that California would come early in the convention roll call, and a strong vote for Kennedy would have an enormous psychological effect.

Brown was uncomfortable with confrontation and preferred that Dutton bargain with the elder Kennedy. "If California goes for Kennedy," Dutton asked, "what are you going to do for California? What about our water problem? What kind of appointments?"

Throughout the campaign the elder Kennedy had watched as his advice was disregarded by his sons and their aides. He had been willing to help finance the costly operation, yet he rarely intervened personally. On this night he wanted to help his son but was limited to his own powers of persuasion. He had no mandate from the candidate. He said he could make no promises.

The meeting broke up inconclusively. No longer trusting Brown to deliver California, the Kennedy team spent the remaining days before the convention trying to pick up individual votes here and there from a fractious delegation.

A Harris survey in Michigan during the first month of the election year found that Kennedy was the only announced Democratic candidate who ran ahead of the likely Republican nominee, Richard Nixon, in the state. Nixon led both Humphrey and Symington by double digits but trailed Kennedy by 6 percentage points. Harris reported that Kennedy's "strong position is striking" and concluded that if Kennedy got a reasonable share of the Catholic vote among Michigan Democrats, he had the capacity to run ahead of Stevenson as well as the governor, "Soapy" Williams, if the state held a primary.

But Michigan did not hold a primary, and Williams, a durable liberal who had led the delegation as a favorite son at the previous two conventions, appeared ready to play the same role in 1960. Kennedy limited his activity in Michigan during the primary season, but one of his congressional allies, New Jersey congressman Frank Thompson, attended a Democratic dinner there and discovered latent support for the Massachusetts senator. Encouraged by the news, the Kennedy campaign stepped up their work in the state. It was apparent Kennedy needed to win over two strong forces in the state's Democratic Party: the labor movement and the civil rights community.

Walter Reuther, president of the powerful United Auto Workers in a state dominated by the automotive industry, had reservations about Kennedy because of his support of the Landrum-Griffin bill. Another union official destined to lead the UAW, Leonard Woodcock, had tried to allay these concerns by inviting Kennedy to speak at a UAW convention in October 1959.

As Kennedy began to sweep through the primaries, interest in his candidacy grew. Sorensen attended a conference of Michigan liberals to speak on Kennedy's behalf and was grilled by the group about Kennedy's commitment to their causes. If Michigan were to support him at the Democratic convention, Governor Williams declared, "we wanted to be sure that we were backing somebody who wasn't going to be a Curley politician," a reference to the infamous Boston politician who had died late in 1958.

In May the state Democratic convention again endorsed Williams as a favorite son, but even the governor recognized a strong Kennedy trend among his constituency.

Williams, Neil Staebler, the state Democratic chairman, and Millie Jeffrey, a well-known figure representing UAW interests in national party politics, traveled to Washington to meet with Kennedy in early June. The trio had originally felt much closer to Humphrey, but he had fallen in the primaries. "We were naturally having our own personal dilemmas," Williams admitted. During the discussion with Kennedy, they suggested that he meet with a larger group from Michigan that would include labor leaders and black civil rights activists.

Kennedy arranged to fly more than a dozen Democrats from Michigan to Washington on his campaign plane, the *Caroline*, to attend a luncheon meeting at his Georgetown home on June 20, three weeks before the start of the convention. For the first time several black leaders joined the party leaders in a frank discussion with the candidate. The visitors were given the full Kennedy treatment. The candidate welcomed them at the door, and Jackie invited them to a buffet lunch on the terrace outside. Still, Kennedy encountered doubts. The black group, which included Esther Gordy Edwards of the Motown musical enterprise and Charles Wartman, editor of the black weekly *Michigan Chronicle*, told Kennedy they were unhappy with his failure to speak out in favor of the sit-ins by black students at segregated lunch counters, a new tactic by the civil rights movement that was spreading across the South.

Following a lengthy discussion the group seemed impressed by the candidate—by his comfortable manner and his attention to their concerns. After Kennedy assured them that he would offer stronger support of civil rights, the group left satisfied. Their state moved into the Kennedy column, with Governor Williams in the lead.

New York was the largest of the dominoes to fall for Kennedy before the convention. In many ways New York—as much as Massachusetts—could be called home to the Kennedys. Discouraged at not being accepted in Boston, where Yankees still controlled commerce and society, Joe Kennedy felt that Boston was "no place to bring up Catholic children." In 1927 he purchased a mansion in Bronxville, New York, where Jack spent his teenage years. In 1960 the elder Kennedy was still firmly connected to Wall Street and other powerful figures in the metropolis.

With 114 votes the state of New York carried enough clout to propel Kennedy close to the 761 he needed at the convention, and from the outset of his long campaign his operatives had been burrowing into an assortment of county Democratic organizations, building a network of supporters.

Much of the preliminary spadework was performed by John Bailey, from nearby Connecticut, and, in a rare example of political effectiveness, Joe Kennedy himself. Bailey knew most of the political figures in the city quite well. The elder Kennedy worked through Congressman

Charles Buckley of the Bronx, believed to be his partner in a real estate investment, to round up additional support for his son.

Once again the Kennedy boosters were able to use favorable surveys in the state. Harris pointed out that Republicans now held the governor's office and both U.S. Senate seats because of bickering among the Democrats. Kennedy was presented as a broadly acceptable candidate who was capable of defeating Nixon in New York by record margins. Harris went on to say that Kennedy "would be the odds-on favorite to carry the day" among Democrats if Stevenson stayed out of the state. Kennedy was strongest in the borough of Queens, the home of many Irish Catholics, and weakest in the Jewish precincts of the Bronx and Brooklyn, where his father had antagonized many people with his unpopular diplomatic stance toward Germany in the days before World War II. Harris also recommended that Kennedy "take steps to become better known in Harlem" and to develop acquaintances among "the leaders of New York's Negro community."

The Kennedy operation recognized the importance of a broad-based approach and set out to establish grassroots alliances not only in the boroughs of New York City but in the cities, small towns, and villages upstate.

Instead of paying fealty to Tammany Hall, the Democratic machine in Manhattan that once controlled the state party, the Kennedys laid siege to Tammany boss Carmine DeSapio's organization by surrounding him with fresh leaders from other counties who were Kennedy loyalists. Even in his own city DeSapio was confronted by Buckley, who controlled the Bronx, and another congressman, Eugene Keogh, who wielded power in Brooklyn. The two men were prepared to deliver their boroughs to Kennedy. The fearsome Tammany Tiger, depicted by the famous nineteenth-century cartoonist Thomas Nast as preying upon a helpless Body Politic, was being reduced to a loud but toothless remnant in New York politics.

During the spring of 1960 Manhattan Democrats were riven over issues that had nothing to do with the presidential race. DeSapio and his loyal state Democratic chairman, Michael Prendergast, were fighting off a reform movement led by Eleanor Roosevelt, former governor Herbert

Lehman, and Thomas Finletter, secretary of the air force in the Truman administration. During the squabbling Tammany even turned on one of its own, Mayor Robert Wagner. Prendergast sneered that "Wagner always played his own game—what was best for Wagner." The mayor used almost exactly the same phraseology, claiming that DeSapio "played little games."

Some of the New York political meetings degenerated into farce. Prendergast, who had a reputation as a lackey to DeSapio, described one encounter between Joe Kennedy and Tammany. There is undoubtedly hyperbole in his account, but it is a funny story and symbolic of the disarray in New York. It took place on the eve of the West Virginia primary.

"My friend, Mr. DeSapio, said to me, 'We have a lunch date.'"

"With whom?" Prendergast asked.

"A guy you'd like, Joe Kennedy." Prendergast had never met the man.

"The meeting was at the Plaza. On the way up, I said to Carmine, 'Look, do what you want, but I'm not going to be beleaguered.'"

Joe Kennedy was accompanied by Charles Buckley and a banker. As soon as the Tammany duo walked in, Prendergast said Kennedy "jumped all over me. He started to give me a song and dance, and he told us that they were only going to get 33 percent of the vote in West Virginia." To salvage the Kennedy campaign from the appearance of defeat, Joe demanded that they immediately endorse his son, warning, "If you don't come out for Jack tomorrow, your votes aren't worth a damn at the convention."

Prendergast replied, "Mr. Kennedy, I'm just as Irish as you are, and if that's all you care about, our votes, you can go to hell!" Joe put on his hat and slammed the door on his way out of the room.

The candidate's father took other initiatives that were probably not authorized by the campaign. He tried to throw his weight around in New York among more dignified personalities, including Francis Cardinal Spellman, the archbishop of the nation's greatest diocese.

Kennedy had scored a big hit in New York earlier in his quest, at the Alfred E. Smith Memorial Foundation dinner at the Waldorf-Astoria Hotel, a Catholic affair that offered an annual stage as important to politicians as Washington's Gridiron dinner. Setting up his audience for a lament about the devastating loss by the Catholic Smith, Kennedy alluded to an earlier presidential candidate who had lost badly. He paused, with a comedian's timing, and said, "Alfred M. Landon, Protestant. . . . The memory of that election still burns deeply in our minds." The crowd howled with laughter.

But the conservative Cardinal Spellman provided no smiles or blessings for the Kennedy campaign. Joe ranted about the slight. He wrote a friend that he was going to unleash his old associate, the *New York Times* columnist Arthur Krock, to launch a newspaper crusade against the cardinal. He even sent word of the threat to Spellman in an effort to keep the Catholic leader quiet during the campaign.

While Joe feuded with the Catholic hierarchy, Manhattan Democrats made war on one another. Tammany was not watching while most of the upstate county chairmen began climbing onto the Kennedy bandwagon after he followed up his critical victory in West Virginia by beating Wayne Morse in Maryland and then in Oregon.

Seeing confusion in the Empire State, Johnson's supporters shipped Texas money there to try to arrest the Kennedy momentum. According to Mayor Wagner, the funds were "given to a couple of fellows who were supposed to deliver, and they couldn't deliver anything because the delegates here were for Kennedy."

Unable to prevent Kennedy supporters from winning seats in the New York delegation, Prendergast announced in early summer that the state would back a favorite son—for vice president. The favorite son would be Wagner. The mayor dismissed the idea. "It was quite obvious you couldn't have two Catholics on the ticket."

Meanwhile Johnson, who had been counting on the New York bosses in his convention mathematics, saw the votes disappearing. Wagner had told him months earlier that Kennedy was making inroads in the counties outside the city, speaking in places like Syracuse and Buffalo, where he recruited another powerful ally, Erie County Democratic chairman Peter Crotty. Johnson confined his activity to New York City. Wagner told him, "Very frankly, that doesn't excite the people of New York City very much. If the majority leader in the Senate goes to Kalamazoo or someplace like that, it's big news. But great people go to dinner in New York every night. The average person doesn't know about it and could care less."

Johnson was displeased by Wagner's observation. He was even angrier when Wagner endorsed Kennedy in June. He telephoned the mayor. "It wasn't a congratulatory conversation," said Wagner. "He was very rough and very unhappy that I had come out. He told me that in the future if he needed anything, he knew where to go for it. He can be very rough if he wants to be."

The internecine battles continued at the state Democratic convention in Albany, where Tammany forces succeeded, for the moment, in denying the former governor Herbert Lehman, a leader in the reform movement, a seat on the New York delegation to Los Angeles.

On June 18 Wagner hosted an event at Gracie Mansion, the traditional home of the city's mayor, to present Kennedy as the champion in the fight for the state delegation. He hoped that the reception might heal the rift among the various factions in the party. Instead Kennedy, angered over the slight to Lehman, would have nothing to do with DeSapio or Prendergast. He showed no interest in a peace treaty with the ultraliberal Stevenson wing of the party, either.

The national convention was little more than three weeks away and Kennedy was closing in on the presidential nomination. He no longer had to lower himself to the snake pit of petty local quarrels. The ouster of Onions Burke in 1956 and the political emasculation of Carmine DeSapio four years later were behind him now. He had more important battles ahead, more formidable enemies to overcome.

CHAPTER SEVENTEEN

Triumph in LA

Five days before the start of the Democratic National Convention Lyndon Johnson finally announced that he would be a candidate, moving from an informal campaign that had all the subtlety of a Texas longhorn into a desperate, highly public effort to wrest the presidential nomination from Kennedy. At the same time Adlai Stevenson, who had claimed the last two nominations, continued to despair over whether to declare himself a candidate again while a cadre of liberal activists worked to build enthusiasm for his third attempt to win the White House.

In Los Angeles, the site of the convention, thousands of delegates and their alternates, party officials from fifty states, members of campaign teams, partisans of candidates who still had breath left, long shots, favorite sons, over-the-hill politicians, camp followers, political junkies, and hundreds of reporters were already gathering, creating a buzz that swept across the country: Could the young senator from Massachusetts be stopped short of victory on the first ballot? If not, who might he choose as his running mate?

On Saturday Kennedy flew west aboard an American Airlines jet, confident that he had the votes necessary to win. As a student of history he knew that two other prominent Democrats had arrived at their conventions earlier in the century with the nomination in hand and somehow failed to get it: Champ Clark in 1912 and William Gibbs McAdoo in 1924. But on those occasions a candidate had to get a two-thirds su-permajority for nomination, a requirement that produced long and de-bilitating roll calls; after Franklin Roosevelt's first nomination in 1932 the rules were changed to require just a simple majority, and that meant Kennedy's target was 761 votes.

Despite his near certainty that the nomination was his, Kennedy re-alized he must spend the four days before balloting began the follow-ing Wednesday locking up the loyalty of his supporters while carefully massaging the pride of various bosses, reminding them that he had the strength to prevail and that they needed to be sure they wound up on the winning side.

Kennedy had enjoyed a flurry of positive media attention a few days before his departure courtesy of Harry Truman. Just prior to the Oregon primary a month earlier, Kennedy had a chance to learn that wit was more effective than feigned outrage in dealing with the hostile former president. While endorsing his fellow Missourian, Stuart Symington, whose fortunes were even then ebbing hourly, Truman said his main complaint about Kennedy was that he was from Massachusetts. Ken-nedy won widespread laughter and appreciation for his comeback: "I have news for Mr. Truman, Mr. Symington was born in Massachusetts."

Over the Fourth of July weekend, with the convention a week away, Kennedy had another tiff with Truman. This time the former president got major television exposure by raising again the question of whether Kennedy was too young and inexperienced to be president, and answer-ing firmly in the affirmative. Suggesting a future candidacy for Kennedy, Truman concluded, "May I urge you to be patient."

Kennedy got extensive coverage for his return volley two days later. From his Cape Cod rest stop he summoned Sorensen, already in LA for convention preparations, to return east to draft a response. Again wit won. Kennedy replied that if fourteen years in national office were in-sufficient, that would rule out every president of the twentieth century, including Woodrow Wilson, Franklin Roosevelt, and Truman himself. And if forty-four was the cutoff age for national leadership, that would have precluded Jefferson from drafting the Declaration of Independence, Washington from commanding the Continental Army, Madison from his work on the Constitution, and even Christopher Columbus from setting sail from Spain. The name of another young man cited in Sorensen's draft, Jesus Christ, was cut by his boss.

Arriving in Los Angeles, Kennedy was met by John Bailey, the veteran of past party wars who had helped steer his friend through the shoals of doubting Democratic leaders to the brink of nomination. One of his jobs that week was greeting and schmoozing with big shots on their way into town. Bailey took the candidate to meet with one of them, Governor David Lawrence of Pennsylvania. The setting was the aging Biltmore Hotel on Pershing Square in downtown LA. Because of its size—more than a thousand guest rooms—the hotel was chosen by the Democratic National Committee as the convention headquarters as well as the command posts for candidates, temporary studios for the television networks, and private rooms for select print reporters. The hotel anchored an unsavory neighborhood described by the novelist John Rechy: "Nervous fugitives . . . pushers, the queens, the sad panhandlers [inhabited] . . . the world of Lonely-Outcast America squeezed into Pershing Square, of the Cities of Terrible Night downtown now, trapped in the City of Lost Angels." For all its sordid surroundings, a world of political glamour would exist for a week inside the Biltmore.

Following Kennedy's meeting with Lawrence, *Time* magazine correspondent Hugh Sidey encountered Robert Kennedy late Saturday afternoon, walking in a hotel corridor toward his office on the eighth floor. "How's it look?" Sidey asked.

"I think we've got him," Robert replied. Lawrence said he would do what his delegation wanted, and it was obvious that the Pennsylvanians wanted Kennedy. "That's the ball game."

Johnson was unable to reconcile himself to the widening belief that Kennedy's nomination was inevitable. He considered Kennedy an undeserving upstart; nearly a decade older, Johnson outranked him in congressional seniority and believed he had better connections in the party hierarchy.

In the days leading up to the convention, Johnson went on the at-
tack in the manner he had learned growing up amid bare-knuckled
Texas politics. He called upon a former Capitol Hill counselor from
his orbit, Donald Cook, now president of the huge American Electric
Power Company, to investigate Kennedy's health. Cook used his contacts
to learn that Kennedy had been treated for Addison's disease. Although
Cook's research lacked definitive details, Johnson decided to go public.
He enlisted his alter ego, John Connally, to hold a press conference with
India Edwards, a leader in women's activities in the Democratic Party,
to announce that Kennedy suffered from the disease. "Doctors have told
me he would not be alive if not for cortisone," she said.

Such roughhouse tactics were familiar to the Irishmen in the Kennedy
operation. Robert responded quickly, describing his brother's ailment as
unrelated to classical Addison's disease. The candidate simply had some
"adrenal insufficiency" that was not dangerous, he countered, and denounced the claims from the Johnson camp as "malicious and false" and
"despicable." Sorensen later admitted that the statement was "literally
true but generally misleading." Nevertheless Johnson was forced to back
away from the issue.

Coupled with his failure to raise apprehensions over Kennedy's
health, Johnson's hopes were set back further on the weekend before the
convention opened, when he learned through a grapevine of political
intelligence at the Biltmore that the New York and Illinois delegations
were staying firmly with Kennedy and that Pennsylvania was likely to
do the same.

Still, Johnson was unwilling to concede. When the convention opened
on Monday, July 11, he spoke at several caucuses. In an appearance before the representatives of the state of Washington, he took a swipe at
Joe Kennedy, who five years earlier had offered to finance a Johnson
presidential campaign that would include young Jack Kennedy on the
ticket. Johnson vowed to stand up for America rather than appease its
enemies. "I wasn't any Chamberlain umbrella man," he bellowed. "I
never thought Hitler was right."

It was a provocative comment, but no Kennedy rose to take the bait.

Dispirited, Johnson watched the convention's first-night events on television in his hotel suite, where he dined privately with his old friend Jim Rowe, an éminence grise in Democratic Party affairs. After failing to lure Johnson into the presidential race the year before, Rowe had become an advisor to Humphrey; when that failed, he returned to Johnson's side. The television set cast flickering images of Senator Frank Church of Idaho delivering the keynote address, but Johnson's mind was on Kennedy. He turned to Rowe and asked, "I don't see how we can stop this fellow, do you?"

"No," Rowe replied, "I guess not."

There was one last trick for Johnson to play. He challenged Kennedy to a debate before a joint meeting of Texas and Massachusetts delegates on Tuesday afternoon, and he made sure that the venue would be on his home turf, the Biltmore's Crystal Ballroom, a site used by the Texas delegation for its caucuses. "I want to get on the same platform with Jack. I'll destroy him," Johnson told an aide.

Kennedy's father questioned the wisdom of engaging in a debate with Johnson. "Isn't that the goddamndest thing you ever heard of? If I were Jack I wouldn't get within a hundred yards of him," the old man told John Seigenthaler, a family friend who was working as a reporter for the *Tennessean*. Seigenthaler had been granted an interview with Joe Kennedy at the estate of Hollywood actress Marion Davies, a star from an earlier era when Joe had dabbled in the movie industry. He was following the convention on television from poolside, wearing a bathing suit, a sports shirt, and a narrow-brimmed straw hat. He offered no retort to Johnson's crack about the "umbrella man." This was his son's fight, he said. "He doesn't need me making wisecracks or making speeches."

And as usual his son's decision differed from his father's about a face-off with Johnson. Bouncing with enthusiasm, Kennedy entered the Crystal Ballroom with his brother Robert and a few supporters from Massachusetts. The scene evoked comparisons with the biblical parable of Daniel in the lion's den. The bareheaded Kennedy found himself surrounded by scores of Texans wearing Stetsons and "LBJ" buttons. Dozens of reporters were pressed against the walls to witness the drama.

In brief opening remarks Kennedy disarmed his rival with praise. He said he had no basic disagreement with his host over major issues. "I come here today full of admiration for Senator Johnson, full of affection for him, and strongly in support of him—for majority leader." There were warm chuckles from the Texas crowd.

Johnson followed with a long recitation of his Senate accomplishments. He hailed his attendance record during one lengthy debate that lasted six days. "Lyndon Johnson answered every one of the fifty quorum calls," he shouted. "Some men who would be President answered none."

When it was his turn to speak again, Kennedy simply grinned and congratulated Johnson for his "wonderful record answering those quorum calls." Then he shook hands with Johnson and walked out of the room.

Jack Valenti, a Houston PR agent who worked on assignment for Johnson, used a Texas idiom to describe how Kennedy's performance destroyed the last vestiges of Johnson's campaign for the nomination: "He just tore Johnson a new asshole is what he did."

Stevenson's indecisiveness as the convention began seemed to reaffirm all of the beliefs about him that swirled among members of the Kennedy team: that he was a two-time loser in presidential politics, incapable of making difficult calls; that he was the epitome of an egghead, a bloodless intellectual, complete with a bald head and a thoughtful, furrowed brow; that dealing with him was, as Robert Kennedy so cruelly put it, like trying to do business with an "old woman." When approached by emissaries from Kennedy asking him to return a favor from 1956 and make a nominating speech for the leading candidate, Stevenson said he must remain neutral.

Even Stevenson's closest supporters grew exasperated over his failure to act. He flatly refused to issue a call to arms, even when his diehard followers begged him to seize the moment, to declare himself a candidate, to draw energy from their passion and lead them in storming the convention.

Stevenson too had arrived in Los Angeles on Saturday, two days before the convention, enjoying a rapturous greeting of several thousand and encouraged by endorsements from such liberal newspapers as *Newsday* and the *New York Post*. That night he attended a glittering reception in Pasadena hosted by Agnes Meyer, a stalwart supporter in a circle of prominent Democratic women that included Eleanor Roosevelt. The wife of financier Eugene Meyer, who had bought the *Washington Post* in the 1930s and saved it from bankruptcy, Agnes was the quintessential model of a Stevenson loyalist. A graduate of Barnard College and the Sorbonne, she was wealthy, seventy-three years old, and one of Stevenson's greatest patrons. She adored his eloquence and his elegance. Her letters to him began with the words "Adlai, My Hero." At the party she and others urged him to move quickly, for time was running out. In less than forty-eight hours the convention would open, and the final weekend was to be filled with private, frenzied deal-making amid the usual round of social events.

While Stevenson was being feted in Pasadena, there was a celebrity-studded dinner party for Kennedy at the Hollywood home of his sister Pat and her husband, Peter Lawford. Bill Blair, torn between his affection for Stevenson and his link to the Kennedy effort, accepted an invitation to attend. Kennedy greeted him warmly, but Blair encountered a different mood when he approached Joe Kennedy. The patriarch stared coldly at him, clenched his fist, and snarled of Stevenson, "Your man must be out of his mind."

The next day Stevenson met with several Democratic movers and shakers at his bungalow at the Beverly Hills Hotel. Phil Graham, now the publisher of the *Washington Post*, and his wife, Katherine, the daughter of Agnes Meyer, suggested that he place Kennedy's name in nomination rather than suffer the humiliation of an ignominious defeat in an attempt to be drafted as the nominee. Stevenson held a separate meeting with several of his friends and advisors, including Mike Monroney, a respected senator from Oklahoma who had become the public voice of the "Draft Stevenson" movement, and Stevenson's long-time associate, John Sharon. They urged the two-time nominee to get to work without delay, to become an active candidate, to speak at delegate caucuses and seek support from wavering party leaders.

But Newton Minow, another of Stevenson's associates from his law firm, managed to pull his friend into a bathroom for privacy. "Governor," Minow said, "you can listen to what you hear from those people or to me. Illinois is caucusing in fifteen minutes and it's almost one hundred percent for Kennedy."

Stevenson's eyebrows arched. "Really?"

"Really," Minow replied. He recommended that Stevenson "come out for Kennedy, be identified with his nomination, and unite the party."

"I know you're right," Stevenson said. "But what can I do with people like Mrs. Roosevelt? Kick them in the ass?"

"You're getting kicked in the ass this way," Minow told him. If Stevenson did not believe him, Minow said, he should talk with some of the power brokers "whose judgment you respect," such as David Lawrence and the leaders of Stevenson's own Illinois delegation.

That afternoon the Illinois group met in caucus. Mayor Daley announced that Kennedy would get at least 59 of the state's 69 votes on the first ballot. At 2 a.m. Stevenson met with Lawrence, who forecast an overwhelming vote for Kennedy in his Pennsylvania delegation. Lawrence suggested that Stevenson give up any dreams of being drafted and nominate Kennedy.

Stevenson did nothing, so his supporters escalated their efforts. During opening ceremonies in the Los Angeles Sports Arena, a basketball facility used by the Lakers and the University of Southern California and a short walk from the yawning LA Coliseum, the site of the 1932 Olympics, Stevensonites displayed banners and chanted, "Win with Stevenson!" Outside hundreds of others sent up a clamor for him.

Throughout the day Stevenson sifted through a sheaf of handwritten notes from his conversations with key players at the convention. Humphrey, reluctant to leave the scene without making an impression, had told him "Make up your own mind" and remember there were forces who "won't go to Jack."

Much of Stevenson's hope sprang from California. The delegation was still split, and Governor Pat Brown had assured Stevenson that he was still their "first love." But Brown acknowledged that he was "obligated" to support Kennedy, "who could have beaten me badly and ruined my career" had he entered the California primary.

Inspired by the enthusiasm of his followers, Stevenson decided to go
to the convention hall Tuesday night to sit with the Illinois delegation, a
departure from tradition, which holds that candidates do not appear before balloting. He was still an undeclared candidate, but he was greeted
like a conquering general by hundreds of his supporters who had packed
the galleries, triggering a floor demonstration that disrupted the convention program. There was a move to bring him to the podium to address
the crowd crying for him. It was an electric moment, but instead of a gallant speech Stevenson delivered a lame joke: "After going back and forth
through the Biltmore today, I know who's going to be the nominee of this
convention—the last man to survive."

Norman Mailer, writing the first of his political essays for *Esquire*,
described the reaction: "The applause as he left the platform was like the
dying fall-and-moan of a baseball crowd when a home run curves foul."

Agnes Meyer was not so lyrical when she was asked about Stevenson's appearance. "Mrs. Roosevelt and I sat there. . . . We had worked so
hard for the demonstration. We had the applause there. But then he went
up on the platform and throws it out the window. He could have swept
that convention. I could have murdered him. He should have told us he
wouldn't fight."

By the third and decisive day of the convention Stevenson still had
not made up his mind. Humphrey took matters into his own hands and
announced that he would support Stevenson. The Minnesota senator did
not have much clout left, but he went to work on people from his Upper
Plains region, members of the North Dakota delegation. The state had
11 votes, and the delegates were bound by the unit rule. Kennedy was believed to have 6 votes inside the delegation, but one person was teetering.
"Humphrey was trying to get the one delegate to flip, which could give
the delegation to Stevenson," reported Bob Wallace, the Kennedy liaison
responsible for tracking the state. As strategists weighed the coming vote
count, even North Dakota's meager 11 votes were considered critical to
the effort to block Kennedy from a first-ballot victory. So could the vote

of one delegate from North Dakota. In the end, Wallace said, "the guy was for Humphrey, but he stuck with us. We had to work on him."

While Humphrey was unsuccessful in North Dakota, Stevenson had no luck changing the verdict in his own home state. He attempted to reach Richard Daley by phone, but Daley did not return his calls. So Stevenson found Jake Arvey, the state party chairman, who interceded on his behalf and persuaded Daley to call Stevenson from his post on the convention floor at the head of his delegation. Daley's tone was abrupt. He told the former Illinois governor that he had no support among the state's delegates. He added that Stevenson had kissed goodbye any hope of votes when he said earlier that he would not be a candidate. For good measure the Chicago mayor reminded Stevenson that he had few friends in the rough-and-tumble delegation dominated by his machine in 1956, but Daley had delivered votes for him anyway. This time he had no intention of doing so.

The "Draft Stevenson" movement was doomed, but that did not stop his supporters from turning its death throes into a final, romantic ending. As nominating speeches droned, floodlights washed over Mrs. Roosevelt as she entered the convention hall. She sat in the balcony with hundreds of Stevenson backers who had infiltrated the hall when allies sneaked entry badges to those without tickets. Authorities had to reinforce police guards to keep others from crashing the gates. Senator Eugene McCarthy, used before as a needle to try to puncture Kennedy balloons, was chosen to nominate the reluctant candidate. McCarthy's speech was an unforgettable political eulogy for the man who had led the Democratic ticket in 1952 and 1956. "Do not reject this man," McCarthy thundered. "Do not reject this man who has made us all proud to be Democrats! Do not leave this prophet without honor in his own party!"

Stevenson's partisans in the galleries stamped and screamed and set off a spectator blitz that veteran reporters compared to the pandemonium of the Republican convention in 1940, sending its nomination to a dark horse, Wendell Willkie. Attempts to control the Stevenson demonstration failed, and for more than thirty minutes the convention hall trembled with noise. Finally it subsided, and so did the surge for Stevenson.

Kennedy's staff let the Stevenson hoopla pass, noticing that hardly any of the people whooping on the floor were actually delegates. The work of Kennedy's team had been quieter and more effective. They had been firming up their delegate majority all week, meeting with delegates from the major states while at the same time monitoring early convention skirmishes over procedure.

With the format, schedule, and rules set in stone, the first genuine challenge at the convention itself involved acceptance of the Democratic Party Platform—a test on Day 2 of Kennedy's ability to control events on the floor. The outcome had been what in politics and bridge is called a lie-down, and it firmly established Kennedy as not only a true Democrat but a liberal one.

In 1960 no issue at the Democratic gathering mattered more, substantively and politically, than civil rights. Under the strong influence of Kennedy (his long efforts to woo southern Democrats and his temporizing on civil rights before 1960 now barely remembered), party officials had for months prepared to issue the most sweeping statement in support of efforts to end Jim Crow that their party had ever considered. Its language was nearly indistinguishable from the most pressing demands of the growing civil rights movement. The political task—of concern to Kennedy himself—was to adopt the platform without provoking a walkout of southern delegates like the one that helped make Truman's election so difficult in 1948.

Platforms could be tricky because they had to be prepared before it was completely clear who the presidential nominee was going to be. Early in 1960 the Democratic national chairman Paul Butler risked trouble by naming as the Platform Committee chairman a prominent Kennedy supporter, Chester Bowles of Connecticut. As it turned out, Butler was lucky in avoiding conflict because the party was not deeply divided ideologically except on civil rights, and Bowles was an acceptable figure. A former governor and a diplomat from the Truman days, Bowles was now a congressman who had been a fixture at Democratic conventions since 1940. It helped that he was known for his ardent support of Stevenson in 1952 and 1956, as well as for his close ties to Humphrey.

But he had expressed agreement with Kennedy's controversial call

for Algerian independence in 1957, and after weeks of wooing by Sorensen, Bowles had publicly come aboard the Kennedy campaign in the
fall of 1959 with the imposing title of chief foreign policy advisor. He
was, however, comfortable with the fact the title was a sham; he said
he never served a day in anything close to that role. What he actually
gave the campaign was a significant name, being the first of the major
Stevenson liberals to publicly support Kennedy at a time when the Massachusetts senator was laboring to establish his liberal credentials before
a suspicious wing of the party.

Kennedy made sure Bowles was surrounded by loyalists. The Platform Committee's staff director was Kennedy's friend, Professor Abraham Chayes of Harvard Law School, and the all-important civil rights
plank was to be drafted by Kennedy's recent hire, Harris Wofford, a
young lawyer with background on the staff of the U.S. Commission on
Civil Rights and one of the earliest white supporters of the movement in
the South who was close to Martin Luther King.

The language could not have been tougher. On his brother's behalf,
Robert Kennedy regularly issued instructions that the plank was not to
be weakened. Kennedy still had miles to travel in the evolution of his
civil rights commitment, but the platform represented his biggest step
yet away from his political pursuit of southerners, whose ranks included
many segregationists. Kennedy's forays into Dixie had troubled many
liberals. Now he was clearly content to let Johnson sweep the region at
the convention; indeed the commitment to allow the South to stand with
him for the nomination was one major reason there was no serious attempt to foment a 1948-style walkout in 1960.

The civil rights plank's sweeping vision was the elimination of all
forms of discrimination based on race, religion, or national origin. The
specifics included a revival of Title III of the 1957 law, which would have
authorized the attorney general to intervene in any court, civil or criminal,
to halt any discriminatory practices, including suppression of voting rights.
On school desegregation, which had proceeded at a snail's pace in the six
years since the historic ruling in *Brown v. Board of Education*, the platform
pledged the next administration to demand basic plans for compliance
from every district in the country affected by that Supreme Court decision.

On jobs, the plank supported the creation of a Fair Employment Practices Commission to combat job discrimination in the private as well as public sectors. It also supported making permanent the new, investigative Civil Rights Commission.

For the first time the party went on record to pledge repeal of the odious, racialist quota system that had been established nearly forty years before to restrict immigration with rules that were overwhelmingly in favor of white, Northern Europeans.

And for good measure, in a symbolic gesture important to the civil rights movement's leaders, the platform endorsed the sit-in demonstrations that had been occurring in many southern cities to protest segregation in public accommodations, calling the tactic "a signal to all of us to make good at long last the guarantees of our Constitution."

The line could not have been more clearly drawn. As expected, delegates from the Deep South cried foul, but there was no move to leave the convention. A series of amendments inside Bowles's 108-member committee had all failed; on each objection raised by the opposition, the pro–civil rights delegates—with Kennedy's troops in the vanguard—mustered 66 no votes in a sign of discipline supervised by Robert Kennedy.

As the platform was shipped off to the floor, nine states signed what they called a statement of "repudiation": Alabama, Florida, Georgia, Mississippi, Louisiana, Arkansas, South Carolina, North Carolina, and Virginia. Interestingly, neither Tennessee nor Johnson's Texas joined them.

On the floor the drama came during the presentation of the minority report, when the southern states had their opportunity to object to the civil rights plank before the platform prepared by Bowles's committee was approved by voice vote. In the process the delegates and a national television audience got close looks at the faces of Jim Crow and the unyielding supporters of "the southern way of life."

The minority report was presented by the chairman of the Georgia Democratic Party, James H. Gray. Through marriage Gray owned a newspaper and television station in the southwestern Georgia city of Albany and was one of segregation's most skillful defenders and publicists.

But it was jarring to listen to Gray make the case against the civil rights movement, since he did so in a distinct Massachusetts accent. He had been brought up in the western part of Kennedy's state and was a Dartmouth College graduate. Even odder, Gray was something of a Kennedy friend and the personification of the white southern element Kennedy had courted during his efforts to win support in the region. Gray had struck up a casual friendship with Kennedy's older brother, Joe, in college and made Jack's acquaintance after the war. In fact he had arranged speaking engagements for Kennedy in the state, and in 1958 had hosted him and his wife over a weekend in Albany.

The following year Gray had been part of a group that included Georgia's newly elected governor, Ernest Vandiver—whose wife was Georgia senator Richard Russell's niece—that negotiated with Robert Kennedy privately on civil rights as a prelude to their possible support of Kennedy's nomination. The effort was thwarted by Russell, Johnson's close friend, and the other Georgia senator, Herman Talmadge, when it became clear Johnson wanted the nomination. The Georgians had therefore come to Los Angeles in support of Johnson, and Gray served as the exponent of their losing cause as he invoked "states' rights" and inveighed against "radicals" in his speech.

Following the perfunctory rejection of the southerners' position the picture got uglier. All year there had been a quiet movement among segregationist politicians in the South. This year they did not plan walkouts from the Democratic or Republican conventions. Instead they plotted to put together slates of "independent" candidates for the Electoral College in the fall. The idea depended on a deadlock in the election that would throw the presidential decision into the House of Representatives, where each state had one vote. In that situation a southern bloc might hold the balance of power.

One of the people in this effort, the new Mississippi governor, Ross Barnett, rose as a symbol of resistance. He was a bumbling segregationist from the old school, malleable in the hands of an organization of wily and bitter-end racists in Mississippi who ensured his election. In a voice dripping with the Leake County molasses of his homeland, he often warned his constituents to guard against the activities of "niggers" and "communists." After seeing Kennedy pass through the Biltmore, Barnett, who wore a fedora everywhere, had another observation: "That young fellow will never get far; he doesn't wear a hat."

To launch Barnett's symbolic stand as a favorite son of Mississippi and a leader of the unpledged electors campaign, the segregationists chose a man well known to both white supremacists and civil rights watchdogs to deliver the last nomination speech of the night. Thomas Pickens Brady (he pronounced his last name with a soft *a*) was one of the founders of the White Citizens Council movement in Mississippi, a resistance organization spreading its tentacles through the South. On the surface its members were respectable business and civic leaders, judges and public officeholders. But many had relationships in the darker and violent world of the Ku Klux Klan; in fact their few detractors in the South referred to the Citizens Council as the "button-down-collar Klan."

Born to money, Brady was a preppie (Lawrenceville Academy) and a Yale man. He was also an avowed racist. In 1955 he had written a popular booklet entitled *Black Monday*, published by the Citizens Council. Its title referred to the day the Supreme Court handed down its school desegregation decision. In Brady's worldview "the loveliest and the purest of God's creatures, the nearest thing to an angelic being that treads this terrestrial ball is a well-bred, cultured, southern white woman and her blue-eyed, golden-haired little girl." He had a lesser opinion of African Americans: "You can dress a chimpanzee, housebreak him and teach him to use a knife and fork but it will take countless generations of evolutionary development, if ever, before you can convince him that a caterpillar or a cockroach is not a delicacy."

Taking the spotlight to propose Barnett for president, Brady denounced the civil rights plank as "communist inspired." Most of the delegates on the convention floor booed lustily. The Kennedy organization, eager to make their man's nomination a reality, let this revealing sideshow pass.

In the final hours before the balloting, Kennedy's major concern was the clock more than the vote. His confidence about the roll call was solid, but he worried that any delays might allow last-minute maneuvers and she-nanigans by his opponents. That required good relations with the convention's chairman so that his gavel could help Kennedy formally record his majority as quickly as possible on a first ballot on Wednesday night, immediately following the last nominating oration.

Kennedy had for weeks assiduously courted the convention chairman, Governor LeRoy Collins of Florida. Sam Rayburn, who had often wielded the gavel in the past, could not do so this time because of his support for Johnson. Kennedy's initial concern involved how Collins would handle switches of state delegation votes following roll calls—a sign of the lingering memories among Kennedy strategists of the convention voting in 1956, when Kefauver-friendly states were recognized to blunt Kennedy's momentum at a critical moment. Collins assured Kennedy that he would recognize any switching delegations in alphabetical order. Johnson's allies made one attempt early in the convention week to get the rules changed, basically to prevent favorite sons from withdrawing in favor of one of the declared candidates until after the first ballot. Their objective would have denied Kennedy votes from friends like Florida's favorite son George Smathers and Iowa's Herschel Loveless in an effort to keep his vote count below the necessary 761. But the Johnson move was soundly defeated, an early clue that Kennedy had command of the floor.

On the evening of the nomination Collins learned that the anti-Kennedy forces wanted to delay the roll call as long as possible, preferably to the next day. The Kennedy camp wanted it to come immediately after the speeches. Collins told both sides there would be just one roll call after the speeches if it was not at "an unreasonable hour." To make sure all was on track, Kennedy himself called Collins at the podium while the speeches were droning on.

With the first ballot only minutes away, the Kennedy confidence at last became visible. On the floor, tally sheets with the names of the states and territories, with numbers next to them, began to appear in the hands of top Kennedy aides and friends. In the Massachusetts delegation Sam Beer, the national chairman of the liberal Americans for Democratic Action, was standing next to Ken O'Donnell, who pulled out one of the tally sheets. Beer watched in awe. As each state's name was called, O'Donnell

called out the number of Kennedy votes just before the totals were announced. He hit the mark on all of them, with the exception of the still-
chaotic California delegation.

From his own post on the floor Robert Kennedy had a final order; it
was for his brother Ted. As the campaign's western states director, Ted
was dispatched to the Wyoming delegation to make one last deal. Sensing from his own intelligence that a first-ballot win could come from
this delegation, Robert wanted a firm commitment. If Wyoming could
have the distinction of putting Kennedy over the top, would the delegation be willing to provide the votes? At that point the Kennedy count
had him with 10½ of the delegation's 15 votes. Ted joined the delegation
on the floor and, in a loud voice so all could hear him, asked them to
pledge a unanimous vote. His main target was the delegation's leader,
Tracy McCracken, a Johnson supporter. McCracken felt Kennedy's calculation was unrealistic, so he quickly said yes, never believing he would
be forced to honor his promise.

In the hubbub on the floor, Robert Kennedy had to dispose of a last-
minute ploy by the Tammany Hall leader Carmine DeSapio, who made
a bizarre request. If Kennedy would release 30 delegates committed to
him on the first ballot, DeSapio promised to return them during a second
ballot. The Kennedys never trusted the Tammany gang. To Robert this
offer was proof that DeSapio as well as his close associate, state party
chairman Michael Prendergast, had been closet Johnson supporters all
along. His response bordered on the contemptuous: "To Hell with that.
We're going to win on the first ballot."

At last there was nothing left to do, and the roll call began.

It followed the pattern the Kennedy campaign expected. The South
generally sided with Johnson, but the Northern giants of New York,
Pennsylvania, Illinois, and Michigan were firm in their commitment to
Kennedy. California's vote splintered, yet Kennedy's early stealthy work
paid off in states such as Arizona, Nebraska, and North Dakota. By
the time the roll call came to Wyoming, with its 15 votes, Kennedy was
within 12 of the nomination.

That prospect had triggered the deal with Ted Kennedy, and Tracy McCracken never hesitated in keeping his word. With no dissent he cast all the votes for Kennedy, to give him 765, enough for the nomination.

After nearly five years in pursuit of national office, Kennedy's victory reminded Sorensen of his boss's summary of the road ahead when the campaign was in its organizational infancy at the beginning of 1959: "New England, plus the primaries, plus the big Northern states, plus half the west and scattered other votes to make up for a near shutout in the south."

That was basically what happened.

CHAPTER EIGHTEEN

Choosing LBJ

O n his way to the Democratic convention, Kennedy fully expected to ask Symington to be his running mate, and he had a solid basis for believing that Symington would accept the offer.

He had equally strong, and wrong, feelings about Johnson, still his opponent for the presidential nomination. He summed them up on the commercial flight he took to Los Angeles with an entourage of top aides and a handful of friends and favored writers. One of them, who sat next to him for part of the trip, was Tony Bradlee, Ben Bradlee's wife, who had some questions from her *Newsweek* workhorse husband to ask if she got the chance. At the time Kennedy was in a no-talking mode on doctor's orders to conserve his voice. In response to her question about Johnson for vice president, he scribbled a curt reply: "He'll never take it."

After arriving at the convention, Kennedy's thoughts about selecting Symington grew stronger, until he was actually the nominee, when everything went haywire.

Kennedy basically bungled the process of choosing his running mate. He operated dogmatically on the faulty assumption that Johnson would never accept an offer from him, neglecting numerous hints to the contrary. And when his assumption proved dead wrong, he failed to execute his ultimate decision after hasty consideration—alone—with his brother Robert. There was considerable vacillation because Kennedy did

258 THOMAS OLIPHANT AND CURTIS WILKIE

not want to run with Johnson. It was both an ironic and a tragic set of calculations—ironic because, as Robert much later acknowledged, the election could not have been won without Johnson, and tragic because of the longer-run consequences in places named Dallas and Vietnam and, later, for Robert, in Los Angeles.

Even before his trip to the convention, Kennedy had heard fresh suggestions about Johnson's value. Just a couple of weeks earlier, feeling secure that the votes for the nomination were in hand, Jack and Robert invited one-page memoranda from senior people in the campaign listing their recommendations for a running mate. Sorensen's memo survives; at the top of the list he wrote, "Johnson—helps with farmers, Southerners and Texas." Sorensen also added a shrewd observation: "Easier to work with in this position than as Majority Leader."

But Symington, uppermost in Kennedy's mind on the plane to LA, seemed perfect national ticket material: good looks and distinguished carriage, a full head of gray hair and a sonorous, senatorial voice. Hollywood would have had no trouble loving him for either of the top roles. And nobody disliked him intensely. He was attached to no controversial position or cause and came from a genuine swing state with more than its share of farmers the Democrats needed to win.

On top of that Symington's résumé was excellent and his record in government outstanding. He was extremely wealthy from a family electronics business he had shepherded, and he won high marks as the country's first secretary of the air force after the cold war reorganization of the military in the 1940s. He had warned of Soviet gains in nuclear armaments long before Kennedy discovered a "missile gap." While he was not known for any important legislation, he had famously stood up to Joe McCarthy—so vigorously in fact that McCarthy sarcastically referred to him as "Sanctimonious Stu."

Symington's presidential campaign had not been hopeless; he was considered a credible candidate. But even as he traveled the country extensively in 1959, he was realistic enough to see that Kennedy had moved ahead too far, too quickly, to make competition in the primaries a plausible option. His fallback position was to become a respectable compromise choice in a brokered convention.

As the summer and its convention date approached, Symington realized that obtaining a presidential nomination by any means seemed
out of his reach, and at Kennedy's initiative he began to think about the
second place on the ticket. At the end of May one of his top advisors—
none other than the Washington attorney, Missouri native, Truman
confidante, and occasional Kennedy family lawyer Clark Clifford—was
summoned to Kennedy's home on N Street in Georgetown for lunch and
a long talk. Up to that point no other possibility for the second spot had
received that kind of personal attention from Kennedy himself.

According to Clifford, Kennedy wanted to be certain that Symington was "available" before proceeding further. The two men chose their
words carefully, but there was no question about Kennedy's interest. Before the Democrats headed west, there was a second contact from Kennedy. Clifford said that during this one Kennedy said "Sen. Symington
was his first choice as his running mate." Clifford was inclined to be suspicious, wondering how many representatives of other potential candidates had heard the same thing. Events, however, persuaded him that
Kennedy's statement was genuine.

On the night Kennedy won the nomination, Clifford spent hours
with Symington, his wife, their two sons, Stuart Jr. and James, and their
wives in the living room of the senator's suite at the Biltmore to discuss
the pros and cons of a possible offer from Kennedy.

The Symington sons had spent much of the past year traveling in
support of their father's presidential quest, and they discovered, in state
after state, that the Kennedy family had been there ahead of them. Fifty-
six years later Stuart Symington Jr. recalled his missions in the western
states. He found repeatedly that Ted Kennedy had already been there,
expressing interest in cattle operations and establishing affinity with the
people in places like Wyoming and New Mexico. The Symingtons were
at peace with Jack Kennedy's victory. It had been well-earned.

Clifford and the six Symingtons talked far into the night. In a separate interview Jim Symington remembered that he and his brother discouraged their father. "We told him, 'You don't want to go and carry
another guy's water for him. Go back to the Senate where you can make
a difference.' He said, 'Thanks, boys.'"

Clifford was ultimately persuasive in convincing Symington to give his assent to second place on the Democratic ticket on the grounds that he could do more for Missouri as vice president than as senator.

They all went to bed waiting for word from Kennedy.

At the top of the Kennedy high command, a similar belief prevailed about Symington's imminent selection. According to Dick Donahue, who spent time with Larry O'Brien and Ken O'Donnell after a brief period of celebration, "We were satisfied it was Stuart Symington. You know, that was it, and there wasn't any doubt about it."

The choice of Symington had actually leaked into public print hours before Kennedy won the nomination. Both Charles Bartlett and John Seigenthaler filed stories for Wednesday citing unnamed sources who confirmed Symington's selection. (Jack and Robert Kennedy were later identified, respectively, as the unnamed sources.) Then all hell broke loose.

The triggering event was a telegram from Johnson after the balloting. He had watched the vote on television in his pajamas with a scotch in hand in his Biltmore suite two floors down from Kennedy's quarters. The instant Kennedy clinched the nomination, Johnson had summoned his aides George Reedy and Horace Busby, ordered the telegram, and approved the draft. Then he went to sleep. The telegram was given to Kennedy after he retired to the apartment he was using in Los Angeles, far removed from the madness at the Biltmore. Johnson's message was warm, full of praise and full of pledges to do all he could to help defeat Nixon. One of its particularly notable lines, which Kennedy read to Dave Powers over a quick, late meal, gushed, "LBJ now means Let's Back Jack."

Until that week Kennedy had never wavered in his certainty that Johnson would not accept an invitation to join him on the ticket, even though he had often voiced the opinion that no other person was better qualified by skill and record. Had he paid more attention to clear hints that Johnson might say yes, he would have been much better prepared to think through the infinitely more important question of whether he *should* make the offer. And there was a further complication: Kennedy did not want to offer Johnson—or anyone—the spot and have him refuse it.

If Kennedy's associates had stayed in closer touch with their counterparts in the Johnson camp that year, they would have picked up more than a few suggestions about his availability. He had asked his staff to research how many vice presidents had become presidents (ten at that point) and how many of the thirty-four presidents had died in office (seven). In June Sorensen was having a bite to eat in the Senate cafeteria with Johnson's confidante, Secretary of the Senate Bobby Baker. When Sorensen mentioned Kennedy's belief that Johnson was unavailable, Baker told him he shouldn't be so certain. Following a dinner party at Joe Alsop's house also in June, Baker pulled Sorensen aside and told him Johnson was "coming around" to accepting the vice presidential nomination if his efforts for the top spot failed, which Sorensen interpreted as a message from Johnson himself. Kennedy was also urged by friends in the news business—notably *Washington Post* publisher Phil Graham, who had a close friendship with Johnson, and Alsop—to test his assumption about Johnson's availability. They believed Kennedy was misinformed.

In June, David Lawrence and a big-time Democratic contributor, businessman Matt McCloskey, met with the two powerful Texans Rayburn and Johnson. When McCloskey, a Kennedy supporter for the nomination, began arguing the merits of a Kennedy-Johnson ticket, Rayburn started to rebuke him, but Johnson interrupted. "Now wait a minute, Sam," Johnson said. "I don't want these boys to go out of here and not know where I stand. First of all, I am a Democrat and I am going to do anything my party wants me to." Lawrence told Kennedy about this conversation at the convention and personally assured him that Johnson would accept the nomination if offered.

Long before his campaign was drawn into combat with Johnson, Kennedy saw the danger of a destructive confrontation and made a peace overture to Johnson's chief Texas ally as early as January. He asked Tip O'Neill to assure Rayburn that they shared the same basic political ideologies and a desire for a Democratic victory. O'Neill was the perfect inter-mediary. He was finishing his fourth term in Congress and had already been invited into the speaker's inner circle as a member of the important Rules Committee. He sat in Kennedy's old seat, moving into it after Kennedy's election to the Senate in 1952. Before that O'Neill had been the first Democratic speaker of the Massachusetts House. Though he had not been allied with Kennedy when he first ran for Congress, in 1946, he had steadily grown closer to the rising politician from his district. The respect, trust, and affection was mutual.

Kennedy sensed Rayburn disliked him, and he feared the speaker would have an influential role if he were chairman of the coming convention, where he could dictate parliamentary judgments that might undercut Kennedy moves on the floor. He believed Rayburn had been behind arbitrary decisions from the podium at the 1956 convention that cost Kennedy momentum and thus his bid to get on the ticket.

Now Kennedy instructed O'Neill on dealing with Rayburn: "I want you to butter him up, win him if you can. Tell him I'm a decent fellow. Tell him I'm a Democrat at heart. Tell him that I'll follow the same philosophies that he believes in, and that I'm a fellow who can be trusted."

Over the course of the 1960 congressional session, O'Neill saw Rayburn regularly. The pair were early risers and often found themselves alone in the Speaker's Lobby in the Capitol, reading the morning newspapers from Boston and Texas. At seventy-eight Rayburn lived alone and never spoke of his brief marriage, which had ended in divorce more than three decades earlier. His waking hours were consumed by his keen interest in Texas politics and his job in the House, where he had been the Democratic leader since 1940. He was a diminutive, balding man. His manner was taciturn. From his outward appearance a stranger would never know he was capable of such power. But he held the House in a tight grip. O'Neill, on the other hand, had an engaging personality, full of Boston bluff, and he would occasionally insert fond references to Kennedy in their conversations. Rayburn would respond with gruff grunts.

One morning O'Neill posed a question. "Mr. Speaker, supposing a candidate throws his hat into the ring, and he can't win the nomination, but the convention wants him for the second spot. What do you think?"

Rayburn said the candidate would be obligated to follow the desires of the convention and accept.

When O'Neill reported the conversation, Kennedy said, "That's interesting. He thinks Johnson's going to win and he wants me for vice president."

Months later, at the convention, O'Neill wound up playing a critical role as a messenger between Kennedy and Rayburn.

On Tuesday, the second day of the convention, he was involved in a discussion with key members of the congressional Boston-Austin axis: Rayburn, House Majority Leader John McCormack of Boston, and Wright Patman, another influential congressman from Texas. They talked of Kennedy's strength in the first ballot, which would come the next night. Rayburn conceded that Kennedy had the votes. "Lyndon didn't get started early enough," he said. "They underestimated this young fellow."

McCormack asked, "Would Lyndon take the vice presidency?"

Rayburn repeated a belief he had shared earlier in Washington with O'Neill: "Once Lyndon goes into the convention and he throws his hat into the ring, he has an obligation." Patman added that no one in the history of the Democratic Party had scorned the mantle of the vice presidency.

"If John Kennedy wins the nomination," Rayburn said, "I'll do everything in my power to make Lyndon Johnson take the [vice presidential] nomination—if Kennedy wants Johnson." He turned to McCormack and added, "If Kennedy wants Johnson for the vice presidency, get in touch with me."

McCormack, the No. 2 man in the House, had a checkered relationship with Kennedy throughout their years together in Massachusetts politics. So he delegated the assignment to O'Neill: "Tom, there's a chore for you. You find Kennedy. Tell Kennedy that if he's interested in Johnson, then Speaker Rayburn will arrange it."

Rayburn gave O'Neill his hotel room number as well as a telephone number where he could be reached. "Jack won't have any difficulty locating me anyway," he pointed out.

But O'Neill had difficulty locating Kennedy. With the convention in recess for the night, he went from one cocktail party to another, trying to find the candidate. At midnight he intercepted Kennedy at a reception run by the Steelworkers union at Chasen's, a popular hangout in West Hollywood for entertainment figures. Breathlessly he told Kennedy, "I've got to talk to you for a minute." He said Rayburn could arrange a Johnson connection.

Kennedy was interested. He told O'Neill, "Lookit! Go out and stand by my automobile. I want to hear this conversation from start to finish."

Pushing away a crowd of party-going delegates, police formed a cordon in the street to provide privacy for the two men. After hearing O'Neill's account, Kennedy said of Johnson, "I want him badly. With him we can carry Texas. We may be able to break the South."

At the convention the next day, with Kennedy's nomination at hand, O'Neill told the speaker he had delivered the message and that Kennedy would be calling him.

Here the history of Johnson's selection as Kennedy's running mate gets shrouded by conflicting accounts from various sources involved in the drama that would take place over the fifteen or so hours between the time Kennedy got Johnson's telegram and his announcement on Thursday afternoon that he would name Johnson. The accounts offered by the Kennedys and members of the Johnson camp are examples of the distrust, deceit, and deviousness practiced by both sides. They said different things to different people. But in the world of Boston and Texas politics, duplicity was never considered a mortal or even a venial sin.

It is conceivable that O'Neill aggrandized his part in the affair or misinterpreted what he heard, for reports persist that until the last hours Rayburn remained an opponent of Johnson's accepting a place on the ticket. Later Jack and Robert Kennedy added to the mystery in separate conservations with friends, both declaring that no one would ever really know how Johnson was chosen. The only people with direct knowledge were also the only people in a position to influence the outcome directly: Jack and Robert, and Johnson and Rayburn.

For a half-century journalists and historians have tried to reconstruct the events that took place in the Biltmore, and all versions have discrepancies. One of the most exhaustive descriptions covers forty-five pages in *The Passage of Power*, the third volume of Robert Caro's biography of Johnson. Yet from the monumental Kennedy archives there are equally credible accounts that deliver a different picture. There is a long, authoritative description of events by Robert Kennedy included in hundreds of pages of an invaluable oral history he gave with the understanding that it would be closed to the public until after his death. At the time he would have thought that would be decades away.

Some of the differing recollections are no doubt skewed by personal enmity. Robert Kennedy had a long-simmering hatred of Johnson. He called him "mean, bitter, and vicious . . . an animal in many ways." And the contempt was mutual. During the frenetic dealings over the vice presidency that day, Johnson referred to Robert as a "little shitass."

What follows is an attempt to draw upon all of the available evidence to tell the story of how Johnson was chosen. It begins in the very early hours of Thursday, with Kennedy, the nomination in hand, decompressing with Powers in his hideaway LA apartment. After reading Johnson's telegram, Kennedy tried to call him, but at 2 a.m. a drowsy aide picked up the phone and mumbled that his boss was asleep. Next, Kennedy tried to reach his own secretary, Evelyn Lincoln, who had not yet arrived back at the Biltmore. Instead he reached her husband, whom Kennedy affectionately called "Abe," to whom he dictated a short note to Johnson saying he would come by his suite at midmorning. Lincoln hand-delivered the message to the Johnson headquarters on the seventh floor.

By the time Kennedy and Powers got to Kennedy's suite on the ninth floor of the Biltmore, at around 8 a.m., Evelyn Lincoln had confirmed with Mrs. Johnson an appointment for Kennedy to meet with her husband later in the morning. Then, like a Shakespearean character introduced to complicate the plot, Robert Kennedy arrived.

From that moment through a crazed, historic day there was a flurry of hurried conversations and meetings, as well as dashes upstairs and downstairs at the Biltmore, involving a bewildering cast of important characters. On both the Kennedy and Johnson sides of this drama, senior members caught bits and pieces of what was unfolding, but timelines were not completely clear, even back then.

Among Kennedy's associates, Dave Powers, his loyal friend from Boston, picked up the first hint that Kennedy might choose Johnson. Between bites of fried eggs and toast at the apartment, Kennedy asked Powers how the southern votes had split the night before. The answer: of 409 in all, Johnson got 307 to just 13 for Kennedy.

Powers caught a second signal about six hours later, after Jack and Robert Kennedy had been alone together in one of the bedrooms at the hotel. As they emerged, he overheard Robert say to his brother, "If you're sure it's what you want to do go ahead and see him."

The third signal was revealed to press secretary Pierre Salinger. He was visiting Robert Kennedy, who was soaking in a bathtub in his hotel room after seeing his brother. Robert wanted to know the number of Electoral College votes projected for states Kennedy was certain to carry in November, and he wanted Texas's number added to the total. Salinger, who objected to Johnson, sensed the situation immediately. "You're not going to do that," he said in a remark representing a statement as well as a question.

"Yes we are," Robert replied, setting off a furious reaction by Ken O'Donnell, who was also in the suite and was "violently opposed to the idea" of Johnson on the ticket.

The fourth hint of the developing storm came in one of the meetings Kennedy had that hectic morning with the scores of people who flocked to his suite. In one gathering, almost certainly just before the nominee went to see Johnson alone, were senior labor union officials, including UAW president Walter Reuther; Arthur Goldberg, the powerful union attorney; and Reuther's right-hand man, Jack Conway. Many members of the labor movement were implacably opposed to Johnson.

According to Conway, Kennedy expressed concern about the special session of Congress that Rayburn and Johnson had scheduled for the next month. Observing that the election was probably going to be extremely close, Kennedy said he felt "obligated" to at least discuss the vice presidency with Johnson. "I don't see any reason in the world why he would want it," he added.

Conway quickly countered, "Lyndon Johnson will accept it if you offer it to him."

A final indication came that morning, supplied by another top Kennedy aide, Larry O'Brien: the separate arrivals of Symington and the young senator from Washington state, Henry "Scoop" Jackson. Besides Symington, Jackson was the only other person the Kennedy team seriously considered a possible running mate. Both had been summoned to be told that they would not be chosen.

Kennedy met privately with Symington, who was accompanied by Clark Clifford. Apologetically Kennedy told Symington he would not be picked. Symington took the news without rancor. His son Jim recalled the family had "a strange mixture of feelings—relief, and at the same time, resentment that he wasn't chosen."

Jackson would be offered the temporary chairmanship of the Democratic National Committee for the fall campaign, displacing John Bailey, who had been promised the position for months. Bailey yielded the post graciously and became DNC chairman a year later.

There is agreement that Kennedy showed up in Johnson's suite downstairs on time, that he stayed alone with the Texan for about thirty minutes, and that he told Johnson he would get back to him after more discussions. Accounts are also compatible that the vice presidency came up in the discussion and that Johnson shattered Kennedy's long-held assumption by declaring he was both available and interested. There is no question that the matter had not been resolved when Kennedy left; influential players in the party had to be contacted.

But at this point accounts and timelines diverge.

Johnson said of the meeting, "He offered me the vice presidency."

But according to Robert Kennedy, "He hadn't offered it to him at that time, he just discussed it." That is also the memory of Sorensen and of others Jack Kennedy spoke to, including Charles Bartlett. Bartlett said Kennedy told him, "I didn't offer the Vice Presidency to Lyndon; I really just held it out there." It was at that point merely a "gesture."

But the subject was now clearly on the table and had to be dealt with. According to Robert Kennedy, after his brother returned from talking with Johnson and they were alone Jack said, "You just won't believe it; he wants it." Robert recited the dialogue: "And I said, 'Oh, my God!' and he said, 'Now what do we do?' . . . We both promised each other that we'd never tell what happened."

But a few years later Robert gave a fuller version in his sealed interview, with the understanding that it had historical value. He explained that what followed for the next few hours after his brother's meeting with Johnson was "the most indecisive time we ever had. . . . That was just terrible." He insisted that Kennedy did not want Johnson. "During the whole three or four hours we just vacillated back and forth as whether we wanted him or didn't want him and finally we decided not to have him, and we came upon this idea of trying to get rid of him and it didn't work."

The real reason "that we'd try to get him out of there . . . [was] because Jack thought he would be unpleasant." There was also a question of trust. Jack's comments over the years were replete with references to Johnson's being untrustworthy. He didn't want to repeat FDR's relationship with Truman. It was only after FDR died, in the last year of World War II and just fifteen years before the 1960 convention, that Vice President Truman learned of the Manhattan Project to develop the atomic bomb. Kennedy wanted to choose someone he trusted. But he knew, based on the Electoral College numbers, he needed Johnson to win.

The plan the Kennedy brothers devised to rid themselves of Johnson would not touch on the bedrock concern of whether Johnson was suitable to serve as vice president. Robert explained, "This is what we worked out, that I'd tell him there was going to be a lot of opposition, that it was going to be unpleasant, that it was going to focus attention and we were going to have trouble with the liberals, and they were going to get up and fight it, and the President [his brother] didn't think that he wanted to go through that kind of an unpleasant fight. . . . But the President wanted to have him play an important role and he could run the party, the idea being that to run the party he could get a lot of his own people in, and then if he wanted to be President [in] eight years or something he could have the machinery where he could run for President or do whatever he wanted."

The two brothers decided that the possibility of Johnson's vice presi-

dential nomination—whether or not an actual offer had been made—
should be pulled back "if we could get him to withdraw and still be
happy."

As it happened, they couldn't.

Robert went to see Johnson in his suite at the Biltmore. "I said [to
Johnson], 'You can run the party [as chairman of the DNC],' and in my
judgment, seeing him since then he is one of the greatest sad-looking
people in the world. You know he can turn that on; I thought he burst
into tears. I mean it was my feeling at the time—although I've seen him
afterwards look so sad I don't know whether it was just an act or anything. But he just shook, and tears came into his eyes and [he] said, 'I
want to be Vice President and if the President will have me I'll join with
him in making a fight for it.'"

Realizing that Johnson could not possibly be "happy" without the
nomination, Robert said he gave up. He told Johnson, "Well, that's fine.
He wants you to be Vice President, if you want to be Vice President, we
want you to know."

By the time Robert gave this account, from a distance of several years,
he may have conflated his meeting with Johnson shortly before the official announcement of his selection with at least one earlier trudge to
Johnson's floor. In accounts from the Johnson perspective, senior Johnson
associates were present for the visits Robert made in the morning and
afternoon, as many as four that day.

There are other complications in reconciling Robert's account with
the recollections of the Johnson team. During Jack Kennedy's first meeting with Johnson no one else was in the room. Johnson maintains he told
Kennedy he could not accept the nomination unless Rayburn agreed to
it. And he warned Kennedy that Rayburn was "dead set" against it at
that moment. When Robert suggested that Johnson become chairman of
the party, Rayburn was said to have a one-word response: "Shit." Despite
what O'Neill reported, there are numerous such examples in the Johnson version of Rayburn's hostility to Kennedy and of his objections to his
protégé's joining him on the ticket.

According to Johnson's allies, after learning of Rayburn's reluctance, Kennedy asked if he could talk to the speaker and try to enlist his

support. The only record of a Kennedy-Rayburn meeting was a tape-recorded statement Rayburn gave months later to one of his aides, D. B. Hardeman, which Hardeman used in a biography of Rayburn he wrote with the writer Don Bacon. In Rayburn's words: "I told him, 'I'm dead set against this, but I've thought it over, and I'm going to tell you several things: If you tell me you have to have Lyndon on the ticket in order to win the election, and if you tell me that you'll go before the world and tell the world Lyndon Johnson is your choice, and you insist on his being the nominee and if you'll make every possible use of him in the National Security Council and every other way to keep him busy and keep him happy, then the objections that I have had, I'm willing to withdraw.' Kennedy told me: 'I tell you all these things.'"

It is not clear when Kennedy saw Rayburn or if they spoke on the telephone. It was at least an hour after the Kennedy-Johnson session at mid-morning, probably even later. The time table is tight, but it would allow for an interpretation that Kennedy retained his initial interest in Johnson and convinced Rayburn of the merits of a JFK-LBJ ticket, remembering what O'Neill had told him Tuesday night. Then, after talking at length with his brother, he changed his mind and agreed that Robert should try to nudge Johnson away from the ticket.

During the same period, at midday on Thursday, there were tales of changed minds among influential figures on the Johnson side in addition to Rayburn. Senator Bob Kerr of Oklahoma, the exemplar of Big Oil interests in the Senate, was said to have come to Johnson and playfully threatened to shoot him between the eyes if he agreed to join Kennedy, then, hours later, threatening to shoot him if he didn't go on the ticket.

What is known is that Kennedy announced his choice of Johnson at about 3:30 that afternoon. Johnson's allies claimed that Robert's last trip to their floor in a final effort to talk Johnson off the ticket actually occurred after Jack had called Johnson and read him the text of his announcement.

When it became evident that Johnson would be the choice, it set off waves of surprise and adverse reaction. Leaders of the party's liberal forces and top officials of the labor movement cried betrayal, for they had been assured repeatedly by O'Donnell—and even Kennedy himself—that Johnson would never be chosen. Even though Johnson's record reflected far more moderation than the records of the champions of segregation from the South, he was still associated with them in the minds of the left and labor.

Trouble began to surface even before Kennedy's announcement. Word that he might choose Johnson had made it to a gathering of union leaders at the nearby Statler Hilton Hotel. Robert Kennedy and O'Donnell were dispatched to soothe them. The UAW's Jack Conway advised the pair to make their points and leave quickly before getting into an argument.

George Meany, the head of the giant AFL-CIO, "went ballistic," according to Conway. He threatened a formal split between the labor movement and the Democratic Party. "Meany just ranted and raved and just cursed Kennedy. It took hours to bleed the emotion off."

Reuther, the host of the meeting at the Statler Hilton, was also critical, reflecting the frustration of a passionate liberal and a man devoted to organized labor. Stevenson had waited too long; Humphrey, loved by union members, had been unsuccessful; and now Reuther was unhappily faced with Johnson on the ticket.

Conway was more philosophical: "My reaction in these things is that it's unimportant. Once the event has taken place, what the hell, you can sit around and drink beer and talk about things like that if you want, but nothing changes. So I just, in effect, wiped it clean. . . . It was an emotional thing. It had to be bled."

The venting and emotional bleeding went on for several hours.

Alex Rose, the boss of New York's Liberal Party, talked of denying the Kennedy-Johnson entry his party's line on the ballot, a move that could jeopardize Kennedy's ability to win the state.

The Michigan delegation, stroked so successfully by Kennedy before summer began, was infuriated by Johnson's selection. Soapy Williams, the third-term governor, talked of forcing a floor fight that focused on civil rights. He was so angry that he burst into a meeting near Kennedy's headquarters at the Biltmore and nearly came to blows with some southern delegates who were elated over the news about Johnson.

Joe Rauh, the leader of Americans for Democratic Action and the face of liberal values in the party, was also beside himself with rage. A member of the District of Columbia delegation, Rauh had been alarmed by a story earlier in the week in the *Washington Post*—planted by Phil Graham—touting Johnson's selection. He sought out Robert Kennedy. "I had the best possible assurance it was not going to happen," Rauh said later, and he passed word to his fellow DC delegates that the ticket would be clean of Johnson. Now he felt he had "been made a liar."

Jack Kennedy sent O'Donnell to calm him. But O'Donnell himself was also upset. "Joe," he told Rauh, "I'm as sick about this as you are, but in the morning we'll all feel better, and we've got a job to do."

O'Donnell had already had his own argument with the man for whom he had labored over the past few years. As a senior aide he had been responsible for making many of the "No Johnson" commitments for months. After his boss's intentions emerged that morning, O'Donnell found himself somewhere between rage and apoplexy. He felt betrayed too, and it showed on his face when he spoke to Kennedy. The nominee pulled O'Donnell into a bathroom at the Biltmore suite to give his trusted aide a chance to vent, and O'Donnell lashed out.

He recalled that Kennedy defused his anger with a lecture of his own: "I'm forty-three years old, and I'm the healthiest candidate for president of the United States. You've traveled with me enough to know that I'm not going to die in office. So the Vice Presidency doesn't mean anything. I'm thinking of something else, the leadership of the Senate. If we win, it will be by a small margin and I won't be able to live with Lyndon Johnson as the leader of a small majority in the Senate. Did it occur to you that if Lyndon Johnson becomes Vice President I'll have Mike Mansfield as the leader of the Senate, somebody I can trust and depend on?"

"I began to soften and see things differently," O'Donnell admitted.

Slowly the negative intensity began to dissipate. A phone call from the meeting of labor leaders to David Dubinsky, a genuine legend in their ranks who had run the International Ladies Garment Workers Union since the Depression, sped up the healing process. The call was put on speaker phone so that Reuther and company could hear Dubinsky call Johnson's selection a "masterstroke." It would give Democrats a shot at winning Texas and the rest of the South, he said.

Reuther was moved to seek an affirmative statement from Johnson. He called Bob Oliver, a Johnson aide who dealt with the unions. Within minutes Johnson responded with the strongest statement on civil rights he had ever made, including an admiring nod to the spreading sit-in movement.

Before he was presented to the convention Johnson was introduced to several of the senior Kennedy staff members who had never met him. One was Larry O'Brien.* Not for the last time in their lives, they began talking tactics, this time for the upcoming nomination vote that evening. To avoid a floor fight on national television, they developed a plan to have convention chairman LeRoy Collins recognize one of their supporters. John McCormack, with Abraham Ribicoff serving as a backup, would move to have Johnson's nomination made unanimous by voice vote. It was pure guile and muscle—second nature to both Johnson and O'Brien—and it worked.

When the moment came, the no votes sounded as loud as the yes votes, but anyone familiar with the way a majority operated in the House of Representatives knew what would happen next. Collins announced, "The ayes have it." He banged his gavel, and it was all over.

The process may have been messy, but for the first time in American history, two sitting senators—opponents just the day before—had been nominated to be president and vice president.

Just a few hours earlier the writer Douglass Cater saw Kennedy walking alone down a corridor at the Biltmore. He asked Kennedy if he was surprised that Johnson ended up on the ticket.

"I was flabbergasted," Kennedy replied.

---

*   O'Brien was the one top Kennedy aide who lasted. He stayed on in the sensitive White House job handling relations with Congress after Kennedy's death, and Johnson later trusted him to run the Democratic National Committee. He ran the party's affairs through the 1972 campaign before going on to help create the modern National Basketball Association as its commissioner; the league's championship trophy is named for him.

CHAPTER NINETEEN

Holy War

The call for assistance, with an ego-boosting hint of history, had gone out near the end of June, reflecting the near certainty at the top of the Kennedy campaign that a first-ballot nomination was in store at the Democratic National Convention. Ted Sorensen, acting on the presumptive nominee's behalf, requested drafts of the traditional climax of the modern convention, an address accepting the presidential nomination. As the staff member who would be both the editor and the ultimate writer, Sorensen asked for no more than ten double-spaced pages. The eleven men of letters who received Sorensen's request were also invited to contribute a short summary of an overall theme for the address, with a few particularly ringing—and hopefully catchy—phrases.

What the note did not disclose was the fact that Kennedy and Sorensen had no intention of producing predictable partisan rhetoric or a checklist of major goals to generate noise from the delegates inside the tight, smoky confines of the convention arena. Instead they intended to concentrate on a theme resembling an inspiring presidential inaugural address and to avoid the trap of a State of the Union recitation of proposals that often sounded like a reading of the Yellow Pages. The message would be aimed at Americans watching on television, not an audience of politicians. It was not designed to put an exclamation point on a convention victory but to launch the general election campaign against Nixon.

Even the setting that was envisaged broke precedent. The speech would be moved from the convention hall to a much larger venue.

The professors and professional writers who received Sorensen's request were a varied lot, known for eloquence as well as erudition. From the academic community: Alan Nevins of Columbia, Walt Rostow, James MacGregor Burns, Sidney Hyman of the University of Chicago, Arthur Schlesinger Jr., Mark De Wolfe Howe of Harvard Law, and two professors from tiny Amherst College, Henry Steele Commager and Earl Latham. From the writing and journalism worlds: novelist Gore Vidal, who was a distant relative by marriage of Jackie Kennedy; *Harper's* magazine editor John Fischer; and Max Freedman, the Washington correspondent for the *Manchester Guardian* and a genuine Kennedy friend.

It turned out that the offerings from Rostow and Freedman jibed best with Kennedy's and Sorensen's lofty intentions, perhaps because both men had been more directly involved with the campaign.

Kennedy's address heralding a "New Frontier" represented the opening offensive in the general election campaign rather than a declaration of victory to claim the nomination and end the convention. His handlers, adept in stagecraft, succeeded in moving his Friday night appearance to the mammoth Los Angeles Coliseum, a short walk from the musty Sports Arena. Rather than restricting seats to delegates and party potentates, the closing ceremony offered free admission to anyone interested. More than eighty thousand came, from the city by bus, from the surrounding suburbs via freeways, creating an attendance record for an American political convention. Open to the skies as the sun went down, the event began at an odd hour to accommodate the different time zones for the rest of the country. The evening was meant to symbolize the fresh direction that Kennedy intended to take the party, demonstrating that it was time, as he said, "for a new generation of leadership."

At the beginning of the speech he hailed Johnson, his new running mate, for bringing "unity and strength to our platform and our ticket." He recognized fallen rivals and new allies Stevenson, Symington, and

Humphrey, and welcomed the support of Truman and Rayburn, aging Democratic leaders who had been suspicious of him. The language was warm, but the bow to the people whose long, often nasty objections Kennedy had overcome was perfunctory—one short paragraph.

It might have been jarring for a television audience to hear the candidate mention his religious faith. But that is what Kennedy provided next, at a time when the jury was still out on whether his Catholicism was an albatross or a spur to his election. Anticipating one of his biggest hurdles, he said simply that the question of his religion had no relevance in the coming campaign because he had long supported public education and the separation of church and state and always would. But the placement of these comments at the top of his speech was a hint that he was prepared to defend his faith and explain his political independence from it. He also took routine, partisan jabs at Vice President Nixon, his Republican opponent, as a candidate unfit to follow Eisenhower.

Kennedy's twenty-two-minute message touched on other topics he and Sorensen had developed over many months. But the speech would be remembered for Kennedy's description of a New Frontier that would become emblematic of his administration in the same way Woodrow Wilson's "New Freedom" and Franklin Roosevelt's "New Deal" symbolized theirs. Those earlier totems were built on promises, he said; in contrast, "[The] New Frontier . . . is not a set of promises. It is a set of challenges." Even more to the point, this New Frontier "sums up not what I intend to offer to the American people but what I intend to ask of them. It appeals to their pride, not to their pocketbook; it holds out the promise of more sacrifice instead of more security."

He was purposely facing west as he spoke of a "last frontier," where "the pioneers gave up their safety, their comfort and sometimes their lives to build our new West." Now the nation stood "on the edge of a New Frontier—the frontier of the 1960s, the frontier of unknown opportunities and perils, the frontier of unfilled hopes and unfilled threats." It would be a "turning point of history."

Near the close of his remarks he said, "It has been a long road from the first snowy day in New Hampshire many months ago to this crowded convention city. Now begins another long journey."

ABOVE: Joseph Kennedy sits with his up-and-coming politician son in an undated picture taken before the quest for national office began. Kennedy typically disregarded his father's usually blunt political advice. (*Getty Images/Pictorial Parade*)

RIGHT: When it all started for real, Kennedy looked more like a young first-term senator. This photograph was taken in the fall of 1955. That was when his father made his proposal to Lyndon Johnson that he run for president in 1956 with JFK as his running mate.

All photos courtesy of the John F. Kennedy Presidential Library and Museum unless otherwise noted.

In a rowdy crowd at Boston's Hotel Bradford, Kennedy woos delegates to the pivotal Democratic meeting in the spring of 1956 where his allies took control of the Massachusetts party and ousted chairman William "Onions" Burke. The tough-looking fellow behind him, probably an off-duty cop, reflects the decorum concerns on all sides that day. *(Courtesy of the* Boston Herald-Traveler*)*

For much of 1957 the country was glued to television screens to watch the hearings of the special Senate committee investigating corruption and organized crime infiltration of major labor unions, especially the teamsters. Here, John Kennedy (a member) shares a private moment with his brother Robert (the general counsel and staff director). On the left is the committee's chairman, Democrat John McClellan of Arkansas.

Jacqueline Kennedy leads a Kennedy foray into Cajun Country in the fall of 1956 at the Rice Festival in Opelousas. The man beaming, at right, is Edmund Reggie, one of JFK's key supporters in a southern state he would carry in 1960. His daughter, Victoria, would one day marry Edward M. Kennedy.

A glimpse from early 1956. To the left at this political dinner is another Catholic possibility that year, New York City mayor Robert Wagner. The man in the middle is Kennedy's friend and Harvard buddy, Massachusetts congressman Torbert Macdonald. *(Courtesy of the Boston Herald-Traveler)*

From the floor of the Democratic convention in Chicago in 1956 the base of Kennedy's last-minute scramble to become Adlai Stevenson's running mate, the Massachusetts delegation.

November 18, 1956

Dear Jack:

I should have thanked you long before
this. I can think of no one to whom we should
all be more grateful than to you. And I am
only sorry that I did not better reward you
for your gallantry in action. I have confident
hopes for your future leadership in our party,
and I am sure you will help immeasurably to keep
it pointed in a positive direction.

With my boundless gratitude, and
affectionate regards,

Cordially,

Adlai

Honorable John F. Kennedy
122 Bowdoin Street
Boston, Massachusetts

Shortly before Thanksgiving 1956, Adlai Stevenson sent this private note to Kennedy, thanking him for his campaign endeavors. JFK was already in the process of deciding to run for the presidential nomination in 1960.

This photograph is from his swamped Senate mail room in 1958 when Kennedy was running for re-election but in the second full year of his presidential activity.

This is a very rare photograph of Kennedy in the small apartment his family kept for decades on Boston's Bowdoin Street in the shadow of the State House. He and his brothers used the apartment as an address for voting purposes but never resided there. It was a hideaway and a site for meetings such as this conversation with a reporter.

The Kennedy brothers in May 1957 in their roles on the Senate committee that held televised hearings into corruption in the labor movement. Robert Kennedy ran the committee's investigative staff and John Kennedy was a member. Between them is Pierre Salinger.

In the spring of 1958, Kennedy, in shirtsleeves on the left, plots strategy on pending labor reform legislation, his most important legislative accomplishment. Ted Sorensen, left; and in the rear on the right is Arthur Goldberg, who would become Kennedy's secretary of labor.

The future of health care for the elderly is symbolized in this rare photograph from the late 1950s of Kennedy and Representative Aime Forand. The Rhode Island Democrat was the first to propose financing hospital insurance via the Social Security payroll tax. Kennedy developed the idea further in 1960 and it became Medicare in 1965.

Kennedy famously enjoyed give and take with national reporters. This photograph from 1958 shows him in a Senate corridor with a young Rowland Evans, then a correspondent for the *New York Herald Tribune*. Evans eventually formed a widely syndicated political column with Robert Novak of the *Chicago Sun-Times*.

BIG JOHN
AND
LITTLE JOHN

"BE SURE TO DO
WHAT YOUR POPPA TELLS YOU."

An example of the cartoon face of bigotry that Kennedy faced because of his faith throughout the campaign. It is one of thousands from the files of aide James Wine, a onetime National Council of Churches official who worked the issue for Kennedy.

With Kennedy a full year before the 1960 primaries is his top policy and speechwriting aide. At the time, Sorensen was twenty-nine, with six years of JFK work already under his belt.

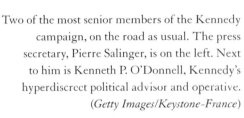

Two of the most senior members of the Kennedy campaign, on the road as usual. The press secretary, Pierre Salinger, is on the left. Next to him is Kenneth P. O'Donnell, Kennedy's hyperdiscreet political advisor and operative. (*Getty Images/Keystone-France*)

O'Donnell, shown here at left, was as close to John Kennedy as anyone in the long campaign. He traveled with him throughout 1960, performing sensitive political tasks by the bucketful. In the middle is William Green III of Philadelphia, scion of a powerful Democratic family and one of Kennedy's key converts in his march to the party's presidential nomination. The man on the right is unidentified. (*Getty Images/Charles H. Phillips*)

Within Kennedy's Irish Mafia, Lawrence F. O'Brien was the quiet, formal one, at least in private. The son of a restaurant/tavern owner in Springfield, Massachusetts, O'Brien designed and ran the elaborate organization that helped propel Kennedy to his surprise Senate victory in 1952; he replicated that operation and supervised it in 1960. (*Getty Images/John Loengard*)

Arthur Schlesinger Jr. was one of the first of the Adlai Stevenson campaign veterans to openly support Kennedy after 1956, giving him an early dose of credibility among fellow liberals who had serious reservations about the fledgling candidate. Schlesinger is shown greeting President-elect Kennedy at Harvard University. Behind Kennedy is Congressman Thomas P. O'Neill Jr. (*Getty Images/Bettmann*)

Senator George Smathers of Florida lights JFK's cigar. Smathers was a friend, occasional boon companion, and valued political supporter. In 1960, his favorite-son candidacy kept the second largest southern delegation to the Democratic convention out of Lyndon Johnson's hands.

Long before anyone else was campaigning, Kennedy was on the road working, as he is here in a 1959 journey to Oregon with Congresswoman Edith Green, a onetime Stevenson supporter and leading liberal. By locking up the state's liberals early, Kennedy was in solid position to swamp Senator Wayne Morse the following spring, making his nomination in Los Angeles a virtual certainty.

Wooing the mooing in Wisconsin. It's hardly unusual for a politician to be seen among the state's most important residents. The key point here is the date, 1959, by which time Kennedy had already made some three dozen appearances in Wisconsin, an important element in his victory over Hubert Humphrey in the pivotal primary early the following spring.

One full year before the crucial California primary Kennedy was hard at work. Shown here in May 1959 with the state's new governor, Edmund G. "Pat" Brown, Kennedy eventually made a deal to not contest Brown's favorite-son campaign. Brown agreed to support Kennedy if he won the pre-California primaries. In the end, Brown could not fully deliver.

The first big coup for Kennedy was the support from Ohio right after he formally announced in January 1960. JFK and his brother Edward flank Ohio governor Mike DiSalle in the spring of 1959, when he first committed to supporting Kennedy's candidacy.

Hardly anyone knew it, but John Kennedy had already been running for president a full six months when this photograph was taken of him being interviewed by a radio reporter in June 1957 in Columbia, South Carolina.

Ever the happy warrior, Hubert Humphrey campaigns in West Virginia against a Kennedy machine that turned out to be a juggernaut. Humphrey lost by roughly 20 percentage points. (*Getty Images/Paul Schutzer*)

In the West Virginia primary campaign, Kennedy had a special weapon—Franklin Delano Roosevelt Jr., shown here with the candidate. In the struggling state there were strong memories of the New Deal's programs and of Eleanor Roosevelt's empathy, all symbolized by the son's constant presence during the final weeks of the campaign.

On the day of the climactic West Virginia primary, campaign manager Robert Kennedy in his trademark, rolled-up white shirtsleeves takes a break from his frenetic schedule for an ice cream at a diner in the Charleston area. He had been in the state continuously since the Wisconsin primary the previous month. (*Courtesy of* Look *magazine*)

This is Ted Sorensen's one-page memorandum to JFK with his recommended options for a running mate, sent two weeks before the Democratic convention opened. Lyndon Johnson's name at the top of his list was in spite of Kennedy's conviction that LBJ would never say yes.

COPY

June 29, 1960

MEMORANDUM

To: Senator John F. Kennedy
        Robert F. Kennedy

From: Ted Sorensen

Subject: Possible Vice Presidential nominees

1. Johnson -- helps with farmers, Southerners and Texas -- easier to work with in this position than as Majority Leader.

2. Stevenson -- on the basis that he would be a sort of "first secretary".

3. Humphrey -- helps with Negroes and farmers -- his primaries' attacks on JFK may be used by the Republicans anyway.

4. Yarborough -- a Southerner liked by the liberals -- good civil rights and agriculture record -- would help carry Texas.

5. Engle -- would help carry California.

6. Symington -- a national figure -- would help with farmers.

    Should be considered, but handicapped by being young and too much like JFK (we don't want the ticket referred to as "the Whiz kids", etc.)

1. Orville Freeman -- also good on agriculture and civil rights.

2. Scoop Jackson -- has acquired stature through inquiry on national security.

3. Also doubtful: Grant Sawyer, Stewart Udall or Gaylord Nelson

    Should be considered, but likely to offend some group in the party

1. Southerners: Collins, Hodges, Gore and Smathers.

2. Hennes Williams

3. Proxmire

4. Kerr (gas and oil)

5. Anderson (suspect among the same farmers that are suspicious of JFK)

6. Governors Docking and Loveless -- both extreme conservatives, inarticulate and sometimes ill-tempered

The debate that fizzled is shown in this photograph of the encounter of Kennedy and Lyndon Johnson before the Texas delegation the day before Kennedy won the nomination. Doing his best as emcee is House Speaker and Johnson mentor and ally Sam Rayburn.

Campaigning in North Carolina late in the 1960 general election, Kennedy actually touches a baby (a rare JFK gesture) in an open car with Terry Sanford, the successful gubernatorial candidate that year. Kennedy led the Democratic ticket to victory in the state, one of six in the south he carried with Lyndon Johnson's help.

As a passionate liberal, Eleanor Roosevelt was hostile to JFK's brief vice-presidential bid in 1956. Mrs. Roosevelt felt JFK had not been there for the fights against Senator Joseph McCarthy's witch hunts. This photograph shows her during the general election in 1960, when she had warmed to Kennedy's candidacy.

Initially suspicious, even hostile, to John Kennedy, the liberal establishment is shown here hard at work on his behalf during the 1960 general election campaign. From the left, former Truman Air Force Secretary Thomas Finletter, former New York governor W. Averell Harriman, Eleanor Roosevelt, and Adlai Stevenson. (*Getty Images/Joseph Scherschel*)

Democratic presidential nominee John Kennedy schmoozes with Hubert Humphrey at a civil rights conference in New York. Standing behind them in his trademark bowtie is a leading civil rights leader, Governor G. Mennen "Soapy" Williams of Michigan.

Kennedy checks the stage at the third debate with Nixon in October of 1960 along with suits from host network ABC. On the left is John Charles Daly, the first radio network voice to report the attack on Pearl Harbor and later the host of the long-running CBS game show *What's My Line*.

This picture of the third debate captures John Kennedy at his podium in the ABC studios in New York, while Richard Nixon observes from his podium in Los Angeles. For the three other debates Kennedy and Nixon shared a stage.

Gossip and reputation aside, this is what Kennedy's support among female voters actually looked like in this photograph of a JFK event in Philadelphia down the stretch of the 1960 general election campaign.

This is the "boiler room" for the Kennedy campaign on election night, 1960. It was set up on the porch of Robert Kennedy's house in the family compound on Cape Cod. *(Courtesy of* Look *magazine)*

After the all-nighter election night in 1960, a reporter naps in the press room at the armory in Hyannis. The result had not yet been called outside of the first edition of the *New York Times*. *(Courtesy of the* New Bedford Standard-Times*)*

The car carrying Kennedy moves through the crowded streets of Hyannis on its way to the local armory where the press was waiting late on the morning of November 9, 1960. Kennedy was ready to make the transition from senator and Democratic nominee to president-elect. *(Courtesy of the* New Bedford Standard-Times*)*

The torch is minutes from passing as John Kennedy and Dwight Eisenhower leave the White House en route to the Capitol and the inauguration. (*Getty Images/Bettmann*)

To the victors go the White House spoils. This is quite likely the last picture taken of President Kennedy and his inner circle of aides, most of them campaign veterans. Taken on October 24, 1963, the president emerges from his Oval Office onto the portico, surrounded by (from left) Ken O'Donnell, Pierre Salinger, science advisor Jerome Wiesner (seated), Larry O'Brien, budget director Kermit Gordon, special counsel Lee White, Tim Reardon (the one member in this group who had been with JFK since his first Congressional campaign in 1946), White House coordinator for DC affairs Charles Horsky, early Iowa campaign organizer and then Office of Emergency Preparedness official Edward McDermott, top economics advisor Walter Heller (leaning on chair), military aide Major General Chester Clifton, Ted Sorensen, Food for Peace director Richard Reuter (he succeeded George McGovern), national security council executive secretary Bromley Smith (the lone Eisenhower holdover) and NSC advisor McGeorge Bundy. The only top people not shown were Bob Kennedy and personal aide Dave Powers. (*Getty Images/Arnold Newman*)

Actually it would be the continuation of a journey that first began in the mind of the candidate and his father five years earlier, a drive that gained legitimacy when he captured the imagination of many Democrats—if not their vice presidential nomination—exactly four years before.

The provenance of the speech is an indication of its fundamental, blended nature. The parlor game that took place afterward to link "New Frontier" to a specific source obscures the important point Kennedy was attempting to make. Beyond a call for party unity and acceptance of his religion, he had a vision of the country's future, and he wanted America, a nation in transition, to be able to identify with a young, vigorous candidate who projected strength at a time of cold war dangers.

Kennedy himself later attributed the phrase "New Frontier" to Rostow. The writer David Wise, who interviewed Kennedy about his vision, also mentioned the influence of Max Freedman, a Canadian by birth who had taken a leave from his newspaper job to work on the campaign; Freedman was in Los Angeles that convention week working on the speeches of other Democratic big shots who were addressing the convention.

According to Freedman, "New Frontier" was a last-minute answer to what had been a multiple-choice test. "You see, we'd been looking for a phrase like this—you know, the New Deal, Fair Deal, the New Freedom, the Square Deal," he recalled. "A phrase that Kennedy wanted was the 'New America,' but that had already been unfortunately chosen as the title for one of Adlai Stevenson's books of speeches, so that was out. And in sheer desperation Ted picked on this and that's how the phrase got in."

According to Sorensen, through whose typewriter all the drafts went, the origin is more fuzzy. He said "New Frontier" appeared repeatedly in various essays. He mentioned material from Alan Nevins about the "old frontier" as America migrated west in the nineteenth century, as well as Sorensen's own family's prairie roots in Nebraska. Kennedy, he said, was determined to find a memorable catchphrase. "The Senator wanted that acceptance address to include a vivid phrase that would reflect his emphasis on the tasks and challenges confronting the American people, combining the need to change with the country's unfinished agenda, while invoking the courage and achievements of the past."

There was no way a short oration could put to rest all the questions surrounding Kennedy's candidacy—his age and relative inexperience at the national level, his religion, his fitness as a cold war president. In the torrent of reactions from a skeptical political world to his convincing triumph at the convention, Kennedy was no longer portrayed as a rookie climber facing Mt. Everest, as he had been just the year before. Yet he was still widely considered an underdog against Nixon. He had just come through a bruising fight for the nomination; his next challenge was the possibility that voters would prefer the stability of an Eisenhower administration in those perilous times. But Kennedy's opponent, wearing the incumbent president's mantle, was controversial, a man who provoked strong distaste among Democrats and held uncertain standing inside the Eisenhower administration.

Nixon, who escaped the primary season without an opponent to test him, would be formally anointed at an orderly, almost placid Republican convention later that month. So the match-up was formalized, and the contest began. A helpful image of the general election campaign between these two completely different products of the Depression and World War II is of two people on an odd teeter-totter; it might move up a foot or so on one side, then move up a foot or so on the other—from start to nail-biting finish.

The rest of July and much of August belonged to Nixon. At the end of the month the first Gallup poll of the nation found Nixon slightly ahead, allowing for statistical error, by 50 to 44 percent. The Kennedy camp viewed the Gallup margin as a tad high because of the poll's closer proximity to the smooth Republican convention. But Nixon's lead was not disputed anywhere among political authorities.

Following the conventions, tradition called for the candidates of both parties to spend the rest of the summer catching their breath to be ready for the fall campaign that would begin on Labor Day. But there were unusual developments in 1960.

Congress was recalled to Washington in early August for a special session. It would be the last time Majority Leader Johnson outranked Senator Kennedy. Johnson and Rayburn had conceived of the session when Johnson still entertained dreams of the presidential nomination for himself. Perhaps, exercising his legendary powers of persuasion and intimidation, he could coerce better behavior from his famously recalcitrant, conservative fellow southerners and show how he could get things done.

But the session failed to produce any significant legislation. As a vice presidential nominee, Johnson wielded no special club in Congress, and the session was a vivid reminder that inside the congressional world even Kennedy himself had little influence. Although the two men atop the Democratic ticket supported several measures, their efforts were frustrated by an increasingly familiar combination of Republicans and conservative Democrats, most based in the South, who held seniority on almost every front. The session was dismissed after a week, and Kennedy left with a sense of disquiet over his chances in the "Solid South," a region that had proved so reliable to Democrats for decades. Most of the southern delegations had opposed the civil rights plank in the Democratic platform, and many of the southern members of Congress seemed determined to block any progressive legislation.

An example of the special session's futility involved a proposal, supported by Kennedy, to raise the minimum wage by 25 cents to $1.25 an hour. In the House the linchpin of the "deadlock" James MacGregor Burns described was its Rules Committee, which controlled the flow of legislation from other committees to the floor. The Rules Committee was dominated by conservative Republicans and Democrats from the South determined, above all else, to resist any progressive challenges. Conservatives in both parties were also pro-business and united in resistance to major domestic initiatives and economic regulation. The House Rules Committee chairman, Howard Smith of Virginia, was as well-known an obstacle as were Richard Russell and James O. Eastland in the Senate.

The minimum wage legislation never had a prayer. Some Kennedy strategists saw the behavior of Democratic leaders that month as payback for the strong civil rights plank in the convention platform. "Whatever their motive," Sorensen later wrote, "the reconvened session only embittered Kennedy.... The results offered fresh evidence of Democratic disarray in the south, where Nixon's initial forays were well-received.... The opposition of powerful southern Democratic senators and congressmen to their party's legislative program, aided by the threat of Eisenhower's veto, rendered the Democratic majorities in both houses uncomfortably impotent and encouraged Republicans to disrupt Democratic plans still further through political and parliamentary maneuvers on civil rights."

In August, with the distraction of the special session out of the way, Kennedy spent time mending fences with venerable Democratic figures who had been uneasy over his quick rise. On a bright Sunday he made a pilgrimage to Hyde Park, the home of Eleanor Roosevelt, ninety miles upstate from New York City, to take part in a ceremony honoring Franklin Roosevelt on the anniversary of the passage of the Social Security Act. More important for Kennedy, he had lunch with the late president's widow, who still commanded a following among Democratic liberals and had withheld her formal endorsement.

Kennedy brought with him William Walton, who would prove to be an exotic figure in the hurly-burly of New York politics. Walton was battle-tested as a correspondent for *Time* magazine, parachuting into Normandy with the 82nd Airborne on D-Day, and spent time after the war with the *New Republic*. But he had quit journalism to become a full-time artist, making a name for himself in the abstract-expressionist field. A Georgetown neighbor of the Kennedys, Walton worked enthusiastically as a volunteer in the primary campaign after Kennedy causally enlisted his services at a small dinner party in January to celebrate the artist's latest one-man show. Now Walton was being asked to serve as the head of Kennedy's Citizens Committee in New York that fall.

Kennedy had a private meal with Mrs. Roosevelt, after which Walton joined them. Naturally gregarious, Walton displayed art world manners that had appealed earlier to Jacqueline Kennedy; he quickly formed a bond with Mrs. Roosevelt too.

She agreed to join Herbert Lehman, a former governor, as honorary chairmen of the Citizens Committee of New York, which would operate independently of the badly fractured Democratic organization in the state. Their presence would ensure the support of liberals, a vital element in state party affairs. There would be citizens groups like this all over the country—some effective, some not so much; some smoothly functioning in tandem with the regular Democratic organizations, and some at war with each other. After Kennedy's visit Mrs. Roosevelt wrote in her journal that she had found him "a likeable man with charm" but "hard-headed." She concluded, "He calculates the political effect of every move."

Walton recalled that Mrs. Roosevelt lectured Kennedy about his speaking style and told him, "You must take lessons right away."

(Actually he had been taking lessons. Kennedy was no longer the skinny young man with a high-pitched voice who spoke in sometimes indecipherable, rushed sentences when he first ran for Congress in 1946. Traces of his youthful habits remained, however, and he worked on eliminating them. A friend, John Saltonstall, member of a Democratic wing of the mostly moderate Yankee Republican family in Massachusetts, recommended that he work with a professor of voice at Boston University, David Blair McClosky. The professor helped Kennedy learn to relax his throat while speaking and to breathe more deeply from his diaphragm. During the special session of Congress, McClosky, positioned in the gallery above the Senate floor, used hand signals when Kennedy was speaking to indicate when he should slow down and when he should use his diaphragm more. Kennedy kept improving.)

Mrs. Roosevelt also surprised her visitors that August day by expressing disappointment in Stevenson, long the liberal paladin, and offered a few more words of advice to the candidate before they left. Walton called her performance a "marvelous, sort of a motherly thing" and admitted that he and Kennedy "were just eating it up. It was very divine."

Large crowds thronged the roads around Hyde Park during Kennedy's visit. In a conversation with Walton in the car leaving the estate, the candidate confided that Mrs. Roosevelt had not only spoken deroga-torily of Stevenson, who failed to rally to the call of the liberal bloc at the convention, but had informed him, "I don't think Governor Stevenson has the qualities that we need for president." At this point, Kennedy told Walton, "I almost peed in my pants."

The appointment of Walton as the nominal head of the Kennedy campaign in New York was fated to set off a series of internecine battles across the state among disparate members of the Democratic coalition already feuding over attempts by the Roosevelt-Lehman branch of the party to reform the cranky, corrupt leadership exemplified by Tammany Hall. The conflict, which was not confined to New York, was predictable because the citizens committees—which worked well for Kennedy dur-ing the primaries—were designed to keep his campaign firmly under the control of Robert Kennedy and to stay independent from the Democratic Party infrastructure, while pursuing less partisan voters.

Despite a postconvention memo from Soapy Williams advocating the merger of the Democratic National Committee apparatus with the Kennedy campaign staff in order to avoid confusion and overlapping, Robert Kennedy chose to establish separate committees in each of the states. Byron White, the Kennedy leader in Colorado, was put in charge.

In a long memo Robert instructed his operatives in each state to quickly form a "Kennedy for President" committee, to invite all factions of the party to become members, and to elect or appoint a loyal chairman. "It is of the greatest importance—and it cannot be over-emphasized," Robert wrote, "that local or state units should work in close liaison with regular Democratic organizations. We should be willing to help them and keep them advised as to our activities."

It was nice advice in theory, but the instructions would be ignored or deliberately countered during the general election campaign—and sometimes at the command of the candidate's brother.

Six days after his lunch with Mrs. Roosevelt, Kennedy cemented his rela-tionship with Truman by traveling to meet with him at the Truman Li-brary in Independence, Missouri. The two men held a press conference that began, in typical Truman fashion, with the former president telling reporters, "Well boys, do your stuff."

Asked what he and Kennedy had been able to achieve in their short meeting, Truman responded, "We have accomplished enough to win the war, that is all."

They were asked about the Gallup poll that showed Nixon leading Kennedy. "It think it was 50 to—" the journalist added, pausing to recall the other number. Kennedy, a dedicated student of polls, grinned and supplied it: "44."

Truman quickly broke in with memories of his own successful battle with Thomas Dewey twelve years earlier. "Do you remember a Gallup poll had showed Dewey to be 60 to 42 in 1948?" When someone pointed out that the numbers added up to more than 100 percent, Truman's point was made: he dismissed polls altogether. "They don't mean a thing," he said.

By the end of an eventful August, an updated Gallup survey had Kennedy tied with Nixon. If nothing else, the new poll meant that it would be a very close race. In Nixon, Kennedy was confronted with an experienced campaigner, supported by the might and know-how of a Republican Party that had controlled the White House for eight years.

The two men had both served in the U.S. Navy during World War II and both were elected to the House of Representatives in 1946, arriving in Washington as freshmen members of the 80th Congress, where Republicans held a majority in both chambers. Truman would brand it the "Do Nothing Congress." Despite their partisan differences, Kennedy and Nixon had a civil, across-the-aisle friendship during their time together in the House.

In many ways Nixon's political ascendancy was more remarkable than Kennedy's. He was the child of a struggling family in one of the sun-parched valleys of southern California, a land of "hardpan reality" and "grit and hue," as described by his biographer Roger Morris. Nixon attended the undistinguished Whittier College, a few miles from home. It was only after he went far away to law school at Duke University on scholarship and served in the South Pacific in the U.S. Naval Reserve during the war that he shed his provincial roots.

He was clearly ambitious, a striver. His first campaign for a House seat and his victorious run for the Senate in 1950 were both textbook cases of a Republican tactic of the day: to link a Democratic opponent to organizations or causes that were considered "red" or at least "pink" in the early years of the cold war. He built on his reputation while a member of the House Un-American Activities Committee, which raised witch-hunting to an art form, with his relentless pursuit of Alger Hiss, a State Department official accused of spying for the Soviet Union.

Before he was forty Nixon was vice president of the United States— but not before he had to beat back charges of a scandal involving a slush fund set up for him by rich Republican businessmen. Two months after being chosen by Eisenhower, and in the midst of their 1952 race against a Democratic ticket of Adlai Stevenson and John Sparkman, a senator from Alabama, Nixon found himself engulfed by news stories about the secret account.

After a layover in Sacramento during a whistle-stop tour of California, Nixon awoke to read an editorial in the *Sacramento Bee* calling him "the pet protégé of a special interest group of rich Californians." He was hounded at his first stop, Maryville, where a voice shouted, "Tell them about the $16,000!" Agitated, Nixon shouted for his agents to stop the train before it pulled away. He said it was an "Alger Hiss crowd," and he wanted to respond. "You folks know the work that I did investigating the communists in the United States. Ever since I have done that work, the communists and left-wingers have been fighting me with every smear that they have been able to do."

He went on to say that the money he received was used for his office expenses, to save taxpayer funds. Some members of Congress "put their wives on the payroll. That's what Sparkman did," he said. "[My wife, Pat,] has worked in my office night after night after night, and I can say . . . proudly, that she has never been on the government payroll since I have been in Washington, D.C."

His ad hoc speech from the caboose was a precursor to his famed "Checkers speech" before a huge national television audience a few days later to extricate himself from the controversy. He talked of how his family lived within modest means: "Pat doesn't have a mink coat, but she does have a respectable cloth coat." The only gift his family had accepted from supporters "was a little cocker spaniel dog" that had been shipped to them from Texas. His children had named the pet Checkers. Defiantly, he declared, "Regardless of what they say about it, we're gonna keep it."

The "Checkers speech" saved his place on the ticket, but Nixon would later write that the experience left "a deep scar which was never to heal completely." The wound persisted because Eisenhower was never particularly comfortable with him. Though the president congratulated him on his TV performance, called him "my boy," and told him, "You've had a hard time, young fellow," Nixon sensed that he could never rely on his patronage. There had been a coldness ever since their first meeting at the convention after he was selected, when Nixon bounded into Eisenhower's hotel suite and said merrily, "Congratulations, Chief!" The general bristled at the salutation. Nixon later told his daughter it was his first hint that Eisenhower "was reserved and protocol-conscious."

Nixon himself was physically awkward; he would walk on the beach in wingtips while Kennedy cavorted in a bathing suit, barefoot in the sand. Nixon's black eyebrows and five o'clock shadow often made him appear dark and glowering. He was saddled with the unflattering nickname "Tricky Dick." Yet despite the scorn of his liberal enemies, he was a highly intelligent man. He had been a cold-eyed poker player who won many pots in the navy. And he was a politician who survived and succeeded on cunning and guile.

While Kennedy had been forced to correct his own careless remark about expressing "regret" to the Soviet Union after the U-2 affair, Nixon was able to bank on the respect he had won the previous year when he stood eye-to-eye with Nikita Khrushchev in a "kitchen debate" over the merits of capitalism and communism at the U.S. Trade and Cultural Fair in Moscow.

While Kennedy had conquered the heroes of the conservative South (Johnson) and the party's liberal bloc (Stevenson) at the Democratic convention, Nixon was able to make peace with the yin and yang of his own party to head off clashes at the Republican convention in Chicago.

Nixon's greatest threat came from New York governor Nelson Rock-efeller, a liberal who had toyed with running for the GOP nomination but stayed out of the primaries. Like Stevenson, Rockefeller fell back on the idea of being drafted at the convention; unlike Stevenson, Rock-efeller was headstrong and did not flinch from conflict. In June he issued a lengthy statement that spelled out his differences from the Republican agenda in foreign and domestic policy. Rockefeller was sharply critical of Nixon, whom he described as a candidate marching under a banner "whose emblem is a question mark." Meanwhile, in advance of the actual convention, the Republican Platform Committee was grappling with the demands of Senator Barry Goldwater of Arizona, the leader of a loud and boisterous conservative movement.

To head off a collision, Nixon flew to New York to see Rockefeller hours before the convention began. They met at the wealthy gover-nor's home at 810 Fifth Avenue and negotiated for several hours before being able to dictate the terms of their settlement to Illinois businessman Charles Percy.* Nixon would prove to be a formidable rival, and Ken-nedy, who had known him and watched him for fourteen years, never underestimated his abilities. In fact, as that July Gallup poll showed, Kennedy had been trailing him. But then Nixon's campaign was thrown off balance by two separate incidents. Kennedy got lucky, very lucky, as the campaign teeter-totter shifted position.

After an appearance in Greensboro, North Carolina, days after the convention, Nixon scraped his knee badly on a car door. He stubbornly ignored the injury until a serious infection set in, whereupon he checked into Walter Reed Army Hospital in Washington. He was given a strong dose of antibiotics and put to bed, a candidate suddenly out of commission for roughly two weeks.

A few days before Nixon became immobilized, he was humiliated

---

* Percy, eventually a senator, was the chairman of the GOP convention's Platform Committee. The pact came to be known as the "Treaty of Fifth Avenue," and much of its language was embodied in a Republican platform that also offered sops to Goldwater's right wing. Nixon not only reconciled the division with Rockefeller; he offered him the vice presidential nomination. Rockefeller turned it down. The position went instead to Henry Cabot Lodge, the respectable politician-diplomat whom Kennedy had displaced from the Senate eight years earlier; his service as ambassador to the United Nations under Eisenhower had won him bipartisan praise.

by the president he had served for nearly eight years. At a White House press conference Eisenhower was asked if he could give any example of a major idea Nixon had contributed to his administration. "If you give me a week, I might think of one," the president replied. "I don't remember."

In addition to widespread print and television coverage of the incident, Kennedy's advertising team spotted the opening Eisenhower had unwittingly—and possibly jocularly—provided. They pounced. One of Kennedy's thirty-second commercials was quickly constructed around the blooper; it was in the Kennedy TV mix after Labor Day and stayed there until the election.

Kennedy himself faced a serious problem later that month that was totally expected, but it handed him an opportunity to draw upon familiar themes in order to deliver a bravura performance before a national audience.

Long before Kennedy's plans to win the White House were fully formed he had to consider the political implications of his Catholicism. He had been dealing with the subject for years. In 1956 his office prepared material for the widely circulated "Bailey Report" that promoted the viability of a Catholic president. In 1959 he contributed his own positive thoughts about a Catholic in the White House in an article for *Look* magazine, his second in four years. When the nationally known Protestant minister Norman Vincent Peale raised objections to a Catholic candidacy during the West Virginia primary, Kennedy responded to the challenge immediately. Noting that his older brother had died in the service of the country—his own wartime heroism was implicit—he wondered out loud how Catholicism could rule out his desire to serve as president. His words struck a chord with his West Virginia audiences, and he raised the level of discussion. Instead of being defensive about his Catholicism, he became assertive. He pushed the issue in a speech to an important audience of American newspaper editors in Washington shortly before the critical primary date in West Virginia. When he won decisively in that heavily Protestant state, the sense grew in the Kennedy campaign that anti-Catholic bigotry could be defeated nationwide, though a hard core of realists believed the issue would never disappear until a Catholic was actually elected.

To handle the Catholic issue, an office was set up at the Washington headquarters under the rubric "Community Relations." James Wine, a Presbyterian layman who had been working on interfaith matters for the National Council of Churches, was hired to take charge of the shop. Sorensen had met Wine while consulting with progressive Protestants during the flap in West Virginia and was impressed by his expertise. He represented a strain of Protestants from mainstream denominations who were sympathetic to Kennedy and contemptuous of the anti-Catholic babble that came from fundamentalist and evangelical groups.

At first Wine's job.was to respond to letters and help write statements on religious matters for the campaign. Hundreds of letters arrived each week, many of them condemning Catholicism. With two assistants and two stenographers, Wine tried to answer the more thoughtful ones. But some were in crabbed handwriting or so weird and virulent that he put them in a file labeled "No answers." Typical of the correspondence was a "Dear Jack" letter from a Staten Island man who wrote, "It has been my observation that bad luck has come to all Roman Catholics who were in the WACs [Women's Army Corps]. You will become a tool of these Cardinals who are a version of Europe's Nazis. . . . Frankly Jack I think you are a Pansy like the Members of the Medical Profession."

Like others in the Kennedy campaign—Bob Wallace working in the primary states, Fred Holborn refining Kennedy's foreign policy views— Jim Wine is unsung in history. But he and John Cogley, a relatively obscure Catholic writer and former executive editor of *Commonweal*, a progressive Catholic magazine, quietly played important roles in guiding Kennedy through a highly publicized threat to his bid for national leadership.

Once again Norman Vincent Peale was involved in an effort to undermine the Kennedy campaign. To Democrats the minister had long been a nettlesome character. In 1956, after he urged, on God's behalf, his followers to vote for Eisenhower, Stevenson famously responded, "I find the Apostle Paul appealing and the Apostle Peale appalling." And during the West Virginia campaign it was Peale who delivered the attack on

Catholicism that sent Kennedy to the American Society of Newspaper Editors' convention in Washington to deliver a highly publicized reply. This time Peale had company. When Kennedy was chosen the Democratic nominee, Peale joined Billy Graham and other politically active evangelicals in a conspiracy with the Nixon campaign to drum up fears of a Catholic president.

Graham, a Baptist minister who drew tens of thousands to his religious crusades in America and abroad, summoned two dozen fellow evangelists to a meeting in Switzerland, where the abominable prospect of Kennedy as president was on the agenda. Peale was there. So was Daniel Poling, a minister from Philadelphia who had been nursing a grievance against Kennedy for more than a decade and had pursued him with the vigilance of Victor Hugo's Inspector Javert because Kennedy had once canceled an appearance at a ceremony Poling had organized. Others at the Montreux conference opposed Kennedy merely because he was Catholic.

As the most popular evangelist in America, Graham was on a first-name basis with the vice president, and at the conclusion of his conclave he wrote a "Dear Dick" letter. He informed Nixon that "a highly financed and organized office" would be opened in Washington in early September. With satisfaction he reported that the organization would "supply information to religious leaders throughout the nation." Had Nixon objected, the office could not have functioned.

The Kennedy campaign was not blind to the evangelical opposition. His staff found "documentary evidence" of the involvement of the Republican Party with the Protestant ministers' political crusade and raised the issue with the Committee on Fair Campaign Practices in New York. They also picked up intelligence that the new group planned an organizational meeting in Washington in early September. "We knew the meeting was going to take place several days in advance," said Wine. "We considered it as a very serious proposition."

About 150 ministers gathered at the Mayflower Hotel in Washington to meet behind closed doors on September 7. The group would be called the National Conference of Citizens for Religious Freedom. Peale was asked to preside. Poling was there too.

Coincidentally John Cogley, who had been hired to join Wine at the Community Relations branch of the Kennedy campaign, arrived in Washington at the same time and stayed at the Mayflower. Cogley recognized some of the conservative Protestant leaders in the lobby and immediately "got wind that something was going on."

Journalists were alerted, and the secrecy of the meeting was breached when two reporters sneaked into a sound booth. They overheard Peale lament, "Our American culture is at stake [in the election]." Other reporters, prepared to link the group with the Nixon campaign, intercepted some of the ministers when they left the room. According to reports reaching Wine, the evangelicals offered "denials and refutations and misleading statements."

Eventually Peale emerged with a manifesto that declared, "It is inconceivable that a Roman Catholic president would not be under extreme pressure by the hierarchy of his church to accede to its policies with respect to foreign policies." The denunciation created an uproar, but it backfired when public perception concluded that the evangelical group was meddling in the campaign. Peale retreated from an active role. Wine's assessment of their clumsy meeting: "They pretty well shot their own bird down."

Ultimately, rather than hurting Kennedy, the evangelical conspiracy inadvertently played into his hands. His Community Relations team was already preparing a speech on the subject, and he had become a specialist on the separation of church and state.

An invitation to speak to the Greater Houston Ministerial Association, a large organization dominated by Southern Baptists, could not have been better timed. Although some of his advisors cautioned against it, Kennedy quickly accepted the offer. His appearance was set to take place within days, on September 12.

Wine and Cogley flew to Houston and had breakfast with representatives of the ministers' group on the morning of the speech to hammer out the rules of engagement. Kennedy would deliver a formal address and also take questions from the audience. "There was an odd part" to the discussion, Cogley remembered. One of the ministerial negotiators "got worried about the fact that the Church of God people, who were extremist, anti-Catholics from Texas, might get on the program and give a bad image of Texas Protestantism on national television. So he was interested in keeping them from asking questions." Realizing that zealotry would backfire on the ministers' organization, Kennedy's representatives insisted that no questions from the audience would be screened.

The Community Relations teammates then flew to San Antonio in time to join the campaign party barnstorming through Texas that day. Lyndon Johnson, in one of his first campaign assignments, was accompanying Kennedy; he made sure that a full complement of Texas political firepower was on hand. The group included Johnson's wife, Lady Bird, Speaker Rayburn, and even Senator Ralph Yarborough, the longtime liberal antagonist of Johnson's political faction in the state.

In his San Antonio prelude to his appearance in Houston that evening, Kennedy spoke at the Alamo, the former Catholic mission on the western frontier that had been used as a Texas fort in the war against Mexico. The Texas defenders were wiped out to the last man. Since that epic battle in 1836, their bravery has been celebrated in Texas history. Kennedy told a crowd of thousands that inside the Alamo more than a century earlier, "side by side with Bowie and Crockett died Fuentes and McCafferty and Brady and Badillo and Carey. But no one knows whether they were Catholics. For there was no religious test there."

While the candidate was speaking, Wine and Cogley had lunch on the campaign plane, sitting on the tarmac, with Sorensen, who was upset that they had agreed to unscreened questions. He feared that would create an even more hostile environment. But Kennedy did not appear too disturbed when he learned of the ground rules. "He seemed to take it as one more ordeal he had to go through," remembered Cogley. On the flight to Houston Kennedy's aides pitched him potential questions. To save his voice he wrote his answers on yellow legal pads. "He was a little nervous about the way he would reply to some of them," Cogley said. "He obviously had two audiences in mind. One was the Protestant audience he was going to talk to; another was this large Catholic audience out there . . . and he didn't want to say anything that would indicate to them that he had somehow sold out his religion or sold out the Church."

Kennedy's meeting with the Houston ministers took place in a ballroom of the Rice Hotel, and the Kennedy-Johnson Texas campaign paid for the first half-hour to be telecast live to a network of twenty-two stations across the state. The candidate's speech lasted only ten minutes, and he made few departures from a prepared text that essentially reiterated the points he had been making for years. He made one firm declaration: "If the time should ever come—and I do not concede any conflict to be remotely possible—when my office would require me to either violate my conscience or violate the national interest, then I would resign the office."

The question-and-answer session provided greater theater. Some of the ministers, with long, convoluted questions regarding the power of the Vatican, served as foils for Kennedy's concise answers. At the end of one lengthy exposition, one of them asked if he would seek approval from the Vatican. The candidate had a six-word response—"I don't have to have approval"—that elicited applause.

He seemed exasperated at only one point, when a minister brought up a hoary conflict between Kennedy and Poling. More than ten years before, Kennedy had accepted an invitation from Poling to speak at a dedication service for the Chapel of Four Chaplains, honoring four clergymen who went down with an American ship, the *Dorchester*, during World War II. One of the lost chaplains was Poling's son. Kennedy later decided against an appearance because, he said, he learned he was being identified as a "Catholic spokesman" in an advance brochure for the interfaith service. He explained at the time that he was not qualified to act as a spokesman for his church. For years Poling—who ran unsuccessfully as a Republican candidate for mayor of Philadelphia—complained that Kennedy canceled after being ordered to do so by the Catholic hierarchy.

"Is this the best that can be done after 14 years?" Kennedy asked his Houston audience of criticism that he would be a puppet of the church. His voice rising, he repeated, "Is this the best that can be shown?"

At the end of his appearance Kennedy was given a respectful standing ovation. His campaign deemed the evening such a success that film of the event was turned into a commercial telecast multiple times in virtually every state before the election.

Sam Rayburn, who watched the event on television in a hotel room upstairs with members of Kennedy's staff, found himself suddenly filled with admiration for the young man he had dismissed for so long. Rayburn had his own earthy description of Kennedy's performance: "He ate 'em blood raw."

CHAPTER TWENTY

Cunning, Cosmetics, and Blue Shirts

Toward the end of 1959 the huge *TV Guide* reading audience was given a reasonably sophisticated analysis of the medium and its increasing influence on politics. It was timed just right for the eve of a political year that would magnify television's power exponentially. But in spite of the article's prescience, it did not anticipate an event less than a year away that would dwarf even those huge expectations.

In the witty analyst's view, "The slick or bombastic orator, pounding the table and ringing the rafters, is not as welcome in the family living room as he was in the town square or party hall. In the old days, many a seasoned politician counted among his most highly developed and useful talents his ability to dodge a reporter's question, evade a 'hot' issue and avoid a definite stand. But today a vast viewing public is able to detect such deception and, in my opinion, willing to respect political honesty."

The analyst noted the success in the 1958, off-year elections of an unusually large number of new, younger faces: "Their youth may still be a handicap in the eyes of the older politicians, but it is definitely an asset in creating a television image people like and (most difficult of all) remember."

The cost of television definitely worried him, but so did a deeper concern: "Political campaigns can actually be taken over by the 'public relations' experts, who tell the candidate not only how to use TV but what to say, what to stand for and what 'kind of person' to be. Political shows, like quiz shows, can be fixed and sometimes are."

On balance, the writer argued, perceptions fed by television and based on reality were mostly in sync, and a person's TV "image" was likely to be "uncannily correct."

The piece concluded with a bit of a dodge, arguing that it is up to the viewer and voter to sort through it all: "It is in your power to perceive deception, to shut off gimmickry, to reward honesty, to demand legislation where needed. Without your approval, no TV show is worthwhile and no politician can exist."

The byline belonged to John F. Kennedy, yet another example of his use of mass-circulation vehicles to promote his presidential candidacy.

By the time *TV Guide*'s November 14 issue came out, featuring Perry Como on the cover promoting his popular variety show, Kennedy was an avid student of the medium. He had been talking to experts and media executives since he started active campaigning in 1957. Three years later his acceptance speech had been planned with television in mind. He had absorbed numerous pointers—that message and appearance are linked; that short, declarative sentences trump pseudo-erudite verbosity; that a dab of makeup improves appearance; and that under harsh stage lights blue shirts are better than white. He was still working on advice to slow his delivery and breathe with his diaphragm more consistently. In the general election campaign his events were planned with television uppermost in mind. His canny advance man, Jerry Bruno, always had an assistant on the rope lines for Kennedy arrivals, departures, and motorcades. At the right moment the assistant was instructed to drop one section of the line so crowds could be seen surging toward the candidate. To aid his efforts in the Wisconsin and West Virginia primaries Kennedy had also worked with a television producer who pioneered the widespread use of thirty- and sixty-second commercials.

For all that, however, nothing could have prepared Kennedy completely for the following words from CBS News correspondent Howard K. Smith, opening an hour of prime-time television on all the commercial networks simultaneously on the evening of September 26, 1960: "Good evening. The television and radio networks and their affiliated stations are proud to provide facilities for a discussion of issues in the current political campaign by the two major candidates for the Presidency. The candidates need no introduction."

They didn't. For a month they had known this moment was coming. They knew it would be sky-high profile, with the stakes as large as they get; they also knew that these four events would be somewhere between possibly and probably pivotal. And the reason they knew all this was embodied in one word: *television*.

Ironically the only event that came within even distant sight of the 1960 debates' viewer numbers was Nixon's thirty-minute Checkers speech. The audience estimate then exceeded 50 million, making it the most-watched television program ever. Eight years later the four one-hour debates between Kennedy and Nixon were expected to attract audiences at least 50 percent larger.

The crucial question of what to do with such an enormous opportunity—which also posed terrible danger—was answered by both Nixon and Kennedy that first night, in the way each probed his opponent, like a boxer, from the opening bell.

For the first debate the rules were set after easy, almost perfunctory negotiations between the two sides. Each candidate would have an opening statement of eight minutes and closing remarks of three. In between they had forty minutes to handle ten questions from a panel of four journalists. This gave them each two and a half minutes for an answer, and their opponent one and a half minutes to respond. Technically it was more a joint appearance than a formal debate; one of the networks, ABC, actually insisted on calling it that.

Both sides agreed that the first debate would focus on domestic policy. But Kennedy chose to ignore the agreement. For his first strike at Nixon, he looked directly into the camera to communicate to the television audience as if there were no one else sharing the stage. "In the election of 1860 Abraham Lincoln said the question was whether this nation could exist half-slave or half-free. In the election of 1960 and with the world around us, the question is whether the world will exist half-slave or half-free, whether it will move in the direction of freedom in the direction of the road that we are taking, or whether it will move in the direction of slavery. I think it will depend on what we do here in the United States, on the kind of society that we build, on the kind of strength that we maintain. We discuss tonight domestic issues but I would not want any implication to be given that this does not involve directly our struggle with Mr. Khrushchev for survival."

Kennedy went on to declare his dissatisfaction with conditions in the United States, using the familiar rhetorical pattern of parallel construction he and Sorensen preferred: "I'm not satisfied to have fifty percent of our steel mill capacity unused; I'm not satisfied when the United States had last year the lowest rate of economic growth of any industrialized society in the world."

Equally important to Kennedy and to the campaign were the first words out of Nixon's mouth when he began his eight-minute reply: "The things that Senator Kennedy has said many of us can agree with. There is no question that we cannot discuss our internal affairs in the United States without recognizing that they have a tremendous bearing on our international position. There is no question but that this nation cannot stand still; because we are in a deadly competition, as Senator Kennedy, I think, has implied. But when you're in a race the only way to stay ahead is to move ahead. And I subscribe completely to the spirit that Senator Kennedy has expressed tonight, the spirit that the United States should move ahead. Where, then, do we disagree?"

In those first few moments Kennedy was communicating to the viewers, and Nixon was debating Kennedy with a good-natured bow, straight out of a debating textbook.

Kennedy could not have appeared more attractive making his points, perfecting a combination of the visual with the message. This was the result not only of his natural good looks but also of a few last-minute wardrobe and makeup adjustments, recommended by a TV consultant on his campaign staff. Bill Wilson, a producer by trade, had done similar work for a less responsive Adlai Stevenson. In contrast, Kennedy appreciated and often followed Wilson's suggestions. That evening, taking account of the light-colored walls semicircling a set with very bright lights,

Wilson suggested Kennedy change his white shirt and necktie for a blue shirt and a tie that would provide better contrast. The consultant also convinced Kennedy that despite his nice tan he would look better with a little makeup. Wilson got permission to dash across Michigan Avenue from the television studio to buy some Max Factor at a drug store.

Nixon could not match his opponent's good looks, but he compounded his problem by ignoring staff suggestions about his appearance. In fact he rarely spoke to his television advisor, Ted Rogers. Before airtime he accepted only a few swipes of a product called Lazy Shave to disguise his heavy beard. On Nixon, however, the cosmetic produced a gray, almost cadaver-like look under the lights.

As the clock ticked toward the debate's opening, Nixon looked around, fidgeting. There was no Kennedy. Even Kennedy's senior staff appeared worried. Then, with no more than thirty seconds to go, Kennedy suddenly strode in and calmly took his seat. Down through the years a myth first advanced by Larry O'Brien took hold that Kennedy had played a mind game on Nixon. In fact, after banishing all his advisors from his dressing room, Kennedy told Wilson he wanted to relieve himself before going on stage. He emerged from the small, nearby bathroom just in time, moving toward the stage past his brother Robert, whose final, uplifting advice was "Kick him in the balls."

Contrary to romanticized reminiscences, the critical first debate was not a one-sided contest between a gallant, gorgeous Kennedy and a Nixon who looked like he'd been living on the streets since the GOP convention. After his initial remarks, Nixon cogently explained that his disagreement with Kennedy began with Kennedy's far too bleak view of the economy. Nixon chose to compare the Eisenhower years with the years of Truman, whose administration had not yet been rehabilitated by history. Truman's name was a dirty word to most Republicans.

Nixon then attacked Kennedy's own ideas from the perspective of a conservative advocating for a smaller government. He said the Democratic platform Kennedy was running on with gusto would cost at least $13.2 billion more per year than Republican proposals costing $4 billion. In 1960 those were staggering numbers.

"It isn't a question," Nixon stated, "of how much the federal government spends; it isn't a question of which government does the most. It is a question of which administration does the right thing. And in our case I do believe that our programs will stimulate the creative energies of a hundred and eighty million free Americans. I believe the programs that Senator Kennedy advocates will have a tendency to stifle those energies."

From that point on, the debate was predictably partisan thrust and parry, except for one important exchange. After Kennedy listed a number of initiatives Nixon had opposed, including federal aid to education and hospital insurance for the elderly, it was Nixon's turn to respond.

"I have no comment" was all he said.

Going into the debate, the campaign teeter-totter had been raising Kennedy up modestly for weeks, eliminating Nixon's postconventions lead. But in the polls the race appeared statistically tied—according to Gallup, 48 percent for Nixon, 47 percent for Kennedy. Nixon's initial advantage after the Republican convention and the ineffectual special session of Congress had dissipated by September. The change was variously attributed to Nixon's absence from the campaign trail because of his leg injury, to Kennedy's success in beating back the latest attacks on his religion; or to both.

Lou Harris's constant polling had detected the same tiny shifts, though in much more detail. His surveys emphasized the situation in key states: California, Illinois, Pennsylvania, and Ohio turned up very small, pre-debate Kennedy leads. But each fell within the statistical margin for error, and the "undecided" numbers seemed "a little high" for Harris's comfort.

The campaign polled continuously on one issue that seemed unlikely to be raised much if at all in the debates: religion. Harris found a general "concern" about Kennedy's Catholicism in about 25 percent of his samples, depending on the state. Roughly half of that number included people whose inclination was already Republican. The campaign's senior officials hoped that putting Kennedy, looking good and sounding forceful, before a huge television audience would dampen negative sentiment among those who were not determinedly prejudiced.

Appearance and message were the focus for the first debate and those that followed. Kennedy was both the challenger and the underdog. Nixon may have been just four years older, but he had been the sitting vice president for nearly eight years. Kennedy had a thin résumé, and amid the tensions of the cold war his lack of hands-on foreign policy experience appeared to be a weakness.

But on television all of that could change in an hour if he looked and sounded like a potential president, appearing to be Nixon's equal simply by being on the same televised stage with him and acquitting himself adequately. Ahead of the stretch drive to Election Day, if Kennedy appeared to be plausible, his position would be strengthened.

This is why more than one prominent Republican, reportedly including Eisenhower himself, thought that Nixon should have avoided the debates altogether when the networks issued their collective invitation at the end of August. Officially the invitation came from Robert Sarnoff, chairman of RCA, which owned NBC, after Congress had passed and Eisenhower had signed legislation suspending for a year the Federal Communications Commission's rule that the networks allow "equal time" for all opposing viewpoints in public affairs. The rule otherwise would have required the presence of all the smaller party candidates, creating an unwieldy event.

Kennedy immediately accepted; Nixon dithered a few days but ultimately agreed to appear out of concern that he would be hurt by a refusal—and because he suffered from the tragic flaw of hubris. Leonard Reinsch, whose prominent position at Cox Broadcasting involved many Republican contacts, heard of a Nixon brimming with confidence while he watched his opponent's acceptance speech on television with friends. As a Kennedy ally and top media advisor, Reinsch reported Nixon's boasts to the candidate.

There was little initial reaction to the first debate. Nationally the newspaper headlines were flat, the commentators full of carefully balanced, safe observations; no one went beyond *New York Times* columnist James Reston's conclusion that the debate "did not make or break either candidate."

In contrast, the public's reaction seemed clear—to Kennedy's modest benefit. By the time of the debates the networks were already addicted to what they called "audience research." One firm reportedly favored by Republicans, the Schwerin Research Corporation, operated a studio in New York and invited up to four hundred people, a cross-section of the metropolitan area, to watch the debates. Kennedy was judged to have bested Nixon in the first debate by 39 to 23 percent. The Schwerin finding was close to the results of a national survey by Gallup, whose respondents picked Kennedy by 43 to 23 percent.

Only gradually, nearly a week later, did a few stories begin to appear of concerns in the Nixon camp—about his comparative pallor, his dark beard despite the Lazy Shave, and his tendency to perspire noticeably around his mouth.

The second debate, on October 7, had no canned openings or closings, just newsmen's questions and the candidates' answers and comments. For the full hour Kennedy and Nixon went back and forth without significant error, primarily on foreign policy issues as well as a few domestic topics. It was an opportunity for a massive audience to see what the two men had been saying on the campaign trail all year—with one whopping exception. The fate of two tiny islands just off the coast of China suddenly dominated the campaign.

Whatever problems Nixon's appearance may have caused in the first debate, they had been resolved by the second. He was wearing makeup, he had gained weight, and the temperature in NBC's Washington studio was adjusted low enough—after silly backstage skirmishing by aides to the two campaigns—to ensure that he would be less likely to perspire. Yet the numbers remained virtually identical, showing a 44 to 28 percent advantage for Kennedy in the Schwerin survey. (Gallup didn't poll after each encounter.)

But what about the large numbers of viewers of the first debate who were either undecided or thought Kennedy and Nixon had debated to a draw? A likely answer is available in numbers produced behind the scenes, confidentially, for Kennedy by Lou Harris. Early each morning after each debate Harris sent his researchers around the country to create a sample of roughly seven hundred people by midevening. The young pollster then spent the night processing the results and writing his analysis for very limited distribution.

In his bottom-line trial heats for the race, Harris reported that Kennedy's percentage had barely budged from after the first debate (48 percent) to after the second (49 percent); similarly Nixon's totals were 43 and 41 percent, while the movement was minuscule among the undecided, from 9 to 10 percent.

Underneath these numbers, though, were the responses to the question of which candidate had been more effective. After the first debate, the answer was Kennedy by 49 percent to 28 percent for Nixon and 23 percent unsure. However, among those who were unsure, Nixon enjoyed a 10-percentage-point advantage. That would indicate that a large number of people saw the debate as an event, not an election; thus their response was different from their voting preference. This would tend to make Nixon's physical appearance much less a factor.

The second debate produced what Harris called "a more balanced assessment": 39 percent found Kennedy more effective, 35 percent Nixon, and 26 percent were unsure. This time the sample of those who were unsure did not contain the pro-Nixon leanings of the first debate's sample.

Additional hints support the conclusion that Nixon's problems in the first debate were not as severe as initially thought. One came from an extremely limited study of the approximately 20 million people who listened to the debate on the radio—still a significant if declining public affairs medium in 1960.

For decades a myth has persisted that Kennedy "won" the debate in the opinion of those who saw it on television and that Nixon "won" among those who heard only the radio broadcasts. Like many myths, this one holds a germ of truth, but upon examination it is at best misleading.

It turns out that the only source for this conclusion—in addition to a few "man in the street" interviews conducted by Ralph McGill for the *Atlanta Constitution*—is a single survey. It was conducted by Sindlinger and Company, a well-regarded market research firm in Philadelphia that dabbled in politics, reflecting the interests of its founder, Albert Sindlinger. The firm did more than two thousand telephone interviews over the course of the debates. The full polling report has yet to be found, but an account was published in *Broadcasting Magazine* on November 7, the day before the election and weeks after the last debate.

In a sample of fewer than three hundred respondents, Sindlinger reported that 48.7 percent of the radio audience believed Nixon had "won" the debates compared to just 21 percent that picked Kennedy. As for the television audience, the result was 30.2 for Kennedy and 28.6 for Nixon. On balance, scholars who have analyzed the survey suggest that skepticism is warranted. The margin for error in the small radio sample was significant; there is no information about the third of the sample that was unsure; and by 1960 radio audiences for a high-profile event like the debates were more likely rural—and thus more conservative, more likely Protestant, and therefore more likely to be Nixon-leaning.

The more lasting point is that the first debate was less of a Kennedy "victory" than it seemed even at the time. His advantage over Nixon faded through the next three debates. Contemporary polling showed a close result, roughly as close as the real race appeared to be. Survey respondents' opinions about debate performance were important, but they did not translate directly into votes.

That may mask the most important conclusion, namely that the original concerns of some Republicans were well-founded. By agreeing to debate, Nixon gave Kennedy a chance to shed what remained of his image of inexperience. A partisan like Sorensen understood the implication: "Even a draw, if it was a draw, was a Kennedy victory. Millions more voters now knew Kennedy and knew him favorably. Doubting, dissident Democrats now rallied to his cause. . . . The fact that large proportions of both parties had expected a Nixon victory made Kennedy's showing all the more effective."

Lou Harris, equally partisan—though a professional in carrying out his duties—only moderately overstated the case in his report to the high command after the first debate: "This is an incredible change in the image of Senator Kennedy. . . . The single biggest change . . . was the deep respect and warmth his fellow Americans now have for him as a forceful and forthright man of considerable ability and experience. Instead of showing the promise of inspirational leadership, now people say over and over again, obviously this man has it."

In Gallup's monthly polling the numbers shifted slightly during the four debates. In late September, Gallup had Nixon's support at 48 percent to Kennedy's 47; after the last debate, on October 21, Kennedy led 49 to 45 percent. The poll showed a movement of 5 percentage points during the month, a figure that was just outside the survey's margin of error. The teeter-totter had moved again, albeit well within its consistently tiny range.

The Kennedy-Nixon debates were not merely about appearance and speaking style. They also featured two clashes over important foreign policy issues that had the potential to influence the election result. On one, concerning America's tense nonrelations with China, Kennedy just barely dodged misfortune. On the other, involving Cuba, he may have scored politically with a position of questionable wisdom.

Both disputes illustrated the pull of the cold war in the real world and in politics. They also illustrated Kennedy's determination to be seen as a potential leader Americans could trust to oppose aggression and oppose communism everywhere—in Joe Alsop's memorably vulgar phrase, an Adlai Stevenson with balls. But this determination had already been undermined once that May, in his ill-considered, off-the-cuff remark when the U-2 spy plane was shot down over the Soviet Union. Kennedy was still being criticized for that four months later, by Nixon and others. After the first debate he blundered again.

Mao's revolution had defeated the Nationalist forces and driven them onto the island of Formosa (today's Taiwan), a hundred miles off the southern China coast. Under their leader, Chiang Kai-shek, and his powerful wife, Soong Mei-ling, the Nationalists had been assisted ever since by Presidents Truman and Eisenhower and were backed by a formal defense treaty ratified by a Congress that was under the considerable influence of powerful and wealthy interests—called the "China Lobby"—allied mostly with the Republican Party.

The Chinese enemies nearly went to war at least twice during the 1950s; the flashpoints were several very small islands just a few miles offshore, still occupied by the Nationalists, who were supplied with advanced weapons by the Americans. To the Nationalists these islands were symbols of their desire to retake the mainland, as well as potential jumping-off points. To Mao the islands were an insult and a prime target for an invasion of Formosa, which he insisted was part of China. Each side periodically shelled the other, causing considerable damage and loss of life. At least one occasion involved fighter jets with air-to-air missiles; the danger of direct involvement by U.S. forces was periodically real.

Instead of steering clear of such a sensitive issue, Kennedy waded into it on the campaign trail and then in a long broadcast interview on a host of political topics with Chet Huntley and David Brinkley, the famed anchors of NBC News. One question was whether, under present policy, the United States was committed to the defense of the two remaining offshore islands, Quemoy and Matsu (another, Tachen, had been abandoned as indefensible years before). Kennedy replied that the two islands were "an unwise place to draw the line. It seems to me that we should draw the line very exactly and precisely so that any aggressor knows that if he moves into this area that it would mean war."

Kennedy acknowledged administration policy, that the United States would act if any attack on the islands "was part of an attack on the island of Formosa." But he questioned the wisdom of such a doctrine: "How are we to make that judgment? On what basis? Quemoy and Matsu are not essential to the defense of Formosa. . . . We want to draw the line in such a way that we can clearly defend it, that it would have the support of the American people as an attack on the United States, and the support of world opinion. . . . I am not convinced we will in the case of Quemoy and Matsu."

Kennedy's answer was both ill-considered and imprecise, especially his suggestion that a new line in the ocean could be drawn without Chiang's acquiescence and that he would be prepared to draw one unilaterally. Sensing an opening, Nixon pounced at once, his anticommunist and attack-dog instincts stimulated. The interview was certain to come up in the second debate, just days away. Kennedy was lucky there was only one question just before the hour ended, from Edward P. Morgan representing ABC, who asked if a "pullback" from a line in front of the islands wouldn't constitute "appeasement."

Kennedy insisted, forcefully, that Formosa was an unshakeable U.S. commitment. However, he listed a number of top U.S. officials, military commanders as well as diplomats from the Truman and Eisenhower administrations, who had declared the islands indefensible against invasion. He then clarified his position somewhat by saying he was not suggesting "withdrawal at the point of a gun" and that any plan to make a defensive line around Formosa only would have to be "a decision finally that the Nationalists should make." Kennedy hardly needed advisors to remind him that any politician who is forced to clarify a position is in effect confessing his initial mistake.

Not surprisingly, Nixon interjected, "I disagree completely with Senator Kennedy on this point."

Actually he didn't, though he skillfully made it appear that he did. They each were opposed to forcing a change on the Nationalists, and they each supported the current policy, that the United States would not fight to help blunt a theoretical Chinese attack that was "merely"—the official word—directed at Quemoy and Matsu.

However, Nixon dressed up his answer in the language of cold war politics he had learned so well over the years. He compared Kennedy to Truman's secretary of state Dean Acheson, whom Nixon had once derided as the "dean" of his administration's "school of cowardly communist containment." Acheson was a favored Republican target for having uttered imprecise words about the U.S. commitment to South Korea just prior to North Korea's invasion in 1950. (Ironically Acheson had been a critic of Kennedy's early foreign policy initiatives.) Nixon also made it appear as if no Chinese attack on the islands could be anything but part of an attack on Formosa itself. That statement was factually absurd. After a quietly arranged cooling of dangerously escalating hostilities in 1958, the two sides actually had an arrangement under which each would lob shells at the other on alternate days in a weird dance.*

The potential political damage was a fact, however. For the next six days, until the third debate, all of political America briefly became

---

* The agreement lasted a decade, until President Nixon negotiated the "normalizing" of relations with the communist mainland, at Taiwan's expense.

pseudo-experts on Matsu and Quemoy as the warring statements went
back and forth.

On October 13, separated by a continent but joined by the ever-expanding
magic of technology, Nixon, in a Los Angeles studio, and Kennedy, in
New York, went at it from the outset of the third debate.

There were three questions on the China issue, gobbling nearly a
third of the hour. In addition Kennedy and Nixon each took time from
answers on two questions on other topics to elaborate on the dispute.

And then it all came to a sudden stop.

The best explanation is that at a time of genuinely serious cold war
tensions cooler heads prevailed.

During the general election campaign, Eisenhower continued what
had essentially become a tradition, giving presidential nominees not in
office a generalized intelligence briefing on situations around the world.
Kennedy had received such a briefing from Central Intelligence director
Allen Dulles. In addition the veteran diplomat and prominent Democrat
Chester Bowles went to the home of Secretary of State Christian Herter
roughly once a week for a discussion of issues for Kennedy's potential
benefit. That connection appears to have been central in this case.

In the rarefied world of bipartisan diplomacy in tense times, a political dispute over contingency plans for military action involving China
was considered dangerous and irresponsible. In his quasi-memoir *Six
Crises*, published two years after the election, Nixon wrote that he was
contacted by the man running his traveling campaign staff, Fred Seaton
(Eisenhower's secretary of the interior), with a message, apparently from
Herter. Nixon falsely claimed that Kennedy had disagreed with the
Eisenhower policy of "not writing off" Quemoy and Matsu and that he
now wanted to change his mind in order to persuade Nixon to back off
his attacks, which were hurting him politically. Nixon specifically mentioned Bowles's visits to Herter's home. He eventually got to the heart of
the matter, a mutual decision to support Eisenhower's policy (no military response if a Chinese attack was "merely" on the two islands) one
more time in public and then drop the issue. In Nixon's words, "It was

important that the Chinese Communists be given no encouragement to start trouble in the Formosa Straits because of a hassle in the American Presidential campaign."

Nixon was at least onto something, however, when he mentioned Kennedy's political concerns about the dispute. According to Harris's report on his polling the day after the debate, Kennedy might have still been inching up in the race at that point, but the argument on China policy was having an impact. This was the poll that showed Nixon and Kennedy basically tied on the question of who was more effective that evening. On the question of who was more effective on the Quemoy-Matsu argument, Nixon got 39 percent and Kennedy 34 percent, with 27 percent not sure.

The problem with the issue, Harris wrote his bosses, was that "no matter how right Kennedy is and no matter how reckless Nixon might be on it, it places Kennedy in the position of wanting to give up something while Nixon wants to retain it."

At the same time Kennedy and Nixon were wrestling over China, Kennedy was beginning to take on another foreign policy issue that had the undeniable potential of helping his campaign. It was already well on its way into the headlines.

In an early September report based on his in-depth study of the political situation in Illinois, Harris wrote that he had discovered something intriguing: "No issue has the intensity that the Cuban situation has commanded here. While six percent singled it out as the most important problem the next President should act on, one voter in ten who is for Kennedy expressed a sense of urgency about Cuba. Put in politically cutting terms, the Cuban issue here works by better than 2–1 decisively in Kennedy's favor. . . . As the anxieties over Cuba seem to mount, the issue appears to work more decisively for the Senator."

Harris also reported that the Cuba issue "more than makes up" for a Nixon advantage when respondents were asked to pick which candidate was preferable on "getting tough" with the Soviet Union.

Harris expanded on his argument in his polling report following the second debate. After noting that Kennedy had not blunted Nixon's assault on Quemoy and Matsu, he asserted that Kennedy was not taking advantage of the opportunities he had on other foreign policy issues. He cited "the Cuban issue, which still remains the best weapon in the Senator's arsenal. . . . In addition, the Senator must pound home repeatedly the fact that communism has now come within 90 miles of our shores and paint a picture of how ridiculous it is for Castro to taunt and demean us, and how unnecessary all this could have been."

Kennedy responded to this recommendation, especially in October, because it dovetailed with his own evolving views during the tumultuous two years since Fidel Castro's dramatic takeover. It also coincided with a series of highly publicized incidents throughout 1960 as the Eisenhower administration and the new Cuban government clashed repeatedly. They argued over Cuba's human rights abuses as scores of people went before firing squads after show trials; some victims were U.S. citizens. And they disagreed over high-profile economic matters as Castro confiscated property and nationalized industries owned by Americans under the ousted dictatorship of Fulgencio Batista. The assets included major Havana casinos run by American Mafia figures.

At first, like many liberals, Kennedy had been hopeful about the successful Cuban Revolution. Early in 1960 he compared Castro to the nineteenth-century Latin American democratic nationalist Simón Bolívar. But as relations began to deteriorate, Kennedy changed his mind. Originally he had harshly criticized the administration and Nixon personally for their warm embrace of Batista in the 1950s, which he said exacerbated the conditions that produced armed insurrection. However, Kennedy was soon criticizing the administration for not recognizing and responding more quickly to Castro's provocations. Eventually he was strongly urging that steps be taken to help Castro's domestic opponents foment even more opposition, including the violent kind.

At first Nixon responded defensively. But he became increasingly aggressive in portraying Kennedy as an opportunistic flip-flopper. A Kennedy speech on October 6 summarizing his Cuban critique and vaguely urging a greater government response virtually guaranteed the subject would come up in the second debate the following evening.

In the one question about Cuba, CBS correspondent Paul Niven got a bit hung up on the idea that Cuba had been "lost" under an increasingly antagonistic Castro. That allowed Nixon to indulge in a favorite conservative mantra about Truman and Mao's China in the late 1940s: Who lost China?

Nixon then turned defensive. He claimed that under Truman eleven dictatorships had flourished in South America, compared to three in 1960—if one counted Castro, and Nixon said he did. But surprisingly Nixon then turned almost dove-like, explaining that the United States was a signatory to the treaty that established the Organization of American States, which explicitly banned interference by one member in another's internal affairs. He finished with a weak criticism of what he called Kennedy's "defeatist talk," but his answer left him open to attack, and Kennedy stepped in.

He hit administration policy before and after Castro's victory, claiming that in the 1950s, under Batista, some twenty thousand Cubans had died while the administration supported the dictator. He also repeated his comment that two of Eisenhower's ambassadors had warned futilely that Castro and his brother, Raoul, were hostile to the United States. "We never were on the side of freedom," Kennedy asserted. "We never used our influence when we could have used it most effectively and today Cuba is lost for freedom." He hoped it would be regained some day but feared that under "current policies" that would never happen.

Nixon's position was quite deceptive. By October the Central Intelligence Agency was nearly a year into a secret, multipronged effort to overthrow Castro that had been approved by Eisenhower in March, with Nixon's enthusiastic participation, after it was already under way. It had begun as CIA-operated subversion that included gunrunning, clandestine broadcasting, even planning Castro's assassination with members of the American Mafia. It soon evolved into the recruitment and training of exiles for insertion as guerrillas from a base in Guatemala.*

At first Nixon responded defensively about the operations and plans.

---

* The actual, disastrous invasion at the Bay of Pigs by more than 1,500 exiles trained, equipped, advised, and transported by the United States did not occur until Kennedy was president, in 1961.

But like virtually every person involved in so-called covert operations, he could not resist the temptation to blab. In *Six Crises* he wrote that he was infuriated by Kennedy's advocacy of "action" in support of Castro's opponents, a position he believed Kennedy reached with the aid of supposedly secret material he had received in candidate briefings by Director Dulles. Nixon also claimed that because the CIA's activities were so secret, he needed to advocate the opposite course to preserve their cover.

Given the wide distribution of knowledge at that point, among both authorized and unauthorized persons, that assertion is absurd. For one thing, Nixon himself had already begun leaking the essence of the administration's plans. On October 9, while his campaign was grounded in Montana by bad weather, he summoned a good friend among the traveling press, Willard Edwards of the *Chicago Tribune*, to his hotel suite. According to Edwards, Nixon told him that the CIA was training exiles for an operation inside Cuba and that the operation was much more aggressive than anything Kennedy had recommended. He also claimed Kennedy already knew about it but was nonetheless attacking the administration for inaction, secure in his awareness that Nixon couldn't respond.

Edwards treated the conversation as being off the record and didn't write about it immediately as news. (Kennedy was not the only politician who had pals in the press.) Instead, three days later, he wrote cautiously of Nixon, "In the field of foreign policy he is privy to certain government operations which he may not discuss when Kennedy attacks the administration for inaction. He accepts this frustration as a penalty of his office."

If Kennedy had known nothing at that point, the Edwards piece was a tipoff. But he knew a lot. As far back as the summer Robert Kennedy had been told the CIA was training Cuban exiles. While working in California for the campaign he was approached by an active Democrat and former senior CIA official, Tom Braden, who mixed politics with his job as the publisher of a newspaper in Oceanside. "I remember at some point or other," Braden said later, "taking a walk with Bobby Kennedy in some hotel yard and saying to him, 'Did you know that we're going to invade Cuba?' I really shouldn't have told him that but my passion was so great for the victory of the candidate that I did tell him. And I said, 'The fellow in charge of it is a great guy and you ought to see him right away. His name is Dick Bissell.' And he raised his eyebrows and said nothing. I don't know whether he'd known about it before or not."

Richard Bissell, whom Jack Kennedy had tried to recruit as a political supporter early in 1960, was then the CIA's director of covert programs and the man in charge of the ever-expanding Cuba operations. He and Dulles always denied that they told Kennedy about any covert programs anywhere in the world, and there is no indication Bissell even talked to him after Kennedy tried to recruit him. When Nixon's memoir was published the Kennedy White House also denied the account.

But Kennedy did have knowledge about the planned invasion of Cuba, and not just from Braden but from two additional sources. One was the governor of Alabama, John Patterson, an early and vocal Kennedy supporter. Patterson had been a young staff officer in General Eisenhower's wartime headquarters in London. As governor he was approached by a CIA officer and the head of his state's Air National Guard for permission to use an Alabama base to train exile pilots and maintain their planes for use over Cuba. Patterson obliged, but he made a quick trip to New York in October to tell Kennedy what was happening. Patterson said he was fearful that some kind of invasion might happen before the election, then less than a month away.

According to Dulles, however, repeated delays and snafus in the program made any early action impossible. Plans were being constantly revised or discarded. At that point the anti-Castro forces included far fewer exiles than the brigade that ultimately invaded.

Robert Kennedy was told of the exiles' activity by one of the campaign's speechwriters during the general election. William Attwood, a Stevenson campaign refugee, had been in touch with a photographer friend, Andrew St. George, who was on an assignment in southern Florida for *Life* magazine. Working among the famously loose-lipped exiles, he heard repeated stories about secret training exercises. St. George called Attwood, who informed the candidate's brother.

A great many people, in short, were aware of what was going on behind the scenes, Kennedy included. His attacks on the administration continued just as the Nixon responses escalated in severity. Just days ahead of the final debate, on October 21, it was Nixon who made an angry speech denouncing Kennedy—not for taking advantage of secret knowledge but for being an unreliable advocate who changed positions for political advantage.

That speech produced the most important statement of all on Cuba, and it came from Kennedy at an especially tense time in the deteriorating U.S. relationship with Castro. His confiscation of Americans' property and nationalization campaign had intensified; at least three U.S. citizens went before Cuban firing squads in October. On the day before the final debate the administration suddenly announced the recall of the American ambassador to Washington, a prelude to the breaking of diplomatic relations, and an embargo on all U.S. trade with the country, which had already decreased sharply since Castro assumed power. The day before, Kennedy had instructed a speechwriting aide, Richard Goodwin, to come up with a very tough press statement for release in the newspapers on October 21. Goodwin obliged and ran his draft successfully past Sorensen and press secretary Salinger; a final call to Kennedy that evening did not go through because he was napping and unavailable, so the statement was released without his having seen it.

The significance of the statement was in its timing more than its content. Warning of growing Soviet influence in Havana, the statement was harshly critical of the Eisenhower administration. "Now the communists have been in power for two years. Yet we have done almost nothing to keep Castro from consolidating his regime and beginning subversive activities throughout Latin America. In fact, our prestige in Latin America has fallen so low that at the recent Inter-American Foreign Ministers Conference we were unable to persuade our former good neighbors to pass a resolution even criticizing Cuba by name.".

And then this: "We must attempt to strengthen the non-Batista democratic anti-Castro force in exile, and in Cuba itself, who offer eventual hope of overthrowing Castro. Thus far these fighters for freedom have had virtually no support from our government."

This was indeed, as Nixon later complained, a call for what the administration was already doing secretly. Such advocacy for U.S.-assisted use of force was astonishing coming from a liberal, and it distressed many liberal Democrats and more than a few liberal columnists. Days later, mildly concerned about the criticism, Kennedy issued a statement in the form of a telegram to Nixon, insisting that he would take no action in violation of treaty commitments.

Nixon didn't mention Cuba in his eight-minute opening statement in the debate. Kennedy did, in the context of an America being challenged all over the world by communism and failing to respond with creative vigor. But in the first question, by Frank Singiser of Mutual Broadcasting, who asked for specifics on Cuba, Nixon found his opening.

"Our policies are very different," he said. "I think that Senator Kennedy's policies and recommendations for handling of the Castro regime are probably the most dangerously irresponsible recommendations made during the course of this campaign." Nixon once again cited the five treaties he claimed unilateral action would violate. He warned that if the United States took such a course "we would lose all of our friends in Latin America," risk condemnation at the United Nations, and invite Soviet intervention.

Kennedy did not respond in kind. Instead he criticized the new embargo as certain to be pointless without widespread international support, which, he noted, the administration had done nothing to promote.

Nixon made one additional point that night, which produced some national head-scratching. To the question of what to do about Castro, he replied, "We can do what we did with Guatemala." He claimed the leftist government of Jacobo Arbenz had been overthrown in 1954 by the Guatemalan people in response to the hardships generated by a similar embargo, which he called "quarantining."* In fact it was already an open secret in Washington that the Arbenz government had been overthrown in a CIA-directed coup not all that different from one being planned with Castro as the target.

---

* The word would become famous after Kennedy used it as president during the Missile Crisis two years later.

On that sour note nearly a month of the campaign that had been focused almost completely on these four debates ended. The teeter-totter had indeed raised Kennedy slightly; his image as a plausible president was also considerably strengthened. But more than three weeks of campaigning remained, with the outcome still in doubt.

CHAPTER TWENTY-ONE

Walking a Tightrope

From the beginning, the Kennedy campaign was confronted with a painful conundrum: how to appeal to the southern states without alienating black voters, who held the balance in many important northern states, and vice versa.

The "Solid South," a collection of former Confederate bastions, had been an essential part of the Democratic Party coalition for nearly a century and segregationist forces, still tied to the Democratic Party, controlled political life there. It was said that if Republicans called a statewide meeting anywhere in the South, it could be held in a telephone booth. Blacks, who made up as much as a third of the population in some states, were kept from voting by a wall of obstacles: poll taxes, literary tests requiring impossibly erudite interpretations of the Constitution, or simply the outright refusal of local officials to permit blacks to register and threats by some whites to resort to violence if they tried.

But the hold of the national Democratic Party on the South was loosening, strained by resentment over Truman's decision to integrate the U.S. military and dramatized by the Dixiecrat walkout at the 1948 Democratic convention. In 1956 Eisenhower captured five of the eleven states that once made up the Confederacy, and the region loomed as a battleground in 1960.

At the same time, black voters were gaining political power elsewhere, and the increasingly liberal Democratic Party was trying to lure them from their traditional affection for the GOP. Inroads had been made, especially in urban areas, where black Democrats were elected to congressional seats, and there was movement toward a political takeover of big cities. By midcentury, with a fairly friendly Truman administration in place and a postwar sense of growing liberation, it was clear to Democrats that black voters could make the difference in a critical arc of industrial states running from New York to Michigan.

Kennedy found himself caught between the old alliances he had made with the southern grandees, the Russells and the Eastlands, and the realization that he needed to court and win over black voters. In Congress he had demonstrated ease in dealing with southerners; he drank whiskey with them in their backrooms and consummated legislative compromises. One of his best friends was George Smathers, a senator from Florida. Yet he displayed little affinity and much less than empathy with black Americans. They represented a world far removed from his own, a culture he did not seem to appreciate and made little attempt to understand.

"He had no close relationship with any Negro, so-called civil rights leaders," asserted Simeon Booker, the well-traveled Washington correspondent for the giant Johnson Publishing Company, which fed *Jet* and *Ebony* magazines to a constituency of black readers across the country. Before he became a presidential candidate Kennedy had made only a few feeble efforts to connect with blacks. There was a perception among African Americans that the son of Harvard and great wealth was uncomfortable with them.

Just after his failed run for the vice presidential nomination in 1956, Kennedy enlisted the help of a socially prominent couple in black circles in Washington, Belford and Marjorie Lawson. Both held law degrees; the husband had argued cases before the U.S. Supreme Court on behalf of the New Negro Alliance, and his wife had written for years for the *Pittsburgh Courier*, one of the nation's leading African American newspapers, located in the city where she grew up. Their role was to boost Kennedy's profile among blacks.

Kennedy was shaping his run for the presidency in the summer of

1959 when Marjorie Lawson approached Martin Luther King Jr., a rising star in the firmament of civil rights leaders, about meeting with him. Although demands on King's time prevented them from getting together, her overture was the first attempt to introduce two young men who soon became historic figures.

At the start of 1960, with his campaign in full throttle, Kennedy invited members of the Capital Press Club, an African American organization distinct from the Washington Press Club in the still-segregated city, to come to his home for a talk. At first it did not go well. The black reporters were suspicious of Kennedy because of his vote on the jury trial provision in the 1957 civil rights bill. To their knowledge, Kennedy had never been closely identified with black issues; on the other hand, his primary opponent, Hubert Humphrey, had been a champion of civil rights for more than a decade. Some of the visitors' remarks were hostile, and Belford Lawson, who had arranged the meeting, tried to intervene. "No, I can speak for myself," Kennedy said, and explained his position on jury trials for recalcitrant white voting registrars facing criminal contempt charges for their misbehavior, as well as other issues, at length. Before the reporters left, they felt better about him.

Kennedy continued to wrestle with issues important to blacks. His victory in West Virginia was tarnished in politically aware black communities, Booker said, by a belief that he had "just bought the Negro vote there" in order to defeat Humphrey, who should have been their real ally. On the eve of the convention Kennedy had to dismiss Belford Lawson, whom Booker called his "top Negro," because it was discovered that he had been on retainer for Jimmy Hoffa, the Teamsters boss and mortal enemy of the Kennedy brothers. Marjorie Lawson remained on the staff, and Kennedy added Frank Reeves, who had worked for the NAACP, and Louis Martin, another well-connected black journalist. But the office was ruffled by bickering between Mrs. Lawson and Reeves, and the staff members who actually had Kennedy's ear on the subject of civil rights were two liberal white men: his brother-in-law Sargent Shriver and Harris Wofford, the idealist who became a valuable advisor.

The first meeting between the candidate and King took place over breakfast at Kennedy's apartment in New York in June 1960, a month before the convention. They talked for an hour, and King came away with the impression that Kennedy "did not have the grasp and the comprehension of the depths of the problem. . . . I could see that he didn't have the emotional involvement. . . . He didn't know too many Negroes personally."

As a gesture to blacks, the Kennedys decided to add a prominent black name to the campaign masthead. They chose Congressman William Dawson of Chicago, but in a roundabout way that only added to racial misunderstanding. At a postconvention staff meeting, Robert Kennedy was complaining about the lack of productivity in a newly formed civil rights office when Louis Martin, who had recently joined the team, spoke up and said, in effect, We're doing things, but I don't think you're doing enough. Martin told Jack Kennedy he needed to give more recognition to Dawson, a leader of blacks in the House since 1944. A meeting between the two was set up; it lasted thirty minutes.

Driving Dawson back to the capitol afterward, Martin asked, "How did it come out?"

Dawson only mumbled, "Well, now, he's a young man. We had a nice uneventful chat."

Despite his congressional seniority, Dawson commanded little respect among activist blacks. He was the product of a Chicago ward ripe with corruption and a cog in Mayor Daley's machine, which relied on him to harvest thousands of black votes each election day. He discouraged use of the term *civil rights* on the grounds it might offend whites. He also advised against "relations with these wild young men like Martin Luther King. That will just get Kennedy in trouble." At seventy-four he seemed aged beyond his years, and some thought he suffered from senility.

The campaign gave Dawson the title of chairman of the civil rights section and a place in their new office space in a K Street building near Robert Kennedy's headquarters. The open layout offended the old congressman, who said he needed privacy. So Shiver arranged for an enclosed office to be constructed in the middle of the open space. Irreverent staffers called it "Uncle Tom's Cabin."

To attract black voters Kennedy would have to find someone—or something—more vigorous than Dawson.

While he fumbled to improve his standing among black voters, Kennedy turned to his running mate to keep the South in the Democratic column. Johnson's influence in these states—especially his own Texas—was the principal reason he had been chosen. Kennedy had looked at the national political equation and concluded that he could not win without the South. With Johnson at his side, he barnstormed through Texas for three days in September, including appearing before the Houston ministers; he made a few stops in the swing states of North Carolina, Tennessee, and Georgia in the last two months before the election. Otherwise Kennedy was done with Dixie and depended on Johnson and the deals and arrangements he himself had made with key southerners.

Georgia got special attention. With 12 electoral votes, it was a richer prize than any of its neighbors, even Florida, and Atlanta represented the spiritual center of the South even though the city never became one of the floating capitals of the Confederacy. The state was the wellspring for conservative dynasties that spawned Senator Richard Russell and Senator Herman Talmadge, who had helped Democratic presidential candidates carry Georgia every four years. But the state was changing. Atlanta was the home of six historically black colleges that produced a counterbalance of black leadership. The sit-in movement that started in North Carolina early in 1960 quickly spread to Georgia, where the tactics of civil disobedience were being encouraged by people like King.

Several members of the Georgia power structure, including Governor Ernest Vandiver and publisher James H. Gray, met with Robert Kennedy at the Democratic convention, seeking assurance that his brother frowned upon sit-ins. Vandiver had been pressing for leniency from Kennedy on traditional southern ways of dealing with blacks. Robert told the group his brother approved of civil rights demonstrations—as long as they were lawful. Since sit-ins were illegal in Georgia, the protestors could expect no support from the Kennedy campaign. Still, the party's platform had specifically singled out the sit-ins for praise. The Georgia Democrats went home withholding support for Kennedy in the fall.

During the special session of Congress, Vandiver—a very vocal critic of racial integration and the sit-ins—met with Kennedy and Johnson in the majority leader's chambers in the capitol. He wanted to talk privately with Kennedy about a matter that he "didn't want to discuss with anybody else." They went into a small bathroom, where Vandiver talked of Eisenhower's dispatch of federal troops to Little Rock in 1957 to ensure the integration of Central High School. Georgia's legal docket was brimming with desegregation cases, and Vandiver wanted Kennedy to pledge not to send troops to Georgia to enforce school integration. "We wanted his cooperation rather than his sending in troops," Vandiver explained.

According to Vandiver, Kennedy said, "Well, maybe marshals could handle the problem."

"We don't want any marshals, either," Vandiver replied, and claimed that Kennedy agreed not to send troops or federal marshals. Days later Vandiver announced that Georgia Democrats would support the Kennedy ticket.

Other Deep South states also posed difficulties. Kennedy was already criticized by blacks for his cozy relationship with John Patterson, the segregationist governor of Alabama. But he faced another threat there and in Mississippi and Louisiana, where the fear of unpledged electors had inspired racist Democrats to spurn their party and get behind uncommitted slates for November. Under that plan southern states voting for unpledged electors would have a bloc in the Electoral College that could affect the election or throw a disputed contest into the House of Representatives, where the coalition of Republicans and southern Democrats still held sway.

The unpledged elector scheme was very popular in Mississippi. Governor Barnett, a tool of the Citizens Councils, had already offered himself as a candidate for the Democratic presidential nomination in Los Angeles. He had wide support among many erstwhile Democrats in the state, and some went to great lengths to undermine their own party's candidate. For example, the Kennedy campaign produced a television spot showing the candidate visiting Harlem and getting the endorsement of Harry Belafonte, a popular black singer and civil rights activist. The commercial was made available to anyone interested in civil rights.

John Bell Williams, a Democratic congressman from Mississippi, bought a copy from Kennedy headquarters for $13.35. On the night Senator John Stennis, a loyal Democrat, went on statewide TV to endorse Kennedy, Williams arranged for time immediately afterward to show Belafonte's endorsement of Kennedy. "Poor Stennis was crushed," said John Seigenthaler, one of Robert Kennedy's closest associates. "Ex-governor [J. P.] Coleman called us that night and said this was a devastating blow to the campaign.... He understood duplicates had been made of the film and that they had been circulated throughout the Southern states." Steve Smith, the campaign manager in Washington, was put to work retrieving copies of the film and within twenty-four hours had recovered eight or ten. Smith and Robert Kennedy then met with the young woman who had unwittingly sold Williams the film and her supervisor in the campaign. "Both of them were literally scared to death," Seigenthaler said. "Bob and Steve told them not to worry about it, just to be careful and diligent." They tightened procedures for distributing the film in the future.

In Louisiana another renegade Democrat was causing trouble, a former legislator named Willie Rainach, who had been a delegate to Los Angeles. In the late 1950s he had used his legislative office to try to purge blacks from the state voting rolls. Alone among the Deep South states, Louisiana had permitted blacks to register during the populist reigns of Huey P. Long and his brother Earl, who was governor at the time of Rainach's maneuver. At their height more than 160,000 blacks were eligible to vote in Louisiana. Rainach succeeded in substantially reducing that number in the conservative northern part of the state. He ran unsuccessfully for governor in 1959 as the Citizens Council candidate in a field that also included a Ku Klux Klan member. After the 1960 convention he bolted the party and led the unpledged elector campaign in Louisiana.

But Kennedy was buoyed by the support of Louisiana Democrats he had first befriended in the days following the 1956 convention. They were his hosts during two memorable trips, when the senator from Massachusetts had gotten an enthusiastic reception in the heavily Catholic parishes of southern Louisiana. With their help, Kennedy's strategists felt, they could negate the unpledged elector bid in Louisiana.

The Kennedy campaign also ran into difficulty with one of the candidate's closest friends, George Smathers. The Florida senator had taken it upon himself to establish a separate southern campaign organization that would sponsor a speakers bureau and, under his command, coordinate Kennedy activity throughout Dixie. It was operating out of the Carroll Arms Hotel, a popular afternoon trysting place for members of Congress in the shadow of the Senate office buildings.

Robert Kennedy learned of the wildcat campaign after a low-level staffer named Howard Haggerud reported to Seigenthaler that the Smathers operation smacked of personal "empire building" and threatened to divert money from the legitimate Kennedy campaign. Robert "immediately saw the potential dangers" and told his brother of the operation. Jack called Smathers and told him to integrate the effort into the larger campaign. But "instead of getting better it got worse," Seigenthaler said.

After failing to rein in Smathers, Robert decided the Florida senator would accompany him on an upcoming trip through the South. Smathers's chief aides in the Carroll Arms advised against it, telling him, "They hate Bob Kennedy in the South, and he shouldn't go on the trip." Robert insisted and wound up in a furious argument with Smathers during the flight, declaring, "Senator Smathers, I can tell you're his friend, but I can tell you Senator Kennedy is not going to submit to this type of operation. We're not running a Southern campaign as a separate wing of this organization." Smathers relented. He was allowed to keep the office at the Carroll Arms, but all speakers, finances, and campaign activities would be handled directly by the formal apparatus headed by Robert Kennedy and Steve Smith.

Kennedy also had to deal with southern white politicians who feared public association with him. One prominent Democrat in Florida, Farris Bryant, was well on his way to being elected governor that fall; Kennedy wanted Bryant to head his campaign in the state, but Bryant turned him down. He said he would do all he could in private, but because of their differing views on desegregation he could not be a public ally.

———

To shore up southern support Johnson was put to work on a five-day whistle-stop train trip that began in the second week of October at Union Station in Washington and wound through eight states before ending in New Orleans. It was an interesting and bold move. Although Texas had been part of the Confederacy and most of the southern delegations had supported the Texas senator at the convention, the question remained whether he would be accepted as a southerner. Most natives of the Deep South considered Texas foreign to their region, a western state with few of the mores of Dixie. Some East Texas towns close to the Louisiana border were unmistakably southern, but in the heartland of the enormous state, in Dallas and Fort Worth and Austin, local values were western and few people considered themselves southern.

Johnson was the perfect person to bridge that gap. When he spoke with emphasis, he shouted, and his speeches from the caboose of the *LBJ Special* rang with a sound familiar to people who went to churches with hellfire-and-brimstone preachers, people who, for generations, had nurtured bombastic politicians braying a blend of populism and racism. There were no traces of racism in Johnson's speeches, but he had an evangelical flair for persuasion, and he hit all the right notes.

At one of the first stops, in a small Virginia town, Johnson established the tone for his trip when he yelled, "What the Hell has Dick Nixon ever done for Culpeper?"

The *LBJ Special* was like the carnival coming to town. Its arrival was accompanied by a loud recording of "The Yellow Rose of Texas," a nineteenth-century song that had been made into a popular hit in the 1950s. Advance men carefully managed the train's procession; at each stop they took on board mayors, aldermen, and county supervisors whose constituency lay in the town ahead, replacing those who had just appeared. When the train stopped, Johnson magically emerged with a group of local officials who publicly endorsed the Democratic ticket.

The Texas senator's real work took place in a parlor car fitted with comfortable chairs, where he lectured the local dignitaries on the importance of sticking with the Democratic ticket. Using the same personal, brow-beating style he employed outside the Senate chamber, he told the officials of the rewards of loyalty and warned of the consequences if

Nixon were elected, or if (he said *when*) Kennedy were elected without their help. He wound up talking to 1,247 various officials along the way, according to a count meticulously kept by his staff.

In his public speeches Johnson appealed to the South's devotion to military service by talking of Kennedy's heroism in the South Pacific and young Joe Kennedy's death in World War II. "Nobody asked him what church he went to," Johnson would add, to allay concerns about Catholicism.

The train plowed through Dixie with only one comic slip-up. As it pulled out of Greer, South Carolina, it seemed as if the blare of "The Yellow Rose of Texas" would never stop. Johnson could still be heard on the public address system when he roared to an aide, "Bobby, turn off that fuckin' 'Yeller Rose.'"

The *LBJ Special* attracted hundreds—sometimes thousands—of spectators in every town. At the final destination, New Orleans, Johnson was the guest of honor at a faux Mardi Gras parade attended by 100,000 people.

The trip was a ringing success.

While Johnson romanced white southerners, Kennedy worked to earn the confidence of blacks in the North. Concerned that questions about his own voting record and the presence of a southerner on the ticket might upset this crucial community, Kennedy made his quest for black votes a top priority. The stronger effort had begun in earnest back in the spring, after Kennedy realized that Johnson would get most if not all the southern delegate votes for the presidential nomination. He was also receiving considerable criticism for his wooing of white southern politicians with Jim Crow ties. According to Walter Reuther's top aide, Jack Conway, Kennedy was presiding over a campaign meeting touching on civil rights one day, when he suddenly stood up and snapped, "All right, there's no question. The Negroes are right." Almost immediately his top advisors Sargent Shriver and Meyer Feldman, as well as Marjorie Lawson, were dispatched to an NAACP meeting in Minnesota with instructions to transmit a more supportive, cogent message.

The fresh push reached a midsummer climax when Kennedy and his brother Robert were observed shaping the strongest civil rights plank a Democratic convention had ever seen and then helping to push it past the delegates. The renewed commitment encouraged advisors who had been lobbying for a greater effort in the face of opposition from such key staff members as Byron White, who argued against an association with civil rights. White called the issue inflammatory and unnecessary. Even the term *civil rights* raised red flags, not only from old Congressman Dawson but from Johnson, who pleaded that the campaign refer instead to "constitutional rights."

In the period between the first and third debates with Nixon, Kennedy went on a dramatic offensive. A few days after the subject of civil rights was broached in the September 26 debate, people around Kennedy detected a sudden change. Going into Indianapolis for a routine campaign event, he shifted the parade route so that he would go through a black neighborhood. "They had Negroes three deep all along there and I think it did something to Kennedy," Simeon Booker recalled.

Three days later, on October 7, Kennedy, accompanied by his pregnant wife, spoke to a student gathering at Howard University in Washington, perhaps the most prestigious Negro school in the country. The program was held under the auspices of the American Council on Human Rights. Nixon too had been invited but did not attend. Louis Martin gloated, "We had the Howard University student body to ourselves." Kennedy's message, Martin said, would reach "every college-trained Negro in America." It was delivered "at a place that tradition had made important to them, and Nixon had failed to show."

If the Howard event provided intellectual fodder for the thinking black voter, Kennedy triggered a visceral reaction among the masses with his performance in New York on October 12 at events surrounding the National Conference on Constitutional Rights, which his staff helped organize. His day began with breakfast with Eleanor Roosevelt at her home on East 75th Street; she would appear by his side later in the day, giving him her imprimatur, but first he had to take part in the city's annual Columbus Day Parade, an event celebrating Italian heritage.

The National Conference on Constitutional Rights was ostensibly a nonpartisan affair, featuring panels for academic and business leaders to discuss the significance of the growing movement among blacks. Hubert Humphrey served as its chairman. In his remarks Kennedy pledged that two of his colleagues, Senator Joseph Clark of Pennsylvania and Congressman Emanuel Celler of New York, were committed to drafting legislation and pushing to passage all of the elements of the civil rights plank of the Democratic Party. It was Kennedy's first strong stand on behalf of civil rights legislation since 1957.

He also pledged to take important actions as president to advance civil rights, without waiting for a stubborn Congress. At the time blatant discrimination in housing was the lynchpin of the North's version of segregation, including in the operation of federal housing programs. Kennedy promised to end it unilaterally, "with the stroke of a pen."

It was during Kennedy's remarks that day in front of the Hotel Theresa in Harlem, a famous local landmark, that his message caught fire. Flanked by Jacqueline Kennedy and Mrs. Roosevelt and joined by scores of Democratic officeholders and civil rights leaders, he faced a crowd of thousands in the nation's most famous black neighborhood. He knew that Castro had recently stayed at the Theresa and that Khrushchev had come there to embrace the Cuban revolutionary. That recent history did not appear to make Kennedy uncomfortable, however. Instead he alluded to the ongoing revolutions against colonialism in Africa and the coming revolution in his own country.

"Beyond the fact of Castro coming to this hotel, Khrushchev coming to Castro, there is another great traveler in the world," he told the crowd, "and that is the travel of world revolution, a world in turmoil. I am delighted to come to Harlem, and I think the whole world should come here, and the whole world should recognize that we all live right next to each other. . . . We should not fear the 20th century, for this worldwide revolution which we see all around us is part of the original American revolution."

Roy Wilkins, the NAACP leader who once clashed with Kennedy over civil rights issues, said he would give the Democratic nominee a grade "above 90."

Kennedy finally earned the unequivocal blessing of America's own La Pasionaria, Eleanor Roosevelt, after four years of feuding coupled with her own reluctance to give up on Adlai Stevenson. She was famous for understatement, but at a news conference a few weeks later in Washington she was blunt in her assessment of Kennedy: "I think he's learned better now. And I think his record in civil rights . . . has had a tremendous influence on Negro leaders."

Kennedy scored a triumph in New York that day, but sometimes his operation in the state looked like a political version of *Guys and Dolls*, though Damon Runyon never conceived a character more roguish than the real-life Democratic congressman from Harlem, Adam Clayton Powell Jr.

A strikingly handsome and dapper man with a thin mustache, Powell doubled as the minister of the Abyssinian Baptist Church, a Gothic Revival icon in Harlem. He was known for his spell-binding sermons; he also flirted outrageously with women and corruption. But he had become a powerful figure in Congress and boasted a following of tens of thousands beyond the boundaries of Harlem. It was important to line him up as a Kennedy spokesman, but doing so came at a cost.

In early negotiations with the Kennedy team, Harris Wofford told Powell the campaign needed his "thrust." Powell delighted in the double entendre because of his reputation for sexual promiscuity. (In his Harlem speech even Kennedy played on Powell's playboy antics. He said that across Africa many children were named for historical American heroes such as Washington and Lincoln. Noting that Powell had traveled there, he added, "There may be a couple called Adam Powell." Powell shouted back, "Careful Jack!," amid roars of appreciative laughter.)

Louis Martin was delegated to deal with Powell. He learned that if Powell agreed to go on the road for Kennedy he expected the campaign to provide him with luxury accommodations and a limousine at every stop. When the congressman suggested that with $300,000 he could set up a voter registration drive, Martin laughed. Powell eventually required "a sizable financial inducement"; it was approved by Steve Smith, cost unknown. Throughout the fall Powell demanded new outlays from the Kennedy campaign. Martin recalled giving him $5,000 one Saturday while the congressman was enjoying a massage in the House of Representatives gymnasium. Martin tucked the money in a book he handed Powell and rationalized, "We were paying for the speeches."

Powell and his associate, Ray "the Fox" Jones, the Democratic Party leader in Harlem, embroiled the campaign in one minor scandal. They claimed to have a copy of a racially restrictive real estate covenant linked to a Nixon-owned property and sent out a flyer underlining its exclusionary language and adding the word "Shame!" Wofford learned that mailing the document was a violation of law and called Jones. "Ray," he said, "we have been distributing something we shouldn't have been."

"You're a little late," Jones told him. "The FBI has just been seeing me this morning."

The Kennedy campaign learned to work with Powell and Jones and other colorful figures, but their vicissitudes with the black politicians in New York paled beside the trouble caused by a four-ring circus of strife featuring Tammany Hall, the state's liberal bloc, a Kennedy Citizens Committee yearning to be free of the party organization, and the reappearance of Paul Corbin, the Kennedy operative who kept showing up like the proverbial bad penny.

The Kennedy brothers, weary of dealing with Carmine DeSapio and Mike Prendergast, exacerbated relations with the New York bosses by fitting into their general election campaign two men who were bound to antagonize them: the artist William Walton, tapped to be in charge of Kennedy's Citizens Committee in the state, and Corbin, the unorthodox character from Wisconsin, sent as a troubleshooter without the hint of a portfolio.

Tammany had already sneered at the selection of Walton; in fact the Democratic organization claimed they had a commitment from the Kennedys that there would be no separate group in the state. Mix into the stew a lot of factional fighting, and New York had all of the ingredients for an explosion. DeSapio and Prendergast were already at war with the reformers. Meanwhile New York's Mayor Wagner was "becoming more and more a source of disrupting things," Prendergast claimed, because he was "playing ball" with Alex Rose, the leader of the Liberal Party, who clearly stood "against the organization."

Matters were made worse when Robert Kennedy introduced the Tammany bosses to two men who would be working for him in New York: Corbin and Ben Smith, a Kennedy friend from Massachusetts who had teamed with Corbin during the Wisconsin primary. "What the hell does a man from Wisconsin know about New York?" Prendergast snorted.

Robert mollified him by saying, "They don't know a thing, Mike. They're just fellows who are sort of making a little survey and looking over the state." In fact Smith and Corbin were being sent upstate to find fresh leadership for the Citizens Committees.*

The Tammany leaders agreed to send one of their allies, Pat Fischer, with Smith and Corbin to help with what they were told was to be a survey. Within a week Fischer, horrified, called Prendergast, insisting, "You better do something about this." Corbin was recruiting upstate voters to overthrow the party organization. "This guy Corbin is drunk. He's at the bar. He says that you and DeSapio are captives of the Italians and the Jews; that you and DeSapio have to go."

Another angry upstate party official warned Tammany Hall of Corbin: "If you don't have this guy out of here in five hours, I'm going to send somebody out to work him over."

In Corbin's version he was a freelance operator unleashed on the New York organization by Robert Kennedy, who told him, "Just do as I told you, just like you're back in Wisconsin," where Corbin had been a disruptive force in some circles. "It didn't take a week before the whole thing spread through the state," Corbin recalled proudly. Word was being passed that "there was a guy coming, Corbin, who was a son of a bitch, who's going to kick out DeSapio and get rid of the gangsters, get rid of the crooks."

The Tammany twosome complained bitterly to the Kennedy campaign. DeSapio and Prendergast made two trips to Washington to meet personally with Robert Kennedy. At another point Robert delegated Seigenthaler to deal with them. "He didn't want to listen to Mike Prender-

---

* After the election Smith was chosen to occupy Kennedy's Senate seat until Kennedy's youngest brother, Ted, came of constitutional age and could run for the position in 1962.

gast mouth about it," explained Seigenthaler. "It was sort of pathetic to see these two so-called powers in the Democratic Party coming down on their hands and knees to plead about the way the citizens' groups were acting in upstate New York."

There was an inherent conflict between independent Kennedy groups and party organizations in other states, Seigenthaler said. "It happened all across the country. . . . By and large, those problems were worked out. But there were times, especially in New York, when they did not work out."

(Most regular Democratic organizations and the citizens operations managed to work smoothly; in Michigan, for example, the two forces respected a strict division of labor between big cities and smaller communities. On the other hand, California remained the same faction-ridden problem it had been all year, and the discord would help cost Kennedy the state.)

In New York hatred boiled over. Prendergast despised Walton: "The guy was a problem. He used to tiptoe around here in a pair of sneakers with his handkerchief up his sleeve. I threw him out once. I told him: 'Don't come around here until you're dressed properly.'" When Walton suggested that Eleanor Roosevelt be invited to speak at an event, Prendergast snapped, "Mind your own goddamn business."

Walton too was harsh in his recollection of the squabble. He referred to DeSapio as "the Italian, evil man."

When Kennedy went to Harlem, all of the belligerent parties were on the dais with him. Walton said the Tammany bosses "openly snubbed Mrs. Roosevelt and Governor Lehman." And Kennedy noticed. "Jack was outraged," recalled Walton. "And he said, 'You know those cannibals. I want nothing to do with them. Nothing to do with them!'"

Behind the farce, however, was an understanding that New York was must-carry territory, the largest electoral vote prize of them all.

CHAPTER TWENTY-TWO

Calling Coretta

It was just a slow, steady thing; you just sat there and had to wonder whether it was slipping away. It certainly felt like it was." That's how Dick Donahue saw it. By November a genuine Kennedy veteran at the ripe young age of thirty, he was one of Larry O'Brien's three assistants in the campaign's nerve center, the place where hard information from every jurisdiction in the country poured in and from which instructions to the operators in the field were issued.

Five hundred miles north, from his ivory tower in Cambridge, Professor Walt W. Rostow had the same sense: "You could feel the margin narrowing."

Not one to sugar-coat anything, the ever-realistic candidate himself could feel something was a little off. As he listened to a new voice on Nixon's team in late October, Kennedy told Red Fay, "With every word he utters, I can feel the votes leaving me. It's like standing on a mound of sand with the tide running out. If the election were held tomorrow I'd win easily, but six days from now it's up for grabs."

That fresh voice belonged to the president of the United States. Ever since Eisenhower had quipped that it might take him a week to think of an important contribution Nixon had made to his administration, the political world had waited for him to make amends. During that time Nixon and his boss had played an ego game: Eisenhower was willing, but insisted on being asked to help, and Nixon kept putting off his entreaty.

Finally, as the debates wound down, Nixon swallowed his pride and asked. The result produced instant success. Ike's lines were hardly difficult to learn: *Nixon is as qualified as any candidate has ever been. He has been a big help. Vote for him.*

Their joint appearances went so well that the Republican National Committee arranged a half-hour of national prime-time television featuring a summary of the administration's record, an upbeat assessment of the country's current condition, and a gushing endorsement of Nixon. According to data collected for NBC, the Eisenhower program attracted the largest viewing audience for a paid event in the entire campaign.

What is more, a vigorous Eisenhower out on the road, flashing one of the best grins in the history of politics, fit perfectly into the communications strategy for Nixon's endgame. It was designed to warn of the dangers ahead in the world, to stress the importance of electing a president with experience, and to emphasize strength as the safest course toward peace.

Like Kennedy, Nixon had fully embraced the brave new world of television advertising. Unlike Kennedy's campaign, however, the Republicans were relentlessly repetitive, beginning with their slogan, "Nixon and Lodge: They understand what peace demands." Henry Cabot Lodge had become a familiar presence in American living rooms after his service as the U.S. ambassador to the United Nations. Nixon's organization used him frequently because their data showed, as did Lou Harris's, that Nixon's choice for vice president was far more popular than Kennedy's, especially outside the South.

In one commercial Lodge was alone on the screen, solemnly intoning, "We must remain strong so that no other nation dare attack us." In another, featuring just Nixon, the candidate reminded voters that both he and Lodge had actually sat across the diplomatic table from Khrushchev, who "feeds upon weakness."

On the road Nixon was offering foreign policy proposals almost on a daily basis—a special commission to study this, a new division of the State Department to take charge of that. He broke no new, substantive ground. But the blizzard of initiatives kept sending the message that there was a dangerous world beyond America's shores and that he was uniquely ready to face it.

In sharp contrast, Kennedy's message grew scattershot. His advertising included dissonant jingles, or his wife speaking in near-fluent Spanish to TV-watching Texans. On occasion something more sweeping appeared, such as a one-minute version of Kennedy's opening statement, his quick tour of the world, in the first debate.

Down the stretch Kennedy's speeches became more substantive. But for him that meant talking about housing one day, agriculture the next, and health care the day after that. He rarely made big news, even though the speech proposing what became the Peace Corps was developed in this period. For the most part he addressed the huge crowds with eloquent, stirring, uplifting platitudes. No phrase was heard more than his vow to "get this country moving again."

To the trained ear it sounded very much like a campaign whose leaders smelled victory and labored not to lose the advantage they believed they had. In the process they widened an opening for Nixon. Kennedy's pace was grueling, frenetic, but it created a curious phenomenon. He was riding a wave, but trying not to make waves.

Ever since Labor Day, Larry O'Brien and his aides had prepared weekly summaries of Kennedy's strengths and weaknesses in each of the states, with estimates of his numbers in the Electoral College. It was sent only to Jack and Robert Kennedy and Ken O'Donnell. Because these reports were extremely influential in making scheduling and advertising decisions, it was critical that they reflect reality.

With so little time left, the report on October 15, two days after the third debate, was the one with the most impact. O'Brien listed sixteen states with 191 total electoral votes where Kennedy was ahead. They included four states with significant electoral votes: Pennsylvania, New Jersey, Michigan, and Massachusetts. In the South advantages were seen in Georgia, Louisiana, Alabama, and Mississippi. In addition seventeen states, totaling 232 votes, were considered even. The major battlegrounds were New York, Illinois, California, and Texas, while in the South the states in play were North and South Carolina and Arkansas.

This was not a static view of the country. Throughout the fall states were moved regularly across the various categories. At one point O'Brien reported, "Since the October report we have elevated Oklahoma, Texas, Idaho and Nevada from losing to even, elevated West Va. from even to losing, and dropped Minnesota from leading to even." The campaign's most valuable resources—the candidate's time and money—were shifted accordingly.

Kennedy was adequately nimble in making the required adjustments. The exception was in California, with 32 precious electoral votes. The campaign's seemingly intractable trouble involved the still grumpy Stevenson liberals and other organizational challenges. With an excruciatingly close contest unfolding, the state cried out for attention. And yet the schedule called for Kennedy to leave the state for the last time with more than a week to go. Kennedy himself noticed the imbalance and quizzed O'Donnell vigorously about it. His top aide didn't disagree with his boss on the merits, but he argued that the schedule had been packed so tightly there simply was no way to make such a drastic change at nearly the last minute.

"I'll be wasting my time in New York," Kennedy said. "I've got New York and I've got Connecticut. But I haven't got California. Give me those two days in California and I'll win there.... You and your damned schedule. If we lose California it will be your thick-headed fault."

As the long campaign hurtled into its final days, the 1960 election was to be rocked by several unexpected events that sent voters swaying one way, then the other.

The Catholic issue could never be completely banished. Kennedy could afford to be whimsical early in the primary season when *L'Osservatore Romano*, the Vatican newspaper, editorialized about the Church's duty to advise its communicants how to vote. "Now I understand why Henry VIII set up his own church," Kennedy quipped privately. The report from Rome was largely ignored by the American public, and the candidate did not have to spend much time dissociating himself from it. In September his partisans felt he had effectively put the issue behind him with his performance before the Houston ministers.

But that was before three American-born Catholic bishops of the archdiocese of San Juan de Puerto Rico attempted to intervene in an election in the American protectorate in late October. The bishops issued a pastoral letter warning Catholics on the island that they would be denied the sacraments of communion if they voted for the Popular Democratic Party, headed by Luis Muñoz Marín. In fact Catholics who sided with Muñoz Marín were told they risked excommunication. The bishops objected to him because he refused to back legislation that would repeal a law permitting the distribution of literature relating to birth control.

The bishops' letter, widely published in the United States, revived the old concern that the Catholic Church was determined to meddle in politics, that it would not hesitate to dictate policy to a Catholic president and insist upon instructing American Catholics how to vote.

Faced with whether to confront the issue with a Houston-like counterattack or to hope that interest would fade without further ado, Kennedy chose to content himself with a third-person news release from his press office on October 23: "[The candidate] considers it wholly improper and alien to our democratic system for churches of any faith to tell the members of their church for whom to vote." The same language was used in form letters Kennedy's office sent to those who wrote asking about his position.

The campaign also quietly arranged for a statement from the official representative of Pope John XXIII in the United States in the period before there were formal diplomatic relations. Papal Nuncio Egidio Vagnozzi obligingly tried to paint the Puerto Rican actions as a strictly local issue. Nothing like that had ever been done in the United States, he noted, and added, "I am confident also that no such action would ever be taken by the hierarchy in this country." The controversy never reached critical proportions, but there was no doubt that it hurt.

The Kennedy campaign was also disturbed by indications that the offensive launched by the old soldier in the White House at the end of October was having an impact. As Sorensen characterized it, Nixon had "unlimbered his biggest weapon, Ike." Once he became engaged, Eisenhower was effective. He was showcased at a televised rally in Pittsburgh on October 29 and at another in New York four days later. Coupled with the dustup over the bishops in Puerto Rico, Eisenhower's entry into the campaign seemed to sap some of the momentum from the Democrats.

Then two totally unrelated, unpredictable events, incalculable in their importance, took place. One originated in Atlanta and came to a climax in the last weekend of the campaign; the other occurred in Dallas on the final Friday.

Throughout the fall Kennedy's beleaguered civil rights office had come up with ideas that were rejected or proved unsuccessful. In Louis Martin's first conversation with Kennedy, he proposed sending Nixon a telegram challenging him to take a stand on several issues. Kennedy responded, "That idea might sound all right, but you just don't know that s.o.b. Instead of answering directly, he will curve and come back with another question. I don't think we can pin the bastard down that way."

At another point the office sponsored a "flying caravan" of black celebrities—athletes, musicians, and actors— who were to travel from city to city to stimulate interest in Kennedy. One of their number was the old prizefighter Henry Armstrong, who had become a preacher. "In the middle of some of these political rallies he got off the electioneering and started preaching," Martin recalled. "It reached the point where they had to get rid of him because he was not always coherent."

A more practical suggestion involved a project to obtain Martin Luther King's endorsement. Following the convention Kennedy had a second meeting with King in Georgetown. The civil rights leader was impressed by Kennedy's learning curve on civil rights and satisfied that he "had been advised rather well." King was now convinced Kennedy "would do the right thing on the civil rights issue, if he were elected President." But as the leader of the nonpartisan Southern Christian Leadership Conference, he was unwilling to lend his name to the Kennedy campaign.

In lieu of an endorsement Kennedy's staff proposed a joint appearance, somewhere in the South, following an SCLC meeting where King would say he appreciated the Democratic Party's strong civil rights platform. But King said Nixon would have to be invited to the affair too. "Nixon may not come, but I would have to invite him," he told Kennedy's staff. They disliked the suggestion because it would convey an impression of King's neutrality. The idea died.

King wrote later, "I spent many troubled hours searching for the responsible and fair decision. I was impressed by [Kennedy's] qualities, by many elements in his record, and by his program. I had learned to enjoy and respect his charm and his incisive mind. But I made very clear to him that I did not endorse candidates publicly."

On October 19, less than three weeks before the election, King and thirty-five students were arrested for trespassing after a peaceful but fruitless effort to be served at the Magnolia Room, a restaurant on the sixth floor of Rich's department store in downtown Atlanta. The group symbolically declined to post bail. It would be the first night King spent in jail. The next day hundreds of demonstrators picketed segregated Atlanta businesses. There were more arrests. On Friday, October 21—the date of the last debate between Kennedy and Nixon—Atlanta officials, anxious to resolve the situation, allowed King to speak to reporters from jail. "I had to practice what I preach," he told the press, pointing out with pride that five of the six student body presidents from the complex of black universities in Atlanta were fellow prisoners.

On Saturday morning Kennedy's most forceful advisor on civil rights matters, Harris Wofford, was at home in a suburb of Washington when he decided to call his friend Morris Abram, an attorney in Atlanta, to see if anything could be done to free King. Abram was part of a liberal coterie of influential whites in Atlanta who were helping to build the city's reputation as a refuge from backwoods violence and injustice. So was the mayor, William Hartsfield, who had called a meeting at that hour with sympathetic whites and a number of black leaders to try to deal with the King case. Abram said he would tell Hartsfield of Wofford's call.

Several hours later Abram called Wofford and told him, "Sit down and hold on to your seat." Hartsfield had just informed the press that as a result of Kennedy's intervention he had reached an agreement that would lead to the release of King and the others. The spur-of-the-moment announcement created a major problem: Kennedy knew nothing of Wofford's call; in fact Wofford had been chastised earlier for trying to take the campaign's civil rights section too far.

The mayor, a moderate in a political sea of segregationists, joined the telephone conversation. "I know that I ran with the ball farther than you expected," he told Wofford, "but I needed a peg to swing on and you gave it to me."

Wofford's dismay mounted after Kennedy's campaign leaders in Georgia began pelting the Washington headquarters with furious complaints. Supporting King, they warned, would cost Kennedy Georgia— and probably other southern states.

Kennedy's precarious standing in Dixie was saved—for a time—by a couple of sudden developments. Reached in Kansas City, where he was campaigning, Kennedy learned of the Atlanta mayor's claim and approved a misleading news release issued by his press secretary, Pierre Salinger. It stated that, after receiving many calls about the King case, Kennedy had "directed that an inquiry be made to give him all the facts on the situation and a report on what properly should be done." Meanwhile Governor Ernest Vandiver and Griffin Bell, the chief of Kennedy's campaign in Georgia, issued their own press release, which declared, "We know that Senator Kennedy would never interfere in the affairs of a sovereign state."*

While the Kennedy campaign was dissembling, Mayor Hartsfield's initiative to free King faltered because the prisoners continued to refuse bail. By Saturday night he had pressured Atlanta businessmen, including Richard Rich, the owner of the giant department store, to drop their complaints of trespassing. In return the black negotiators agreed there would be no demonstrations on the following Monday. A sense of relief swept the city, but King and his followers would remain in jail through the weekend.

On Monday morning, October 24, jubilation among King's followers waiting outside the jail turned to anger when they learned he was being detained on still another charge, of violating the terms of the settlement of a traffic ticket he received in May in neighboring DeKalb County.

---

* Bell later became attorney general under President Jimmy Carter.

King and his wife had been driving the critically acclaimed Georgia novelist Lillian Smith to Emory Hospital for cancer treatment when the car was stopped by a patrolman—a common practice by police officers spotting racially mixed groups. King was found to be driving with an Alabama license after he had moved to Georgia. Charged with a misdemeanor, he was fined $25 and given a twelve-month suspended sentence by Judge Oscar Mitchell. Five months later King was now being charged with breaching the "good behavior" provision of the suspended sentence. The next day he was transferred to DeKalb County for a new hearing before Judge Mitchell.

Dozens of King's supporters, including his wife and Roy Wilkins, crowded into the little courtroom. They were stunned when the judge sentenced King to four months of hard labor. A Morehouse College philosophy professor, Samuel Williams, who protested loudly, was thrown to the floor by DeKalb County deputies and pitched into a holding cell with King. Coretta King was five months pregnant.

There were suspicions that Governor Vandiver was behind the decision, a belief reinforced when the governor's spokesman said, "I think the maximum sentence for Martin Luther King might do him good, might make a law-abiding citizen out of him and teach him to respect the law of Georgia."

The stern sentence was quickly condemned by civil rights supporters. In Washington, Wofford prepared a strong statement for Kennedy, but his draft disappeared into the campaign bureaucracy. Democratic leaders in Georgia felt it would sink their ticket if Kennedy expressed support for King. Wofford learned that Vandiver privately guaranteed "to get the son of a bitch out of jail if Kennedy would promise not to issue any public statement."

Fearing her husband's life was in danger, Coretta King called Wofford, whom she knew from his civil rights activities before he joined the Kennedy campaign. Years earlier she had told Wofford's wife of a "recurring dream that her husband would be killed in the movement, lynched or shot." Her voice breaking, she asked for help. Wofford decided to ask Kennedy to call Mrs. King but was unable to reach him.

He concluded that Kennedy's aides were thwarting his efforts to get the candidate involved.

Wofford thought of Chester Bowles, the Kennedy advisor who had once served as ambassador to India. As a fellow admirer of Gandhi's tactics of civil disobedience, Bowles had a good relationship with the Kings. Wofford called Bowles at his home; he was dining with Adlai Stevenson. Bowles immediately called Mrs. King and expressed sympathy, but he could not persuade Stevenson to speak to her. In another example of Stevenson's paralyzed judgment, he said he couldn't talk to her because he had never met her.

King's attorneys prepared a writ of habeas corpus to present to Judge Mitchell the next morning, but around 3 a.m. King was rousted from his DeKalb County jail cell and driven away, in handcuffs and leg shackles, into the darkness, to the state penitentiary in Reidsville, 230 miles from Atlanta. In a letter dated October 26 that began "Hello Darling," he wrote his wife, "This is the cross that we must bear for the freedom of our people. So I urge you to be strong in faith, and this will in turn strengthen me."

Learning that he had been moved to a prison notorious for racism and brutality, Coretta King called Wofford again. Her desperation provoked him to call the one person who might convince Kennedy to act: Sargent Shriver, the candidate's brother-in-law. Shriver had been head of the Catholic Interracial Council of Chicago and knew King. Wofford pleaded with him: "The trouble with your beautiful, passionate Kennedys is that they never show their passion. They don't understand symbolic action." He expressed frustration that he had been unable to reach Kennedy, confessing that he had turned to Bowles, who had the fortitude to call Mrs. King.

Shriver was in Chicago with Kennedy, who was resting in a hotel room at O'Hare Airport. Shriver waited until three other aides— Sorensen, O'Donnell, and Salinger—left the room before raising the subject with Kennedy because he knew all three would object to his advice.

He told Kennedy of King's treatment at the hands of Georgia officials and quietly suggested that he phone Mrs. King. "Negroes don't expect everything will change tomorrow," Shriver said, "but they do want to know whether you care. If you telephone Mrs. King, they will know you understand and will help."

Relenting, the candidate asked for her number, placed the call, and spoke with her briefly. It turned out to be a two-minute conversation that validated five years of Kennedy's political toil.

Overjoyed, Coretta King and her father-in-law, the Rev. Martin Luther "Daddy" King Sr., the patriarch of the family, went to Morris Abram's office to tell him about the call. Abram phoned Wofford. "It's happened!" he shouted. "Kennedy's done it. He's touched the heart-strings."

Kennedy casually mentioned his phone call to Mrs. King to Salinger on the flight out of Chicago. The press secretary's reaction differed drastically from Abram's. He alerted Robert Kennedy in Washington about the upsetting development. They both knew reports of the call would be leaked to the press, provoking unpleasant repercussions in the South. Robert's mood turned into cold fury. He instructed John Seigenthaler to usher the civil rights staff into his office. As he rounded them up, Seigenthaler warned, "Bob wants to see you bomb throwers right away."

Robert exploded when Wofford, Martin, and the others assembled before him. "Do you know that three Southern governors told us that if Jack supported Jimmy Hoffa, Nikita Khrushchev or Martin Luther King, they would throw their states to Nixon?" he hissed. "Do you know that this election may be razor close and you have probably lost it for us?" He ordered the civil rights staff to do nothing else of substance for the remainder of the campaign.

By late evening on Wednesday, October 26, news of the call had been made public. Coretta King told reporters in Atlanta, "It certainly made me feel good that he called me personally." She had heard nothing from Nixon or his staff. "Daddy" King, himself a powerful force in the nation's black community, declared that he had been planning to vote for Nixon because he was skeptical of Kennedy's Catholicism; now he intended to vote for Kennedy.

But "Daddy" King's son was still in prison.

At this point conflicting accounts muddle the story of the Kennedy calls made on King's behalf. One thing is clear: the attitude of Robert Kennedy, the most mercurial of the brothers, changed dramatically in twenty-four hours.

On the afternoon of October 27, a wire service bulletin out of Georgia reported that Judge Mitchell had gotten a call from Robert Kennedy asking for King's release. When Seigenthaler heard this, he confidently instructed the campaign press office to put out a release strongly denying it. Robert had told him that morning he was "not going to get into it." However, Seigenthaler recalled, Robert had been boiling after talking with his brother overnight and learning that the Georgia judge had denied King bond. When Seigenthaler drove him to the airport for a flight to New York, Robert seemed "particularly upset" about the lack of due process.

That afternoon, on Long Island for a speaking engagement, Robert went to a pay phone and made a call he told no one about.

Later in the day he checked in with Seigenthaler, who said, "Bob, you'd never believe the story that the AP has got out. . . . That crazy judge—he's going to be a real idiot—he says you called him on the telephone complaining about this."

Robert was silent. Then he replied, "John, you'd better get Tubby [a press aide] to put out another statement. I did call him."

"It just burned me all the way up here on the plane," he told Seigenthaler. "It grilled me. The more I thought about the injustice of it, the more I thought what a son of a bitch that judge was. I made it clear to him that it was not a political call; that I am a lawyer who believes in the right of all defendants to make bond, and one who had seen the rights of defendants misused in various ways."

That night Robert called Louis Martin, one of the men he had bawled out the day before, and informed him of his call to the judge. Delighted, Martin told him, "We now make you an honorary brother."

In an oral history he recorded several years later, Robert acknowledged for the first time that he had been motivated to call the judge after a conversation with Governor Vandiver. "The suggestion came from him either directly or indirectly. The judge was a good friend of the governor and the judge said that if I called and it was a matter of importance he'd make the arrangements." Robert said he had never told anyone of the call from Vandiver because he "thought it would destroy the governor" politically. But he made no mention of the conversation with his brother that may have been the decisive factor.

Vandiver confirmed some of the details much later in interviews he had with various authors. He said that Jack Kennedy had first called him to ask if there was any way to get King out of jail. The governor turned to his brother-in-law, George Stewart, who was a nephew of Senator Richard Russell and deeply involved in Georgia politics. According to Maurice C. Daniels's *Saving the Soul of Georgia*, Vandiver said that Stewart "went out and talked with Judge Mitchell. Judge Mitchell agreed, and I do not know what George told the man. He might have told him that he would get him appointed Federal judge or something. Anyway, he agreed that if either Senator Kennedy or Bobby Kennedy would call him personally and ask him to release Dr. King, that he would release him. I called Bobby Kennedy and relayed the message that George Stewart brought back to me. Bobby Kennedy called Judge Mitchell, and Martin Luther King was released from jail."

Despite their significance, the Kennedy phone calls caused relatively little excitement in the establishment press; however, the news reverberated far beyond Atlanta, through black communities across America. With ten days left before the election, Kennedy's civil rights team suggested a way to exploit the case. Again they turned to Shriver for approval of a brochure. To shield the Kennedy campaign from involvement, a Freedom Crusade Committee, associated with two black ministers from Philadelphia, was formed to sponsor the publication of a single sheet printed on both sides. It was called "The Case of Martin Luther King," and it juxtaposed "No-Comment Nixon" with a "Candidate with a Heart, Senator Kennedy." The Kennedy staff called the piece, printed on cheap, light blue paper, the "blue bomb."

During the next to last weekend before polls opened, 50,000 copies were mailed in bundles to blacks across the country. On Tuesday, November 1, Shriver printed 500,000 more copies for distribution to every black church in Chicago. Before the next Sunday, two days before the election, shipments of thousands more "blue bombs" were heading south on Greyhound buses. The same campaign that less than two weeks earlier had deplored any attempt by the clergy "to tell the members of their church how to vote" was now flooding black churches with campaign propaganda and working to persuade ministers to recommend that their faithful vote for Kennedy.

The Sabbath reception was staggering. The campaign got reports from black churches across America where virtually every worshipper seemed to be carrying a "blue bomb." Ray "the Fox" Jones even called to say the brochure had also touched a secular community; bars in Harlem, Jones reported, were abuzz with enthusiasm for Kennedy.

At the same time the blue bombs were being distributed, the Kennedy-Johnson ticket was the beneficiary of an ugly incident in Dallas. Johnson had gone to the biggest city in his home state to speak on the final Friday of the campaign only to be met by a mob of right-wing extremists who nearly knocked him and his wife, Lady Bird, off their feet.

Dallas was a likely setting for violence directed at the Kennedy campaign. The city was the regional headquarters for the John Birch Society, a far-right organization whose membership detected communists under every carpet and accused every president from Franklin Roosevelt to Dwight Eisenhower of being dupes of an international communist conspiracy. The Rev. W. A. Criswell, pastor of the city's largest congregation, the First Baptist Church, preached that "the election of a Catholic as president would mean the end of religious freedom in America." H. L. Hunt, the city's wealthiest oil baron, liked the sermon so much he had 200,000 copies printed and sent to like-minded ministers around the country. Hunt believed Catholics should be prevented from holding any public office. (In a mid-October Harris survey of Texas, Kennedy was leading 48 to 40 percent, but Harris said he was troubled by the high number of undecided voters, 12 percent, and even more disturbed by a finding that 37 percent of the respondents said religion would make a difference in their vote.)

In Dallas the hostility was palpable, even for the state's native son.

The angry reception for Johnson was organized by Bruce Alger, a conservative Republican congressman from Dallas. He recruited several hundred well-dressed women, some of them Junior Leaguers wearing mink coats, to hand out GOP campaign tracts on downtown sidewalks before Johnson's appearance. The women called themselves "Tag Girls." Others were encouraged to carry posters calling Johnson a "traitor" and "Judas." Alger himself held a sign proclaiming, "LBJ Sold Out to Yankee Socialists."

When the Johnsons arrived outside the Baker Hotel, where they usually stayed in Dallas, they were set upon by women screaming insults and spitting at them. One snatched Lady Bird's gloves from her hands and threw them in a gutter. Johnson, a head taller than his female adversaries, held his wife protectively as they struggled across Commerce Street toward the swanky Adolphus Hotel, where he was scheduled to speak. The couple was accosted again inside the Adolphus by Alger's corps of Tag Girls. Lady Bird appeared stricken by their vehemence. It took Johnson thirty minutes to push his way from the hotel entrance to the elevators.

Television cameras captured the melee, and when it was shown by the networks that night it caused tremors. Among northerners suspicious of Johnson's credentials, aversion was replaced by admiration for a man fending off a mob. For many Texans outside Dallas, the scene elicited embarrassment for their state and sympathy for their senator. It may have affected enough votes to swing the state to Kennedy. According to the Texas writer Lawrence Wright, the election "was decided that day in the lobby of the Adolphus Hotel. People said afterwards they were not voting for Kennedy so much as they were voting against Dallas."

Nevertheless the final weekend passed with no hint of the election's likely outcome. Public polling information available during those hectic days indicated the basic structure of the race had not changed since Labor Day. In critical California, Mervin Field's final statewide survey showed Kennedy at 49 percent, Nixon at 47. The situation was just as murky nationally. Gallup's final preelection survey showed Kennedy at 49 percent to Nixon's 48. Princeton Research called it 52 percent for Kennedy, 48 for Nixon. At CBS Elmo Roper (Lou Harris's mentor) ended the campaign with a survey giving 49 percent to Kennedy and 47 to Nixon, and he judged the 4 percent undecided to be leaning toward Kennedy.

All of the poll results fell within a statistical margin of error. That meant their outcomes could be reversed.

Not having any irrefutable grounds for optimism, Kennedy displayed a Black Irish penchant for pessimism at the end. On Election Eve he chatted very briefly after an appearance in Rhode Island with John Cauley, a pool reporter on the *Caroline* that climactic day. Cauley asked the candidate to size up his chances.

"The one question that I'm asking myself, frankly, is whether this country is ready for a Catholic President," Kennedy replied. "I don't know. Look at Oklahoma. We should never lose that state but I'm afraid we will."

CHAPTER TWENTY-THREE

The Squeaker

Kennedy was right about Oklahoma. But not about the rest of the evenly divided country.

Oklahoma went for Nixon early and decisively on November 8. With an advantage for the Republican nominee of more than 160,000 votes, or fully 18 percent of the 900,000 votes cast, it turned out to be Nixon's third largest margin (after Nebraska and Kansas) in the entire election. Indeed Oklahoma was one of very few states where Kennedy's vote count in 1960 was actually lower than Stevenson's in the Eisenhower landslide four years earlier. But contrary to Kennedy's dark election-eve analysis, his religion was not the only factor in his Oklahoma loss. By 1960, its prairie populism more fading memory than active force, Oklahoma was becoming a conservative state where Nixon's smaller government and stern, cold war–fighting image could resonate.

Elsewhere Kennedy was more fortunate. In the end his five-year quest for national office against enormous odds just barely succeeded. In political terms, all that traveling, speaking, maneuvering, and writing enabled his "positives" (fresh, vigorous, new thinking, Catholic, activist) to keep his "negatives" (inexperienced, unknown risk, bigger government, Catholic) at bay.

The popular vote was the closest since 1888, when the country actually elected the man who got fewer votes, Benjamin Harrison. The

Electoral College margin was the smallest since Woodrow Wilson's second squeaker in 1916. Kennedy got fewer votes than Eisenhower had in 1956 (34.2 to 35.6 million), despite the presence of some seven million additional, eligible voters. In twenty of the states the margin was below 5 percentage points; Nixon took six of them, and one state (Mississippi) went to a slate of Jim Crow–supporting, "independent" electors. Of the thirteen cliffhangers that went to Kennedy, only his advantage in North Carolina was above 4 percent and in five it was below 1 percent.

This was not what Kennedy and his campaign leaders had expected. There had been no preelection boasts of a landslide, but between Harris's polls and O'Brien's organizational high command, there had at least been an expectation of a clear if not solid victory. The price of the optimistic mood after the debates was a rough election day and night.

"We started getting down to the nuts and bolts of it and it was just terrible," recalled Donahue, whose desk was inside O'Brien's lair. "We were leaking and there was just a little bit of leaking all the time and the leak was just enough to keep you behind. . . . Although I never really thought we could lose—mere stupidity more than anything else—I just started to lose confidence that we could make it big and [then] confidence that we were going to be good and then you just want to win."

After voting in Boston, once again using his family's Beacon Hill apartment as his legal address, Kennedy and his wife arrived on Cape Cod in midafternoon. He was on the telephone frequently but not constantly. On this day he was not talking economics with Walt Rostow or domestic policy with Meyer Feldman or rhetoric with Ted Sorensen. His attention was focused solely on Donahue's nuts and bolts. And his major henchmen were focused on precincts and counties, not Kennedy himself.

Recalled John Bailey, who had traveled with Kennedy from the start, "On election day, Abe Ribicoff and I were sitting in the headquarters in Hartford. I was busy. I had a private telephone on my desk and we were trying to do some things, figure out how much we were going to win by and the rest. The telephone rang. I impatiently picked it up and said Hello. A voice said, 'Hello, John.' And I said, 'Who is this?' He said, 'This is Jack.' 'Jack who?' Then he said, 'It's the candidate, who do you think it is.' That day my mind wasn't on him. It was on Jack Somebody who was running the second or third ward someplace in the city."

Bailey told Kennedy he would take Connecticut by 90,000 votes. Bailey was not called a master of his craft for nothing; the margin was actually 91,000.

Much, much more was at stake than 8 electoral votes, or even the fact that not counting the four FDR victories Kennedy would be gaining Connecticut for the Democrats for the first time since 1912.

Ever since the advent of national radio networks in the 1920s, election nights in the United States had been paced by the time zones, with results reported east to west. That created the possibility that results in the first states to report, from the eastern third of the country, might influence the voting farther west, where the polls were still open.

The evidence supporting this possibility has always been skimpy, but the Kennedy campaign was nevertheless paying close attention to the incoming numbers. Even a month earlier O'Brien's weekly national report focused on the reason he was so concerned about Connecticut: "The need for an organizational effort in Connecticut is becoming increasingly more apparent. Polls in Connecticut close at 7 p.m. EST and, because Connecticut is an all [voting]-machine state, results will be known by 8 p.m. (5 p.m. on the West Coast, 6 p.m. in the Mountain Time zone, and 7 p.m. in the Central Time zone). A smashing triumph in Connecticut probably can influence 100,000 to 200,000 votes."

O'Brien's analysis was only half right. It neglected the other significant state with a relatively early poll-closing time, Kentucky, which his report had listed in the "even" column. Just as the dimensions of Kennedy's victory in Connecticut were becoming clear, it became equally clear that Nixon was winning in Kentucky by 80,000 votes, or more than 7 percentage points.

His broader point, however, was theoretically valid. Through midevening a torrent of solid Kennedy victories was reported in the eastern time zones, above all on television. The list was impressive: southern New England, New York, Pennsylvania, Maryland, Delaware, the South as far down as Georgia, as well as Michigan. Someone watching it all unfold on television saw a string of positive Kennedy showings and a clear lead in the popular and electoral vote totals.

The Kennedy compound in Hyannis Port at the end of a quiet street contained multiple dwellings. The main house, just inside the entrance off the street, was the redoubt of the candidate's parents, who mostly stayed there throughout the long evening and night. It was nearby, in the house used by Robert Kennedy, that the nerve center was established: thirty special telephone lines plus four teletype machines, most ending up in a large, first-floor sun porch. There the campaign's most important political people and more than a few useless hangers-on gathered, along with a half-dozen secretaries. In addition to following the action and making the occasional phone call himself, Kennedy punctuated his frequent visits to the command center with occasional solitary strolls on the large lawn outside.

The house he typically used in the compound was behind the command post. In an effort to provide a form of sanctuary, his wife had invited just one guest that night, William Walton. The three of them had an early meal. But Kennedy's inquiries about the numbers were constant.

"I told him a couple of lies about how things were going," recalled Donahue. "I made up a couple of stories which weren't totally inaccurate about the fact that the voting turnout was heavy in a lot of the cities and it was raining in some of the farm areas. . . . He was really relaxed. He was in and out of the house while I was doing some other things there. . . . I think that I was rather surprised that he could remain quite as calm as he did."

In addition to the dose of reality supplied by Kentucky, the first shock and keen disappointment was the result in Ohio. It had been the first major state to break Kennedy's way in the slog to the nomination, and it had been a major focus of effort in the general election. Throughout the final month Harris's surveys consistently showed a small Kennedy lead, and O'Brien's weekly surveys of polls and pols just as consistently put the state in the "ahead" column.

And they were all wrong—by a lot. By late in the evening Nixon was well on his way to a near-landslide in Ohio, with a margin of more than

270,000 votes, or 6.5 percentage points. This was one result that produced a worried huddle of the Kennedy brothers and O'Donnell to share the pain and to wonder what had gone terribly wrong. Was it anti-Catholic sentiment in the smaller communities in the southern part of the state? A lighter than expected turnout in Cleveland and other cities? More important, they worried about what the drubbing portended in the other industrialized states of the Midwest as well as Pennsylvania, where the returns at that point were inconclusive.

"We just could not figure it out," said O'Donnell. "Perhaps that was what was the most frightening. Was it the Catholic thing again? And if it was, what does that mean for the rest of the industrial states? After Ohio, Bobby and I took nothing for granted."

The second shock came from Wisconsin, another state to which there was a sentimental attachment dating from the primaries, but at least one where the expectation had been of a very close vote. Instead Nixon's victory margin was 65,000 votes, or more than 3.5 percentage points. O'Donnell recalled, "This meant Minnesota was in trouble; Minnesota was a seesaw right up until the very end."

As the returns came in from the Midwest and then the West, Kennedy's leads were shrinking steadily. He appeared to have won in Johnson's Texas, but tiny margins in New Mexico and Nevada were more than balanced by clear defeats in Oregon and Washington. The first major break came around midnight, not on television but in the print press. The *New York Times*, probably imprudently, put its first edition to bed with the banner headline "Kennedy Elected President." Coming just a dozen years after the *Chicago Tribune*'s historic goof, "Dewey Defeats Truman," it was an odd decision, more hunch than conclusion, and one not shared in either the Kennedy or the Nixon camp.

The second major break turned out to be a false alarm. Included in the array of machines in use on election night were direct, open telegraph lines connecting the Nixon and Kennedy campaigns with each other and with their national party headquarters in Washington. Their purpose, by agreement, was solely for the transmission of congratulatory or concession statements from the candidates and from President Eisenhower. Shortly after midnight the machine on Cape Cod came alive and printed out a message from Eisenhower congratulating "President-elect Kennedy." Fortunately Salinger had the presence of mind to look before leaping into the air. He contacted his White House counterpart, James Hagerty, who explained that one of the statements he had prepared in advance had been transmitted through a horrid error. He asked Salinger not to say anything about it; in an example of long-ago comity, Salinger complied.

The Kennedy group was just as surprised three hours later when Nixon himself appeared before cameras and supporters from his encampment at Los Angeles's fabled Ambassador Hotel to declare that the trends favored his opponent, but not by enough to produce a formal concession statement. Standing behind Donahue while watching Nixon on the television, Kennedy was his familiar detached self, murmuring at one point that his opponent was doing exactly what he would have done. But Kennedy could not have been serious; he had not been anywhere near a television camera at that point precisely because he knew the outcome remained in doubt.

At that tense point in the early morning hours, Kennedy was ahead, but only narrowly. Where counts had been completed he could depend for certain on 161 electoral votes to Nixon's 135. There were, however, eight states with 141 total votes where counts were still ongoing in extremely tight situations: Pennsylvania, Missouri, Illinois, Minnesota, Michigan, California, Hawaii, and Alaska. To get to the magic number of 269, Kennedy had several possible routes available to him; by contrast, Nixon could not afford to lose more than 6 of the electoral votes at issue, meaning he had to sweep all of the larger states and could lose only the two newly enfranchised ones.

The information available to both sides suggested a Kennedy advantage at that hour; in fact the television showed Kennedy ahead, with 262 electoral votes. That helps explain Nixon's appearance but also supports Kennedy's decision to remain mute.

Nixon's pessimistic statement, however, catalyzed a realization that there was nothing vital to be done before the sun came up. Almost immediately the set was temporarily struck on the sun porch as the senior people sought places for a nap. Kennedy himself walked next door, kissed his mother goodnight, and then returned to his own house and dozed for perhaps three hours.

The first clue that it might be over was the arrival around 6 a.m. of the first carloads of Secret Service agents, who in those days didn't start protecting a candidate until his election appeared certain.

The second clue was the conclusion of the count in Illinois, with Kennedy ahead by the infinitesimal margin of 8,800 votes out of more than 4.6 million cast. The controversies that would engulf the integrity of that count then and for decades afterward had yet to erupt; for the moment, 8,800 votes seemed an unlikely total to be overturned in a recount. He had also finished narrowly ahead in Pennsylvania, Missouri, Minnesota, and Michigan.

"We were satisfied," said Donahue. "We knew it was locked."

At the time, Kennedy's victory appeared more solid than it actually was. The election-night count had him ahead in California by roughly 35,000 votes out of more than 6.5 million, and he was trailing in Hawaii by well under 1,000 votes. But the California count included none of the absentee ballots cast by what was then a traditionally Republican constituency. By mid-November, when they were all counted, Nixon had come back to win the state by roughly the same margin Kennedy had enjoyed on November 9. And the inevitable recount in Hawaii produced Kennedy's smallest margin of victory in the entire election: 115 votes.

In addition the slates of "independent" electors that were on the ballot in three southern states had decidedly mixed results. They were walloped in Louisiana, where Kennedy won overwhelmingly. They very narrowly won in Mississippi, getting 8 electoral votes in the process. And they achieved a small plurality in Alabama, which, under an anomalous state law, produced 6 electoral votes for the segregationist slates and 5 for Kennedy. The 15th electoral vote was collected when one of the people on the Nixon slate in Oklahoma decided to join their cabal. Their standard-bearer was one of the Senate's most powerful segregationists, Harry Byrd of Virginia. The southern fourteen chose South Carolina's senator Strom Thurmond (the presidential nominee of the Dixiecrats in 1948) as their vice president; the renegade from Oklahoma chose Senator Barry Goldwater of Arizona.

THE ROAD TO CAMELOT   355

There was one more anomaly in the 1960 election. For the first and only time there were 537 electoral votes. The reason involved the enfranchisement of Alaska and Hawaii after they became states in 1959. From the total of 531 in 1956, each state got two votes for its new senators; in addition, as prescribed in a transitional statute, each got one new member in the House of Representatives until the 1960 Census laid the foundation for congressional reapportionment, at which point the total became 535 (Washington, DC's citizens got three more subsequently.)

The evenly split popular vote in 1960 was thus 34,220,984, or 49.72 percent, for Kennedy; 34,108,157, or 49.55 percent, for Nixon; and 610,409, or 0.42 percent, for the "independent" slates.

In the Electoral College the result was somewhat more clear-cut: 303, or 56.4 percent, for Kennedy; 219, or 40.8 percent, for Nixon; and 15, or 2.8 percent, for Harry Byrd.

Or was it?

Before the week was over, Nixon, at the start of a postdefeat vacation, announced that he would not contest the result by political means (essentially recounts) or through legal proceedings (lawsuits or investigations of alleged irregularities). However, at almost the same moment he was visited by the Republican national chairman, Thruston Morton, who not only urged Nixon to support a national campaign of challenges but also informed him that the party would undertake efforts in eleven states, beginning at once.

Over the decades that followed, much has been made of the Nixon statements, but only recently has more attention been paid to what the party's leaders actually did with Nixon's full awareness. In his first memoir, *Six Crises*, Nixon put on the cloak of statesmanship to describe his claimed refusal to use challenges to contest the election result. He said he decided not to act, even against the recommendations of senior Republicans, President Eisenhower included.

But Nixon's narrative is false. When Morton outlined his plans, Nixon could have stopped him on the spot with a simple, forceful request. He didn't, making him tacitly complicit in what followed. When his book was published two years later, he also neglected to note that after a very brief, fighting urge, Eisenhower had changed his mind and never supported the Republican actions that followed. Among the first people into the field to stir up challenges were such close and longtime Nixon friends as Robert Finch, Leonard Hall, and Peter Flanagan.

Any campaign of the sort the Republican Party put together in the days following a presidential election must proceed with a large clock ticking away. Typically state laws require some form of official certification of the Election Day numbers as a prelude to the actual casting of votes in the quadrennial meeting of the Electoral College; in 1960 that was to occur on December 19.

With Nixon's acquiescence, Morton's challenge was to come up with 50 electoral votes at Kennedy's expense once California's official result had flipped to Nixon and Hawaii's had flipped to Kennedy. That meant at least two of the larger states on his original list of excruciatingly close results, or at least one of the larger states plus nearly all of the smaller ones: Illinois, Texas, Delaware, Michigan, Minnesota, Missouri, New Jersey, New Mexico, Nevada, Pennsylvania, and South Carolina.

Almost immediately three of the states—Delaware, Michigan, and Minnesota—were taken off the list because of reassessed possibilities, legal or recounting obstacles, or both. In fact recounts in general quickly proved unworkable for the Republican protagonists.

The best example was in New Jersey, where, when the counting stopped on Election Day, Kennedy was ahead for its 16 electoral votes by the underwhelming margin of barely 0.8 percent. The Republicans quickly got recounts going in five counties, but by the end of the month they had failed to turn up any major deviations from the initial count. The process quickly came to a halt, as happened in five of the other states. That meant as a practical matter that the Republican campaign would have to concentrate on Texas and Illinois (with 51 electoral votes between them) and would have to prove fraud to prevent state certification and affect the Electoral College result in both states.

The Texas effort was unsuccessful almost immediately. State law did not have statutory provision for recounts. That meant the only recourse was the federal courts if the Kennedy margin of roughly 46,000 votes, or 2 percentage points, was to be reversed.

The hurdle the Republicans could not clear was jurisdictional. In what amounted to a civil rights lawsuit, they could not persuade a federal judge that he had the authority to intervene in what was after all a state election to select twenty-four electors. They did not bother to appeal.

That did not mean, however, that there was no factual basis for an attempt to challenge the result on grounds of fraud; there was, though it was anecdotal. For example, in East Texas a precinct was found in Angelina County (Lufkin is the seat) that had 86 registered voters but recorded 147 for Kennedy. And in another county farther north (Fannin, Sam Rayburn's home), there were 4,800 official voters who somehow cast 6,100 votes for Kennedy. These anecdotes, however, are just that. Not then, nor in subsequent decades, has any direct evidence of fraud surfaced that would come within a country mile of overturning the official result.

And that meant as a practical matter that the Republican effort could not have succeeded even if it had changed the result in the state about which experts and laymen have argued the most for more than fifty-five years. Tiny as it was, Kennedy's 8,800-vote margin in Illinois was actually only the second smallest of the election in percentage terms. (The margin in Hawaii was barely measurable.) But it was and is by far the most controversial.

As in Texas, there is anecdotal evidence supporting suspicions of fraud. It was found in Chicago wards as far apart as the Sixth, on the largely African American South Side, and the 28th, encompassing some of the city's white ethnic communities. In 1962 three people involved in the 28th ward (two precinct workers and a captain in Mayor Daley's powerful Democratic organization) pled guilty and served brief jail terms for their roles. In addition a Nixon friend and national correspondent for the *New York Herald Tribune*, Earl Mazo, found scores of matches between names on tombstones in one cemetery and those on voter registration rolls. He also visited a vacant, boarded-up house in the city that nonetheless recorded 56 Kennedy votes.

The Republican effort in Chicago and surrounding Cook County was connected to the efforts of the county's top prosecutor, Republican and vociferous Daley foe Benjamin Adamowski, to challenge the official result of his own reelection campaign, which left him trailing Democrat

Daniel Ward by 26,000 votes. A recount began at the end of November and covered nearly a thousand precincts. Two weeks later the effort had produced less than one vote per precinct more for Nixon, and in 40 percent of precincts the Nixon vote turned out to have been overcounted.

With these meager results the Republicans had no choice but to head to court, where the result was the same as in Texas. Though investigations would continue well past Kennedy's inauguration, the results were always the same. Through the ensuing years opinions, usually loudly argued, have been all over the place about Illinois in general and Chicago in particular.

Some analysts have simply assumed the very ground in contention. In addition to partisans on both sides, a more prudent approach has been to cite the very real anecdotal evidence with the awareness that, while no negative can ever be proved, what evidence there is remains far from conclusive.

After a month of accusations and defenses, as well as the accumulation of anecdotal evidence, Nixon finally appeared to have had enough. Not long before his death Mazo told the *Washington Post* that Nixon summoned him in mid-December, shortly before the Electoral College met and after the Illinois numbers had been certified by a Democrat-dominated, official board. Nixon asked him to stop reporting on the election in order to help avoid "a constitutional crisis."

"I thought he was kidding but he was serious," Mazo remembered. "I looked at him and thought he's a goddam fool."

Nixon then called Mazo's editors at the staunchly Republican *Herald Tribune*, whereupon he was pulled from the story, which at that point included four articles of what was to be twelve. Exactly to whom at the paper Nixon spoke has never been made known.

But that was that. On December 19 the Electoral College met and Kennedy was awarded his 303 votes. He had just barely won the election, but he had won legitimately.

The question remains, however, how the result can responsibly be interpreted and explained.

It is axiomatic in a very close election that theoretically almost anything can be cited as an event or situation that is dispositive. For example, many liberals and older voters were attracted to Kennedy because he proposed universal hospital insurance for the elderly, financed through the Social Security system; they probably numbered more than Kennedy's tiny margin in the popular vote. That, however, begs the question of how many voted for him only because of this proposal and how many voted for Nixon only because they disliked it. Similarly Kennedy's proposal to increase the minimum wage to $1.25 an hour from $1.00 was popular, but there is no evidence it swung the election his way.

A more productive exercise could be conducted with the two nominees' decisions on running mates to gauge the extent to which Johnson helped in the South (quite a bit in Texas and the South generally). By contrast, there is no evidence Johnson hurt the ticket even marginally in certain of the northern states; Lodge was better liked in general, but it is speculative to argue that a more liberal alternative would have delivered a single state Kennedy lost to make up for the opportunity Johnson helped provide in the South.

The list of specifics could be extended endlessly with no hope of producing a *Eureka* moment. It's probably more prudent to focus on the bottom lines, the basic architecture of the results.

Kennedy's election represented a shift of 8 percentage points from Eisenhower's large total of 57.8 percent to Nixon's losing share of 49.8 percent. In popular vote terms, Nixon and Kennedy had modestly fewer supporters than the personally popular Eisenhower did in 1956.

The partisan split is revealing. According to the final preelection Gallup polls that the firm later adjusted to reflect the election results, Democrats do not appear to have voted much differently in 1960 than they did in 1956. In Eisenhower's landslide, Stevenson actually increased his vote among Democrats over 1952, winning by 85 to 15 percent. The numbers were not statistically different for Kennedy in 1960, though there were more Democrats in the mix than there had been four years earlier.

The real difference was among Independents, already a growing force in national politics, particularly in the country's explosively expanding suburbs. According to Gallup, the margin among Independents in 1956 for the war hero president with a nonpartisan image was an overwhelming 70 to 30 percent as he won reelection. But four years later the more traditionally Republican Nixon, who had a highly partisan image, fell to a much more competitive 57 to 43 percent.

A few days after the election Meyer Feldman penned a memorandum to his fellow senior staff members attempting to make the case that Kennedy's victory was meaningful, that a mandate could be discerned in the numbers. "On November 8, 1960, 22 states representing 103,750,000 people gave Senator Kennedy a majority," Feldman wrote. "These states represent 58.1 percent of the population of the United States."

It was a lame point, and no top Kennedy person, much less Kennedy himself, attempted to make it in public. The evidence suggests the victory was much more personal than political or ideological. Yet even the personal nature of Kennedy's victory demands qualification. It is not even clear that he won the popular vote, given the unique peculiarities of the voting in Alabama, where the votes for individual electors are maddeningly difficult to characterize.

Two years earlier, in the off-year election that occurred at a time of economic downturn and in the sixth year of a presidency, when the "in" party normally suffers losses, the Democrats had achieved a substantial victory. Some correction might have been expected in 1960, but in modern times the much higher voter turnout for a presidential election has usually favored Democrats.

However, on the day he was elected, Americans also voted in two Republican senators and twenty-one Republican representatives; Republicans also increased their standing in state legislatures as well as state and local offices. That is hardly evidence of a clear mandate to "get his country moving again."

Much more important is the simple, overarching fact that outside of his native Massachusetts more Americans voted for Nixon than Kennedy. It is hard to claim a mandate from facts like these, and he did not. Indeed as president Kennedy sometimes had a small piece of paper in his suit jacket pocket on which he wrote his infinitesimal popular vote margin—to remind himself and others pressing him for "bold" action. (His one such move after the election was confined to his Democratic congressional majority. In an effort to make it much harder for the Republican-Dixiecrat alliance to block legislation he successfully expanded the membership of the House Rules Committee, which regulates the flow of legislation to the floor for votes. Kennedy was well aware that among the 63 freshmen elected to the 435-member House in 1960, his committee-packing proposal was opposed 44 to 19.)

At the margin or tipping point of Kennedy's election, two elements—race and religion—stand out as having had a significant impact on both the result and the margin. There was a spike in the African American turnout in northern, urban areas, overwhelmingly in Kennedy's favor, that was a factor in his victories in New York, Pennsylvania, Michigan, and Illinois. And the issue that never seemed to go away, religious bigotry directed at a candidate who happened to be Catholic, loomed larger than any other, costing him millions of votes but also probably helping him achieve his clear Electoral College victory even as it reduced his popular vote total.

In 1960 what came to be called "exit polls" did not yet exist. However, similar work was done at the time that provides at least some relevant information. One was a series of polls conducted just before and just after national elections beginning in 1948 under the aegis of the University of Michigan's Survey Research Center. Another is Gallup's historical data. Still another began inside the Democratic Party and then the Kennedy campaign, sparked by three MIT political scientists— Ithiel de Sola Pool, Robert Abelson, and Samuel Popkin—with support from a New York businessman, Edward Greenfield, and evolved into an academic project after the election. It involved combining all of the campaign year's polling data as they were collected and projecting trends forward from this massive amount of information with the aid of computers using simulation, then a new technique. In 1959 top party officials responded favorably to a proposal by the group, and preliminary data collection work began. The involvement with the Kennedy campaign, including at least two meetings with Robert Kennedy, took place between late spring and Election Day, intensifying as strategies for the general election were being put together before Labor Day.

The very first report by the group, "Negro Voters in Northern Cities" was issued in June; it strongly urged vigorous support of the civil rights movement, a position toward which Kennedy was already moving after years of temporizing and as it became apparent that despite his best efforts Johnson would get nearly unanimous southern support at the Democratic convention. "In a close election, even a moderate shift in Negro votes could be decisive in eight [key northern states]," it read in part. "Any shifts in the Negro vote could determine the outcome."

Kennedy's support for the civil rights movement increased even more at the convention and subsequently and reached its zenith with the two phone calls to Georgia in late October by his brother Robert and Kennedy himself that helped gain Martin Luther King's release from prison. The campaign was decidedly low key in its handling of the incident in the national media but worked hard to get the word out through the African American press and in the distribution of at least one million "blue bombs" at churches the weekend before the election. According to the analysis by the MIT group, "That helped to push the Negro Democratic [vote] in 1960 from the two-thirds to which it had fallen to something like three-quarters of the total Negro vote." This analysis was confirmed by the Gallup poll numbers. In 1956 the nonwhite vote broke 61 to 39 percent for Stevenson over Eisenhower; four years later the late-moving spread was 68 to 32 percent of a larger turnout.

In addition to race, the other major undercurrent in the election (arguably the most significant in terms of both the result and the margin) was religion. In the ensuing decades some have argued that Kennedy's Catholicism hurt and some that it helped his campaign. Upon close examination, the more complex answer is that it both hurt and helped; it helped supply his Electoral College victory, and it prevented his margin in popular and electoral votes from being greater and more solid.

The Gallup data showed that between 1956 and 1960, the Republican margin in the Protestant vote stayed basically the same—a bit more than 60 percent to a bit less than 40 percent. But among the roughly one-fourth of the electorate that was Catholic—traditionally a Democratic constituency—there was a dramatic shift, from a basically even split in 1956 to a 78–22 percent Kennedy margin in 1960.

As the MIT analysts explained, "Millions of Protestants and other non-Catholics who would otherwise have voted Democratic could not bring themselves to vote for a Catholic. In total—so our model says—

roughly one out of five Protestant Democrats or Protestant Independents who would otherwise have voted Democratic bolted because of the religious issue."

On the flip side, the MIT group also calculated the votes Kennedy gained because he was Catholic. Using its enormous database and computers, the group concluded, "Taking Congressional voting as a base for estimating normal party vote, over one-third of Catholics who would otherwise have voted Republican seemed to switch to Kennedy. The best guess is around 40 percent."

According to the Michigan survey, 10.8 percent of all voters, or about 7.3 million people, switched votes because of religion. Kennedy's net loss was calculated at 1.5 million. However, those anti-Catholic votes were not evenly distributed. They were bunched more heavily in the southern part of the country, relatively safer territory for the Democrats back then; and they were less of a factor in the more closely contested west and north, where Catholics were more prominent.

The MIT team used data from every state to make judgments about the Electoral College impact. The states Kennedy would have lost had it not been for Catholic voters: Connecticut, New York, New Jersey, Pennsylvania, Illinois, and New Mexico. That is, 132 electoral votes. And the states Kennedy lost because of his religion: Kentucky, Tennessee, Florida, Virginia, Oklahoma, Montana, Idaho, Utah, California, Oregon, and Washington. That is, a net gain of 10 electoral votes.

It is silly to speculate about how the election would have turned out had Kennedy not been a Catholic; had he not been, he wouldn't have been Kennedy. But it is not silly to take Kennedy's religion as a given and recognize that his popular vote and electoral vote margins were held down by widespread religious bigotry that was almost instantly marginalized by his historic victory.

Five years of hard work—intellectual and political—had helped him win the Democratic nomination and then the presidency. He had begun seeking national office because he discovered a way forward politically; his ambition, as he saw it, had not been about some cause or issue. It was to be in Theodore Roosevelt's arena, to be in a position to wrestle with the biggest issues and make a difference.

And politics and the issues aside, his "intellectual blood bank"—his aide Ted Sorensen—never stopped reminding friends after Kennedy was murdered why his victory mattered. "We're still here," he would say. For thirteen days in October 1962 Kennedy used the same attributes he displayed during the marathon of his campaign to figure out how to keep a nuclear confrontation with the Soviet Union from becoming a nuclear war.

ACKNOWLEDGMENTS

This book grew from separate ideas by two good friends who worked together for the *Boston Globe* for more than a quarter-century.

As a teenager, Curtis Wilkie had watched on TV the frantic battle for a vice presidential nomination at the 1956 Democratic convention, intrigued by the raw politics of that afternoon and the emergence of a young Massachusetts senator who lost the fight. Nearly fifty years later he drafted a proposal for a book about it. He and his agent pitched the idea to several publishers, but there were no takers. He even met in New York with a revered editor at Simon & Schuster, Alice Mayhew, who told him, "Not big enough." Come back with something bigger, she advised.

Ten years passed, and other books were written by Wilkie and his *Globe* running mate during eight presidential campaigns, Tom Oliphant, who as a teenager in 1960 had canvassed in southern California for six months on behalf of Kennedy. In 2013 Oliphant was visiting Wilkie in Oxford, Mississippi, and told of a conversation he once had with Ted Sorensen, who had wistfully wondered why no one had ever written a book about Kennedy's long run to the White House, an audacious undertaking that actually began when Kennedy was thirty-eight years old. He believed one could make a case that the five-year-long Kennedy campaign revolutionized the American political process by employing a successful grassroots operation that bypassed the party bosses who once controlled the conventions and also introduced the use of polls and thirty-second television spots. At the same time the Kennedy operation skillfully developed several issues that became important laws, including Medicare and federal aid for local education, and defied the dictum that no Catholic could be elected president in this country.

As Oliphant talked, he generated an epiphany. Wilkie retrieved from his campus office a dusty file bulging with material on the 1956 convention as well as notes from interviews in 2002 and 2003 with surviving associates of Kennedy and reporters who knew him back then. The concept for this book started that day.

We knew that any book that led to Kennedy's triumph in 1960 would be laboring under the shadow of Theodore H. White's *The Making of the President 1960*. We were both admirers of White and his book, which changed the way reporters covered presidential campaigns as much as we discovered the Kennedy effort changed the way campaigns are run. Over the course of our own careers as political reporters, both of us became friends with Teddy White. This book is not an attempt to emulate his work but to take up a challenge he laid down in his own author's note when he suggested that later writers "would tell the story of the quest for power in 1960 in more precise terms with a greater wealth of established fact."

Over more than a half-century tens of thousands of articles and hundreds of books have been written of the Kennedy era. More important for our purposes, the John Fitzgerald Kennedy Library in Boston assembled a vast collection of material, including more than 23 million pieces of paper and 1,600 invaluable oral histories from those who dealt firsthand with Kennedy. Some of them were well-known figures; others played important roles in the Kennedy campaign, but their stories would be lost were it not for the oral histories.

We do not purport to be historians. But as journalists we have always tried to keep a sense of historical perspective in our writing. As Kennedy's daughter, Caroline, said not long ago, her father's time in the political arena is slowly but surely slipping into history, past the comments and memoirs of contemporaries. This book, published in the year Kennedy would have been one hundred, is our effort to weave these tales from that critical period between 1955 and 1960 into a narrative that tells the story of how he set out—much earlier than most people know—to win the presidency

This was a true collaboration. We talked the idea through together, we proposed it together, we researched together, we wrote together, and we revised and rewrote together. In the process we had the guidance and direction of two astonishing women who helped shape the idea as well as the manuscript: our literary representative, Deborah Grosvenor, and our editor at Simon & Schuster, none other than the legendary Alice Mayhew. We are also forever grateful to Mayhew's assistant, editor Stuart Roberts, as well as to Susan Spencer, who in addition to being a correspondent for CBS News, Oliphant's wife, and Wilkie's dear friend, contributed greatly to curbing her husband's verbosity and suggesting gently that he get to the point.

Our collaboration was greatly aided by the twenty-first century, especially the wonders of the computer and modern health care. In past projects each of us would have scores of stacks of papers filled with research notes, manuscript drafts, and other writing detritus arranged in occasionally logical piles all over our offices. This time, though typically separated by hundreds of miles between Oxford, Mississippi, and Washington, DC, we could read our collective notes, figuratively look over each other's shoulders as we wrote and revised, and moved chunks of our writing within the manuscript with the touch of a few buttons. Neither of us claims anything remotely resembling computer literacy; this project would have been infinitely more complex had it not been for the patient assistance of people who actually know what they're doing in this daunting technology. Oliphant was happily dependent on the ministrations of Sherry Ellis. Wilkie relied on Chi Kalu, a talented graduate assistant at the Overby Center for Southern Journalism and Politics at the University of Mississippi, where he works.

In the early stages of the writing Oliphant never lost a beat despite a vicious case of flu and pneumonia. For that he will never cease being grateful to the geniuses at the Washington Hospital Center; his recovery to alert productivity was also greatly aided by the constant tortures of his skilled trainer, Melissa Toohey.

Wilkie's diversion due to a health issue had a much sadder ending. During the last year of the project his beloved wife, Nancy, a close friend of Tom and Susan, became seriously ill. Though she battled her illnesses through two lengthy hospitalizations and three trips to Mayo Clinic, Nancy died on September 1, 2016, two weeks after our manuscript was turned in.

Ambassador Caroline Kennedy's point that history is slowly but surely taking over the treatment of her father's time in the public square means that research via the documentary record is gradually becoming the route to more information and to a better understanding of how he became a national figure and then president. Nearly everyone who played an important role is now gone. Gradually personal memories are being enhanced and often supplanted by direct, recorded evidence. In particular the Kennedy Library is a stunning resource that we were somewhat surprised to learn has only begun to be fully searched for information and insights.

The assistance we received at the library was immense. As the director of archives, Karen Abramson could not have been more kind. The same goes for colleagues at the library who have moved on, above all the incomparable Heather Campion, the former chief executive of the Kennedy Library Foundation; and two former colleagues at the library itself, Tom Putnam and Amy Macdonald. But no superlative is adequate for the archivists themselves, who combine encyclopedic knowledge of John Kennedy with a friendly ability to help novices like us work with this gargantuan collection. No author can claim more knowledge or understanding of Kennedy than Stacey Chandler, and she has equally amazing colleagues to whom we will always be grateful: Abbey Malangone, Laurie Austin, and Michael Desmond.

Aside from the Kennedy Library, we extend our thanks to Judy Greenwood and her staff at the Inter-Library Loan Office as well as Jennifer Ford and Leigh McWhite at the J. D. Williams Library at the University of Mississippi; to the Center for Oral History at the University of Southern Mississippi; to Special Collections at Mississippi State University Library; and to the Seeley G. Mudd Library at Princeton University.

We also were greatly aided by those in the Kennedy world as we began to think, plan, and work. Ambassador Jean Kennedy Smith, the president's younger sister, could not have been more gracious and helpful, as was her son, Stephen.

Before he died, Ted Sorensen was a continual source of guidance, goading, and mentoring, as was his widow, Gillian, and the assistant who helped assemble his final memoir, Adam Frankel.

We are grateful to Dick Donahue, the last survivor from the legendary Irish Mafia, who before his death was a gracious supplier of both anecdote and insight. Along with his widow, Nancy, Dick was at Kennedy's elbow from his first race for the Senate through his presidential campaign.

John Seigenthaler, who retained his reporter's eye during his service to John and Robert Kennedy, was an engaging source of stories while he lived, and his lengthy oral histories are full of inside information.

From our own experience as reporters for the *Boston Globe* we knew personally and benefited greatly from many of the characters from Kennedy's political wars, including his brother Ted, Eugene McCarthy, Tip O'Neill, Walter F. Mondale, Edmund Muskie, John Brademas, Morris Udall, Edward Boland, William Winter, Frank Church, and George McGovern.

Others who lived through those days and acquired significant knowledge, whose information and insight aided us, have our gratitude forever. They include Charles Daly, Newton Minow, James Symington and his brother, Stuart Symington Jr., Russell Baker, Sander Vanocur, Christine Sullivan, Melody Miller, Martin F. Nolan, Robert Shrum, and Nick Littlefield.

For all that gratitude, however, any error discovered in this work is our responsibility alone.

BIBLIOGRAPHY

This bibliography is not meant to be an extensive guide to Kennedy books but rather a list of those books that were helpful to us in writing *The Road to Camelot*.

Abramson, Rudy. *Spanning the Century: The Life of W. Averell Harriman 1891–1986.* New York: William Morrow, 1992.

Beatty, Jack. *The Rascal King: The Life and Times of James Michael Curley (1874 1958).* New York: Addison-Wesley, 1992.

Bradlee, Benjamin C. *Conversations with Kennedy.* New York: Norton, 1975.

Branch, Taylor. *Parting the Waters: America in the King Years 1954–63.* New York: Simon & Schuster, 1988.

Bruno, Jerry, and Jeff Greenfield. *The Advance Man.* New York: Morrow, 1971.

Burns, James MacGregor. *John Kennedy: A Political Profile.* New York: Harcourt Brace 1960.

Caro, Robert A. *The Years of Lyndon Johnson: Master of the Senate.* New York: Knopf, 2002.

Caro, Robert A. *The Years of Lyndon Johnson: The Passage of Power.* New York: Knopf, 2012.

Cohen, Adam, and Elizabeth Taylor. *American Pharaoh: Mayor Richard J. Daley. His Battle for Chicago and the Nation.* Boston: Little, Brown, 2002.

Cohen, Dan. *Undefeated: The Life of Hubert H. Humphrey.* Minneapolis: Lerner, 1978.

Dallek, Robert. *Lone Star Rising: Lyndon Johnson and His Times 1908–1960*. New York: Oxford University Press, 1991.

Dallek, Robert. *An Unfinished Life: John F. Kennedy 1917–1963*. New York: Little, Brown, 2003.

Eisele, Al. *Almost to the Presidency: A Biography of Two American Politicians*. Blue Earth, Minn.: Piper, 1972.

Fay, Paul B. *The Pleasure of His Company*. New York: Harper & Row, 1966.

Goodwin, Doris Kearns. *The Fitzgeralds and the Kennedys*. New York: St. Martin's, 1987.

Goodwin, Doris Kearns. *Lyndon Johnson and the American Dream*. New York: Harper & Row, 1976.

Guthman, Edwin, editor. *Robert Kennedy in His Own Words*. New York: Bantam, 1991.

Haygood, Wil. *The King of the Cats: The Life and Times of Adam Clayton Powell*. Boston: Houghton Mifflin, 1993.

Hersh, Seymour M. *The Dark Side of Camelot*. Boston: Little, Brown, 1997.

Humphrey, Hubert H. *The Education of a Public Man: My Life in Politics*. New York: Doubleday, 1976.

Kennedy, Edward M. *True Compass*. New York: Twelve, Hachette, 2009.

Kennedy, John F. *Profiles in Courage*. New York: Harper & Brothers, 1956.

Kennedy, Rose Fitzgerald. *Times to Remember*. New York: Doubleday, 1974.

Martin, John Bartlow. *Adlai Stevenson and the World: The Life of Adlai E. Stevenson*. New York: Doubleday, 1977.

Martin, Ralph, and Ed Plaut. *Front Runner, Dark Horse*. New York: Doubleday, 1960.

Merry, Robert. *Taking on the World: Joseph and Stewart Alsop—Guardians of the American Century*. New York: Viking Penguin, 1996.

Nasaw, David. *The Patriarch: The Remarkable Life and Turbulent Times of Joseph P. Kennedy*. New York: Penguin Press, 2012.

Nixon, Richard M. *Six Crises*. New York: Doubleday, 1962.

Novak, Robert D. *The Prince of Darkness: 50 Years Reporting in Washington*. New York: Crown, 2007.

O'Brien, Lawrence F. *No Final Victories: A Life in Politics from John F. Kennedy to Watergate*. Garden City, NY: Doubleday, 1974.

O'Donnell, Kenneth, and David Powers, with Joe McCarthy. *Johnny We Hardly Knew Ye: Memories of John Fitzgerald Kennedy*. Boston: Little, Brown, 1972.

Risen, Clay. *The Bill of the Century: The Epic Battle for the Civil Rights Act*. New York: Bloomsbury Press, 2014.

Roberts, Gene, and Hank Klibanoff. *The Race Beat: The Press, the Civil Rights Struggle, and the Awakening of a Nation*. New York: Knopf, 2006.

Schlesinger, Arthur M., Jr. *Robert Kennedy and His Times*. Boston: Houghton Mifflin, 1978.

Sorensen, Theodore C. *Counselor: A Life at the Edge of History*. New York: Harper-Collins, 2008.

Sorensen, Theodore C. *Kennedy*. New York: Harper & Row, 1965.

Thomas, Evan. *Robert Kennedy: His Life*. New York: Simon & Schuster, 2000.

White, Theodore H. *The Making of the President 1960*. New York: Atheneum, 1962.

Wofford, Harris. *Of Kennedys and Kings: Making Sense of the Sixties*. New York: Farrar, Straus & Giroux, 1980.

NOTES

CHAPTER ONE

2   To underline his seriousness: Thomas G. Corcoran, unpublished memoir, Corcoran Papers, Library of Congress. See also Robert Dallek, *An Unfinished Life: John F. Kennedy 1917–1963* (Boston: Little, Brown, 2003).

3   "Kennedy was then": Abram Chayes, Oral History, pp. 13–14, John F. Kennedy Library, Boston (hereinafter JFKL).

3   "We all underestimated Kennedy": Joseph Clark, Oral History, p. 88j, JFKL.

4   "The Senator's own interest": Theodore C. Sorensen, *Kennedy* (New York: Harper & Row, 1965), p. 83.

4   "I think he just wanted to see": Robert F. Kennedy, Oral History, p. 660, JFKL.

4   One of the very first articles: Ralph G. Martin and Ed Plaut, *Front Runner, Dark Horse* (Garden City, NY: Doubleday, 1960), p. 27.

5   an earlier Sorensen memorandum: Sorensen, p. 81.

5   Kennedy was thinking of entering the New Hampshire primary: Sorensen, *Kennedy*, p. 81.

6   "We all know that all 96 Senators": Theodore C. Sorensen, Personal Papers, Box 11, JFKL.

CHAPTER TWO

8   "Sometimes you read": Charles Bartlett, Oral History, p. 3, JFKL.

8   it was a "mistaken impression": James G. Colbert, Oral History, pp. 1–3, JFKL.

8   "It's often been said that his father": Andrew Dazzi and John Harris, Oral History, pp. 23–24, JFKL.

9   To the extent Kennedy had a campaign manager: Mark Dalton, Oral History, pp. 1–18, JFKL.

11   "I thought I might be governor": Michael Widmer and Caroline Kennedy, *Listening In: The Secret White House Recordings of John F. Kennedy* (New York: Hyperion, 2012), p. 235.

12   "the only game in town": Theodore C. Sorensen, *Counselor: A Life at the Edge of History* (New York: HarperCollins, 2009), p. 169.

12   "As I told JFK": Ibid., p. 170.

12   The first words of encouragement: Quigley letter to JFK and Kennedy response, Pre-Presidential Papers, Box 507, JFKL.

14   "We have at the banquet table tonight": Sorensen, Personal Papers, Box 9, JFKL.

14   "You have to remember": John M. Bailey, Oral History, p. 3, JFKL.

14   "Early in '56": Fletcher Knebel, Oral History, p. 3, JFKL.

15   Knebel's visit motivated Sorensen: Fletcher Knebel, Oral History, p. 4, JFKL; Sorensen, *Kennedy*, p. 85.

15   "I got the credit": John M. Bailey, Oral History, p. 5, JFKL.

15   the document "caused many people to think": Ibid.

15   "The widespread attention accorded its contents": Sorensen, Kennedy, p. 83.

16   "All indicate that there is": Theodore C. Sorensen, "The Catholic Vote in 1952 and 1956." All quotations that follow are from the "Bailey Report" and notes that Sorensen wrote, to be found in Sorensen, Personal Papers, Box 9, JFKL.

19   "While I think the prospects are rather limited": Kennedy letter, June 29, 1956, in *The Letters of John F. Kennedy*, edited by Martin W. Sandler (New York: Bloomsbury, 2013) p. 54.

20   In the face of: Sorensen, *Kennedy*, p. 84.

21   But according to McCarthy's top aide: Roy Cohn, Oral History, p. 3, JFKL.

22   When the roll-call vote that destroyed McCarthy: Sorensen, *Counselor*, p. 163.

22   Sorensen always insisted it was his own decision: Ibid.

22   The last word, ironically: Sorensen, Personal Papers, Campaign Files, Box 25, JFKL.

23   Farmers, liberals, and his father aside: Sorensen, Personal Papers, Box 9, JFKL.

CHAPTER THREE

24   Burke "was controlled wholly": John E. Powers, Oral History, JFKL.

25   In private conversations with friends: John Sharon, Oral History, JFKL.

25   McCormack had circulated a petition: Thomas P. O'Neill, Oral History, JFKL.

25   His mother, Rose, had passed on a bit of family history: Gerard O'Neill, *Rogues and Redeemers: When Politics Was King in Irish Boston* (New York: Crown, 2012), p. 97.

26   with Joe McCarthy: Kenneth O'Donnell and David Powers, *Johnny, We Hardly Knew Ye: Memories of John Fitzgerald Kennedy* (Boston: Little, Brown, 1972), p. 105.

26   "Leave it alone": Ibid.

27   Kennedy supported Adlai Stevenson: Ibid., p. 106.

27   Without revealing that he planned: Ibid.

28   "We can't let Burke or McCormack know": Ibid.

28   the elder Kennedy loaned Fox $500,000: Herbert S. Parmet, *Jack: The Struggles of John F. Kennedy* (New York: Dial Press, 1980), pp. 242–43.

28   But Fox broke with the Kennedys: O'Donnell and Powers, *Johnny, We Hardly Knew Ye*, p. 108.

28   The skirmish over control of the state committee: Joseph Rauh, Oral History, JFKL.

29   The morning after the primary: O'Donnell and Powers, *Johnny, We Hardly Knew Ye*, p. 109.

29   The following day Kennedy drove: Ibid.

29   Burke provoked one story: Ibid., p. 110.

29   Kennedy had been so preoccupied: Ibid., p. 111.

30   "They want an old familiar face": Ibid., p. 112.

30   Mired in the ferocious culture of Boston politics: Sorensen, Personal Papers, JFKL.

30   to avoid "further disruption": *Boston Globe*, May 17, 1956.

30   "McCormack Rebukes Kennedy, Dever": *Boston Globe,* May 18, 1956.

30   Republican senator Jacob Javits: O'Neill, Oral History, JFKL.

31   The Hotel Bradford: Parmet, *Jack*, p. 353.

31   The Kennedy team believed they had 47 votes: O'Donnell and Powers, *Johnny, We Hardly Knew Ye*, p. 114.

31   While Kennedy worked the crowd: Ibid., p. 115.

32   For their first maneuver: *Boston Globe,* May 20, 1956.

32   "Paddy, I ought to knock you": O'Donnell and Powers, *Johnny, We Hardly Knew Ye*, p. 115.

32   Meanwhile Knocko McCormack looked as ominous: Lawrence O'Brien, *No Final Victories: A Life in Politics from John F. Kennedy to Watergate* (Garden City, NY: Doubleday, 1974).

32   The room teetered toward riot: *Boston Globe*, May 20, 1956.

33   Pat Lynch took 47 votes: Ibid.

33   "The will of United States Senator John F. Kennedy prevailed": Ibid.

33   A month later Kennedy met with McCormack: John F. Kennedy, Senate General Papers, Box 504, JFKL.

33   The victory put Kennedy in a commanding position: Sorensen, Personal Papers, JFKL.

34   Kennedy had "plunged into the fray": Ibid.

34   O'Brien felt it had been a mistake: O'Brien, *No Final Victories*.

34   it was a "turning point in his career": O'Donnell and Powers, *Johnny, We Hardly Knew Ye*, p. 104.

CHAPTER FOUR

35   "I think I have the best chance": Evelyn Lincoln, *My Twelve Years with John W. Kennedy* (New York: David McKay, 1965), p. 75.

36   His father owned Chicago's enormous Merchandise Mart: David Nasaw, *The Patriarch: The Remarkable Life and Turbulent Times of Joseph P. Kennedy* (New York: Penguin Press, 2012), p. 403.

36   Stevenson talked of his fondness for Jack: Ralph G. Martin, *Ballots and Bandwagons* (Chicago: Rand McNally, 1964), p. 379.

36   "all the family at one time or other": Thomas P. O'Neill Jr., Oral History, JFKL.

36   Sarge Shriver stayed close to the Stevenson operation: Donovan L. Luhning, "Prelude to Power: John F. Kennedy and the Democratic Convention of 1956" (graduate thesis, Vanderbilt University, 1991), p. 20; Ralph G. Martin, *A Hero for Our Time* (New York: Macmillan, 1983), p. 107.

36   "We were lobbied to death": Luhning, "Prelude to Power," p. 16.

36   He was anything but passive: Robert Troutman, Oral History, JFKL.

37   Paul Butler, the national Democratic chairman: Dore Schary, Oral History, JFKL.

37   Kennedy remained publicly coy: *Boston Globe,* August 11, 1956, p. 1.

38   The idea of an open convention: Martin, *Ballots and Bandwagons*, p. 373; John H. Sharon Papers, Series 2, Democratic Party Files, 1954–1955, Box 7, JFKL.

38   Sharon had gotten to know Kennedy: John H. Sharon, Oral History, JFKL.

38   Through his backchannel contact: Luhning, "Prelude to Power," p. 20.

38   The nationally syndicated political columnist Doris Fleeson: *Boston Globe,* August 9, 1956.

38   When he withdrew from his failing campaign: Charles L. Fontenay, *Estes*

Kefauver: A Biography (Knoxville: University of Tennessee Press, 1980), pp. 266–67.

39 Stevenson disliked Kefauver: Sharon, Oral History, JFKL; Parmet, *Jack*, p. 373.

39 Frank Clement, who had visions: Fontenay, *Estes Kefauver*, p. 279.

39 "The Democrats last night smote": Interview with Russell Baker by author, 2003.

40 Humphrey was convinced he would be chosen: Max Kampelman, reflections on Hubert H. Humphrey, private letter published in Dan Cohen, *Undefeated: The Life of Hubert Humphrey* (Minneapolis: Lerner, 1978), p. 192; Martin, *Ballots and Bandwagons*, p. 381.

40 But Stevenson had been put off: Arthur M. Schlesinger Jr., *Robert Kennedy and His Times* (Boston: Houghton Mifflin, 1978), p. 131.

40 During opening night ceremonies: Parmet, *Jack*, p. 367.

41 Washington lawyer Abba Schwarz: Ibid., p. 368.

41 She had disliked his father for years: Martin, *A Hero for Our Time*, p. 107.

41 he found Mrs. Roosevelt's suite: Ibid.; Martin, *Ballots and Bandwagons*, p. 415.

41 "That was so long ago": Ibid., p. 416.

41 Kennedy asked flatly whether that meant: Ibid., p. 395.

41 "I think I should know": Ibid.

42 a draft was delivered to Sorensen: Ibid., p. 396.

42 Kennedy looked at his copy of the speech: Thomas Winship, Oral History, JFKL.

42 Winship went to the press room: Ibid.

43 In a session with his closest advisors: Martin and Plaut, *Front Runner*, pp. 58–60.

43 Rayburn, who presided over the convention: Ibid., pp. 60–61.

43 They felt it reflected Stevenson's indecisive nature: Martin, *Ballots and Bandwagons*, p. 400.

43 "I have either done the smartest thing": Martin and Plaut, *Front Runner*, p. 62.

43 "the goddamndest, stupidest move": Doris Kearns Goodwin, *The Fitzgeralds and the Kennedys* (New York: St. Martin's, 1987), p. 784.

43 "I have decided that the selection": Official Proceedings of the Democratic National Convention, 1956, published by the Democratic National Committee, JFKL.

43 Kefauver felt betrayed: Alex Rose, Oral History, JFKL.

44 "At least talk to Adlai": Fontenay, *Estes Kefauver*, p. 270.

44   Kefauver agreed to accompany Roper: Ibid; Martin, *Ballots and Bandwagons*, p. 403.

44   the Tennessee delegation refused to endorse Kefauver: Fontenay, *Estes Kefauver*, p. 271.

44   A similar situation prevailed in the Texas delegation: Martin, *Ballots and Bandwagons*, p. 420.

44   Humphrey was actually writing his acceptance speech: Cohen, *Undefeated*, p. 193.

44   A cross-current of machinations: Robert Wagner, Oral History, JFKL; Rudy Abramson, *Spanning the Century: The Life of W. Averell Harriman 1891–1986* (New York: Morrow, 1992), pp. 540–42.

44   Following his unplanned meeting: Parmet, *Jack*, p. 376.

44   it seemed to be "a fixed convention": Martin, *Ballots and Bandwagons*, p. 404.

44   Kennedy had a short, private talk: Robert Wagner, Oral History, JFKL.

45   The warring New Yorkers agreed: Martin and Plaut, *Front Runner*, pp. 66–75.

45   Robert Kennedy who tackled the unpleasant duty: O'Donnell and Powers, *Johnny, We Hardly Knew Ye*, p. 122.

45   Armed with a pen and a legal pad: Martin, *Ballots and Bandwagons*, pp. 407–8.

45   When Carmine DeSapio: Goodwin, *The Fitzgeralds and the Kennedys*, p. 783.

46   "a way of knocking down Kefauver": Terry Sanford, Oral History, JFKL.

46   the irony of a Jew advocating a Catholic: Martin, *A Hero for Our Time*, p. 106.

46   Smathers felt a sharp pain: George Smathers, Oral History, JFKL.

46   Robert Kennedy had approached his brother's rival: O'Donnell and Powers, *Johnny, We Hardly Knew Ye*, pp. 121–23.

46   "a spectacle that might have confounded": Russell Baker, *New York Times*, August 18, 1956.

46   Given space to watch the proceedings: Tom Winship, Oral History, JFKL.

47   At the end of the balloting: Martin, *Ballots and Bandwagons*, p. 428.

47   Calculations were difficult: J. Leonard Reinsch, Oral History, JFKL; Martin, *A Hero for Our Time*, p. 114.

48   He expressed delight over the unanimous vote: *Boston Globe,* August 18, 1956.

48   After his second-place finish: Martin and Plaut, *Front Runner*, p. 75.

48   Kennedy partisans roamed the Amphitheater: Martin, *A Hero for Our Time*, pp. 112–13; O'Donnell and Powers, *Johnny, We Hardly Knew Ye*.

48   Robert Kennedy grabbed at the arm: G. Mennen Williams, Oral History, JFKL.

48   Humphrey had watched the first roll-call vote: Hubert H. Humphrey, Oral History, JFKL.

48   he began to cry: Martin, *Ballots and Bandwagons*, p. 435; Fontenay, *Estes Kefauver*, p. 273.

48   Learning that Kefauver himself: Interview with Ted Sorensen by author, 2003.

49   "Hubert, I've just got to have those delegates": Fontenay, *Estes Kefauver*, p. 273.

49   Humphrey croaked instructions: Ibid.

49   James Roosevelt, Eleanor's son: Don Rose, Oral History, JFKL.

50   Though Johnson had lobbied: Martin, *Ballots and Bandwagons*, pp. 420, 423.

50   Robert Kennedy could be seen on the convention floor: Tom Winship, Oral History, JFKL.

50   Gore had retreated from the floor: Interview with John Seigenthaler by author, 2003.

51   Now Evans reminded Gore: Ibid.; Fontenay, *Estes Kefauver*, p. 275.

51   some of Kennedy's advisors privately complained: *Boston Globe*, August 18, 1956; Sorensen, *Kennedy*, p. 92.

51   simply said, "Let's go": Parmet, *Jack*, p. 380.

52   "Will the convention be in order?": Official Proceedings of the Democratic National Convention, 1956, published by the Democratic National Committee, JFKL

52   he perceptibly slumped: Interview with Arthur M. Schlesinger Jr. by author, 2003.

CHAPTER FIVE

54   It was an example: Jean Kennedy Smith interview with author, 2015.

54   Instead of plunging back into Senate business: Ibid.

54   "We tried to get Kennedy to speak": John Sharon, Oral History, JFKL.

54   "I took over a briefcase": Sorensen, *Kennedy*, p. 100.

55   This was the beginning of an intimate association: Ibid.

55   "Perhaps the most striking contrast": John F. Kennedy, Speeches and Press Releases, 1956, Pre-Presidential Papers, JFKL.

55   "Sen. Kennedy asked me to obtain": John F. Kennedy, General Senate Files, Box 504, JFKL.

56   "We were conscious that he was going to run": Robert F. Wagner, Oral History, JFKL.

56   "He wasn't quite that definite": Frank Thompson, Oral History, JFKL.

56   an October foray into Louisiana: Edmund Reggie, Oral History, JFKL.

57   his brother Robert joined Stevenson's traveling staff: Schlesinger, *Robert Kennedy and His Times*, p. 133.

57   Sharon said the idea of enlisting Robert: John Sharon, Oral History, JFKL.

58   As Schlesinger put it, "From my own viewpoint": Schlesinger, *Robert Kennedy and His Times,* p. 133

58   "I know he felt": William M. Blair, Oral History, JFKL.

58   "Bob learned what not to do": Newton Minow, Oral History, JFKL.

58   "He spent all day long": Robert F. Kennedy, Memorandum on Stevenson, January 25, 1957, RFK Papers, JFKL.

59   he voted for Eisenhower: Schlesinger, *Robert Kennedy and His Times,* p. 136.

59   By October, however: A tape of the *Meet the Press* broadcast is in the audiovisual collection, JFKL.

60   Sorensen described "a steady turning": Sorensen, Personal Papers, Box 25, JFKL.

61   "my first major speech": John F. Kennedy, Speech and Press Releases File, Pre-Presidential Papers, Box 896, JFKL.

61   As hints go, that was fairly strong: Jean Kennedy Smith, interview.

62   Off the living room was a small room: Goodwin, *The Fitzgeralds and the Kennedys*, pp. 787–88; Edward M. Kennedy, *True Compass* (New York: Twelve, Hachette, 2009), p. 116.

62   Jean Kennedy Smith described the father-son meeting: Interview with author, 2015.

63   "If we work our asses off": Martin, *A Hero for Our Time*. Martin's book was published in 1983, four years before Goodwin's book.

63   Some people, of course, didn't need to be told: Sorensen, *Counselor*, p. 172.

64   "My very appearance here": Ibid.

CHAPTER SIX

65   The telephone call came: Leonard Reinsch, Oral History, JFKL.

66   "Jack, if you're still interested": Newton Minow interview with author, 2015.

67   "And of course that was the time": Wayne Aspinall, Oral History, JFKL.

67   Aspinall was not the only westerner: Teno Roncalio, Oral History, JFKL.

68   Raskin was unusual in believing: Hyman B. Raskin, Oral History, JFKL.

69   "I will work out plans": Francis X. Morrissey, from a collection of writings in a tribute to Joseph P. Kennedy assembled by his son Edward and privately published as *A Fruitful Bough* in 1965, pp. 125–30.

70   "I started early": Widmer and Kennedy, *Listening In*, p. 287.

70   "In 1952," Kennedy recalled: Ibid.

71 Kennedy turned in no fewer than 232,324: Lawrence F. O'Brien, Personal Papers, JFKL.

72 Kennedy money was being spent: Robert Troutman, Oral History, JFKL.

75 He and Sorensen did agree, however: Theodore C. Sorensen Papers, Box 2, JFKL.

77 "Most people didn't take Kennedy very seriously": Robert Donovan, Oral History, p. 3, JFKL.

78 "It's not that I have": Douglass Cater, Oral History, p. 4, JFKL.

78 "How can you say a thing like that?": Washington Reporters Peter Lisagor, George Herman, and Mary McGrory, Oral History, JFKL.

79 several pages of Fletcher Knebel's copy: Theodore C. Sorensen, Personal Papers, Box 22, JFKL.

79 "to the hosts of becalmed voters": Lawrence F. O'Brien, Personal Papers, JFK Campaigns, Box 11, JFKL.

79 Probably the most eyebrow-raising example: Theodore C. Sorensen, Personal Papers, Box 23, JFKL.

80 "I contracted malaria during the war": Theodore C. Sorensen, Personal Papers, Box 22, JFKL.

80 As it turned out, no one really noticed: Robert Caro, *The Years of Lyndon Johnson: The Passage of Power* (New York: Knopf, 2012), p. 46. (Travell also treated Caro for his own back issues.)

81 "I waited until he finished this long tirade": Clark Clifford, Oral History, p. 6, JFKL.

82 The ABC executives had nothing to counter: Sorensen, *Kennedy*, p. 70.

82 For perspective, Sorensen said, he found insight: Sorensen, *Counselor,* p. 177.

83 "One hour of work in 1957": Sorensen, *Kennedy*, pp. 76–77, 96.

CHAPTER SEVEN

84 he coveted a seat on the Foreign Relations Committee: Horace Busby, Oral History, p. 4, JFKL.

85 assignments to the committee went to "team players": Caro, Master of the Senate (New York: Knopf, 2002), p. 564.

85 "No other Democratic Senator": John F. Kennedy, Pre-Presidential Papers, 1960 Campaign Files, Box 996, JFKL.

85 "I kept picturing old Joe Kennedy": Goodwin, *The Fitzgeralds and the Kennedys*, p. 790.

85 the Foreign Relations Committee represented a public platform for his ideas: Joseph Alsop, Oral History, JFKL; Peter Collier and David Horowitz, *The Kennedys* (New York: Summit Books, 1984), p. 233.

86   "a Stevenson with balls": Alsop, Ibid.

88   As the committee's junior member: "Why England Slept," typescript, John F. Kennedy Personal Papers, JFKL; Michael O'Brien, *John F. Kennedy* (New York: Macmillan, 2005), pp. 107–8.

89   Even as war in Europe approached: O'Brien, *John F. Kennedy*, p. 94.

89   Kennedy seemed reluctant to take daring positions: John Sharon, Oral History, JFKL.

90   In 1951, during his third term in the House: Edwin Guthman, ed., *Robert F. Kennedy in His Own Words* (New York: Bantam, 1991), pp. 436–37; Schlesinger, *Robert Kennedy and His Times*, p. 92.

90   "He didn't like him much": Guthman, *Robert F. Kennedy in His Own Words*, p. 437

91   From the Subcontinent: O'Brien, *John F. Kennedy*, p. 235.

91   Although the three Kennedy siblings were treated royally: Guthman, *Robert F. Kennedy in His Own Words*, p. 437

91   to fight communism "by merely the force of arms": Schlesinger, *Robert Kennedy and His Times*, pp. 92–93.

92   The speech marked the beginning of another rupture: Ibid.

92   "I couldn't possibly have a worse argument": Ibid.

93   It was not difficult for him to speak out: O'Brien, *John F. Kennedy*, p. 352.

93   Kennedy had called upon the considerable academic community: Parmet, *Jack*, p. 401.

94   one young academic, Fred Holborn: Fred Holborn, Oral History, JFKL.

95   The Algeria speech became a major production: Ibid.

95   "He had handled relatively safe subjects": Ibid.

95   Kennedy's office made sure that an advance copy: Tom Wicker, Oral History, JFKL.

95   "The most powerful single force": *John Fitzgerald Kennedy: A Compendium of Speeches, Statements and Remarks Delivered During His Service in the Congress of the United States* (Washington, DC: U.S. Government Printing Office, 1964), JFKL.

96   The speech triggered more reaction: Goodwin, *The Fitzgeralds and the Kennedys*, p. 790; Algeria Speech File, 1957, Box 919, Pre-Presidential Papers, JFKL.

96   But Kennedy was rebuked: Schlesinger, *Robert Kennedy and His Times*, p. 199; Joseph P. Kennedy Collection, Box 225, JFKL.

97   "For years the political sharpshooters": Nasaw, *The Patriarch*, p. 711.

97   "[You are] dead right": Chester Bowles, letter to JFK, Algeria Speech File, 1957, Box 919, Pre-Presidential Papers, JFKL.

97   "I do not see that anything is to be gained: JFK, letter to Chester Bowles, Algeria Speech File, 1957, Box 919, Pre-Presidential Papers, JFKL.

97   "one of the historic events of post-war Europe": Ibid.

98   Within a month of his Algeria speech: Sorensen, *Kennedy*, p. 108.

98   a "geopolitical map of the world": John F. Kennedy, "A Democrat Looks at Foreign Policy," *Foreign Affairs* 36, no. 1 (October 1957).

99   Kennedy made a major speech in the Senate: Joseph Alsop, Oral History, JFKL.

99   "it is no longer true that the best defense": John F. Kennedy: A Compendium of Speeches . . . Aug. 14, 1958.

99   "one of the most remarkable speeches": Column by Joseph Alsop, Aug. 17, 1958, cited in Kaiser's 2015 article cited below.

99   the incestuous ties between writers and politicians: Robert G. Kaiser, "The Great Days of Joe Alsop," *New York Review of Books*, March 12, 2015; Robert W. Merry, *Taking on the World: Joseph and Stewart Alsop—Guardians of the American Century* (New York: Penguin, 1996), p. 342.

CHAPTER EIGHT

101   "The automobile–durable consumers' goods–suburbia sectoral complex": Walt W. Rostow, *The Stages of Economic Growth: A Non-Communist Manifesto* (Cambridge, UK: Cambridge University Press, 1960).

101   In comments destined to be associated with Kennedy: The question of the origin of Kennedy's trademark phrases from the campaign has intrigued writers for decades. Shortly after he became president he told the writer David Wise that the source was Rostow, and Wise reported this in the old *New York Herald Tribune*. Rostow, by then McGeorge Bundy's deputy, helping him run the National Security Council in the White House, called him up to acknowledge "get this country moving again" but questioned the attribution of "New Frontier." Walt Rostow, Oral History, p. 138, JFKL. But Wise surprised him with the quotations from Rostow's book. The record tends to support Kennedy on the former, but it is more complicated and fuzzy on the latter

101   But he resisted Rostow's entreaty: Rostow, Oral History, JFKL.

102   Kennedy's "remarkable computer of a mind": Ibid.

102   "I like to think of myself": Martin and Plaut, *Front Runner*, p. 187.

104   "The base of support": Meyer Feldman, Oral History, p. 36, JFKL.

104   "Now if he couldn't get the south": Ibid., p. 32.

105   The well-known liberal lawyer Joseph Rauh: Joseph Rauh, Oral History, p. 8, JFKL.

106 "Whenever the UAW needed John Kennedy": Ibid.

107 "Unlike so many public figures": Archibald Cox, Oral History, pp. 9, 20, JFKL.

109 "When we came back in '59": Stewart Udall, Oral History, p. 7, JFKL.

114 a campaign "to get the country moving again": Arthur Schlesinger Jr., "The Shape of National Politics to Come," in Theodore C. Sorensen, Personal Papers, Campaign Files, Box 25, JFKL.

CHAPTER NINE

115 "I'll be singing Dixie": Arthur Krock, *Memoirs* (London: Cassell, 1968).

117 was being "dealt with very satisfactorily": Transcript, *Face the Nation*, July 1, 1956.

118 When Rosa Parks refused: Taylor Branch, *Parting the Waters: America in the King Years 1954–63* (New York: Simon & Schuster, 1988).

118 white mobs thwarted the *Brown* decision: Ibid.

118 Blacks composed less than 2 percent: U.S. Census Bureau statistics, 1950.

119 an interesting assortment of segregationist leaders and virulent racists: Official proceedings of the Democratic National Convention, 1956, published by the Democratic National Committee, JFKL

119 "I appreciated the help and support": John F. Kennedy, letter to John Bell Williams, Mississippi File, Pre-Presidential Papers, JFKL.

120 "highest regards and best wishes": John F. Kennedy, letter to Judge George C. Wallace, and reply to JFK from Wallace, Alabama File, Pre-Presidential Papers, JFKL.

120 "the darling of the South": Edmund Reggie, Oral History, JFKL.

120 "Let me assure you that my vote": William Winter, letter to John F. Kennedy, Mississippi File, Pre-Presidential Papers, JFKL.

121 the man he expected to be one of his chief rivals: Robert Caro, *The Years of Lyndon Johnson: Master of the Senate* (New York: Knopf, 2002).

121 The Sphinx-like Eastland: Clay Risen, *The Bill of the Century: The Epic Battle for the Civil Rights Act* (New York: Bloomsbury Press, 2014).

122 "under this bill": Caro, *Master of the Senate.*

122 the senator "wanted to be on both sides": Joseph Rauh, Oral History, JFKL.

123 Kennedy was ambivalent: Parmet, *Jack.*

123 would not "constitute a betrayal of principle": Paul Freund letter, Campaign Files, Pre-Presidential Papers, Box 994.

123 Kennedy "misused the letter": Joseph Rauh, Oral History, JFKL.

123 "Frank did a great thing today": Frank Church, Oral History, JKFL.

123 "It appeared to me that the senator": Roy Wilkins, Oral History, JFKL.

124 "The feeling in Washington": Tom Wicker, Oral History, JFKL.

124 "are in love with death": Robert F. Kennedy, Oral History, JFKL.

124 "You showed you were for civil rights": Ibid.

125 The son of a fiery socialist: Roy Reed, *Faubus: The Life and Times of an American Prodigal* (Fayetteville: University of Arkansas Press, 1997).

125 As a product of the northwestern part: Jim McDougal and Curtis Wilkie, *Arkansas Mischief: The Birth of a National Scandal* (New York: Henry Holt, 1998), p. 58.

125 It seemed logical for Kennedy to consider him: Ibid., p. 41

125 a politician "who would trade your daughter": Ibid.

126 But when the "Little Rock Nine" reappeared: Gene Roberts and Hank Klibanoff, *The Race Beat: The Press, the Civil Rights Struggle, and the Awakening of a Nation* (New York: Knopf, 2006).

126 make a political appearance: Sorensen, *Kennedy*.

126 As many as two thousand Mississippians: Parmet, *Jack*. p. 413

126 "Is it not a fact," Yerger asked: Ibid.

126 Kennedy had planned to again laud: O'Brien, *John F. Kennedy*, p. 375.

127 One spectator spoke afterward of his wonder: Ibid.

127 he talked until 2 a.m. with Governor J. P. Coleman: J. P. Coleman, Center for Oral History, University of Southern Mississippi Library; interview with J. P. Coleman by Connie Lynnette Cartledge, Special Collections, Mississippi State University Library.

128 "He is too intelligent": Parmet, *Jack*, p. 413

CHAPTER TEN

129 "He just asked for my help": Bernard Boutin, Oral History, p. 2, JFKL.

130 "Let us face it frankly": John F. Kennedy, 1960 Campaign Files, Pre-Presidential Papers, Box 996, JFKL.

131 "It is my hope": John F. Kennedy, letter to Louis Harris, January 8, 1958.

131 In a five-page memorandum to Sorensen: Louis Harris, letter to Theodore C. Sorensen, December 9, 1957.

131 "While the degree to which these primaries are binding": Theodore C. Sorensen, Personal Papers, 1960 Campaign Files, Box 25, JFKL.

132 commissioned a survey in California: John F. Kennedy, Senate Files, Pre-Presidential Papers, Box 815, JFKL.

133 The California survey: Information on the 1958 polls is from Louis Harris & Associates.

134 "the largest single handicap": Ibid.

134 "When one out of every four voters is anti-Catholic": Ibid.

135 Bernard Boyle was not an elected official: Bernard Boyle, Oral History, p. 2m, JFKL.

136 Colorado had Joe Dolan: Joseph Dolan, Oral History, pp. 11–12, 17–18, JFKL.

137 "the consensus . . . of the working politicians": Robert P. McDonough, Oral History, pp. 1–21, JFKL.

137 Another example of the success: Harvey Bailey, Oral History, pp. 1–11, JFKL.

138 "I think the most remarkable thing": Patrick Lucey, Oral History, pp. 1–49, JFKL.

139 "Senator Kennedy came out to Wisconsin": William Proxmire, Oral History, pp. 1–17, JFKL.

141 "the itty bitty group": Marguerite Benson, Oral History, p. 2, JFKL.

142 "A man's record": *Berkshire Eagle,* April 28, 1958.

142 Kennedy chose not to respond: A file containing the Kennedy-Wilkins material was retained by Ted Sorensen in his Personal Papers, Box 19, JFKL.

144 "I can't be sure of the political future": A file containing the Kennedy–Eleanor Roosevelt correspondence, along with news clippings, was retained by Sorensen in his Personal Papers, 1960 Campaign Files, Box 25, JFKL.

147 shortly after the 1958 election: Theodore C. Sorensen, Personal Papers, Box 8, JFKL.

147 "In the interest of taking up": Lawrence F. O'Brien, Personal Papers, Box 6, JFKL.

149 It was understood that an endorsement: Jack Conway, Oral History, JFKL.

CHAPTER ELEVEN

150 "Discussions with Jack and Bobby": Wallace memo, Theodore C. Sorensen, Personal Papers, 1960 Campaign Files.

151 "I think your main problem": Robert A. Wallace, Oral History, JFKL.

152 In 1959 Iowa was on a short list: Undated 1959 file, "Prospectus for 1960," Sorensen, Personal Papers, JFKL.

152 "I opposed him quite violently": Herschel Loveless, Oral History, JFKL.

153 What the governor was not aware of: Edward A. McDermott, Oral History, JFKL.

153 Geography was a principal reason: John Blatnik, Oral History, p. 11, JFKL.

153 "Some early work": Edward A. McDermott, Oral History, JFKL.

154 Kennedy's advisors did not believe Humphrey had a credible path: Sorensen, Personal Papers, Campaign Files, Box 21, JFKL.

155 "He hoped to be nominated": J. Edward Day, Oral History, JFKL.

156 Daley "indicated strong support": Theodore Sorensen, memorandum to Robert Kennedy, October 23, 1959, in Sorensen, Personal Papers, Campaign Files, Box 24, JFKL.

156 calling him "a first-rate intellect": Paul Douglas, Oral History, JFKL.

156 Symington decided against running in the primaries: Martin and Plaut, *Front Runner*, pp. 428, 432.

157 "In the case of Kennedy," Clifford said: Ibid.

157 "there was no great groundswell": O'Brien, *No Final Victories*.

158 Sorensen called it "the Summit": Sorensen, *Counselor*, p. 180.

159 More levity and eye-rolling: Paul Fay, *The Pleasure of His Company* (New York: Harper & Row, 1966).

159 "Our main conclusion": O'Brien, *No Final Victories,* p. 139.

161 The outlook Sorensen had presented at Palm Beach: Theodore Sorensen, Summary of Sorensen Talk (another copy bears the handwritten title "Summary of Talk by Kennedy Men"), Personal Papers, Campaign Files, Box 22, JFKL.

163 a "southern candidate who did not play": Ibid.

164 "Kennedy Delegate Count (Confidential)": Lawrence F. O'Brien, Personal Papers, Campaign Files, JFKL.

165 "If he had to put his foot on us": John Patterson, Oral History, JFKL.

CHAPTER TWELVE

167 Christie didn't hesitate: Sidney L. Christie, Oral History, pp. 1–2, JFKL.

168 Kennedy was already entrenched: Alfred Chapman, Oral History, p. 14, JFKL.

168 "My feeling that Stevenson": James E. Doyle, Oral History, p. 1, JFKL.

168 To boost his standing in Wisconsin: Martin and Plaut, *Front Runner*, pp. 218–46.

169 "All these people who say I might be influenced": Ibid.

169 religion had become one source of political frustration: Jack Bell, Oral History, pp. 9–10, JFKL.

172 So Kennedy contradicted it: Martin and Plaut, *Front Runner*, pp. 218–46.

172 "It would seem to me that the man": Ibid.

172 saying he was "deeply disturbed": Sorensen, Personal Papers, Campaign Files, Box 24, JFKL.

173 Kennedy's idea about Pennsylvania: Ibid.

173 In Kennedy's judgment nothing about Ohio:

175 Bailey reported that the governor had been unequivocal: John Bailey, Oral History, p. 18, JFKL.

175 "see DiSalle and make sure": Sorensen, *Kennedy*, p. 113.

177 "My hints were to keep him unsure": O'Brien, *No Final Victories*, p. 60.

177 O'Brien's best ammunition: John F. Kennedy, Senate Files, Pre-Presidential Papers, JFKL.

177 "They met to pledge to the Senator": Joseph Cerrell, Oral History, JFKL.

177 "It was a very hard delegation": Don Bradley, Oral History, JFKL.

178 "I told Pat I had no desire": Paul Fay, *The Pleasure of His Company* (New York: Harper & Row, 1966).

179 he was getting 34 percent support among Protestants: Sorensen, Personal Papers, Campaign Files, Box 25, JFKL.

180 Joseph Walton, was more than willing to help: Sorensen, Personal Papers, Campaign Files, Box 21, JFKL.

181 "Son, you've got to learn": Caro, *The Passage of Power*, p. 71.

181 The Kennedy camp described vulgar Texas yahooism: Robert Kennedy, Oral History, JFKL.

182 In O'Brien's files at the end of the year: Lawrence F. O'Brien, Personal Papers, JFK Campaigns 1954–1960, Box 6, JFKL.

CHAPTER THIRTEEN

185 But the beleaguered New Hampshire Democrats were stirring: Bernard Boutin, Oral History, June 3, 1964, pp. 1–2, JFKL.

185 Kennedy spent a few days in New Hampshire: Bernard Boutin, Oral History, April 27, 1972, pp. 15–16, JFKL.

186 Elton Britt, a country singer: Fred A. Forbes, Oral History, February 16, 1966, pp. 9–10, JFKL.

186 Kennedy ignored him: Ibid.

186 Other attacks on Kennedy: Ibid., p. 20.

187 he had "not the slightest idea": Sorensen, *Counselor*.

187 "Like his father before him": Ibid., p. 116.

187 There is a credible story: Ibid., p. 120.

188 "Stop spreading the word": Seymour M. Hersh, *The Dark Side of Camelot* (Boston: Little, Brown, 1997), p. 120.

189 Kennedy quickly penciled a two-page statement: Ibid., pp. 115–16.

189 Kennedy approached Clark Clifford: Clark Clifford, Oral History, JFKL.

189 somebody "who could destroy him": Hersh, *The Dark Side of Camelot*, p. 117.

189 J. Edgar Hoover summarized her file: Ibid.

191 Kennedy "never permitted the pursuit of private pleasure": Sorensen, *Counselor,* p. 121.

191 "No one has ever so understood": Ibid.

191 Kennedy had to shift quickly: Cohen, *Undefeated,* p. 212.

191 "An awful lot is fortune": Widmer and Kennedy, *Listening In*.

191 "the Protestant vote immediately reacted": Harris Polls, Pre-Presidential Papers, Box 819, JFKL.

191 Humphrey meanwhile seemed at home: *Primary*, a documentary by Robert Drew.

192 Kennedy knew Wisconsin would be a major test: Sorensen, *Kennedy*, p. 137.

192 found Kennedy ahead 54 to 46: Harris Polls, Pre-Presidential Papers, Box 819, JFKL.

192 Robert Kennedy sent a detailed memo: Robert F. Kennedy, State Files, Wisconsin Primary Miscellaneous folder, Pre-Administration Papers, Box 50, JFKI.

193 Once a reliably Republican state: Cohen, *Undefeated,* p. 214.

193 William Proxmire's election: William Proxmire, Oral History, JFKL.

194 a faux Irishman who went by the name of Paul Corbin: Evan Thomas, *Robert Kennedy: His Life* (New York: Simon & Schuster, 2000), p. 94.

194 Corbin hung around the fringes: Paul Corbin, Oral History, November 18, 1965, pp. 10–11, JFKL.

194 Corbin's career with the Kennedys: Paul Corbin, Oral History, November 27, 1967, p. 24, JFKL.

194 "He took cheerful delight": Schlesinger, *Robert Kennedy and His Times*, p. 196.

195 a controversial documentary called *Primary*: Thom Powers, "The Kennedy Films of Robert Drew & Associates: Capturing the Kennedys," Criterion Collection, April 26, 2016, online.

196 "Tell Humphrey to lay off": Al Eisele, *Almost to the Presidency: A Biography of Two American Politicians* (Blue Earth, MN: Piper, 1972), p. 147.

196 "The next two weeks of campaigning": Harris Polls, Box 819, JFKL.

196 the campaign proceeded to "bungle" expectations: O'Brien, *No Final Victories*, p. 65.

196 Edwin Bayley, later blamed himself: Edwin Bayley, Oral History, pp. 1–17, JFKL.

197 Proxmire hosted a dinner party: William Proxmire, Oral History, JFKL.

197 Robert took the returns personally: Thomas, *Robert F. Kennedy*, p. 93.

197   Kennedy was more verbal: O'Donnell and Powers, *Johnny, We Hardly Knew Ye*, p. 160.

CHAPTER FOURTEEN

198   He had begun cultivating support: Robert McDonough, Oral History, JFKL.

198   "low on our list": O'Brien, *No Final Victories*, pp. 66–76.

199   "It's a nothing state": Nasaw, *The Patriarch*, p. 733.

199   "Take this decision about the West Virginia primary": Rostow, Oral History, JFKL.

199   Kennedy was heartened by a Harris poll: O'Donnell and Powers, *Johnny, We Hardly Knew Ye*, pp. 160–78.

199   As the filing deadline of February 6: Robert McDonough, Oral History, JFKL.

200   Kennedy was meeting in his Georgetown home: Alex Rose, Oral History, JFKL.

200   The next day Goldberg and Rose met with Humphrey: Ibid.

200   not Humphrey's only visitors: Jack Conway, Oral History, JFKL.

201   Rev. Norman Vincent Peale: Robert McDonough, Oral History, JFKL.

201   "The fact that I was born a Catholic": Ibid.

201   William Battle, who had been a fellow PT boat commander: William Battle, Oral History, pp. 6, 7–9, 11, JFKL.

202   When Ted Kennedy submitted to an interview: Kennedy, *True Compass*, p. 143.

203   "Beat Humphrey over the head": Robert Wallace, Oral History, JFKL.

203   Wallace had second thoughts: Ibid.

203   Convinced that the rapidly expanding new medium: Jean Kennedy Smith interview with the author, 2015.

203   Devine was quickly hired: A collection of Devine's commercials is available in the audiovisual department at the JFKL. A larger collection is housed at the University of California, Los Angeles.

205   Matt Reese, a local political consultant: Matt Reese, Oral History, JFKL.

205   "I'd give my right testicle": Charles Bartlett, Oral History, p. 47, JFKL.

206   he relied on a gimmick: John Seigenthaler, Oral History, #2, JFKL; Vito N. Silvestri, *Becoming JFK: A Profile in Communication* (Westport, CT: Praeger, 2000).

206   yet if he spoke openly about Kennedy's Catholicism: James Rowe, Oral History, JFKL.

206   A damaging perception: Charles Bartlett, Oral History, p. 47.

206 Strapped for funds to combat Kennedy's riches: Ibid.

207 Rowe acknowledged trying to raise money: James Rowe, Oral History, JFKL.

207 The son seemed to enjoy the long hours: Frank Forbes, Oral History, March 4, 1966, p. 35, JFKL.

207 an explosive bit of opposition research: Ibid., p 36.

207 In the last days of the West Virginia effort: Ibid., p. 37.

208 On Roosevelt's final day in West Virginia: Ibid., pp. 37–38.

208 Roosevelt had charged that Humphrey: *Charleston Daily Mail*, May 7, 1960.

208 "Any discussion of the war record": Ibid.

209 "I have no suitcase filled with money": Memo to Kenneth O'Donnell, including verbatim descriptions of news stories, Robert F. Kennedy Memos Folder, Box 39, JFKL.

209 "By golly, we've come this far": Robert Wallace, Oral History, JFKL.

209 Larry O'Brien was given the task: O'Brien, *No Final Victories*, pp. 66–76.

209 Dick Donahue, did some firsthand negotiating: Donahue, in interview with the author, 2015.

210 "The facts are that both sides": Robert Wallace, memo to Robert Kennedy, May 27, 1960, Pre-Administration Papers, JFKL.

210 "For West Virginia . . . nobody gives a damn": Donahue, Oral History, JFKL.

210 The question of where the cash: Burnhardt, Oral History, JFKL.

211 a "carefully documented report": Robert D. Novak, *The Prince of Darkness: 50 Years Reporting in Washington* (New York: Crown, 2007), p. 65.

211 "I was paid out of private funds": Robert Wallace, Oral History, JFKL.

212 Contingency planning may be wise: See, for example, Theodore H. White, *The Making of the President 1960* (New York: Harper Perennial, 2010), p. 101, in which the attribution is made to "the citizens of Kanawha County (which encompasses Charleston)." Sorensen, in *Kennedy*, written after his murder in 1964, repeated this supposed Harris projection of "a 60–40 landslide for Humphrey" statewide.

212 "Sen. Hubert Humphrey has taken": Bob Mellace, *Charleston Daily Mail*, April 15, 1960.

212 he gave one local official in the Charleston area: Richard Donahue, Oral History, pp. 22–25, JFKL, and in an interview.

212 Kennedy himself chose to spend the evening: Benjamin C. Bradlee, *Conversations with Kennedy* (New York: Norton, 1975), p. 27.

213 He had expected a whipping: Joseph Rauh, Oral History, JFKL.

213 At 12:08 a.m.: Associated Press bulletin, May 11, 1960.

CHAPTER FIFTEEN

214 Johnson had already arranged for changes: Robert Dallek, *Lone Star Rising: Lyndon Johnson and His Times 1908–1960* (New York: Oxford University Press, 1991), 546.

214 There was more evidence of his intentions: Caro, *The Passage of Power*, pp. 71–73; Jack Valenti, Oral History, JFKL.

214 Then there were the whispers from Capitol Hill: Hugh Sidey, Oral History, JFKL.

215 Johnson's friends were puzzled: Dallek, *Lone Star Rising*, p. 559.

215 "I understand you're having a state convention": Stewart Udall, Oral History, JFKL.

216 He turned immediately to Maryland: Fred Forbes, Oral History, JFKL.

216 Governor J. Millard Tawes: Bernard Boutin, Oral History #2, JFKL.

216 The commitment had been made: Ibid.

217 The day after West Virginia: Joseph Tydings, Oral History, JFKL.

217 For style points: "John F. Kennedy forever part of the Harford Co. legacy," *Baltimore Sun*, Nov. 22, 2013.

217 He had been shown the results: Harris Polls, Senate Files, Pre-Presidential papers, Box 816, JFKL.

218 "It is obviously important": Robert F. Kennedy Pre-Administration papers, Memos, Outgoing Folder, Box 34, JFKL.

218 "the loneliest man in Washington": *Oregonian*, April 24, 2016.

219 In spite of his embarrassing defeat: Associated Press, May 20, 1960.

219 a strange feud with Morse: Mason Drukman, *Wayne Morse: A Political Biography* (Portland: Oregon Historical Society, 1997), pp. 285–89.

221 Kennedy and Smathers, "together or singly": Roger Mudd, *The Place to Be: Washington, CBS, and the Glory Days of Television News* (New York: Public Affairs, 2008), p. 95.

221 On the morning of March 1: George Smathers, Oral History, JFKL.

224 The former first lady issued a public statement: Adlai Stevenson Collection, Box 68, Correspondence with Eleanor Roosevelt, Seeley G. Mudd Manuscript Library, Princeton University.

224 After agonizing over the proper wording: Ibid.

224 "You ask when I am 'going to make a direct move'": Ibid.

224 "different types" who "never got along": Robert F. Kennedy, Oral History, JFKL.

224 Stevenson was equally suspicious: John Sharon, Oral History, JFKL.

225 Stevenson met secretly with Johnson: Ibid.

225 privy to "the most anti-Kennedy diatribe": Ibid.

225 Johnson's loyalist in Texas, John Connally: Ibid.

225 Stevenson sent a "Dear Jack" letter: Adlai Stevenson Collection, Box 68, Correspondence with Eleanor Roosevelt, Seeley G. Mudd Manuscript Library, Princeton University.

225 In a combustible political environment: John Bartlow Martin, *Adlai Stevenson and the World: The Life of Adlai E. Stevenson* (Garden City, NY: Doubleday, 1977), pp. 506–11.

226 "Guess who the next person": Ibid.

226 he had made a "dire mistake": Ibid.

226 regarded Stevenson as "a pain in the ass": Robert F. Kennedy, Oral History, JFKL.

227 "The insults and distortions of Mr. Khrushchev": John F. Kennedy, Speech to the Senate, June 14, 1960, JFKL.

227 But Kennedy quickly pivoted into sharp criticism: Widmer and Kennedy, *Listening In*, p. 213.

CHAPTER SIXTEEN

228 Kennedy developed a bond with Chicago's Mayor Daley: Adam Cohen and Elizabeth Taylor, *American Pharaoh* (Boston: Little, Brown, 2000), p. 250.

229 Winning elections meant winning power: Curtis Wilkie, "Chicago without Daley," *Boston Globe Sunday Magazine*, May 4, 1980.

229 Daley called him "highly qualified": Cohen and Taylor, American Pharaoh, p. 248.

229 Robert Meyner, had proved intractable: Center on the American Governors, Eagleton Institute of Politics, New Brunswick, NJ.

230 Serious allegations arose: Seymour Hersh, *The Dark Side of Camelot*, pp. 110–11.

230 he had been "particularly incensed": Rose Fitzgerald Kennedy, *Times to Remember* (Garden City, NY: Doubleday, 1974).

230 Kennedy believed he had reached an understanding: Frederick Dutton, Oral History, JFKL.

230 remained sentiment for Stevenson: Hyman Raskin, Oral History, JFKL.

230 Brown was shocked: Frederick Dutton, Oral History, JFKL.

231 In the five weeks between the California primary: Ibid.

231 subjected to intense efforts: Ibid.

231 Ten days before the convention: The dinner meeting is described in ibid.

232 Kennedy's "strong position is striking": Harris survey

233 "we wanted to be sure": G. Mennen Williams, Oral History, JFKL.

233 The trio had originally felt much closer to Humphrey: Ibid.

234 For the first time several black leaders: Ibid.

234 In many ways New York: Ira Stoll, "John F. Kennedy: A New Yorker," *New York Post*, November 22, 2013; Nasaw, *The Patriarch*.

234 Much of the preliminary spadework: Robert Wagner, Oral History, JFKL.

235 Once again the Kennedy boosters: Harris Polls, Pre-Presidential Papers, Senate, Polling Box 816, JFKL.

235 Manhattan Democrats were riven over issues: Michael Prendergast, Oral History, JFKL.

236 DeSapio "played little games": Robert Wagner, Oral History, JFKL.

236 "My friend, Mr. DeSapio": Michael Prendergast, Oral History, JFKL.

236 Kennedy had scored a big hit in New York: Nasaw, *The Patriarch*.

237 Seeing confusion in the Empire State: Robert Wagner, Oral History, JFKL.

237 Unable to prevent Kennedy supporters: Ibid.

237 Wagner had told him months earlier: Ibid.

238 Johnson was displeased by Wagner's observation: Ibid.

238 Wagner hosted an event at Gracie Mansion: Ibid.

CHAPTER SEVENTEEN

239 confident that he had the votes: O'Brien, *No Final Victories*, pp. 79–83.

239 As a student of history: Sorensen, *Kennedy*, p. 155.

241 Arriving in Los Angeles: Hugh Sidey, Oral History, JFKL.

241 "Nervous fugitives": John Rechy, excerpt from *City of Night*, in *Big Table 3*, ed. Paul Carroll (San Francisco: Bolerium Books, 1959).

241 "How's it look?" Sidey asked: Hugh Sidey, Oral History, JFKL.

242 Johnson went on the attack: Ibid., pp. 96–97.

242 "literally true but generally misleading": Sorensen, *Counselor*, pp. 192–93.

242 he took a swipe at Joe Kennedy: Caro, *The Passage of Power*, p. 95.

242 Dispirited, Johnson watched: James Rowe, Oral History, JFKL.

243 There was one last trick: Caro, *The Passage of Power*, p. 102.

243 "Isn't that the goddamndest thing": John Seigenthaler, Oral History, JFKL.

243 Bouncing with enthusiasm, Kennedy entered: Caro, *The Passage of Power*, p. 103.

244 "He just tore Johnson a new asshole": Jack Valenti, Oral History, JFKL.

245 The wife of financier Eugene Meyer: Jean H. Baker, *The Stevensons: A Biography of an American Family* (New York: Norton, 1997), p. 350.

245   While Stevenson was being feted: Martin, *Adlai Stevenson and the World*, p. 522.

245   Stevenson met with several Democratic movers and shakers: Ibid.

246   "Governor," Minow said: Ibid., p. 523.

246   Mayor Daley announced that Kennedy would get: Cohen and Taylor, *American Pharaoh*, p. 259.

246   Much of Stevenson's hope: Ibid.

247   "After going back and forth through the Biltmore today": Norman Mailer, "Superman Comes to the Supermarket," *Esquire*, November 1960.

247   "The applause as he left the platform": Ibid.

247   "Mrs. Roosevelt and I sat there": Martin, *Adlai Stevenson and the World*, p. 525.

247   Kennedy was believed to have 6 votes: Robert Wallace, Oral History, JFKL.

248   He attempted to reach Richard Daley: Martin, *Adlai Stevenson and the World*, p. 526.

248   As nominating speeches droned: W. H. Lawrence, "Kennedy Nominated on the First Ballot; Overwhelms Johnson 806 Votes to 409," *New York Times*, July 14, 1960.

248   "Do not reject this man": Mailer, Superman Comes to the Supermarket.

249   agreement with Kennedy's controversial call: Chester Bowles, Oral History, p. 6, JFKL.

252   they plotted to put together slates of "independent" candidates: Curtis Wilkie, *Dixie: A Personal Odyssey through Events That Shaped the Modern South* (New York: Scribner, 2001), pp. 92–93.

253   "That young fellow will never get far": Mississippi folklore abounds with tales of Barnett's curious comments and malapropisms. This is one of them; others appear in Wilkie, *Dixie*.

253   "button-down-collar Klan": Ibid.

253   "the loveliest and the purest of God's creatures": Thomas P. Brady, *Black Monday* (Winona, MS: Association of Citizens' Councils, 1955), p. 12.

254   Kennedy had for weeks assiduously courted: LeRoy Collins, Oral History, pp. 11–13, JFKL.

254   With the first ballot only minutes away: Samuel Beer, Oral History, p. 3, JFKL.

255   Robert Kennedy had a final order: Kennedy, *True Compass*, pp. 148–50.

255   Robert Kennedy had to dispose of a last-minute ploy: Robert F. Kennedy, Oral History, p. 240, JFKL.

256   After nearly five years in pursuit: Sorensen, *Kennedy*, p. 181.

CHAPTER EIGHTEEN

257 Kennedy was in a no-talking mode: Bradlee, *Conversations with Kennedy*, pp. 30–31.

258 "Johnson—helps with farmers": Sorensen, Personal Papers, Campaign Files, Box 25, JFKL.

259 Kennedy wanted to be certain that Symington was "available": Clark Clifford, Oral History, p. 8, JFKL.

259 The Symington sons had spent: Interview with Stuart Symington Jr. by author, 2016.

259 "We told him, 'You don't want to go' ": Ibid.

260 "We were satisfied it was Stuart Symington": Richard Donahue, Oral History #2, JFKL.

260 Both Charles Bartlett and John Seigenthaler: Charles Bartlett, Oral History, JFKL; John Seigenthaler, Oral History #1, JFKL.

260 The triggering event was a telegram: O'Donnell and Powers, *Johnny, We Hardly Knew Ye*, p. 214.

261 If Kennedy's associates had stayed in closer touch: Caro, *The Passage of Power*, pp. 113–14; Sorensen, *Counselor*, p. 242

261 In June, David Lawrence: Thomas Donaghy, *Keystone Democrat: David Lawrence Remembered* (New York: Vantage Press, 1986), pp. 138–41.

261 Long before his campaign was drawn into combat: Thomas P. O'Neill, Oral History, JFKL.

263 "Lyndon didn't get started early enough": Ibid.

264 Later Jack and Robert Kennedy added to the mystery: John Seigenthaler, Oral History, JFKL; Dallek, *Lone Star Rising*, p. 578.

265 "mean, bitter, and vicious": Guthman, *Robert Kennedy in His Own Words*, p. 417.

265 a "little shitass": Caro, *The Passage of Power*, p. 139.

265 After reading Johnson's telegram: O'Donnell and Powers, *Johnny, We Hardly Knew Ye*, p. 214.

266 the first hint that Kennedy might choose Johnson: Ibid., p. 215.

266 Powers caught a second signal: Ibid.

266 The third signal was revealed to press secretary Pierre Salinger: Pierre Salinger, Oral History, JFKL.

266 The fourth hint of the developing storm: Jack Conway, Oral History, JFKL.

267 A final indication came that morning: O'Brien, *No Final Victories*, p. 84.

267 "a strange mixture of feelings": Interview with James Symington by author, 2016.

267 Jackson would be offered the temporary chairmanship: O'Brien, *No Final Victories*, p. 84.

267 "He offered me the vice presidency": Caro, *The Passage to Power*, p. 123.

267 "He hadn't offered it": Sorensen, *Kennedy*, pp. 163–66.

267 "I didn't offer the Vice Presidency": Caro, *The Passage to Power*, p. 124.

267 "You just won't believe it": Schlesinger, *Robert Kennedy and His Times*, p. 208.

268 "the most indecisive time": Robert F. Kennedy, Oral History, p. 619, JFKL.

268 The real reason, "that we'd try": Ibid., p. 616.

268 The plan the Kennedy brothers devised: Ibid., p. 619.

268 The two brothers decided: Ibid., p. 616.

269 "I said [to Johnson]": Ibid., 619.

269 In accounts from the Johnson perspective: Caro, *The Passage to Power*, p. 129.

269 he could not accept the nomination: Ibid., pp. 122–23.

269 a one-word response: "Shit": Dallek, *Lone Star Rising*, p. 580.

270 "I told him, 'I'm dead set'": Caro, *The Passage to Power*, p. 128.

270 there were tales of changed minds: Dallek, *Lone Star Rising*, p. 579.

270 Johnson's allies claimed that Robert's last trip: Caro, *The Passage to Power*, pp. 132–34.

271 Trouble began to surface: Jack Conway, Oral History, JFKL; Caro, *The Passage to Power*, p. 136.

271 Alex Rose, the boss of New York's Liberal Party: Caro, *The Passage to Power*, p. 136.

271 The Michigan delegation, stroked so successfully: G. Mennen Williams, Oral History, JFKL; Caro, *The Passage to Power*, p. 137.

271 Joe Rauh, the leader of Americans for Democratic Action: Joseph Rauh, Oral History, JFKL.

272 O'Donnell had already had his own argument: O'Donnell and Powers, *Johnny, We Hardly Knew Ye*, p. 217.

272 Slowly the negative intensity: Ibid., p. 219.

273 One was Larry O'Brien: O'Brien, *No Final Victory*, p. 85.

273 "I was flabbergasted": Douglass Cater, Oral History, JFKL.

CHAPTER NINETEEN

274 requested drafts of the traditional climax: Sorensen, Personal Papers, Campaign Files, Box 25, JFKL.

277   Kennedy himself later attributed the phrase: Rostow, Oral History, JFKL.

277   According to Freedman, "New Frontier": Max Freedman, Oral History, p. 44, JFKL.

277   According to Sorensen, through whose typewriter: Sorensen, *Counselor*, p. 218.

278   Nixon, who escaped the primary season: Kennedy, *True Compass*, p. 158; Sorensen, *Kennedy*, p. 153.

280   "Whatever their motive": Sorensen, *Kennedy*, p. 170.

280   Walton was battle-tested as a correspondent: William Walton, Oral History, JFKL.

281   she had found him "a likeable man": Eleanor Roosevelt journal, August 17, 1960, Eleanor Roosevelt Papers.

281   (Actually he had been taking lessons: Silvestri, *Becoming JFK*, p. 96.

282   Despite a postconvention memo: Robert F. Kennedy Papers, Pre-Administration, Political Files, 1960, Special Collection, JFKL.

282   Six days after his lunch with Mrs. Roosevelt: Presidential Campaign, Speeches, and the Press through 1960–1961, subsection 15-09, Pre-Presidential Papers, JFKL.

283   He was the child of a struggling family: Roger Morris, *Richard Milhous Nixon: The Rise of an American Politician* (New York: Henry Holt, 1990), pp. 40–44.

284   After a layover in Sacramento: Ibid., pp. 772–73.

284   His ad hoc speech from the caboose: Ibid., pp. 831–33.

285   the experience left "a deep scar": Richard M. Nixon, *Six Crises* (Garden City, NY: Doubleday, 1962), p. 128.

285   The wound persisted: Jeffrey Frank, *Ike and Dick: Portrait of a Strange Political Marriage* (New York: Simon & Schuster, 2013), p. 60.

285   There had been a coldness: Morris, *Richard Milhous Nixon*, p. 733.

285   Nixon was able to bank on the respect: Frank, *Ike and Dick*, p. 191.

286   In June, he issued a lengthy statement: Richard Norton Smith, *On His Own Terms: A Life of Nelson Rockefeller* (New York: Random House, 2014), pp. 340–48.

286   After an appearance in Greensboro: Frank, *Ike and Dick*, p. 208.

286   A few days before Nixon became immobilized: Ibid., p. 205.

288   To handle the Catholic issue, an office: Sorensen, *Counselor*, pp. 161–62.

288   At first Wine's job: James Wine, Religious Issue Files, 1960, Box 1014, JFKL.

288   Once again Norman Vincent Peale: Karl Keating, *Catholic Answers*, blog, February 5, 2013.

289   Graham, a Baptist minister: Nancy Gibbs and Michael Duffy, *The Preacher and the Presidents: Billy Graham in the White House* (New York: Hachette, 2007; Shaun A. Casey, *The Making of a Catholic President: Kennedy vs. Nixon 1960* (New York: Oxford University Press, 2009), pp. 124–136.

289   "a highly financed and organized office": Casey, *The Making of a Catholic President*, p. 124.

289   The Kennedy campaign was not blind: James W. Wine, Oral History, JFKL.

290   Coincidentally John Cogley: John Cogley, Oral History, JFKL.

290   Journalists were alerted: James W. Wine, Oral History, JFKL.

290   "It is inconceivable that a Roman Catholic president": Robert P. Jones, *The End of White Christian America* (New York: Simon & Schuster, 2016), p. 64.

290   Wine and Cogley flew to Houston: John Cogley, Oral History, JFKL.

291   In his San Antonio prelude: Chan Miller, "Remembering the Alamo," Gilder Lehrman Institute of American History, New York.

291   Wine and Cogley had lunch on the campaign plane: John Cogley, Oral History, JFKL.

291   Kennedy's meeting with the Houston ministers: Film of John F. Kennedy's address to Greater Houston Ministerial Association, September 12, 1960, JFKL.

292   Kennedy had accepted an invitation from Poling: James Wine, Religious Issues files, Subject: Chapel of the Four Chaplains, JFKL.

292   Kennedy was given a respectful standing ovation: Robert F. Kennedy, Pre-Administration Papers, Media Campaign, Film of Houston Ministers Folder, Box 37, JFKL.

293   "He ate 'em blood raw": O'Donnell and Powers, *Johnny, We Hardly Knew Ye*, p. 210.

CHAPTER TWENTY

294   "The slick or bombastic orator": John F. Kennedy, "A Force That Has Changed the Political Scene," *TV Guide,* November 14, 1959.

296   "Good evening. The television and radio networks": Ibid. The debate quotations are from transcripts kept by the Commission on Presidential Debates, online.

296   "In the election of 1860": Ibid.

298   "Kick him in the balls": William Wilson, interview with author, 2016.

299   Lou Harris's constant polling: Lawrence F. O'Brien, Personal Files, Box 11, JFKL.

300   This is why more than one prominent Republican: Leonard Reinsch, Oral History, JFKL.

301 numbers produced behind the scenes: Louis Harris polls, in Lawrence F. O'Brien, Personal Papers, Box 11, JFKL.

302 It turns out that the only source: *Broadcasting Magazine*, November 7, 1960, p. 28.

303 "Even a draw, if it was a draw": Sorensen, *Kennedy*, p. 201.

303 "This is an incredible change": Louis Harris polls, in Lawrence F. O'Brien, Personal Papers, Box 12, JFKL.

305 Kennedy was lucky there was only one question: "The Campaign and the Candidates," part 3 of NBC News series, interview with Senator and Mrs. Kennedy, September 30, 1960, for broadcast the following day.

305 "an unwise place to draw the line": Ibid.

307 During the general election campaign: Chester Bowles, Oral History, JFKL.

307 In the rarefied world of bipartisan diplomacy: Richard M. Nixon, *Six Crises,* excerpt in *Life,* March 20, 1962, p. 76.

308 "No issue has the intensity": Louis Harris polls, in Lawrence F. O'Brien, Personal Papers, Box 11, JFKL.

308 "no matter how right Kennedy is": Ibid.

309 He cited "the Cuban issue": Ibid.

310 Nixon's position was quite deceptive: Tim Weiner, *Legacy of Ashes: The History of the CIA* (New York: Doubleday, 2007), pp. 155–66.

310 At first Nixon responded defensively: Nixon, *Six Crises* excerpt in *Life*, p. 78.

311 Nixon himself had already begun leaking: David Pietrusza, *1960: LBJ vs. JFK vs. Nixon* (New York: Union Square, Press, 2008), pp. 370–71.

311 According to Edwards, Nixon told him: *Chicago Tribune*, Oct. 12, 1960.

311 "In the field of foreign policy": Ibid.

311 "I remember at some point or other": Thomas and Joan Braden, Oral Histories, JFKL.

312 As governor he was approached by a CIA officer: John Patterson, Oral History, JFKL.

312 According to Dulles, however, repeated delays: Allen Dulles, Oral History, JFKL.

312 Robert Kennedy was told of the exiles' activity: William Atwood, Oral History, JFKL.

CHAPTER TWENTY-ONE

317 "He had no close relationship": Simeon Booker, Oral History, JFKL.

317 Just after his failed run: Clayborne Carson, ed., *The Papers of Martin Luther King Jr.* (Berkeley: University of California Press,), p. 276.

318   Marjorie Lawson approached Martin Luther King Jr.: Ibid., p. 277.

318   Kennedy invited members of the Capital Press Club: Simeon Booker, Oral History, JFKL.

318   bickering between Mrs. Lawson and Reeves: John Seigenthaler, Oral History, JFKL.

318   The first meeting between the candidate and King: Clayborne Carson, ed., *The Autobiography of Martin Luther King Jr.* (New York: Hachette, 2001).

319   the Kennedys decided to add a prominent black name: Louis Martin, Oral History, JFKL.

319   Despite his congressional seniority: Harris Wofford, *Of Kennedys and Kings: Making Sense of the Sixties* (New York: Farrar, Straus & Giroux, 1980), p. 61.

320   Several members of the Georgia power structure: Jeff Roche, *Restructured Resistance: The Sibley Commission and the Politics of Desegregation in Georgia* (Athens: University of Georgia Press, 1998), p. 176.

321   a matter that he "didn't want to discuss": Ernest Vandiver, Oral History, JFKL.

321   the Kennedy campaign produced a television spot: John Seigenthaler, Oral History, JFKL.

322   a former legislator named Willie Rainach: Amanda Leigh Russell, "Ballots, Barriers, Purges and Surges: African-American Voting Rights in Shreveport and Caddo Parish, Louisiana, 1958–1969," *North Louisiana History* 40, no. 1 (Winter 2008).

323   difficulty with one of the candidate's closest friends: John Seigenthaler, Oral History, JFKL.

323   After failing to rein in Smathers: Ibid.

323   One prominent Democrat in Florida, Farris Bryant: Farris Bryant, Oral History, JFKL.

324   "What the Hell has Dick Nixon ever done": Caro, *The Passage to Power*, pp. 145–48.

325   1,247 various officials: Ibid.

325   only one comic slip-up: Ibid.

325   While Johnson romanced white southerners: Theodore Sorensen, Oral History #5, JFKL.

325   "All right, there's no question": Jack Conway, Oral History, JFKL.

326   In the period between the first and third debates: Simeon Booker, Oral History, JFKL.

326   Three days later, on October 7: Louis Martin, Oral History, JFKL.

326   the National Conference on Constitutional Rights: John F. Kennedy, Speeches, JFKL.

327 a grade "above 90": Roy Wilkins, Oral History, JFKL.

328 the campaign needed his "thrust": Wil Haygood, *King of the Cats: The Life and Times of Adam Clayton Powell Jr.* (Boston: Houghton Mifflin, 1993), p. 270; Harris Wofford, Oral History, JFKL.

328 Louis Martin was delegated: Wofford, *Of Kennedy and Kings*, p. 60; Haygood, *King of the Cats*, p. 270; Evan Thomas, *Robert Kennedy*, manuscript, p. 100, JFKL.

329 his associate, Ray "the Fox" Jones: Harris Wofford, Oral History, JFKL.

329 Tammany had already sneered: Robert Wagner, Oral History, JFKL.

329 Wagner was "becoming more and more a source": Michael Prendergast, Oral History, JFKL.

330 Matters were made worse when Robert Kennedy: Ibid.

330 "They don't know a thing, Mike": Paul Corbin, Oral History, JFKL.

330 "You better do something about this": Michael Prendergast, Oral History, JFKL.

330 "If you don't have this guy out of here": Ibid.

330 In Corbin's version: Paul Corbin, Oral History, JFKL.

330 "He didn't want to listen to Mike Prendergast": John Seigenthaler, Oral History #2, JFKL.

331 Prendergast despised Walton: Michael Prendergast, Oral History, JFKL.

331 Walton too was harsh in his recollection: William Walton, Oral History, JFKL.

CHAPTER TWENTY-TWO

332 "It was just a slow, steady thing": Richard Donahue, interview with author, 2015.

332 "You could feel the margin narrowing": Walt W. Rostow, Oral History, p. 135, JFKL.

332 Not one to sugar-coat anything: Fay, *The Pleasure of His Company*, p. 65.

334 Ever since Labor Day: Lawrence F. O'Brien, Personal Papers, Box 12, JFKL.

334 Throughout the fall states: O'Donnell and Powers, *Johnny, We Hardly Knew Ye*, pp. 243, 245.

335 "I'll be wasting my time in New York": Ibid.

335 The Catholic issue could never be completely banished: Sorensen, *Kennedy*.

336 Faced with whether to confront the issue: Press release, Presidential Campaign folder, JFKL; James Wine, Religious Issue Files, 1960, JFKL.

336 Nixon "unlimbered his biggest weapon": Sorensen, *Kennedy*, p. 207.

337 he proposed sending Nixon a telegram: Louis Martin, Oral History #1, pp. 12–13, JFKL.

337   the office sponsored a "flying caravan": Louis Martin, Oral History #2, pp. 45–48, JFKL.

337   a project to obtain Martin Luther King's endorsement: Carson, *The Autobiography of Martin Luther King Jr.*

338   "I spent many troubled hours": Ibid.

338   King and thirty-five students were arrested: Branch, *Parting the Waters*, p. 351.

338   Kennedy's most forceful advisor on civil rights matters: Wofford, *Of Kennedys and Kings*, pp. 14–15.

339   While the Kennedy campaign was dissembling: Branch, *Parting the Waters*, pp. 355–56.

339   On Monday morning, October 24: Ibid., pp. 357–58.

340   The stern sentence was quickly condemned: Harris Wofford, Oral History, p. 17, JFKL.

340   Fearing her husband's life was in danger: Ibid., p. 18.

341   King's attorneys prepared a writ of habeas corpus: Carson, *The Autobiography of Marin Luther King Jr.*

341   a prison notorious for racism and brutality: Wofford, *Of Kennedys and Kings*, pp. 18–19.

341   "Negroes don't expect": Ibid.

342   Overjoyed, Mrs. King and her father-in-law: Ibid.

342   Kennedy casually mentioned his call: Ibid.

342   "Bob wants to see you bomb throwers": John Seigenthaler, Oral History, JFKL.

342   news of the call had been made public: Wofford, *Of Kennedys and Kings*, p. 20.

343   On the afternoon of October 27: Ibid., p. 21; John Seigenthaler, Oral History #2, pp. 231–32, JFKL.

343   made a call he told no one about: Robert F. Kennedy, Oral History, JFKL; Guthman, *Robert Kennedy in His Own Words*, p. 70.

343   "Bob, you'd never believe the story": John Seigenthaler, Oral History #2, pp. 233–34, JFKL.

343   "We now make you an honorary brother": Louis Martin, Oral History, p. 512, JFKL.

343   "The suggestion came from him": Robert F. Kennedy, Oral History, JFKL.

344   Vandiver confirmed some of the details: Jack Bass, *Taming the Storm: The Life and Times of Jude Frank M. Johnson and the South's Fight over Civil Rights* (Garden City, NY: Doubleday, 1993), p. 170; Maurice C. Daniels, *Saving the Soul of Georgia: Donald L. Hollowell and the Struggle for Civil Rights* (Athens: University of Georgia Press, 2013), p. 118.

344 Despite their significance: Information on the "blue bombs" and their effect is in Wofford, *Of Kennedys and Kings*, pp. 23–25.

345 In a mid-October Harris survey of Texas: Harris Poll of Texas, Oct. 17, 1960, JFKL.

345 Bruce Alger, a conservative Republican congressman from Dallas: Caro, *The Passage of Power*, p. 149.

346 When the Johnsons arrived at the Baker Hotel: Lawrence Wright, "Why Do They Hate Us So Much," *Texas Monthly*, November 1983; Scott K. Parks, "Extremists in Dallas Created Volatile Atmosphere before JFK's 1963 Visit," *Dallas Morning News*, October 12, 2013; Caro, *The Passage to Power*, p. 151; Harris poll of Texas, October 17, 1960, JFKL.

346 the election "was decided that day": Wright, "Why Do They Hate Us So Much."

347 Not having any irrefutable grounds for optimism: John Cauley, Oral History, p. 7, JFKL.

CHAPTER TWENTY-THREE

349 "We started getting down to the nuts and bolts": Richard Donahue, Oral History, p. 135, JFKL.

349 "On election day": John Bailey, Oral History, p. 56, JFKL.

350 "The need for an organizational effort in Connecticut": Lawrence F. O'Brien, Personal Papers, Box 6, JFKL.

351 "I told him a couple of lies": Richard Donahue, Oral History, JFKL.

351 And they were all wrong: Helen O'Donnell, *The Irish Brotherhood: John F. Kennedy, His Inner Circle and the Improbable Rise to the Presidency* (Berkeley: Counterpoint, 2015), Kindle edition.

352 "We just could not figure it out": Ibid.

352 The second major break: White, *The Making of the President 1960*, pp. 22–23.

352 Shortly after midnight the machine on Cape Cod: Ibid.

358 Some analysts have simply assumed: See, for example, Dallek, *An Unfinished Life*, p. 295: "Daley's machine probably stole Illinois from Nixon." In lieu of even anecdotal evidence Dallek then simply wrote that Daley "reported" the result "before the final tally was in." In fact Daley reassured the Kennedy nerve center on the telephone all evening that the senator would carry the state, but again, there is no evidence that Daley's standard-politician's confidence was anything more than that.

358 After a month of accusations: Peter Carlson, "Another Race to the Finish," *Washington Post*, November 17, 2000.

360   "On November 8, 1960": Theodore C. Sorensen, Personal Papers, Box 7, JFKL.

360   the simple, overarching fact: White, *The Making of the President 1960*, p. 361.

361   "Negro Voters in Northern Cities": Ithiel de Sola Pool, Robert P. Abelson, and Samuel Popkin, "Candidates, Issues and Strategies: A Computer Simulation of the 1960 and 1964 Elections," p. 94.

INDEX

ABOUT THE AUTHORS

Thomas Oliphant is a Pulitzer Prize–winning journalist. He was a political reporter at *The Boston Globe* for forty years and is the author of four books. Al Franken says "Oliphant brings more to the table than anyone I know." Madeleine Albright called him "the Will Rogers of our times."

Curtis Wilkie was a national and foreign correspondent for *The Boston Globe.* He teaches journalism at the University of Mississippi. He is the author of *The Fall of the House of Zeus,* which *The Wall Street Journal* wrote "reads like a John Grisham novel." Tom Brokaw described Wilkie as "one of the best journalists of our generation."